D1808008

Women under the Bō tree examines the tradition of female world-renunciation in Buddhist Sri Lanka. The study is textual, historical, and anthropological, and links ancient tradition with contemporary practice. Tessa Bartholomeusz utilizes data based on her field experiences in many contemporary cloisters of Sri Lanka, and on original archival research. The author explores: the history of the re-emergence of Buddhist female renouncers in the late nineteenth century after a hiatus of several hundred years; the reasons why women renounce; the variety of expressions of female world-renunciation; and, above all, attitudes about women and monasticism that have either prohibited women from renouncing or have encouraged them to do so. One of the most striking discoveries of the study is that the fortunes of Buddhist female renouncers is tied to the fortunes of Buddhism in Sri Lanka more generally, and to perceived notions of Sri Lanka as the caretaker of Buddhism.

CAMBRIDGE STUDIES IN RELIGIOUS TRADITIONS 5

WOMEN UNDER THE BŌ TREE

CAMBRIDGE STUDIES IN RELIGIOUS TRADITIONS

Edited by John Clayton (University of Lancaster), Steven Collins (University of Chicago) and Nicholas de Lange (University of Cambridge)

WOMEN UNDER THE BŌ TREE

Buddhist nuns in Sri Lanka

TESSA J. BARTHOLOMEUSZ

Department of Religion, Florida State University

CAMBRIDGE
UNIVERSITY PRESS

Published by the Press Syndicate of the University of Cambridge
The Pitt Building, Trumpington Street, Cambridge, CB2 1RP
40 West 20th Street, New York, NY 10011-4211, USA
10 Stamford Road, Oakleigh, Melbourne 3166, Australia

First published 1994

Printed in Great Britain at the University Press, Cambridge

A catalogue record for this book is available from the British Library

Library of Congress cataloguing in publication data

Bartholomeusz, Tessa J.
Women under the Bō tree: Buddhist nuns in Sri Lanka/Tessa J.
Bartholomeusz.
p.   cm. – (Cambridge studies in religious traditions: 5)
Includes bibliographical references and index.
ISBN 0 521 46129 4 (hardback)
1. Buddhist nuns – Sri Lanka.   2. Monasticism and religious orders
for women, Buddhist – Sri Lanka. I. Title. II. Series.
BQ6150.B37   1994
294.3′657′082 – DC20   93–33586 CIP

ISBN 0 521 46129 4 hardback

TAG

For my parents

Contents

ix

x   *Contents*

Preface

Nur Yalman's book, *Under the Bō Tree* (Berkeley: University of California Press, 1967), focused on Buddhist social structures in Sri Lanka. Playing on that title, I shall explore gender and social structures that have been challenged or reversed in Buddhist Sri Lanka.

In 1983, on holiday in Sri Lanka, I met some extraordinary Buddhist women who had challenged contemporary notions of gender and social structure: they had exchanged their white *sārīs* for orange robes. In doing so, they had usurped the monks' sole claim to monastic legitimacy. As acting members of a self-declared monastic community, these women have become necessary components of contemporary Buddhist society. I wondered what it would be like to live cloistered as they did, what Buddhist monks and laity thought of such women? Moreover did these cloistered women's views on Buddhism differ from those of monks?

When I returned to America, I discovered that very little had been written on the robed Buddhist women I had met in Sri Lanka though much had been written on Buddhist monks. In order to fill that lacuna, I slowly began translating Pāli texts that were relevant to the topic of Buddhist female monasticism; texts that helped me link the Buddhist classical tradition with living practice. I then returned to Sri Lanka to conduct a field study of the women I had met in 1983. That study and those translations have evolved into the account that I offer below.

My study of cloistered Buddhist women in Sri Lanka is somewhat timely; historians of religion over the past few years have produced many studies that focus on the religious experience of women. There are too many to list, yet among them are: Caroline Walker Bynum's *Holy Feast and Holy Fast: The Religious Significance of Food to Medieval Women* (Berkeley: University of California Press, 1987); Thomas

xi

Cleary's edited *Immortal Sisters: Secrets of Taoist Women* (Boston: Shambala, 1989); Frederique Apffel Marglin's *Wives of the God-king: The Rituals of the Devadasis of Puri* (Delhi: Oxford University Press, 1985); and Fatima Mernissi's *Beyond the Veil: Male-Female Dynamics in Modern Muslim Society* (Bloomington: Indiana University Press, 1987). All these books address what it means for a woman to be religious; they discuss why women's religious experiences are often different from those of men; and they debate how women express their religiosity. My study enters these discussions and debates; in the pages that follow I explore what it means for a woman to devote her life to religion.

This study focuses upon Buddhist women in Sri Lanka, particularly those who have revived and reinvented an ancient Buddhist vocation for women, namely monasticism. Like monks, they plant near their cloisters a sapling of the Bō tree. Tradition alleges that the Buddha sat under such a tree when he attained enlightenment; thus the tree symbolizes both Buddhist and clerical affiliations. For Buddhist cloistered women, however, the Bō tree symbolizes much more. It is believed that a woman much like them made an arduous journey in the third century, BCE, from north India to Sri Lanka with a branch of the Bō tree. She then arranged for it to be planted in Anurādhapura, and according to tradition that very tree continues to thrive. Like the Bō tree that survives despite conditions that have been prohibitive for its growth, women in contemporary Sri Lanka continue to choose the monastic life despite the protests of their families. They devote their lives to Buddhism and live near or under the Bō trees of Sri Lanka.

Acknowledgments

I have profited immensely from the contributions of those I met while conducting my field study in Sri Lanka in 1988–89 under the auspices of a Fulbright-Hays Fellowship. It is impossible for me to thank every one of them, yet there are a few who deserve special mention. My warmest thanks go to my family in Sri Lanka, namely: Mr. and Mrs. C. S. E. Gunasekera, Mr. and Mrs. Charles Gunasekera and Tamara, Mr. C. S. C. Gunasekera, Mr. and Mrs. Izeth Hussain, Mr. and Mrs. Peter Weerakoon, Mrs. H. Woutersz, and Fr. Eric Bartholomeusz. From the day that I landed in Colombo until the day that I left, my aunts, uncles, and cousins showed me unparalleled kindness. I would also like to thank Ranmali Perera and Maureen Fernando for their thorough work in the Colombo National Archives and for accompanying me on my interview trips.

My friendships with the lay nuns among whom I conducted my research were an invaluable source of comfort. It is impossible for me to express how indebted I am to each lay nun I interviewed. Special thanks, however, are in order for the lay nuns of the Madivala Upāsikārāmaya; without the help of Kotmalee Dhīrā Sudharmā and her pupils in the midst of the critical events in Sri Lanka during 1988–89, I do not think that I would have continued with the research.

I am grateful to the former president of Sri Lanka, J. R. Jayewardene, for granting me access to the Presidential Archives and for supplying me with invaluable contacts. In addition, I would like to extend my gratitude to: Mr. Paranavitane of the Colombo National Archives for permitting me access to rare manuscripts; Mr. Gamini Jayasuriya, of the Mahā Bodhi Society, who has granted me permission to quote from Anagārika Dharmapāla's diaries; and the staff of the Young Men's Buddhist Association, who helped me plow through nineteenth-century sources. I am also indebted to Mr. David

xiii

Koch of the Morris Library, Southern Illinois University, who has allowed me to quote from "The Open Court Publishing Company Archives."

The computer experts at Indiana University, Indianapolis, deserve special mention; Melody Johnson helped me sort out innumerable gliches in the book's printing process and was patient all the while. Evelyn Oliver of the Department of Religious Studies, Indiana University, Indianapolis, helped with the photocopying. I also am indebted to Indiana University for providing me with a generous grant that supported the final editing process. With regard to the editing, Daya de Silva patiently checked my footnotes against my bibliographies and expertly composed the index. For that, I am especially grateful.

The scholarship and friendship of fellow South Asianists such as William Harman, Vijay Pinch, Meena Khandelwal and Chandra R. de Silva have been a source of inspiration for me. I have also profited gratefully from my friendships with Aline Kalbian, Tracy Fessenden, Cynthia Hoehler, Steven Weinberger, and Donald Davison, all of whom encouraged me to write this book. I am also indebted to Phil MacEldowny for suggesting the title. This book would have been impossible without the insights of Professors Karen Lang, H. L. Seneviratne, Paul Groner and Jeffrey Hopkins, all of the University of Virginia. I have also benefited from the advice of Professor Steven Collins of the University of Chicago, and Professor Charles Hallisey of Harvard University, who both read through later drafts of this work. However, any errors found herein I claim solely as my own.

Notes on pronunciation

In this work, Sinhala, Pāli, and Sanskrit terms are romanized according to the generally accepted system. I have made efforts to keep spelling as consistent as possible. However, as I have quoted from many different sources, the spelling of place and personal names may be inconsistent. The following notes on transliteration may be useful to those unfamiliar with Sanskritic languages:

Vowels

a	as in Americ*a*
ā	as in y*a*cht
ä	as in h*a*t
ee	as in p*ay*
i	as in s*i*t
ī	as in m*ee*t
ō	as in r*o*w
u	as in p*u*t
ū	as in l*oo*t

Consonants are to be pronounced as in English, except for the following:

c	as in *ch*apter
ch	as in enri*ch h*er, when spoken quickly
d	as in brea*d*th
dh	the aspirate of d
ṃ	a hard nasal, pronounced with lips closing
ň	a nasal, pronounced with tongue at top of mouth
ñ	as the Spanish ñ
ṇ	as in pi*n*, but with tongue further back
t	as in *th*at, but without aspirating
th	as in *th*in

ṭ	as in pi*t*, but with tongue further back
ś	as in *s*ugar
ṣ	as in *s*ugar, but with tongue further back

Dramatis personae

Many of the figures we meet in the pages that follow have names that can be confusing to those unfamiliar with Sinhala and Pāli. I have thus provided a short description of the most important figures below. Some contemporary Sri Lankan lay nuns are known by a monastic name preceded by the name of their village. Others are known by a monastic name followed by a title. Contemporary western lay nuns resident in Sri Lanka are also known by a monastic name; their names, however, are preceded by a title. In all cases, I have placed the monastic names first. Moreover, as much as possible I have conformed to spellings that the lay nuns use; these spellings do not always correspond to the Pāli textual tradition.

Anulā: Anulā was a consort of King Devānampiyatissa. According to the Sri Lankan chronicles, she donned the ochre robe, took the ten precepts, and remained cloistered while awaiting the arrival of the nuns' lineage in the third century, BCE. See chapter 1.

Bhadrā, Ayyā and Dhammā, Ayyā: In 1986, two young German women by the clerical names of Bhadrā and Dhammā travelled to Sri Lanka; their intention was to be granted admission into the monastic community (*saṅgha*). They were eventually committed to a mental institution and were asked to leave the island. See chapter 8.

The Countess: Later known as Sister Saṅghamittā, Countess Miranda de Souza Canavarro was an American woman who opened an *upāsikārāmaya* (lay nunnery) in Colombo in 1898. She and Anagārika Dharmapāla worked closely together for two years trying to revive interest in female renunciation toward the turn of the twentieth century. See chapters 3 and 4.

xvii

Dhammādinnā, Kotagoda: Kotagoda Dhammādinnā, who established the Dhammādinnārāmaya in Matiambalama, Etulkotte, renounced lay life because her family life was unsatisfactory. See chapter 7.

Dharmapāla, Anagārika: Anagārika Dharmapāla, formerly Don David Hewavitarane, helped to redefine the role of the layperson in Buddhist Sri Lanka. He was born in 1846 and died in 1933. Just before his death, he became a Buddhist monk. See chapters 3 and 4.

Dhīrā Sudharmā, Kotmalee: Kotmalee Dhīrā Sudharmā was the incumbent of the Madivala Upāsikārāmaya, my primary research site. See chapters 7 and 8.

Indrāṇi Mäniyo: Indrāṇi, who lives at the Rahula Upāsikārāmaya in Grand Pass, Colombo, became a lay nun at the age of eleven. She spends most of her time taking care of her teacher, Hewavitarane Mäniyo, who claims to be a relative of Dharmapāla. See chapter 7.

Khemā, Ayyā: Ayyā Khemā is the German born American nun who established a meditation retreat at Parappaduwa Island, near Dodonduva, Sri Lanka. Before taking the vows of the *bhikṣuṇī*, Ayyā Khemā was a leading lay nun in Sri Lanka. See chapters 7 and 8.

Khemindā, Ayyā: Like Ayyā Khemā, Ayyā Khemindā is one of the western lay nuns who renounced the home life in Sri Lanka. Originally from Holland, Ayyā Khemindā has made Kandy her home. See chapter 8.

LaBrooy, Sybil: Sybil LaBrooy, whose clerical name was Sister Padmavati, was a Burgher who became the Countess's closest ally when their lay nunnery closed in 1899 due to moral and financial scandals. See chapters 3 and 4.

Ñānasīrī, Ayyā: Ayyā Ñānasīrī is an American lay nun who renounced lay life in Sri Lanka in 1987. She organized the Convocation of Buddhist Nuns held in Sri Lanka in 1989. See chapter 8.

Saṅghamittā, Bhikkhunī: Tradition alleges that Bhikkhunī Saṅghamittā was the daughter of the great Indian king, Asoka. Tradition also holds that she established the order of Buddhist nuns in Sri Lanka in the third century, BCE, and that she arrived on the island with a branch of the Bō tree. See chapter 1.

Śāntā Sil Mātā: Śāntā's ordination was the first of two ordinations that I witnessed in Sri Lanka. Śāntā, formerly Līlāwatī, is a pupil of Mahāgoda Sumettā and renounced aged forty-five. See chapter 8 for a description of her ordination.

Shearer, Catherine: Catherine Shearer, whose clerical name was Sister Padmavati, was an American nurse who travelled to Sri Lanka in 1899 to assist the Countess with the lay nunnery work. See chapters 3 and 4.

Subhodānanda: Subhodānanda, like Dharmapāla, advocated an active role for the laity in the religious life of his people. Formerly a Buddhist monk, Subhodānanda encouraged the laity to don the ochre robe, keep the precepts of the renunciant, and live cloistered without changing formal status. See chapter 2.

Sudāsikā: The youngest of Mahāgoda Sumettā's pupils, Sudāsikā renounced at the age of four. She is the youngest lay nun I met. See chapter 7.

Sudharmā, Kotmalee: Kotmalee Sudharmā is the fifth incumbent of Lady Blake's Upāsikārāmaya in Kandy, which is mistakenly considered to be the first "nunnery" of the modern period. See chapters 5 and 7.

Sudharmā, Sister: Sister Sudharmā is at present the incumbent of the Vihāra Mahā Devī Upāsikārāmaya in Biyagama, Kalaniya. She has had the patronage of some of the most influential members of Sri Lankan society, including former President J. R. Jayewardene. See chapters 6 and 7.

Sudharmācārī: Sudharmācārī (Sudhammācārī), formerly Catherine de Alwis, was a wealthy socialite who established Lady Blake's Upāsikārāmaya in Kandy in 1907. Contemporary lay nuns consider the former Anglican to be the first lay nun of the modern period. See chapter 5.

Sumanāsīlī Sil Mātā: Sumanāsīlī is one of Sister Sudharmā's students. She was "ordained" at the Vihāra Mahā Devī Upāsikārāmaya in Anurādhapura. Like the lay nunnery by the same name in Kalaniya, it is in the care of Sister Sudharmā. Like many of her peers, Sumanāsīlī has attended a school set up by the government with the sole purpose of educating lay nuns. See chapter 8.

Sumedhā Sil Mātā: Sumedhā was known as Soma until she was ordained at the Susilārāmaya in Mahāragama in 1989. I attended her ordination, which was presided over by Madihee Paññāsīha, the leader of the Amarapura Nikāya. See chapter 8.

Sumettā, Mahāgoda: Mahāgoda Sumettā established the Yaśodārā devī Upāsikārāmaya in Dehivala and still presides over it. She has also opened an orphanage for victims of ethnic strife on the premises of her lay nunnery. See chapters 7 and 8.

Theranā: Theranā, also known as Śāntinī, is considered to be a *bhikkhunī* by her teacher, the controversial Battaramulle Uttama. She lives at his *vihāra* in Rattanapitiya, Nugegoda. See chapter 9.

Uttama, Battaramulle: Battaramulle Uttama, also known as Uttama Sādhu, is the controversial self-ordained monk who has ordained over twenty women as "*bhikkhunīs*," or fully fledged nuns. He presides over a temple in Rattanapitiya, Nugegoda. See chapter 9.

Uttarā Mäniyo, Kagalle: Kagalle Uttarā Mäniyo presides over a lay nunnery in Kataragama and has established a forest hermitage for lay nuns in the Ruhuu National Forest. At the forest hermitage, lay nuns live in caves, secluded from the distractions of village life. See chapter 8.

Vāyāmā, Ayyā: Ayyā Vāyāmā, Australian by birth, was "ordained" by Ayyā Khemā at Parappaduwa. Like most western lay nuns, she is known as Ayyā, that is "honorable lady," the term by which the members of the ancient order of nuns were known. Ayyā Vāyāmā lives in Ambalangoda with a Sinhala lay nun. See chapter 8.

Wikramasinghe, Ayoma Kotalāwala: Though most of the contemporary lay nuns of Sri Lanka come from economically depressed families in rural Sri Lanka, Wikramasinghe, who lived for a short period as a lay nun, is related to some of the most powerful and aristrocratic families in the island. See chapter 8.

PART I

Introduction
The tradition of Buddhist female renunciation in Sri Lanka

This is a book about Buddhist women in Sri Lanka who have "renounced the world,"[1] or exchanged their lay identity for monastic life. The sources indicate that an order of nuns, a *bhikkhunī saṅgha*, played a significant role in the development and spread of Buddhism in its early history in the island.[2] Though there is not an officially sanctioned order of nuns in Sri Lanka today, there are women who set themselves up in the role of the ordained nun, the *bhikkhunī*, without changing formal status. These I shall call "lay nuns." Whether they renounced lay life in the third century, BCE, or in the twentieth century, CE, female renunciants – both lay and ordained – have faced hardships unknown to men. Primarily, this is because for the most part Buddhist Sri Lankans throughout history have been ambivalent about women who renounce conventionally accepted social roles. For instance, the Pāli *Dīpavaṃsa*, which chronicles the formative years of Buddhism in Sri Lanka, records that women who entered the monastic community became great Buddhist teachers, and even became *arahants*, or enlightened beings. It also claims that they were renowned for their scholarly acumen and that kings honored them.[3] In short, the *Dīpavaṃsa* values nuns and their contribution to the establishment of Buddhism in Sri Lanka. However, according to the Pāli *Mahāvaṃsa*, Buddhists considered monks more worthy of support than nuns. Though the *Mahāvaṃsa* mentions that nuns attained enlightenment,[4] references to them are sporadic; rather, the *Mahāvaṃsa* is replete with references to monks, and especially to the beneficence on the part of many kings to the order of monks. In the *Mahāvaṃsa*, when kings make donations to the monastic community, the largest share goes to the male order.[5] Aside from the story of the founding of the female monastic order in the island, nuns are never mentioned unless in conjunction with monks. Essentially, the order of nuns is an appendage to the order of monks.[6]

3

Why is this paradoxical? (for readers who don't know)

Thus, implicit in the *Mahāvaṃsa* is the message that men are more
suited to the monastic life than women. Paradoxically, that same text
tells us that women can and did become *arahants*.

This ambiguity is presaged in many Indian canonical Buddhist
texts, such as the Pāli Canon.[7] Some texts suggest that women are
equal to men in their abilities to progress along the Buddhist path to
enlightenment. Others imply that women are incapable of doing
little else except tempting men away from that very path. This
paradox is illustrated by the Buddha's proclamation in the canonical
Samyutta Nikāya that women are able to attain *nibbāna* (Pali; *nirvāṇa*,
Sanskrit), the soteriological goal of Buddhism: "Whoever has such a
vehicle, whether it is a woman or a man, by means of that vehicle
shall come to *nibbāna*."[8] Many passages, however, belie the egalitarian message of the Canon; instead, they bespeak misogyny. For
instance, the *Anguttara Nikāya* records that the Buddha directed his
monks to beware of women, and to be ever vigilant of the women who
may try to entrap them:

Monks, I see no other single form so apt to rouse excitement, so desirable, so
intoxicating, so apt to bind, so distracting, such a hindrance to winning the
unsurpassed peace from effort[9] ... as a woman's form. Monks, whosoever
clings to a woman's form – infatuated, greedy, enslaved, enthralled – for
many a long day shall grieve, snared by the charms of a woman's form.

Monks, a woman even when going along, will stop to ensnare the heart of
a man; whether standing, sitting, or lying down, laughing, talking or
singing, weeping, stricken or dying, a woman will stop to ensnare the heart
of man ... Truly one may say of womanhood: "it is wholly the snare of
Māra."[10]

How do we reconcile such passages? Allan Sponberg has argued
convincingly that this ambiguity about women in the early Buddhist
texts reflects "the multiplicity of voices" that express "a different set
of concerns current among members of the early community" of
monks.[11] Many of these concerns arose after the death of the Buddha,
when the male dominated monastic order had to cope with regulating
a lifestyle suitable for both monks and nuns in cenobitic communities.

Among these various attitudes toward women in the texts,
Sponberg has isolated four. Though the four attitudes build upon one
another, they are not mutually exclusive. The first is soteriological
inclusiveness, or the view that one's gender "presents no barrier to
attaining the Buddhist goal of liberation from suffering."[12] The texts
record that the Buddha himself believed that women were capable of

attaining *nibbāna*. The second attitude is institutional androcentrism, or the belief that "women indeed may pursue a full-time religious career, but only with a carefully regulated institutional structure that preserves and reinforces the conventionally accepted social standards of male authority and female subordination."[13] The *Mahāvaṃsa*, with its emphasis on monks and casual reference to nuns, articulates this view. The third attitude is ascetic misogyny, or the condemnation of women "as a threat to male celibacy."[14] The *Anguttara Nikāya* contains a passage that exemplifies this tendency. The fourth attitude toward women in Buddhist texts is soteriological androgyny, or the "dramatic revalorization of the feminine, ... a reevaluation of all those qualities and expectations culturally ascribed to male and female."[15] In this view, qualities normally associated with the feminine are considered indispensable for the successful practitioner. I also include in this attitude the general glorification of the feminine.

Sponberg's analysis of these four views in early Buddhist texts is a useful tool for assessing attitudes toward women and world-renunciation that have prevailed in Sri Lankan Buddhist history. In the pages that follow, I discuss the ways that these attitudes have influenced the choices women make, and the choices made for women, in relation to the monastic vocation. As much of the rest of this book is devoted to explaining why this is the case, I shall only outline the answer here.

Generally, in Sri Lankan history, women have either been allowed to fulfill their spiritual capabilities as renunciants, or they have been discouraged from it, depending on historical exigencies. Sri Lankan Buddhists have occasionally drawn on positive canonical images of female renunciation, images that reflect soteriological inclusiveness, and have encouraged women to preach and renounce lay life, despite the contradictory misogynous attitudes in those very texts. It is important to note at the outset of this study that in several periods of Sri Lankan history, the third century, BCE, the late nineteenth century, CE, and later in the 1940s, Buddhists have called upon women to rediscover their vocation as world-renouncers. They have done this by highlighting inclusive passages of the Pāli Canon. Encouragement of this type was most marked in the 1890s, a time when people such as Anagārika Dharmapāla encouraged women to play leading roles in the Buddhist revival.

During Dharmapāla's day, Buddhists used positive canonical images of women to affect various religio-political agendas, such as the re-establishment of Buddhist institutions that were deemed necessary for the welfare of the country. Women-centered religious activity became a striking feature of Sri Lanka and was hailed in the newspapers. To use Sponberg's term, the feminine was "revalorized;" drawing upon favorable images of women as nurturing mothers *and* as nuns, Dharmapāla argued that women were able to "reproduce" Buddhism by "going forth from home into homelessness."[16] He himself became a celibate revivalist and advocated that some women should also remove themselves from physical reproduction and become nuns. In effect, he encouraged women to engage in the *social* reproduction of Buddhism by preaching and awakening others to their Buddhist heritage.[17] At a time when the task of resuscitating Buddhism was of paramount importance for many Buddhists, women performed any service they could, including preaching in ochre robes. In Part I of this study, I recount this period of religious experimentation in which feminine institutions, such as the order of nuns, were to a large degree revalorized.

On the other hand, women have been discouraged from playing an active, visible role in religious life, such as in contemporary Sri Lanka. Many monks argue that women need not renounce the world in order to be exemplary Buddhists; this can be done while remaining a laywoman or a householder: an *upāsikā*. *Upāsikā* is a term that has many different meanings in contemporary Sri Lanka. I shall have more to say about the term in chapter 5. However, we should keep in mind that in its broadest use, *upāsikā* refers to all Buddhist laywomen; and in its more specific use, it refers to the pious women and female children who keep the Buddhist precepts on the full-moon days (*pōya*). Buddhists also use it to refer to females who keep the precepts for extended periods of time. The contemporary lay nuns of Sri Lanka fall into the latter category; because they are not members of the *sangha*, the monastic order, Buddhists often refer to them as *upāsikās*. I further discuss the lay nuns' status in Part II below. Here I need only say that many contemporary monks, referring to the great female lay benefactors of the Pāli Canon, pre-eminent among them, Visākhā, claim that it is more important for women to support Buddhism by cultivating their roles as laywomen, and nurturers.[18] In other words, women are expected to conform to the stereotype of the loving, selfless female who worships, supports monks by offering alms, and acts as the foundation of the family. Related to this is the way in which these monks also claim that the female lay community has an important role to play in the life of Buddhism in Sri Lanka. They argue that the Buddha himself proclaimed that *upāsikās* – female householders – are among the four-fold community of followers that he envisaged.[19] The other three are: pious laymen, or male householders (*upāsakas*); monks (*bhikkhus*); and nuns. These monks also argue that as women cannot become nuns, (a problem I explore in chapter 1), women should behave like Visākhā. However, this nurturing householder is the antithesis of the world-renouncer who conducts worship services, receives alms, and leaves her family. In spite of such polarization, many women in Sri Lanka renounce lay life and argue that they have every right to do so. In Part II, I offer their life stories in addition to exploring why monks are opposed to the lay nuns' vocation.

While exploring the attitudes of Buddhist Sri Lankans toward women and world-renunciation, I ask the following question: how does contemporary female renunciation, as a movement, fit into the broader developments in Sri Lankan Buddhism that Richard Gombrich and Gananath Obeyesekere, Stanley Tambiah, and others have recently documented?[20] Among these developments are Protestant Buddhism, which "originated as a protest against the British in general and against Protestant Christian missionaries in particular. At the same time, however, it assumed salient characteristics of that Protestantism."[21] Though, as we shall see, this new ideological Buddhism that emerged in the late nineteenth century was a response to the British, it has continued to shape Buddhism to the present. Thus, there have been many expressions of that new ideology, all of which we can call Protestant Buddhism. I shall explore in the chapters that follow the nature of Protestant Buddhism, especially as it relates to the recent resurgence of female renunciation in Sri Lanka.

Another development that is related to the contemporary movement of female renunciation in Sri Lanka, is the claim that Buddhist Sri Lankans have an historical and sacred role to protect Buddhism from dangerous and alien forces. Though this point of view has created divisions between the various ethnic groups of the island, it has also fostered a positive valuation of female renunciation, especially in the late nineteenth and early twentieth century.

A third development in Sri Lankan Buddhism that is connected to the revival of the nuns' vocation is the "rediscovery" of various traditional Buddhist paradigms. Among them are: the socially active, yet celibate layman, the *anagārika*; the forest monk; and the lay meditator.[22] While exploring these developments as they relate to the movement of contemporary female renunciation, I also ask other questions, namely: what is the relationship between sexual stereotypes and religious views? Do sexual stereotypes and religious views help to determine the roles that Theravādin Buddhist women play in Sri Lankan society? If so, how? In what ways, if any, are western women who become Buddhist world-renouncers influenced by traditional Buddhist images of the feminine? What is the relationship between Buddhist texts and behavior, especially with regard to female world-renunciation?

Like many major world-religions, Buddhism has been guided almost predominantly by men. Consequently in the Pāli canonical texts, women are frequently characterized as helpless, vulnerable, profane, and weak (both morally and physically). As such, they are not suited to the life of the world-renouncer. Nevertheless, in almost every corner of Buddhist Sri Lanka, at least one shaven-headed, ochre-clad woman, is part of the landscape. She may live in a village cloister with other women like herself, or choose to live in a cave and spend hours in solitary meditation. Whether she lives in a cave or in a village, she relies on alms for sustenance; she conducts worship services for the laity, teaches the Buddha's message, and hopes to attain *nibbāna*. According to the Buddhist canonical texts, many of the activities of contemporary female world-renouncers, or lay nuns, are reminiscent of the activities of the ancient ordained nun. Like her, the contemporary female renunciant has eschewed worldly luxuries in favor of a life of service or contemplation. However, unlike the *bhikkhunī*, the female renunciant such as Sudharmā who lives in Madivala, and Sumettā who lives in Dehivala, is technically a laywoman because Sri Lankan women are at present unable to enter the *saṅgha*. Nonetheless, lay nuns invariably base themselves on models of female renunciation found in the canonical texts, though their responses to those models differ widely.

In contemporary Sri Lanka, women are not encouraged to renounce. Instead, as we shall see in Part II, they are expected to marry and nurture a family. However, in spite of societal pressures urging them not to renounce, lay nuns have created viable religious roles for themselves. Moreover, they are supported to one degree or another by Buddhist society, yet never in the same explicit manner as the monks. Among the lay nuns I interviewed, not one related that her family supported her decisions to leave home. They were all expected to marry, have children, and abide by the precepts of the householder, the *upāsikā*. The precepts of the householder are a variation of the ten precepts of the *bhikkhu* and the *bhikkhunī*. For the monk and nun, the ten precepts consist of restraint from injury to creatures, restraint from stealing, restraint from unchastity, restraint from lying, restraint from the occasion of sloth from liquor, restraint from eating at the wrong time, restraint from seeing shows of dancing, singing and music, restraint from the occasion of using garlands, scents, and wearing finery, restraint from using high beds and large beds, and restraint from accepting gold and silver. Occasionally, very devout laymen and laywomen abide by the ten precepts for extended periods of time, though the way that the laity "takes" the ten precepts differs from the way the monks recite them. I shall have more to say on this in chapter four. What must be kept in mind here, however, is that most laity keep the first five precepts, while the particularly pious among them may keep the first eight. The majority of contemporary lay nuns, unlike most laity, abide by the ten precepts for life. Though the lay nuns have chosen to abide by the ten, each lay nun I interviewed told me that before her renunciation, her family expected her to conform to the stereotype of the pious Buddhist woman who keeps the five precepts and remains in-the-world. Nonetheless, it is estimated that in contemporary Sri Lanka 5,000 women, albeit as laity, have chosen to walk in the footsteps of the ancient *bhikkhunī*, who kept the ten precepts in addition to the 311 monastic rules.[23] Their life histories emphasize the deep contradictions and constraints under which many Buddhist women live in their dual role as *upāsikās* and world-renouncers.

The history of Sri Lankan Buddhist women who renounce the world without changing formal status is relatively recent. It can be traced to the late 1800s, a time in which the laity, both men and women, experimented with new roles, and in which the West became increasingly interested in Buddhism. The late nineteenth century witnessed great social change in Sri Lanka, or Ceylon as it was then called,[24] which fostered a Buddhist revival that continues to the present day. As a response to centuries of colonial rule, beginning with the Portuguese in 1505, the Buddhist revival was a seed-bed for experimentation and innovation.[25] Many Buddhist laypeople responded to the sense of decline in the island by attempting to return Buddhism to an "ideal" pristine, or pure, form. Michael Carrithers has documented the fascinating careers of monks and laymen whose

order of nuns depicted ~ (11ᵗ (fn.27) — would be
nice to have this more systematically laid out by
now

10   *Women under the Bō tree*

responses to such times revived and reformed the ancient practice of
forest-dwelling asceticism;[26] much like the personalities who are the
subject of Part I below, the forest monks asked themselves: "how can
Buddhism be revived?"

During the 1890s, women engaged in activities that were to
breathe new life into Buddhism. Women began preaching Buddhist
sermons and, much to the dismay of many, they began wearing robes
of ochre, the color associated with the *sangha*. Some Buddhists
considered such activities revolutionary, yet necessary; for others,
they were anathema. The sources from the period inform us that
preaching in robes had traditionally been the prerogative of the
monk only.[27] The sources also tell us that some women nonetheless
donned the robe and became exemplars of religious enthusiasm. One
such woman traversed the southern part of the island preaching and
teaching, while others concentrated their activities in Colombo. I
recount their activities in Part I below.

Though it is impossible to tell how many there were – it is likely
that their numbers were few – the lay nuns of the 1890s became the
focus of numerous editorials and articles. At least one of them was
ethnically Sinhala, while another was a Burgher, a descendant of the
Europeans who colonized Sri Lanka in the seventeenth century. Two
of these renunciants became students of Dharmapāla, who helped to
direct the Buddhist enthusiasm of the late nineteenth century.
Dharmapāla and an American woman he had recruited for Buddhist
work, Countess Miranda de Souza Canavarro, organized female
renunciants into a Buddhist cloister where meditation, service, and
the revival of Buddhism were features of their daily life; however,
they never gained entrance into the *sangha*. The "Countess," as she
was referred to in the press, renounced lay life herself, donned an
ochre robe, and travelled around the island to raise money for
Buddhist projects.[28] According to his diaries, Dharmapāla encouraged the Countess's activities. In fact, he argued that the women
of the 1890s should be more like the women in the Pāli Canon who
had served Buddhism by renouncing lay life. For several years he
entertained the idea of re-establishing the order of nuns in the
island.[29] He worked closely with the Countess and dedicated his
energies to establishing a cloister for religiously motivated women. In
1898, his dream came true. The history of the first cloister for lay
nuns, or "lay nunnery," of the modern period, and the social history
that gave rise to it, are documented fully in Part I. This episode of

Dharmapāla's life challenges assumptions that interest in female renunciation in the modern period was primarily the product of cultural exchange between Burma and Sri Lanka.[30] Rather, interest in female renunciation was one consequence of Buddhist cultural awakening in the island, which was precipitated by internal developments.

Since the 1890s, Sri Lankan women have continued to renounce the world, while western women have continued to be drawn to the vocation of the female Buddhist renunciant. Though there are marked differences between the practice of western female renunciants and their Sri Lankan counterparts, both groups renounce the world without changing formal status. They are not *bhikkhunīs*, yet they have established themselves in the role of this defunct order of nuns. As in the 1890s, contemporary female renunciants are the focus of many articles and editorials that center around their contradictory status as lay monastics. The newspaper debates do not take place between lay nuns and monks; rather, laypeople and monks challenge each other to counter charges of misogyny, on the one hand, and heterodoxy, on the other. Much of the controversy surrounding the lay nuns is over their lack of status in the *saṅgha*, as well as the feasibility of re-establishing an ordination lineage for them. As Gombrich has remarked, it is likely that many people would welcome the re-establishment of an order of nuns in Sri Lanka;[31] however, as I learned during the course of my study, there are just as many who would not. Though monks and laity – both men and women – continue to debate the issue over the ordination of women, the majority of the lay nuns I interviewed would not choose to enter the *saṅgha*, even if it were possible. They argue that membership in the monastic order is not a prerequisite for leading a monastic life. I explore this and other reasons for their disinterest in entering the *saṅgha* more fully in Part II.

BUDDHISM FROM A DIFFERENT VIEW

This book is not only about female renunciants in Buddhist Sri Lanka; it is about Buddhism from the perspective of those women who have renounced the world. Although few words have been preserved of the women who renounced the world when the lineage was introduced to the island in the third century, BCE,[32] or for that matter, in the nineteenth century, their voices echo throughout the

sources I have used. In addition to culling voices from historical
documents, I offer contemporary lay nuns' opinions about their own
tradition. Moreover, I discuss their attitudes about Buddhism in Sri
Lanka in general, including attitudes about monks, especially
political monks and their activities.

The vision of Buddhism that female renunciants offer – both
ordained and lay – has been blurred throughout the centuries by
both a patriarchal religion disinterested in women's views, and by
scholars, ever since the pioneering days of Buddhist scholarship. If
scholars explored the religious experience of Buddhist women in Sri
Lanka, more often than not, it was as an afterthought, an appendix,
or a footnote. Only recently have we begun to view Buddhist
women's religious experience as something other than as a sup-
plement to men's. This recent trend is long overdue.[33]

Though Buddhist Studies have, for the most part, kept the religious
experience of women on the periphery, there are notable exceptions.
Any study of Buddhist women, such as the one I offer here, is
indebted to I. B. Horner's classical study of women during the
formative years of Buddhist history.[34] In this work, Horner not only
analyzed the rules that governed the ancient order of nuns, but
included the life histories of many of its members based upon their
own poems: the *Therīgāthā*. In Horner's (1930) work, the religious
experience of women does not provide supplementary information
about the experience of men; rather it is seen as truly representative
of Buddhism and the Buddhist monastic community. Horner's
contemporaries had already paved the way for studies that are
sympathetic to the woman's point of view. In the 1890s, Caroline A.
Foley, i.e., Mrs. Rhys Davids, and Mabel Bode provided insights into
the lives of the women leaders of early Buddhism. Bode explored the
position of women in Buddhism as reflected in the *Manoratha Pūraṇī*,
while Foley focused upon the condensed biographies of ancient nuns
recorded in the *Paramattha Dipānī*.[35]

Both Bode's and Foley's accounts of the Buddhist nun in ancient
Indian society offer valuable insights into women and renunciation
in early Buddhism. D. N. Bhagavat's study of the early Buddhist legal
system also provides a complete picture of the life of the woman who
had renounced the world in favor of monastic life; it devotes an entire
chapter to women and renunciation.[36] Along these lines, Meena V.
Talim's study of the rules that governed the life of the nun places the
Buddhist female renunciant in the context in which her tradition

arose. By suggesting that the Buddhist nun must be viewed as one expression of female renunciation among many in ancient India,[37] she paints a broad picture of the religious life of women in early Buddhism.[38] Among recent studies, Mi Mi Khaing's work is noteworthy because it offers a comprehensive account of Buddhist women in Burma.[39] Similarly, Chatsumarn Kabilsingh's study of Buddhist women in Thailand extends our knowledge of the contribution made by women to Buddhism in Southeast Asia.[40] Susan Murcott's work on the ancient order of Buddhist nuns in India is also commendable, for it fully explores the goals, aspirations, and lives of women who renounced lay life at the time of the Buddha.[41] In addition, Mohan Wijayaratna's admirable exploration of the ancient order of nuns in India offers a comprehensive look at the "ideal" life of the ancient nun.[42] It is my hope that what follows will complement Wijayaratna's book by offering instances of the "actual" state of female renunciation in Theravāda Buddhism.

While Buddhist female renunciants slowly move from the margins and the footnotes of scholarly works into the texts themselves, they continue to move from the periphery and boundary into mainstream religious life in Sri Lanka. Though female renunciants such as Sudharmā and Sumettā, whom we meet in Part II, have defied conservative monks by establishing themselves in the role of the ancient nun, they have also helped to create newer, more powerful roles for women in Buddhism. These experiments in new roles, no matter how much they are fashioned upon classical images, are a challenge to the orthodoxy and institutional conservatism of Sri Lankan Buddhism.

THE CONSERVATIVE BUDDHIST TRADITION OF SRI LANKA

The history of female renunciants in Sri Lanka provides a case study of religious revival and reform in a country that makes claims to Buddhist doctrinal purity. Many of the Buddhist monks I interviewed believe themselves to be the conservators of "true" Buddhism. They argue that their counterparts who have preceded them throughout Sri Lanka's Buddhist history have had a similar responsibility.[43] These monks claim that the Buddhist tradition in Sri Lanka, the Theravādin tradition, has understood itself to be conservative since its inception in the island.[44] For instance, by establishing an order of nuns shortly after Buddhism was introduced to the island, Buddhists conformed to conservative notions of Buddhism. According to the texts the Buddha declared that there are four Buddhist communities, namely: monks, nuns, laymen, and laywomen. Thus, when the first Buddhist Sri Lankan king's female folk asked to enter the monastic order, the king acted conservatively by arranging the establishment of the order of nuns in Sri Lanka. The order attracted many women,[45] though it never prospered as much as the order of monks. Nonetheless, the nuns of the island contributed to the growth of Buddhism and, as we have seen, the chronicles claim that many achieved reputations as great teachers and religious adepts. However, the fortunes of *bhikkhunīs* changed in the turbulent decades of the eleventh century. References to them end at this time, thus bringing to a close the history of the ordained nun in Sri Lanka. Though it is impossible to reconstruct with any accuracy the demise of the *bhikkhunī saṅgha*, it is possible to reconstruct the controversy surrounding its re-establishment.

As I have noted above, many Theravādin Buddhist monks in Sri Lanka understand themselves to be *the* conservators of Buddhism; this is also true of the lay nuns and much of the laity. They are heir to what H. L. Seneviratne calls the Sinhala-Buddhist or "Mahā-vamsa-view" of history that "defines the world-historical role of Sri Lanka as the stronghold of Buddhism and Buddhist civilization."[46] Based on the fifth-century *Mahāvaṃsa*, but in many respects the product of the nineteenth century, this view has been bolstered by research "mingled freely with the revivalist-inspired restoration of ancient monuments and the re-discovery of the splendour of the lost cities..."[47] The Mahāvaṃsa-view thus legitimates the idea that Sri Lankan Buddhists have had a sacred mission: to maintain the purity of the Buddha's message and teachings in a world that is constantly changing. Although the *Mahāvaṃsa* does not suggest that Sri Lanka is uniquely the defender of Buddhism, many contemporary Sri Lankan Buddhists claim that their island was destined to be the bastion of orthodox Buddhism and that the history of their island is, therefore, a sacred history. In short, my informants tell us that there is an irrefutable connection between Buddhism and Sri Lanka.

How does this idea of Sri Lanka as sacred Buddhist isle and its Buddhist inhabitants as the conservators of "true" Buddhist tradition relate to the discussion of the controversy over the re-establishment of the order of nuns? When the order of nuns disappeared in the eleventh century, it was not resuscitated by bringing ten nuns from

Burma – the quorum of nuns required by monastic rules to ordain a woman into the *saṅgha*[48] – even though such an action would have been possible. (There is not at present an order of nuns in any Theravādin Buddhist country.[49] However, there was an order of nuns in Burma in the eleventh century that Buddhists could have called upon to aid in the re-establishment of the nuns' lineage in Sri Lanka. According to the sources, it became defunct roughly two hundred years after the demise of the order of nuns in Sri Lanka.[50]) The order of monks was similarly affected in the eleventh century, yet the king revived it by bringing Burmese monks to Sri Lanka to re-establish the lineage; the order of nuns, however, was never revived.

Attempts to revive the order of nuns in the present are quashed by monks who argue that in order to do so, monastic rules would have to be broken. Because they see themselves as heirs to the Theravādin tradition, which they argue has not condoned altering or amending the rules that govern the monastic community,[51] they are opposed to the ordination of women. According to their rationale, as it is impossible to assemble the requisite quorum of Theravādin nuns to ordain a woman into the *saṅgha*, they cannot ordain women without abrogating the rules. The majority of the Sri Lankan monks I interviewed, therefore, represent a conservative tradition that they claim has traditionally endeavored to protect Buddhism from change and any divisive threats to its preservation.[52]

Despite their belief that they walk in the footsteps of the *bhikkhunī*, the lay nuns represent change. Though they carry out the traditional services of the ordained nun, and though they are for the most part conservative in respect to their practice,[53] they pose a challenge to orthodoxy. Chapter 1 explores more fully the tension between orthodoxy and the tradition of female renunciation, with special reference to the establishment of the order of nuns in Sri Lanka in the third century, BCE. In chapter 2, I present the rise of the unordained nun in the nineteenth century, within the context of the social, political, and religious climate of the period. I also make special reference to ambiguous models of the laity in the canonical works, models that have served as springboards for innovation, and include the category of the lay nun. In chapters 3 and 4, I examine Dharmapāla and the Countess's attempts to re-establish and institutionalize the tradition of Buddhist female renunciation in Sri Lanka. The early twentieth-century institutionalization of the unordained female renunciant is the subject of chapter 5, while the effort to reinvigorate the institution is the focus of chapter 6. Chapters 7, 8, and 9 are concerned with contemporary Sri Lanka. In these chapters, I offer biographies of many lay nuns and explore their reasons for choosing the monastic lifestyle, the problems that they face, their goals and aspirations, as well as their own interpretation of their vocation.[54] Their life histories demonstrate that though the lay nuns face hardships, they do have access to power which is normally not within the realm of rural laywomen from whom they are drawn. It is the power to chart their own destinies. In order to understand the contemporary scene, we must first turn our attention toward the story of the formation of the ancient order of nuns in Sri Lanka, for it is often invoked in the present.

The ancient order of nuns in Sri Lanka

INTRODUCTION

Early Buddhist Sri Lankan attitudes toward women and world-renunciation resonate throughout the *Dīpavaṃsa*, the *Mahāvaṃsa*, and the later *Cūlavaṃsa*,[1] as well as in the Chinese sources, which immortalized the nuns' missionary activities in the fifth century. In this chapter, I explore these attitudes and relate them to the present debate over the re-establishment of the nuns' lineage. This chapter is intended chiefly as the background for understanding that volatile debate, a debate that is rooted in traditional stories. As we shall see in Part II, contemporary Sri Lankans – both lay and monastic – legitimate their views about the ordination of women by citing the ancient stories of nuns and laywomen. And, as we shall see in chapter 2 and chapter 3, late nineteenth- and early twentieth-century Buddhists used the *Mahāvaṃsa* and *Dīpavaṃsa* stories about nuns and laywomen as their charter for a reformation of Buddhism. Indeed, the Mahāvaṃsa-view of history has helped define the way that female renunciants have been perceived from the 1890s to the present.

THE NUN IN ANCIENT SRI LANKA

According to the *Dīpavaṃsa* and the *Mahāvaṃsa*, the Indian King Asoka was responsible for the introduction of Buddhism into Sri Lanka. His son, the monk Mahinda, established the order of monks in Sri Lanka, and his daughter, the nun Saṅghamittā, established the nuns' lineage.[2] Though the *Mahāvaṃsa* account of the establishment of the order of nuns in Sri Lanka agrees with the *Dīpavaṃsa*, it does not follow the development of the order. The *Dīpavaṃsa*, however, alludes to the expansion of the order of nuns from Anurādhapura, the north-central capital, to the southern-most reaches of the island.[3]

Moreover, it records that kings both listened to the advice of nuns, and saw to their material comforts.[4] Indeed, nuns, rather than monks, are the focus of the *Dīpavaṃsa*; as R. A. L. H. Gunawardena has pointed out, very few monks appear in the chronicle, while the larger number of clerics mentioned by name are nuns.[5]

The *Dīpavaṃsa*, in contrast to other sources, teems with allusions to the order of nuns; a few Pāli scholars have, therefore, speculated that it might be one of the few literary pieces that nuns composed.[6] According to the *Dīpavaṃsa*, not only did women desire to renounce lay life when inspired by the example of the monk Mahinda, they were also the first in the island to obtain the fruits of the Buddhist path: "Having listened to the best doctrine, the consort Anulā, who was faithful and full of insight, and the five hundred maidens, then established themselves in the fruit of the *sotāpatti*; it was the first insight ... "[7] Anulā then asked the king to arrange for the ordination of women as he had for men. The king, in turn, requested that Mahinda ordain Anulā and the others. However, Mahinda responded by insisting that it was outside of his power to ordain women into the monastic community: "Oh, king, it is not in accordance with the rules for monks to give entrance to women.[8] My sister, Saṅghamittā, will come and bestow admission upon Anulā; she has caused her release from all fetters [that is, she had attained *nibbāna*]."[9] The text then describes how Mahinda sent a message to Asoka, who agreed that Saṅghamittā and the proper quorum of nuns should make the arduous journey to Sri Lanka in order to establish the nuns' lineage. In the meantime, the Sri Lankan king made arrangements to accommodate Anulā and the other women in a special place of residence suited for their new vocation: "Then the king caused a house to be built on one side of the city. The five hundred maidens with Anulā as their leader, who was noble of birth and resplendent, undertook the ten precepts."[10]

Though the *Mahāvaṃsa* does not contain as many references to the Sri Lankan order of nuns as the *Dīpavaṃsa*, it does include a narrative of Anulā's life not found in the latter. According to the *Mahāvaṃsa*,

Anulā with the five hundred maidens and the five hundred harem women then kept the ten precepts; she dressed in yellow, was pure, and looked forward to admission into the *saṅgha*; she remained in the *upāsikāvihāra* until the nuns arrived from India. The king built that accommodation for her and she was content. Because *upāsikās* [laywomen] dwelled in it, it was famous in Lanka as the "*Upāsikāvihāra*."[11]

Based on the narrative, Anulā and the other women donned the yellow robe,[12] observed the ten precepts, and remained sequestered for six months while awaiting the arrival of Saṅghamittā and the quorum of nuns needed to initiate them. Although their residence, attire and precepts approximated that of the order as they awaited Saṅghamittā's arrival,[13] Anulā and the other women had not completely renounced their lay identity nor had they become members of the Buddhist order. Until Saṅghamittā bestowed formal initiation upon them,[14] these women remained "betwixt and between" two social groups, namely, the laity and the *saṅgha*. Such a position is best described as "liminal."[15] This powerful image of Anulā and her retinue in the third century BCE – especially with regard to their liminality – was to have ramifications more than two thousand years later when other women began to assume a similar status for different reasons.[16] As far as I know, this is the only such case of women being sequestered without formal initiation into the *saṅgha* until the latter decades of the nineteenth century. The narratives of both the *Dīpavaṃsa* and the *Mahāvaṃsa* suggest that Anulā's liminal status was the result of specific historical consequences and ended once women were granted entrance into the order.

According to the chronicles, Saṅghamittā eventually arrived with the other members of the *bhikkhunī saṅgha*. In addition, she brought with her a branch of the Bō tree under which the Buddha was enlightened. She immediately began to ordain the island's women: "The five hundred royal women who were high born and successful, entered the *saṅgha* and then attained *nibbāna*. Anulā, surrounded by the five hundred maidens, also attained *nibbāna*. The king, by the name of Arittha, also entered; he too attained *nibbāna*. All attained to the level of *arahant* and were fulfilled."[17] In this way the order of nuns was established in Sri Lanka.

The *Mahāvaṃsa* account of the arrival of Saṅghamittā and the Bō tree to Sri Lanka ends by glorifying the nun and her brother Mahinda, both of whom were responsible for the spread of Buddhism throughout the island. In a touching scene in which the king learns of the passing of Mahinda, we also are informed of Saṅghamittā's death: "Saṅghamittā, the great nun who was very wise, having fulfilled her obligation to the religion and having benefitted so many people, at fifty-nine in the ninth year of King Uttiya attained final *nibbāna* while dwelling in the tranquil Hatthalhaka Vihāra for nuns.

The king performed the highest *pūjā* in honor of her for an entire week,[18] and all of Lanka was adorned as it was for the monk,"[19] or Mahinda, when he died. Although the *Mahāvaṃsa* glorifies Saṅghamittā, the implication of its silence in regard to the development of the order of nuns is that it was an afterthought of the monk author. The Chinese sources, however, pick up the narrative of the nuns where the *Mahāvaṃsa* leaves off.

Though the Sri Lankan sources do not mention the missionary activities of nuns, Chinese sources record that Sri Lankan nuns were responsible for introducing the Theravāda nuns' lineage in China in 434, CE.[20] In fact, "according to the Biography of the Bhikṣuṇīs,[21] in the year 429, AD, there was a captain of a foreign ship, Nandi by name, who brought *bhikṣuṇīs* from the Sinhala country (Shih-tzu-kuo) to the Capital of the early Sung Dynasty at Nanking. They [stayed] in the Chin Fu Monastery and their purpose in coming to China was to form a *bhikṣuṇī saṅgha* ... "[22] A few years later, a larger delegation of Sri Lankan nuns arrived in China, thereby supplying the number of nuns needed to confer ordination,[23] and consequently "over 300 nuns were ordained by them."[24] Thus, the missionary activities of Sri Lankan nuns were not limited to the furthermost reaches of the island; nuns were also responsible for the spread of Buddhism as far away as China.

The Sri Lankan inscriptions and literary works from the centuries following the missions of nuns to China indicate that royalty patronized the nuns, and that the order of nuns continued to flourish.[25] According to one inscription, the king built them a grand nunnery, while another inscription records the usual privileges that accompanied land belonging to a nunnery.[26] Another tenth-century inscription informs us that the nuns performed the duty of nurturing the sacred Bō tree that tradition claims Saṅghamittā had carried with her to Sri Lanka:

A stone pillar inscription ... records a decree of amnesty granted to a certain village which had been set apart for the supplying of the necessities of life to the nuns who daily sprinkled water on the Great Bodhi-tree of the Mahavihara ... We note from the inscription under reference that the *bhikkhunis* who poured water on the Great Bodhi-tree were held in the highest esteem and respect because they are spoken of a *meheni-vat* hambuvan, "the *bhikkhuni* ladies." *Vat-hambu* is the feminine of *vat-himi* (Sanskrit: *vastu svami*) a term of very high honour.[27]

From late tenth- or early eleventh-century inscriptions,[28] we learn that King Mahinda V (982–1029) built a large residence for nuns, thus suggesting that their numbers were on the increase at this time.

The *Cūlavaṃsa* also affords glimpses of the ancient nun in Sri Lanka and her interaction with the culture around her. According to the *Cūlavaṃsa*, King Mahinda IV (956–972) was a patron of the order of nuns and built them a nunnery.[29] Though this is the last literary reference to the ancient order of nuns in Sri Lanka, it implies that the order was a viable force in the tenth century; it seems unlikely that the king would have built residences for an order of nuns in decline.[30]

As we saw in the Introduction, the order of nuns ended mysteriously in the eleventh century or, as Gunawardena has remarked, the nuns "left the stage of history as quietly as they had occupied it."[31] The order of monks, too, became defunct at this time. According to the chronicles, King Vijayabāhu of the late eleventh century began the process of restoring the order of monks by soliciting help from the Burmese to reintroduce the lineage to Sri Lanka. However, the chronicles are silent about attempts to re-establish the order of nuns in Sri Lanka. That the chronicles do not mention attempts to bring nuns from Burma to re-establish the order, does not necessarily mean that no attempts were made. Yet, there is no mention of attempts to restore the order of nuns in later inscriptions. Certainly King Parakramabāhu (1153–1186), the great Buddhist monarch, would have availed himself of Burmese aid if the restoration of the order of nuns had been a priority. History, however, is silent about any attempts during his reign or later.

The contemporary debate over the re-establishment of the nuns' lineage hinges upon the eleventh-century demise of the order of nuns, and the lack of interest in resuscitating it at that time. This debate also centers upon the nuns' fifth-century missionary activities in China. Hema Goonatilika, a proponent of the re-establishment of the nuns' lineage in Sri Lanka, has argued that it can be revived with the aid of Chinese nuns, the direct spiritual descendants of Sri Lankan nuns.[32] Others, including D. Amarasiri Weeraratne, a vocal Buddhist layman, agree with her.[33] However, such a joint venture is resisted by many monks in Sri Lanka who claim that the Chinese tradition is now too corrupt to be introduced in Sri Lanka. For instance, the Venerable Madihee Paññāsīha argues that though Sri Lankan nuns introduced the Theravāda nuns' lineage to China: "it is the accepted view of the *Maha Theras* [senior monks] of the Theravada tradition that it [the present ordination lineage in China] does not conform to the Theravada Vinaya rules."[34] In short, conservative Sri Lankan monks, like the Venerable Madihee Paññāsīha, believe that the ordination of women by the Chinese would threaten the integrity of their Theravādin heritage. One consequence of this fear is that women at the present time cannot enter the *saṅgha*.

CONCLUSIONS

In contemporary Buddhist Sri Lanka, the ideal woman is she who nurtures her family and the monastic order, not she who renounces the world.[35] The majority of the lay Buddhists I interviewed remarked that even though they do, or would, offer *dānaya* (alms) to female renunciants, they believe that world-renunciation is not a suitable concern for women. Their ideas about women and world-renunciation thus, in many ways, echo the monks. Therefore, it is not surprising that all contemporary efforts to reestablish the order of nuns are quashed.[36] In short, from the point of view of most monks and many lay Buddhists I interviewed, women can (and should) be religious by remaining "in-the-world."

Attitudes about women in the Pāli Canon as the embodiment of *saṃsāra*[37] legitimate inequality and send a negative message to Buddhist communities. When I asked various monks around the island about the possibility of re-establishing the order of nuns, many invoked the canon as proof that the Buddha did not consider women worthy of entering his monastic community. The Sri Lankan chronicles, too, have shaped the thinking of monks. For instance, in my conversations with a senior monk about the issue of ordination for women, I mentioned that according to the chronicles, nuns had been an important factor in the spread of Buddhism in Sri Lanka. He countered by claiming that those very chronicles also suggest that nuns were not indispensable for the success of Buddhism. Some monks also mentioned that the often pitiable condition of women who have renounced the world in the present, a topic to be explored more fully in Part II below, is proof that they should not be allowed to enter the *saṅgha*. Though it can be argued that the plight of these women is due largely to their *lack* of status in the *saṅgha*, one such monk suggested that if a woman "really wanted to live like a *bhikkhunī*, she would, even though the lineage has ended. That the lineage has ended and was never revived is proof that women should not renounce."[38] Though it is impossible to know exactly why the order of nuns ceased to exist in Sri Lanka or, for that matter, exactly what the Buddha's attitudes were toward women and renunciation, ideas about each exist in the present. These ideas provide parameters for the choices made for women who renounce the world, as well as the choices such women make.

Sri Lankan Buddhists allege that the Bō tree which Saṅghamittā brought with her to Sri Lanka continues to thrive, yet, the lineage she introduced, as we have seen, has disappeared. It is difficult to determine whether there was a tradition of female renunciation – lay or "legitimate" – during the centuries that followed the demise of the order of nuns in the eleventh century. However, the sources of the modern period suggest that Buddhists made attempts toward the turn of the twentieth century to revive the vocation of the nun. In chapter 2, I document the first attempts in the recent period to revive the tradition of Buddhist female renunciation, and the attitudes toward women, in particular, and Buddhism, in general, that such revivals reflect.

Nineteenth-century Ceylon: the emergence of the lay nun

INTRODUCTION

Toward the end of the nineteenth century, Buddhist female renunciants once again became a prominent part of the Ceylonese landscape. In this chapter, I describe the conditions that allowed women to participate more fully in Ceylonese Buddhist life at that time. The development of Protestant Buddhism, which redefined the role of the Buddhist laity in the island, was particularly influential.[1] "The most important ingredient" of Protestant Buddhism "was the very idea of the layman's responsibility, both for the welfare of Buddhism and his own salvation."[2] The essence of Protestantism in the new Buddhist ideology of the late nineteenth century was the claim that the individual could seek his or her ultimate goal "without intermediaries."[3] Protestant Buddhists thus blurred the distinction between laity and *saṅgha*; they denied that "only through the Sangha could one seek or find salvation, *nirvana*."[4] In short, much like Protestant Christians, they claimed that "the religious rights and duties are the same for all."[5] Women, as much as men, were heirs to this new way of thinking.

The erosion of the Goyigama caste's virtual monopoly of the monastic order also facilitated the increased participation of both women and lower caste men in public religious life. For our purposes, it is most relevant to note that in the late 1790s and the first two decades of the nineteenth century, Salāgama, Durāwa, and Karāva castes introduced many new monastic lineages into Ceylon. This undermined the Goyigama's exclusive claims to the *saṅgha*.[6] This general liberalization of the religious atmosphere in the nineteenth century gave impetus to the rise of the lay nun at the turn of the twentieth century. The "disestablishment of Buddhism,"[7] which created a new relationship between *saṅgha* and state, and the

24

"purification" or restoration of Buddhism, also set the stage for the emergence of the lay nun.

According to the sources, many late nineteenth-century Buddhists perceived that Buddhism had reached a critical ebb due to the christianizing campaigns of three waves of colonization. They responded to the plight of Buddhism in innovative ways, thus spawning a Buddhist revival.[8] Late nineteenth-century Buddhists drew on all their resources to resuscitate Buddhism, especially the untapped resources of laymen and laywomen. One Buddhist summed up the the query of many Buddhists of his day and asked who should resuscitate Buddhism: "From every side we hear of the necessity for a reformation. Is the reformation to come from within by a Council of the priests, or from without by the people themselves?"[9] For him, reformation was the responsibility of the laity.[10] We shall explore more fully in chapter 3 the general trends of the Buddhist revival, trends that, among other things, helped to institutionalize new religious roles for Buddhist men and women. Here it suffices to say that Buddhists who became active in the Buddhist revivalism of the period did not consider women limited either in regard to their ability to attain *nibbāna*, or in their contribution to the resuscitation of Buddhism.

The latter half of the nineteenth century was a period of religious experimentation, and there were various responses to the social and religious upheaval of the period. Carrithers has traced the contemporary forest hermitage movement to this time, a time in which Buddhists argued that the *saṅgha*, and other Buddhist institutions, had decayed. Carrithers describes that one of the pioneers of the forest movement, Paññānanda, searched for two years trying to find a virtuous teacher, that is, one who was not "sedentary" like the majority of the *saṅgha*.[11] Deeply affected by the laxity of the monastic community, Paññānanda devoted his life to its well-being. Paññānanda and his teacher went so far as to bring what they considered a proper monastic lineage from Burma, which was not associated with the lax and corrupt lineages of their day. In doing so, they established in 1863 the strict Rāmañña Nikāya.[12] Their stress on purity of practice was symptomatic of the late nineteenth-century return to "traditional" Buddhist values and practices. The message of the revival of traditional values was that if Buddhism was to survive, the *saṅgha*, as well as the country, must be reformed along Buddhist lines. As we shall see, re-

newed interest in the role of women in Buddhism also reflects this
tendency.

Rather than worshiping at their local temples and supplying alms
to monks – traditional female roles – a few Buddhist women donned
yellow, or ochre, robes and began to preach. These women moved
from the private sphere, the sphere of temple worship and support,
into the public sphere and became religious exemplars. Guided by
the laity who drew upon ambiguous canonical and post-canonical
models to encourage them, such women significantly contributed to
the late nineteenth-century Buddhist revival. As laywomen who
preached and wore the ochre robe, they eloquently expressed
Protestant Buddhism in both word and deed. Like other Protestant
Buddhists these women "undercut the importance of the religious
professional, the monk, by holding that it is the responsibility of every
Buddhist both to care for the welfare of Buddhism and to strive ... for
salvation."[13]

In addition to the 1890s, there have been at least two other cases
in Sri Lankan Buddhist history where the traditional paradigms of
renunciant and laity have been conflated. In this chapter, I refer to
these cases and to the social and historical milieu in which they arose.
I also offer the canonical viewpoint on the traditional roles of clergy
and laity, by exploring the early Buddhist conception of both. The
development of these themes provides the background for the
institutionalization of the tradition of female renunciation in the late
nineteenth century, the subject of chapter 3. To set the stage for the
rise of the lay nun, I begin with foreigners' accounts of Buddhism in
the island, accounts that trace the emergence of social upheaval in
late nineteenth-century Ceylon.

NINETEENTH-CENTURY IMPRESSIONS OF CEYLON

Travellers, including European missionaries and adventurers, were
not aware of female renunciants of any type at all in Ceylon during
the early and middle nineteenth century. For instance, Helen Ford,
who wrote a travellogue in 1889, offered impressions of Buddhist
monks,[14] but was silent about female renunciants. M. Bremer, an
English planter who lived in Ceylon, dedicated several pages of his
travel guide to the activities of monks and temple life in Colombo and
out-station areas. Like Ford, Bremer made no mention of female

renunciants in his account of Ceylon during the middle of the nineteenth century.[15] The eighteenth-century explorer, Captain Basil Hall, not unlike Ford and Bremer, was aware of religious life in South Asia, yet devoted nothing to female religiosity in Ceylon.[16]

As may be expected, the travellers who were most interested in the religious history of Ceylon, and South Asia in general, were the clergy. William Knighton, who wrote in the 1840s, dedicated much of his *History of Ceylon* to an analysis of Buddhism. In his description of the introduction of Buddhism to the island, Knighton gave credit to Saṅghamittā, who established the nuns' lineage in Ceylon:

It is not to be supposed that the female sex would have been behind the other in enthusiasm at such a time. They came in crowds to hear the divine messenger, and headed by the king's sister in law, they demanded to be made priestesses of the faith of Buddho. Mahinda professed himself unable to comply with their demand; at the same time informing them that, in his capital of his father's kingdom, there was a celebrated priestess named Sanghamitta, who was also his sister.[17]

Knighton continued his narrative with Saṅghamittā's attempts to persuade her father that it was her duty to travel to Ceylon to introduce the order of nuns there. Then follows a description of her function in Ceylon:

The ceremonies and offerings being concluded, Sanghamitta entered upon the office of ordaining and converting with zeal and success. Numbers of devoted females, headed by the queen, presented themselves as candidates for the female priesthood. Nunneries were established, and at length, Sanghamitta satisfied with the amount of her labours and their efforts, retired to spend the remainder of her life in seclusion and retirement, devoting herself to the exercise of her religious duties ...[18]

What is glaringly absent from Knighton's meticulous account of Saṅghamittā's contribution to Ceylonese culture, is mention of a similar tradition during his tenure in Ceylon. If there had been a tradition of female renunciation during the period in which Knighton was involved in the Methodist Mission in Ceylon, he surely would have mentioned it in his accounts.[19]

W. Osborn Allen, a Christian minister who toured India, Ceylon and Burma during 1882 and 1883, was also intrigued by the position of women in Buddhist history. In a chapter of his work replete with descriptions of Anurādhapura, the ancient capital of Ceylon, Allen

mentioned the contribution made by "Mahinda's sister," Sanghamittā: "Soon after the building of the *dagoba* [relic chamber] other
missionaries came from India to Ceylon, and one of them, the sister
of Mahinda, brought with her a branch of the Sacred Bo Tree then
flourishing at Buddha Gaya."[20] Allen's descriptions of Buddhist
women in Ceylon were confined to the historical past. However, in an
earlier chapter containing an account of his journey to Burma, Allen
included a contemporary account of female religiosity in Burma:
"The great *pagoda* at Rangoon is called the Shway Dagohn ... Up
and down the steps pass throngs of men, women and children, monks
with their shaven heads and yellow robes, and sometimes a nun also
shaven but dressed in white, looking old and ugly."[21] Allen was not
only aware that a tradition of female renunciation existed in Burma,
he also thought it important enough to include in his description of
religious life in Rangoon. Thus, if there had been a similar tradition
in Ceylon during his tenure there, it is quite probable that he would
have commented upon it.

Bishop Reginald Stephen Copleston, who wrote in 1892 guided by
his intense interest in the history of the clergy in Ceylon, offered an
account of the ancient order of nuns. Copleston argued that the order
of nuns in the early period of Ceylon's Buddhist history was already
disintegrating:

The period under consideration appears to have witnessed the gradual
decline in Ceylon of the institution of the Community of Nuns. In the
fabulous description of the days of Dutthagamini and Vattagamini [the first
and second centuries, BCE] the nuns are constantly mentioned as attending,
and as being provided for, in enormous numbers, bearing no unconsiderable
proportion to those of the monks. On these legends little truth can be
founded, except that the institution was believed some centuries later to
have flourished in those early days.[22]

Copleston did not limit his analysis of the female community to the
early and medieval period. In fact, after mentioning that there were,
indeed, nuns in Ceylon in former times, he categorically stated that
their tradition no longer existed: "There are *none* in Ceylon now; and
the received opinion I believe agrees with the conclusion to which I
have been led, that the institution of female mendicants was never
much developed ... in Ceylon."[23] Thus, according to Copleston who
wrote in the early 1890s, there were no Buddhist female renunciants
in Ceylon at that time.

John Ferguson, another missionary with a keen interest in Buddhism, devoted a chapter of his book about Ceylon to the present state of Buddhism in the island. Writing in the early 1890s, he reiterated Copleston's contention that the tradition of female renunciation was defunct: "there are no nuns in Ceylon now."[24] Ferguson mentioned the "energetic attempts made to revive Buddhism during the past ten years"[25] under British rule, attempts which were revolutionary and creative. However, he did not witness the resurgence of interest in Buddhism at its height, for he left Ceylon shortly after completing his book. The outcome of this resurgence included an interest in reviving the order of nuns in 1897, and the laity's concurrent revolutionary appropriation of the robe and vocation of the clergy. In the next section, I set the scene for the creation of the laity's new vocation.

THE SAŇGHA, THE STATE, AND THE DISESTABLISHMENT OF BUDDHISM

When the British in 1815 seized power from the Kandyan king, they also became heir to one of his former duties – the maintenance of Buddhism. In order to establish suzerainty over the ancient Kingdom of Kandy, which the colonial powers before them had failed to achieve, the British drafted a "convention" that, among other things, guaranteed the protection of Buddhism in Ceylon. The fifth clause of this convention was concerned solely with Buddhism: "The religion of the Boodhoo professed by the chiefs and the inhabitants of these Provinces is declared inviolable, and its Rites, Ministers and Places of Worship are to be maintained and protected."[26] Essentially, the traditional *saṅgha*-state relationship was to be upheld by the British governor who, by virtue of the convention, had assumed the responsibilities of the deposed king.

According to some early correspondence between Kandy and London, the British had forseen the necessity of maintaining this traditional relationship. In a letter General Brownrigg of Ceylon attempted to explain the contents of the fifth clause to the Earl of Bathurst, and also evaluated the Kandyan Convention:

... the fifth confirms the superstition of the Boodhoo in a manner more emphatical than would have been my choice. But as the reverence felt toward it at present by all classes of the inhabitants is unbounded and mixed with a strong shade of jealousy, and doubt about its protection – and that in our secure possession of the country hinged upon this point, I found it necessary to quiet uneasiness respecting it, by article of guarantee couched in more qualified terms.[27]

Thus, at least one Englishman acknowledged that without this guarantee for the protection of Buddhism, the British would not have be able to have gained control of the entire island.

For hundreds of centuries prior to British rule – in fact, since the inception of Buddhism in Ceylon in the third century, BCE – the symbiotic relationship between the Buddhist clergy and the state had been a perennial problem for each and every king. Though there is nothing in the *Vinaya* that condoned such a relationship, the king, who upheld order in society at large, similarly upheld order in the monastic community.[28] It was his duty to protect the order of monks and ensure the existence of a peaceful land in which the religion could prosper.[29] This frequently included the need to take direct action in monastic affairs by purifying Buddhism – the order of monks – to ensure its prosperity.[30]

Until the British annexed Kandy, each king, as political authority, had acted to ensure that the monks abided by the *Vinaya* following allegations of laxity and corruption, perhaps made only by the kings themselves. This incursion of political authority into monastic affairs, or "purification," is evident as early as the Anurādhapura period. It continued until the eighteenth century, when King Kirti Srī Rājāsinghe sponsored the re-establishment of higher ordination of monks with Siamese (Thai) help.[31] In fact, until Kandy was annexed, the king litigated all the matters of the monastic order including higher ordination proceedings, the appointment of ecclesiastical offices, and the protection of monasteries.

For the first three decades of their rule, the British maintained the "religion of the Boodhoo" in accordance with the Kandyan Convention of 1815. Moreover, in 1818, a new proclamation further strengthened the clause of the Convention pertaining to Buddhism. In order to assure the people of their loyalty, the British added these words: "As well the priests all the ceremonies and processions of the Buddhist religion shall receive the respect which in former times was shown to them."[32] In keeping with their proclamation, the British began to take a more active role in Buddhist affairs. They took custody of the Tooth Relic of the Buddha and began appointing chief priests, both of which had been acts of royalty in the past and, therefore, remained the prerogative of the British. However, within a few decades, British citizens living on the island began to question their Christian government's patronage of Buddhism and forced the British government to respond. Their sentiments reached the Queen of England who in 1846 commanded the British government in Ceylon to remove their influence from Buddhist affairs. The policies were changed in no uncertain terms: "First, ... the Government is to withdraw from all direct interference in their religious observances. Second, ... the custody of the relic is to be given up to themselves. Third, ... no more priests will be appointed by the government. Fourth, ... all pecuniary payments to the priests will cease. Fifth, ... all lands recognised and registered as temple property will be entirely exempted from taxation."[33] In this way, the state withdrew all its connections with Buddhism, that is, they "disestablished" it, even if their withdrawal took several years. In order to completely sever themselves from any involvement in Buddhism, the government in 1853 provided Buddhists with an organization to control their own affairs that later proved to be ineffective.[34] The government's new relationship to Buddhism prompted repercussions that continue to the present.

One of the ramifications of this new and impersonal relationship was that the Buddhist clergy lost the powers traditionally guaranteed to them by the king including the selection of appointments to temple offices. The honor and power that had been entitled to chief monks by virtue of their office was no longer guaranteed. Consequently, "the chief monks themselves had to do their best to assert their authority in relation to their subordinates," including the laity.[35]

Aside from the crisis experienced by the ecclesiastical establishment, another ramification of the new policies was that the state would no longer perform purifications of Buddhism when needed. Thus, pious laity and monks lost recourse to the state, which had traditionally rectified problems in the monastic order. Therefore, after the 1840s when the need arose to purify the monastic order, it was done without help from the state. As I have suggested elsewhere,[36] purification in Buddhist literature can only be understood in the context of the king as the protector and defender of the religion.[37] In spite of this traditional meaning, however, I believe that purifications of a sort continued to exist in Ceylon, even after the fall of the king and the disestablishment of Buddhism. Whether considered in its traditional meaning, or in its broader application, purification implies not only purging, but restoration and re-vitalization, as well.[38]

After Buddhism was disestablished, the laity launched many campaigns to breathe new life into Buddhism that were both innovative and revolutionary. At such a time when Buddhists, as we have seen, argued that the Buddhsit clergy were in need of reform,[39] the laity became motivated to purify the religion themselves, thereby assuming the former responsibility of the government. As specific examples of this type of purification in the 1890s indicate, many laypeople began to assume the vocation of the monk. These Protestant Buddhists called into question "the traditional monastic monopoly in withdrawal from the world";[40] this created conditions that allowed laypeople to act and present themselves in a clerical capacity. According to the sources, these Buddhist laymen and laywomen chose to remain "in-the-world" rather than becoming recluses, one prerogative of the monk. In regard to this, they also argued that the *sangha*, like Christian clergy, should play a larger role in the lives of their *dāyakas*, their supporters.[41] In other words, laypeople advocated a "this-worldly" asceticism.

BUDDHISM AND THE LAITY

At this point, I need to explain some fundamental, traditional distinctions between the monk and the layperson. Though canonical and non-canonical works, for the most part, address the monastic community, they also contain advice to the laity. Such advice, however, is sporadic at best and limited to only a few of the discourses.[42] Among the canonical texts, one stands out as somewhat unique – "The Sigālovāda Suttanta" – for it is concerned solely with the proper behavior of the laity. The text, the "*Vinaya* of the Laity,"[43] covers issues such as the proper relationship of: parents to children, and children to parents; pupils to teachers, and teachers to pupils; wife to husband, and husband to wife,[44] to name but a few. The Buddha's counsel to a young householder, Sigāla, on how to be a good layman contains the core of the text's teachings: "If indeed, young householder, the Ariyan disciple has put an end to the four vices in conduct, he does no evil actions ... ; he has practiced so as to control both this, and the next world. At the dissolution of the body, after death, he has a happy rebirth in heaven ... "[45] According to the text, the Buddha exhorted Sigāla (and all laypeople) to aspire to heaven, rather than to *nibbāna*, the goal of the monastic community.

The laity's pursuit of *nibbāna*, however, is not unknown to Buddhism; in fact, references to the abilities of laypeople to achieve the *summum bonum* of the clergy are a feature of canonical and post-canonical literature. For instance, the early post-canonical *Milindapañho*[46] suggests that early Buddhists credited the laity with the ability to attain *nibbāna*. Somewhat preoccupied with the abilities of the householder, the Greek king, Milinda, asks Nāgasena, a scholarly monk, if the layperson can realize the fruits of the Buddhist path: "Revered Nāgasena, is there any householder living in a house, enjoying sense-pleasures, living as master in a house surrounded by wife and many children, accustomed to Vārānasī sandal-wood, using garlands and perfumes, who uses money, whose turban is decorated with a variety of jewels, pearls and gold, by whom the peaceful, highest goal of *nibbāna* has been realised?"[47] Nāgasena answers that thousands of people had attained *nibbāna* while in lay life.[48] "If this is so," asks the king, "What is the purpose of becoming an ascetic monk?" Nāgasena explains that the practices of a monk are the "base for those who desire purification:... those householders living in a house, enjoying sense-pleasures, who realise the peaceful and highest goal of *nibbāna*, have all in former births finished the practice of the thirteen stages of asceticism."[49] In other words, *nibbāna* can be attained by a householder, albeit one who lived as a monk in a previous birth.[50] Thus, according to the *Milindapañho*, the householder can achieve the fruits of the Buddhist path to liberation.[51] Yet, unlike the ordained clergy who have the *Vinaya* to guide them – to prohibit them from lapsing into lay life – the laity are not bound by convention to follow one specific example, as the tensions and ambiguities in canonical and post-canonical works indicate. The "Sigālovāda Suttanta" offers the laity advice only, not rules and regulations to guide the devotee through every aspect of life. Thus, the meaning, goals, and proper mode of religious activity for the laity are ambiguous in the canonical works and have remained ambiguous throughout Buddhist history in Ceylon. In short, canonical and post-canonical works, as well as the people who have interpreted them, have never been able to agree on what the lay community stands for.

The traditional relationship between the monk and laity in Ceylonese Buddhism has nonetheless been reciprocal and well-defined, while Theravāda Buddhism has traditionally maintained a distinction between the path of the lay devotee and the monk/nun. The path of the monk/nun requires renouncing the world and following the monastic code, both of which are considered most appropriate for the attainment of *nibbāna*. The laity provide the clergy with material comforts to aid them in their pursuit of *nibbāna*, while the clergy in turn offer those who give to them a chance to reap merit. In other words, the *saṅgha* acts as a "field of merit" for the laity. This symbiosis, however, has not always remained intact. Some Buddhists in the 1890s, for instance, were dissatisfied with the lax behavior of many monks, and no longer considered monks worthy of alms. Instead, as we shall see in the next section, they found a few laymen and laywomen more worthy of their support than monks. Thus, with the collapse of the traditional safeguards that protected Buddhism, Ceylon entered a period of creativity and reform; one in which the roles of the *saṅgha*, the state, the laity, and especially women, were redefined.

CEYLONESE BUDDHISM IN THE 1890s

Those members of the laity laity who took a much more active role in the religious life of the island authenticated their new roles by claiming continuity with past traditions. According to the newspapers of the 1880s and 1890s, Buddhist revivalists self-consciously modelled themselves upon ancient exemplars of Buddhist piety immortalized in canonical and post-canonical works, as they attempted to purify and restore Buddhism. For instance, an 1898 letter from an ex-monk to a daily newspaper reveals that at least one person attempted to construct a category of religious specialist that drew on the lifestyle of both the clergy and the layperson. In his letter filled with fiery invectives against the traditional clergy in need of reform, Subhodānanda, an ex-monk, supported his proposed new status with historical precedence:

> July 28, 1898
> Pooreupāsakārāmaya
>
> With kindness, we were glad to receive your letter.
>
> According to Buddhism, if one wants to attain *nibbāna*, one must give up worldly goods and become a priest or an extremely pious layman [*upāsaka*] and, because of that, I am at the moment an *upāsaka*.[52] I was for a short period a monk, and now I have given that up. One should respect the

followers of the Buddha without taking into account whether they are monks or laity.

You can see from the old documents that there were in the past thousands of people who abided by the ten precepts while in lay life; they wore yellow robes. There are others who received their livelihood from going on begging rounds while in lay life. There is proof that there were about 500 women including Anulā who observed the ten precepts during the reign of King Devānampiyatissa in Ceylon. The king made them places to stay, which were like temples. These were called *upāsikāvihāras*, and they were famous in Ceylon. This is evident from reading the *Mahāvaṃsa*,[53] and the old document, *Atuwawa*, mentions this. In the *Paramatajotika*, people other than novices observe the ten precepts [as if they are one] in the same manner as monks; some, however, observe each one individually.[54]

Since white clothes and the things like them are liked and are pleasing to everyone, they lead us toward the five passions.[55] Thus we should wear the yellow robes even in lay life. The white clothes are also an obstruction to the austerities. They are not suitable for us. We are *upāsakas* who are followers of the Buddha.

In the past a monk at Oruwalla and Athurugiriya has not approved of pious laypersons who observe the eight precepts, and he has told so many lies, whatever came to his mouth, thus destroying most of the Buddhist tradition. His views have been published before.

By writing this letter, I am not writing lies against the religion. Such is done by so-called scholars. It is better for you to find out the truth.

Sincerely,
A dweller at the
Pooreupāsakārāmaya[56]
Ballāgama Subhodānanda[57]

Subhodānanda's glorification of Anulā and her lifestyle undoubtedly drew attention to women and world-renunciation. Indeed, to use Sponberg's terms, he "valorized" Anulā's liminal status, and advocated it for himself and other laity.

According to Carrithers, Subhodānanda became the leader of an ascetic group of itinerant "monks" who were the forerunners of the present-day forest monks of Sri Lanka.[58] Subhodānanda did not advocate *tapas* (asceticism) in his 1898 letter to the editor, a facet of his (perhaps later?) practice that Carrithers documents. Yet, he did condone a much more active role for the laity. He justified his position by citing continuity with the past.

Though the accounts that Subhodānanda cited are unclear,[59] they are suggestive of the claims he made. What Subhodānanda envisaged for the Buddhist laity – ochre robes and cloisters for the pious – he put into practice in his own life. Though a layman, he wore the robes of the clergy, which helped to undermine the sole claim of the monk to the robes. Moreover, he believed *nibbāna* to be within the laity's reach. In short, he was a champion of Protestant Buddhism. While cloistered in a lay monastery not unlike Anulā in the *Dīpavaṃsa* and *Mahāvaṃsa*, he preached this doctrine to other lay Buddhists.[60] In fact, to my knowledge, this is the first reference in the modern period of Ceylonese history to the cloistering of the laity in special abodes for religious purposes.

An 1899 article about a laywoman who kept the ten precepts, Jitadharmadūta Sīlavatī Upāsikā, suggests that there were also women preachers at the time Subhodānanda began his reforms. Sīlavatī, who had made a pilgrimage to Anurādhapura with "her six year old" in a rickshaw, stopped at resthouses and preached to the crowds. She had travelled to Anurādhapura from Galle at the invitation of a group of laypeople in order to "advise many people on religious principles,"[61] despite the fact that the order of nuns had been defunct for centuries. The account does not inform us whether Sīlavatī donned a monastic robe, but it does suggest that she took a clerical name. Moreover, she was "an advisor" like Subhodānanda who observed the precepts incumbent upon particularly pious Buddhist laity and members of the monastic order. A later, critical article suggests that Sīlavatī, or a woman like her, preached in the monk's robes:

It has been prohibited for laymen and laywomen who observe the ten precepts to don the yellow robes, and attachment to money is also prohibited. In spite of this, I have seen in many places those who observe the ten precepts wearing the yellow robe while preaching and collecting money. One laywoman collects money at the various places, among them, Colombo, in which she preaches. We would like to know what becomes of this money. The answer to this question is that she puts it in the bank in her child's name and will use it in the future for a cloister. This lady collects money by preaching in various parts of the country.[62]

Despite the misgivings of some, the idea of a pious layman or laywoman undergoing a change of name, lifestyle, residence, and appearance had been established by the late 1890s. While some people considered Sīlavatī and Subhodānanda's activities to be defiant, there were others who considered them necessary and offered encouragement. In an editorial from late 1898, a Buddhist named Gunasekera made an interesting propositon: "It is no doubt that the producing of pure, knowledgeable pious laywomen and pious laymen will spread the Buddhist religion in the world. I don't think anyone would contest this fact. Therefore we should set up schools in the hope of setting up cloisters for pious laity."[63] For Gunasekera, the reformation of Buddhism was the responsibility of pious laymen and laywomen, both of whom should be trained properly in cloisters. It is striking that he condoned women renouncing the world. For Gunasekera, there was no conflict of models; rather, women, like men, were able to actively support Buddhism. What is noticably absent from Gunasekera's plea is any mention of the ordained clergy who were traditionally held to be responsible for the spread of Buddhism. The Sinhala newspapers of the period were replete with other tacit criticisms of the monastic order, as well as confrontational accusations against the order, such as Subhodānanda's.

In this period of heightened lay activity, newspapers were used as a forum to discuss the role of the monk and the role of the laity. For instance, Kadavaduwa Tilakumāra asked whether "there is any difference in observing the eight precepts in a temple, or from a layman, if the practitioner is unable to find a pious monk."[64] The columnist responded "If you do not know how to observe the precepts, it is good to get advice from a teacher. There is nothing wrong with doing so on your own if you know the precepts. The pureness of *sil* [correctness of practice] does not depend on the person who is advising you."[65] In other words, the practitioner does not need a monk in order to be placed on the proper path of practice; emphasis is shifted from persons to actions. Indeed, according to a subsequent response to a similar query, a monk is not needed at all: "If the pious layman and pious laywoman are unable to find a monk to assist them in observing the precepts, it is correct to find the assistance of a pious layman who observes the eight precepts."[66] According to these writers, there were very few monks to assist the laity in their spiritual quest, the monk's traditional role. Therefore, the laity advocated that some in their own group should appropriate the function of the monk in society.

Buddhists addressed the crisis in the monastic order in other articles and attributed it to the peculiarities of "popular" Ceylonese Buddhism. A writer in an 1898 newspaper editorial suggested that the crisis was due to novitiates' lack of proper motivation. He demanded that those who had not entered the monastic order for bona fide reasons should disrobe. Among the list of reasons for the acceptance, and continued persistence, of unworthy novitiates into the monastic order, are some of particular interest to this study. According to the editorial:

3 Useless people who have bad horoscopes are ordained and this destroys the religion. They should leave the priesthood.[67]

5 If a monk is unable to observe *sil* as a monk, it is better to observe *sil* as a layman. He should not continue to be a monk.

6 In countries like Siam and Burma, small children are being ordained. They study the religion as much as possible while they are in robes. Later, they leave their robes. They live as laymen. They are able to come back to the priesthood if they desire. It is much better if we could have the same system in Ceylon.[68]

Points five and six suggest that in the 1890s at least one Buddhist no longer considered formal status a prerequisite for leading a religious life. This commentary is only one example that is indicative of the changing views of many Buddhists in the 1890s.

An article from 1897 provides a description of some of the activities of pious laymen at the turn of the nineteenth century, as well as advice about how to provide for them: "The Buddhist laymen who chant *pirit* [efficacious sutras] are given food, oil, rice, and robes. These should not be considered as wages but as *dānaya* [alms]. It is improper to accept or give alms with this attitude."[69] Thus, the laity by the 1890s had not only begun to preach in robes, they had also begun to assume another of the roles traditionally associated with the ordained clergy: the chanting of *pirit* performed by monks at times of crisis and during rites of passage. Moreover, such pious laymen were rewarded for their role in the form of donations, or *dānaya*, a word traditionally used only in association with the monastic order. The laity's behavior toward other members of their own religious group defied the orthodox code of religious behavior and weakened the role of the monk.

A series of newspaper articles that appeared in December, 1898, and January, 1899, further attest to the late nineteenth-century attenuation of the monk. The also suggest that Sīlavatī and Subhodānanda were not isolated proponents of innovation. According to a letter published in a Sinhala newspaper, at least a few laypeople in the 1890s preached in robes:

It has been about 2000 years since the Buddhist religion was established in Ceylon. During this time, I have not been made aware of pious laywomen and pious laymen taking the eight precepts and wearing the yellow robes. I have seen the above-mentioned people recently in Colombo and other parts. A lot of people think that this may cause division. Some say there is no harm in this. This is not a question to be taken lightly. The Buddhist monks should say whether it is customary or not and whether it should be done. I ask that my question will be answered in this paper.

A Follower of Buddhism[70]

The letter suggests that the laity's new vocation was a topic of conversation among at least some Buddhists. Within a few days, a letter containing similar queries appeared in the same newspaper; this time, such activities were condemned:

I have not seen pious laymen and pious laywomen from Siam, Burma, Tibet, Cambodia and other Buddhist countries wearing the orange robes. Nor do those pious laymen and pious laywomen from other countries who visit Ceylon wear the yellow robes. In fact for the past 2000 years, the laity has not worn the yellow robes. If those who take the five and the eight precepts have the right to wear yellow robes, then are all people from Buddhist countries *tripitakadāra* [versed in the Pāli canon]? It is a wonder that the *mahāsthaviras* [elder monks] of our country do not point this out. If those who observed the *pehevasa* [fasting on the quarter day of the lunar cycle] wore yellow robes, it should be mentioned in the *Tripiṭaka* [the Pāli Canon]. Yellow robes donned by the monks is a great possession and people accept that the monks who wear the robes are worthy of them. The respect they command is being destroyed. On the days that the eight precepts are observed, both men and women are in the monasteries at night listening to religious talks. The yellow-robed monks are also there. While travelling, if a monk does not wear his robe, there is room for much calamity [sic]. Even a riot could take place [if his status is not recognised]. It is no doubt that women donning the yellow robes and shaving their heads will at some time establish a nuns' lineage.

It is not the custom of great men to keep silent at these times of conflict even when misdeeds are being committed by monks. It is in fact the responsibility of Buddhist people to consult the world famous, knowledgeable monks of Lanka and to listen to their advice. Whether those who keep the five precepts and the eight precepts should wear the yellow robes is my question.

S. W. G. Pragñāratna
13/12/98
Kurunagalla[71]

Pragñāratna's arguments contribute much to this discussion of the role of the laity in Ceylon during the period under question. According to his letter, it seems that in addition to the laity who kept the ten precepts, those who kept only the five or the eight precepts,

too, appropriated the robes of the clergy. Moreover, Pragñāratna
implied that the laywomen of his day wore the yellow robe. What
Pragñāratna witnessed in the 1890s conflicted with his world-view in
which monks, rather than laywomen and laymen, acted in a clerical
capacity. One of the outcomes of the activities of such women,
Pragñāratna predicted, could be an attempt to re-establish the nuns'
lineage. History suggests that Pragñāratna's speculations were
correct.

THERAVĀDA BUDDHISM AND MONASTIC MARGINALITY

The layperson cum preacher discussed in the publications of the
period, found himself or herself on the periphery of both the clerical
and lay communities and belonged to neither.[72] In other words, he or
she occupied a "marginal" position in Buddhist society.[73] The 1890s
were not unique with respect to this type of innovation. At other
times in the history of Buddhism in the island, laypeople have created
marginal positions for themselves by assuming the vocation of the
monk without changing formal status. For instance, during the early
Kandyan period, there was a type of "quasi monk who was resident
in a monastery but who had not been formerly admitted to the order
as a *sāmaṇera* [novice] and who was not necessarily celibate."[74] This
lay monk, or *gaṇinnānse*, seems to have worn "white or saffron cloth
instead of the orthodox robe prescribed for Buddhist monks."[75] He
"represented a new type of monk peculiar to the early Kandyan
period, not known before that time or since in the history of
Buddhism in Ceylon."[76]

The rise of the *gaṇinnānse* resulted from a decline in the standards
of piety among the ordained members of the monastic order.[77] As the
development toward private property among the monastic order
increased[78] and as pupils were often chosen from the teacher's kin
group, many men became monks in order to become heir to land
grants. In short, they "entered" the *saṅgha* without being properly
ordained as dictated by the *Vinaya*. "Indeed, most of the monks in the
late sixteenth, seventeenth and early eighteenth centuries belonged
to the category of *gaṇinnānses*."[79] One consequence of this was that in
the middle of the eighteenth century, monks had to be brought from
Thailand to reintroduce higher ordination. When in 1753, proper
ordination procedures were reintroduced in Ceylon by a purification
of the monastic order, the category of *gaṇinnānse* ceased to exist.

The Sri Lanka Vinaya Vardena Society (VVS), which was founded in the 1930s and continues to the present, presents another instance of people who have renounced the world in innovative ways. This movement started as a protest against orthodox clergy and resulted in the formation of a society vowing to produce a pristine form of Buddhism. The organizers of the VVS believed that such purity in Buddhism was only possible if Buddhist monks were reformed; a conviction that eventually led to a total disapproval of the monastic order in favor of self-ordained monks: "the Society regarded as properly ordained, *bhikkhus* who took the robes on their own or under the direction of a teacher who himself had not received initiation."[80] Like the pious laywomen and laymen of the 1890s, the members of the VVS appropriated the vocation of the clergy. In fact, according to Stephen Kemper, "the happiest innovation has been the attempt on the part of the Society's membership to take on the role of religious virtuosos themselves."[81] When invited, "the Society's members accept the veneration of other laypeople, say *pirit* (chant *sutras*), perform ... *pūjās* (worship services), and take *dāna* (donations offered to monks). On ordinary *poya* days, too, householders give *dāna* to invited members of the Society and gloat over their superior *sīla* (virtue)."[82] In short, the VVS advocates that the laity appropriate the role of the monk in Sri Lankan Buddhist society.

From this look at the *ganinnānse* of the Kandyan period, the marginal men and women of the 1890s, and the Vinaya Vardena Society of the 1930s, various elements common to all emerge. First of all, conditions of social change gave rise to each of the three marginal groups. Secondly, in each case, this social change resulted in a type of quasi-monk or nun who existed in uncertainty between two social worlds. Thirdly, the outward appearance of the members of each of the three marginal groups tended toward that of the clergy.[83] However, they all (at least in theory) observed the ten precepts, rather than the ten precepts and the 227 and 331 monastic rules of the monk and nun, respectively. Indeed, as we shall see in the next section, their vision of monastic Buddhism was inevitably very different to that of the *Vinaya*, the monastic code.

ORTHODOX BUDDHISM

In spite of the innovations of the Kandyan period, the 1890s, and the 1930s, the editor(s) of the *Vinaya* did not condone the marginal status of the monk/nun cum layperson. In fact, the *Mahāvagga*, a *Vinaya* text, addresses this phenomenon and categorically states that such "imposter behavior" is to be circumvented without exception. It records an incident in which monks, "having left the order ... , pretended to be novices, ... pretended that they were living in communion, though it was by theft."[84] "Having assumed the status of the monk, *without* undergoing the training,"[85] these men "stole" their new career as monks. According to the text, the Buddha responded to the incident by stating that the vocation, and the right to live in the order, as well as the rules of the monks, belong to the monastic order alone. In other words, "The order is the owner"[86] of the lifestyle and vocation of the monk.

Other canonical and non-canonical references are equally as clear as the *Vinaya* in prohibiting the "going forth" of persons without the permission of the order. The *Milindapañho*, for instance, does not condone the idea of people renouncing the world independently of the *saṅgha*. In a dialogue in which Milinda questions Nāgasena as to the fate of the householder who achieves *nibbāna*, we learn that the householder has only two destinies. Nāgasena explains that: "... either that same day he goes forth or he attains *parinibbāna* [death, without the possibility of rebirth]. That day is not able to pass without one or other of these events taking place."[87] Two important points emerge from Nāgasena's answers to the king's queries. First of all, Nāgasena states that the enlightened person cannot share the householder's life: he must either become a monk or put an end to the cycle of rebirth that very day. A more important theme emerges from the king's follow-up question: "If, reverend Nāgasena, he receives neither a teacher or a preceptor, nor a bowl and robe on that day, could that *arahant* go forth himself, or could he allow that day to pass ...?"[88] Nāgasena responds succinctly: "An *arahant*, sir, cannot go forth on his own. On going forth by oneself, one falls into theft."[89] According to Nāgasena, even an *arahant* cannot "go forth" without becoming a member of the monastic order. In short, even he or she who has attained *nibbāna*, "falls into theft," having renounced the world alone. Though circumvented in the *Vinaya*, the type of innovation discussed in this chapter is a recurrent feature of

Theravāda Buddhism. The community of lay nuns of the present day may again remind us that the *Vinaya's* iron-clad distinction between clergy and laity is ambiguous.

CONCLUSIONS

The laity's late nineteenth-century appropriation of the dress and vocation of the monk in an attempt to revive Buddhism was revolutionary. In breaking down the barriers between monks and laity, the laity created a new category of religious practitioner. On the other hand, their activities were conservative: their "charters" were canonical and post-canonical works. In other words, the laity found their precedent in tradition. Women, as much as men, consciously conflated the traditional paradigms of clergy and laity; their activities were also both revolutionary and conservative. From one point of view, the lay nuns' vocation was conservative; its precedent was the post-canonical *Mahāvaṃsa* and *Dīpavaṃsa* story of Anulā who kept the ten precepts, renounced the world, and wore the ochre robe, even before entering the *saṅgha*. By setting themselves up in the roles of nuns, these pious laywomen, and those who encouraged them, considered that their activities maintained and revived Buddhism. Yet, unlike Anulā, they had "gone forth" without the possibility of becoming members of the *saṅgha* and, as we see in the next chapter, they were encouraged to do so. In fact, the hints of soteriological inclusiveness in Subhodānanda's writings were echoed in the writings of others in his period. Indeed, their advocacy of the laity renouncing the world helped to revolutionize the way people would view the role of Buddhist women in the generations that followed.

Though Subhodānanda and Sīlavatī represent individual lay efforts to revive Buddhism, there were collective efforts to do the same. In chapter 3, I explore these efforts and the trends in late nineteenth-century Sri Lankan Buddhism that they reflect.

Theosophists, educators, and nuns

INTRODUCTION

Some of the women who renounced the world in the late nineteenth century went so far as to join women like themselves in a lay nunnery. Ceylonese patriots, foremost among them the celibate Anagārika Dharmapāla, a Buddhist Theosophist and a symbol of religious and national pride,[1] encouraged their activities and wrote that they were necessary for the welfare of Buddhism in the island.[2] Since his early years, when he was known as Don David Hewavitarane, Dharmapāla had maintained an interest in Buddhism, especially as it relates to the daily life of the laity. As a youth, having witnessed the Pānadura debates of 1873, in which a Buddhist monk emerged the victor in a series of debates with a Methodist minister, Dharmapāla developed the courage to fight in the moral battle for his country.[3] Though the Pānadura victor was a monk, Dharmapāla argued that both monk and laity should be involved in the revival and maintenance of Buddhism. In other words, he maintained that Buddhism was meant as much for the monk as for the layperson (upāsaka); indeed, in the context of his day, the duties of the upāsaka needed as much reinterpretation as the role of the monk.[4] Dharmapāla argued that Ceylon Buddhism needed to be reformed, and that it should be reformed in accordance with the ancient texts. He wrote, for instance, that canonical Buddhism offered women far more freedoms than other religions, and that women should reclaim those freedoms.[5] In addition to encouraging women out of their domestic sphere, he urged Buddhists of different caste affiliations to unite in the struggle against the British.[6] He argued that Buddhists should not only resuscitate Buddhism, they should also purge it of superstition;[7] and he encouraged economic development that would enable Buddhists to compete with the West.[8] Dharmapāla retrieved many of these

44

themes from canonical Buddhism, which became his blueprint for an "ideal" Buddhist society: a society in which Buddhist female renunciants would play a major role. By appealing to the glories of Buddhist civilization celebrated in the Canon and the Pāli chronicles of Ceylon, Dharmapāla contributed to a new nationalist identity and sense of self-esteem that empowered Buddhists to challenge the perceived discriminatory policies of the British. Dharmapāla's interest in scripture and text "led progressively to the ideologization of religion as charter which represented a shift from "religiousness" to "religious-mindedness," from religion as moral practice to religion as cultural and political possession."[9] In other words, interest in Buddhist female renunciation in the latter decades of the nineteenth century originated in the same revivalism that has shaped contemporary Sinhala Buddhist national identity. In this chapter, I discuss Dharmapāla's attitudes toward female renunciation, attitudes that were shared by a good many Buddhists of his day, and relate them to the formation of the new Sinhala Buddhist nationalism.

THE LATE NINETEENTH-CENTURY BUDDHIST REVIVAL

The period of Buddhist revivalism in late nineteenth-century Ceylon that stimulated the rise of the unordained nun has been adequately documented elsewhere.[10] Thus, in this chapter, I need only outline the main points. Swept along by the tide of change in the 1890s, lay Buddhists became involved in chartering Buddhist organizations, the goal of which was the revival or purification of Buddhism. Among the most notable of the societies that mushroomed in the 1890s was the Mahā Bodhi Society (MBS), established by Dharmapāla himself in 1891. The purpose of the MBS was the "resuscitation of Buddhism in the land of its birth," and in all Buddhist countries.[11] This resuscitation included, among other things, the development of a Buddhist education for females so that they would be able to work for the Buddhist cause. This goal was not merely of local concern; Ceylon Buddhists solicited western women to teach Buddhist children, which resulted, as we shall see, in the establishment of the first documentable cloister for Buddhist women in centuries.

Another lay organization drafted in the 1890s was the Young Men's Buddhist Association (YMBA) in Colombo. Founded in 1898 by D. Baron Jayatilake, who was to become involved in that same year with the organization of the first lay nunnery in modern history, the YMBA encouraged this involvement of the laity in the revival of Buddhism.[12] Both the MBS and the YMBA continue to function today.

By far the most important and influential layman of the 1890s was Dharmapāla, who was among those intrepid adventurers such as Allen, who set out to explore south and south-east Asia in the late nineteenth century. Like many travellogues of the period, Dharmapāla's records and diaries of his journeys are replete with details of religious life in India, Burma, and Thailand. Similarly to Allen, whose impressions of the Buddhist lay nuns of Burma are a central feature of his writings, Dharmapāla was aware of the contribution of the lay nun to other Buddhist cultures. Writing in 1891 for an English weekly journal published by the Buddhist Theosophical Society in Colombo, Dharmapāla offered his impressions concerning education and female monasticism in Burma:

Education is an important factor among them. Every boy and girl is made to learn, – the former in a *pansala* [temple school], the latter in a Buddhist Convent – the home of the *dasa sil upāsikās* [devout laywomen who keep the ten precepts, i.e. lay nuns]. They are taught to read and write on a purely Buddhistic basis. *Jathakas*,[13] Pāli *sutras* and the like are given to be read; and the child not only learns its language but learns its religion, too.[14]

In a subsequent issue, Dharmapāla related other impressions of Buddhist lay nuns in Burma, including specific details of their daily life, as well as their appearance:

The *upasikas* who observe the *dasa sīla* [the ten precepts] are greatly respected by the laymen for their purity of life and knowledge of the *dharma*. It is an edifying spectacle to behold in the pavements and courtyards of the temple these revered women, with their pure white robes and shaven heads, slowly walking up and down, rosary in hand, and their thoughts concentrated on some enobling subject. Some of these *upasikas* are quite young, but as a rule they enter the order when they are over 40...[15]

His discussion of lay nuns in Burma suggests that he valued the contribution that women were able to make to Buddhism; he hoped that the women of Ceylon would be able to make a similar contribution. Some of Dharmapāla's writings bespeak a misogynous prejudice because women, from his point of view, could tempt him away from his commitment to celibacy;[16] however, they also reflect a glorification of the feminine, as his writings on lay nuns in Burma suggest.

Writing in 1891, Dharmapāla made no reference to similar groups of lay nuns in Ceylon. His silence in this regard is telling; had there been a tradition of female renunciation in Ceylon in the early 1890s, it surely would have captured his attention.[17] His diaries and travel articles indicate that he was fascinated with the idea of Buddhist female renunciation, and continued to be, for decades. Indeed, in an 1897 diary entry, Dharmapāla wrote that the establishment of the Theravādin order of nuns was one of his priorities: "In 1890 in the month of July, I believe," Dharmapāla wrote, "I suggested the resuscitation of the *bhiksuni* order in Ceylon.[18] Seven years later the idea suggests itself again. I wrote to Mr. James Dias of Panadura about it..."[19] If we can take this diary entry at face value, rather than as a reflection of an idealized past, Dharmapāla entertained the idea of re-establishing the order of nuns in Ceylon even prior to his tour of Southeast Asia. At the same time, he wrote that Ceylon Buddhists needed to be ever vigilant of the ways in which pagans, especially Christians, debased Buddhism.[20] He argued that "in Ceylon, Buddhism [had] lived uninterrupted through all [the] 2200 years" before his mission, but that its influence had ebbed.[21] The elevation of Buddhism in Ceylon meant the elevation of the Sinhalese, and the re-establishment of traditions associated with Ceylon Buddhists, including the order of nuns.

While in the United States as a Buddhist missionary in 1897 for the Colombo Theosophical Society, Dharmapāla was once again reminded of his earlier interest in the order of nuns in Ceylon. The circumstances of his renewed interest in the defunct order of nuns are fascinating and filled with all the makings of a good novel. According to his diary, Dharmapāla's earlier interests were rejuvenated after meeting a colorful American socialite in San Francisco who, by all accounts, was just as eager as he to advance the cause of women in Ceylon by resuscitating the defunct order of nuns. Countess Miranda de Souza Canavarro,[22] the "Countess," a lapsed Catholic and the American wife of the Portuguese ambassador to the Sandwich Islands, had spent many years as a student of Theosophy. But it was not until she met Dharmapāla in 1897 that she was able to completely renounce lay life and immerse herself in the study of eastern religions, an intellectual interest of late nineteenth-century America.

By the 1880s, "a significant trend toward Buddhism was under-

T. Soc.

way" in America.[23] The Theosophical Society, founded in the United States in 1875, was perhaps most responsible for this trend. In fact, the co-founders of the Theosophical Society, Colonel Henry Olcott and Madam Blavatsky, both formally became Buddhists in Ceylon in 1880, a pattern which was to be repeated by other American Theosophists. Buddhism had permeated American society to such a large degree that in 1883, Phillips Brooks, an American Episcopal priest, was able to write of the 1880s as the "days when a large part of Boston prefers to consider itself Buddhist rather than Christian."[24] Like quite a few others of her time, the Countess found that her ideas were compatible with the Theosophical Society, which emphasized the Buddhist religion and espoused the unity of all faiths.

belief in degenerat E. relig's

The Countess, like most Theosophists of her day, believed that the eastern religions had degenerated. For instance, Blavatsky and Olcott argued that even eastern Buddhists did not understand Buddhism any more, due to the efforts of Christian missionaries to eradicate it. Moreover, the members and co-founders of the Theosophical Society insisted that education was the key to restoring Buddhism to its former glory. These ideas compelled Olcott during

T. Soc. desire to restore Budd.

his presidency of the American Branch of the Theosophical Society, to return to Ceylon in 1886 for the very purpose of pressing upon the Buddhists of Ceylon the necessity of a Buddhist education for their youth. An English Theosophist accompanied him and, by the end of their tour, they had raised enough funds to begin to establish Buddhist schools around the island, albeit for boys only.[25] The Countess was a part of this migration from the West, though she had volunteered to develop a Buddhist curriculum for girls.

The Countess was not the first western female Theosophist to travel to Ceylon; others, at the request of Olcott, had journeyed there a few years earlier to help propagate "true" Buddhism among the

women

Buddhist womenfolk. Such western women contributed to the changing social and religious scenario of nineteenth-century Ceylon. Like the Countess and her Ceylonese Buddhist colleagues, they were interested in the advancement of South Asian women through Buddhist education.

educ

Education became a very important rallying point around which Buddhists protested against the policies of the British. Among these policies was the Quarter Mile Clause, the law imposed by the British to ensure that schools could not be built within a quarter of a mile of an already existing school;[26] in effect the policy prohibited Buddhists from establishing rival schools to Christian missionary schools. Education has continued to be a political issue in Sri Lanka, even after independence from Britain in 1947.[27] In much the same way that Buddhists in the post-independence period have argued that education is a primary vehicle for instilling traditional Buddhist values, Buddhists in the 1880s and 1890s argued that education could promote traditional culture.

While Buddhists, as we have seen, took an interest in the education of boys in the 1880s, a Buddhist education for girls was sorely lacking. However, this void was filled by the founding of the first institution in Colombo to accommodate young Buddhist women – The Saṅghamittā School for Girls. This institution, which was later affiliated with the first Ceylonese lay nunnery, the Saṅghamittā Upāsikārāmaya, no longer exists today. However, extant records of the School and Upāsikārāmaya indicate that the Countess was the administrator of both. As principal and "mother superior," the American Buddhist helped to plant seeds for the resurgence of the tradition of female renunciation in Ceylon, something Ceylon Buddhists had already begun, as we saw in chapter 2. The Saṅghamittā project became the focus of the attention for the Colombo Buddhist elite and the Theosophical Society of Ceylon for an entire decade. Its *raison d'être* was the Buddhist re-education of christianized Buddhist girls.

THE SAṄGHAMITTĀ SCHOOL FOR GIRLS

One of the first full-time principals of the Saṅghamittā School was an Australian Theosophist, Kate Pickett, who was also the first Australian Theosophist to teach in Ceylon.[28] Pickett arrived in Ceylon in 1890 at the invitation of Olcott, who had placed an advertisement in an Australian Theosophical publication requesting Buddhist teachers for Ceylon's girls.[29] Little did Pickett realize when she began her tenure as principal that the Saṅghamittā School for Girls, named after the first *bhikkhunī* to arrive in Ceylon from India, would become Ceylon's first Buddhist lay nunnery in recent history.

Prior to Pickett's arrival, a group of women in Colombo argued that the future of Buddhism in Ceylon, which seemed doomed due to the great organizational powers of Christian missionaries, was in the hands of their children. However, according to these Colombo women, the future of Buddhism in Ceylon was not the sole responsibility of male children, but also of young girls. Organizing themselves into a group in 1889, which became known as the Women's Educational Society of Ceylon (WES),[30] these Colombo women began the work of educating their daughters in Buddhist schools.

The WES's chief aim, according to a Buddhist publication, was "to open, as soon as funds [were] available, an institution at Colombo for the higher education of Sinhalese girls ... under European supervision and to establish as many girls' schools as possible in the country."[31] Another description of the goals of the WES appeared in the same magazine; it, however, was less restrained:

The object of this Society is to rescue the rising generation of the daughters of Ceylon from the wily snares of the cunning missionary, and to ensure that the mothers of the future shall be actuated not merely by traditional devotion but by an intelligent faith in their religion, and when that object is fully achieved the honey-tongued deceivers, who try with such diabolical art to seduce the weak-minded into apostasy, may pack up their trunks and go back to Christianize and civilize their own land (which sadly needs their help by all accounts) for their occupation here will be gone forever.[32]

No matter how they articulated their goals, the members of the WES did achieve their primary purpose: they opened a Buddhist high school for girls in Kandy, followed by the opening of the Saṅghamittā Girls' School in Colombo.[33]

Even before the founding of the Saṅghamittā Girls' School, Olcott championed the advancement of women through education. In an address to the inaugural meeting of the WES in 1889, Olcott gave an account of his visit to the alleged tomb of Bhikkhunī Saṅghamittā and admonished the women of the WES to undertake the restoration of the tomb, and of a Buddhist education for girls.[34] This dual theme of the nun, on the one hand, and the education of young women, on the other, was reiterated in the history of the Saṅghamittā School for Girls. The School was founded in October, 1890, and among those who participated in its opening ceremony was the young Dharmapāla.[35] Mallika Hewavitarane, Dharmapāla's mother, was one of the organizers of the event; she was a member of the WES and later served as its president. The accounts of the opening, presided over by Olcott, suggest that it was a huge success.[36]

Lay Buddhists generally agreed in the 1880s that the decline of Buddhism in Ceylon could be remedied by the advancement of women. A commentary from the period under review succinctly stated the views of many Colombo Buddhists:

...the work which the Women's Educational Society of Ceylon has undertaken is of the very greatest importance and entitled to universal approbation. The examples offered by ancient and contemporaneous history prove that the true greatness and prosperity of a state or country are largely dependent upon the intellectual and moral elevation of its women.[37]

Essentially, the advancement of women could affect the socio-political agenda by strengthening Ceylon and contributing to its prosperity. The writer's inclusive attitude toward women is echoed throughout the journals and newspapers of the period under review.

Late nineteenth-century Christians, not unlike Buddhists, argued that the responsbility of religious education resided with women. Though the two groups disagreed on many issues, they both agreed that the future of Buddhism was in the hands of women. For instance, the writer of the 1888 report of the Wesleyan Mission in the Galle District stated that Buddhist women were the major supporters of religious life in Ceylon: "But the greatest force of Ceylonese Buddhism is not in the Bo-Tree, the priesthood, the wealth of temple lands, or even in the sacred books... The dominant force for Buddhism in the Island is Woman."[38] Thus, at least one Christian considered that Buddhist women, rather than Buddhist institutions, and even monks, were the backbone of Buddhism in Ceylon. The women of the WES undoubtedly agreed.

Be that as it may, the WES's Saṅghamittā Girls' School was ill-fated from its inception. Just two weeks after Pickett's arrival in Ceylon, a fellow Buddhist found her dead in the bottom of a well in Maradana, a district of Colombo.[39] The circumstances surrounding her death, to date, remain uncertain, though there was much speculation at the time. Many believed that she had committed suicide; others believed that she had been murdered.[40] Among those who gave eulogies for Pickett was Dharmapāla who, like Pickett, was a champion for the education of Buddhist children.[41] The account of Pickett's funeral, whether or not the historical allusions are accurate, attests to the high esteem in which she was held. According to descriptions: "Miss Pickett's cremation was the first instance of a lady's remains being cremated in Ceylon. Even queens of the Island were not cremated, only *bhikkhunīs* (ordained nuns)."[42] That Pickett, a female educator, was given honors due only to Buddhist nuns, is significant. As we have seen, Buddhists such as Olcott believed that in ancient times it was one responsibility of the nun to educate pious laywomen and children; as Dharmapāla's accounts suggest, Buddhists in other countries held that nuns were responsible for the religious education of children. It is not surprising, then, that Buddhists aligned Pickett, a female educator, with the *bhikkhunīs* of ancient days.

In spite of Pickett's untimely death two weeks after her arrival in Ceylon, the WES carried on with its project to educate Buddhist girls. After a brief respite, the WES began an active search for a replacement for Pickett. The second western woman the WES found to become principal was Marie Museus Higgins, a German-born American Theosophist who travelled to Ceylon to help in the "emancipation of Buddhist women."[43] Unfortunately for the Saṅghamittā School, Higgins' tenure as principal was short-lived; due to various administrative reasons, she resigned on December 15, 1893.[44] She later established her own school in the elite Cinnamon Gardens area of Colombo, which continues to operate to the present.[45]

Pickett's mother assumed the position of head-mistress for a short while after Higgins had resigned.[46] Not much is known about Mrs. Pickett's career in Ceylon, although Dharmapāla does refer to her occasionally in his diaries. On one such occasion, he wrote "Mr Wickramaratna ... says that Mrs. Pickett had violated the precepts by destroying eggs and that the sacred name of Saṅghamittā was profaned."[47] The newspapers also took an interest in Mrs. Pickett. A Sinhala Catholic newspaper ran an article about her, which included a reference to the Countess: "The Principal at this School, the Lady Pickett, will be terminating her work there as she feels that this school is not functioning to her satisfaction. 'We hope that lady who became a Buddhist recently will not follow the same example, when she takes over,' says the 'Messenger' newspaper."[48] Another newspaper kept readers abreast of new developments: "Mrs. Pickett, the Lady Principal of the Saṅghamittā School, severs her connection with that Institution, and will be leaving for Adelaide a fortnight hence by the Friedric dher Grosse. The M. M. Steamer Melbourne which arrived here this morning from Marseilles brought out Countess Canavarro, the recent convert to Buddhism who has come out at the request of Mr. Dharmapāla, to study Buddhism in Ceylon and to help the Buddhist cause."[49] Thus, as Mrs. Pickett made preparations to depart from Ceylon, the Countess approached the shores of Colombo;

and we enter the final chapter of the history in the Saṅghamittā School for Girls.

THE COUNTESS AND DHARMAPĀLA

When the Countess arrived in Colombo in 1897 on her mission to elevate Buddhist women, she was greeted by an elite crowd of Buddhists. Prior to her arrival, the newspapers requested that "the respectable Buddhist ladies" of Colombo should greet the Countess at the harbour "dressed up in white," and "should kiss and welcome her."[50] Among the ladies who greeted the Countess was Dharmapāla's mother, who welcomed the recent convert to Buddhism into the Hewavitarane family home. In fact, it was at the Hewavitarane mansion in Slave Island, Colombo, that the Countess drafted the original plans for the Upāsikārāmaya. The Countess arrived approximately two weeks before Dharmapāla, and she remained busy until his arrival by meeting the Buddhists and Theosophists of Colombo and planning for the opening of a "convent," as she called it.[51] After Dharmapāla's arrival in Ceylon, together they set about trying to find a suitable location for their historic joint venture, the Saṅghamittā Upāsikārāmaya. According to Dharmapāla, the Upāsikārāmaya work was to be the "first priority."[52]

As soon as she arrived on the island, the Countess became the center of attention of the Colombo elite,[53] and later, the center of controversy and scandal. The figure who emerges from the diary of the young Dharmapāla is a very complex and tantalizing woman. When we are first introduced to the Countess in his diaries, she seems like a frustrated, and rather eccentric, housewife. Of course, we are viewing her through the eyes and words of Dharmapāla, whose mistrust of women certainly colored his perceptions. Yet, it could not have been very commonplace in late nineteenth-century America, for a middle-aged, Catholic housewife to renounce the comforts of home in order to travel to Ceylon to become a Buddhist missionary.

Young Dharmapāla's encounters with the Countess occupy a good deal of his diary entries from March 1897, when they first met in San Francisco, until her stormy departure from Colombo, in October, 1900.[54] From the moment that they were introduced, Dharmapāla was struck by her intense manner: "Mrs. Canavaro [sic] called on me. I handed the relic to her. She has been victimised by her passion for phenomena. Ah the selfish nature of man. I warned her not to expend her psychic energy in the experiments as it would end in disaster for her and the world. "[55] Deeply concerned for the welfare of his new friend, Dharmapāla urged her not to experiment with her "powers." He often wondered to himself how he could "save her," and "channel her energies for the good of the world."[56] He spent the next few months of their relationship instructing the Countess and sending her long letters "full of suggestions about spiritual progress."[57] As early as June, 1897, just four months after their initial meeting, Dharmapāla expressed his desire for her to travel to Ceylon to educate Buddhist women, as well as other plans for their future.[58] In June, 1897, Dharmapāla wrote that he had high hopes for the Countess. He had "received under registered cover a long letter from Mrs. Canovarro [sic] as well as MS [manuscript] of her 'Aura of Diseases.' Replied to her that there is work to be done in Ceylon re-establishing the Order of Nuns in the Island."[59] The Countess, who believed that the "women of India [sic] have lapsed from the Buddhist faith,"[60] was very willing to journey to Ceylon to help resuscitate Buddhism and elevate the position of women. Dharmapāla had finally found the person who could fulfill his desire of restoring women to their rightful place in Buddhism, a preliminary and necessary step, he argued, toward restoring Ceylon as the bastion of Buddhism.

In June, 1897, the Countess wrote to Dharmapāla, who had been travelling throughout the United States drumming up support for his MBS, that she was ready to leave for Ceylon. Dharmapāla, well aware that others might object to the Countess's rather sudden commitment to him and to Buddhism, warned her that she should travel to Ceylon "alone, just as HPB and A. Besant did."[61] After receiving the invitation, the Countess left Horritos, California, "the home of her childhood, for the sake of the Buddha,"[62] and arrived in New York City, where Dharmapāla formally inducted her into Buddhism. What followed three weeks later was, by all accounts, quite remarkable and of historical noteworthiness: "In the evening at 8:30 the unique ceremony of admitting the Countess M. de Canavarro as an *upāsikā* was celebrated. It was a decided success. For the first time on American soil a lady was admitted to the Order."[63] At first glance, the "Order" of *upāsikās* might be one of the four Buddhist communities that the texts recommend for the continuance of Buddhism, namely: the *bhikkhu*; *bhikkhunī*; *upāsāka* (pious layman); and *upāsikā* (pious laywoman). However, Dharmapāla was interested in "reinventing" a special category of *upāsikā*, that is, one who keeps the moral precepts and renounces family life but who nevertheless stays "in-the-world." In fact, as early as 1891, Dharmapāla thought of "forming the Order of *Anagārikas*," celibate persons who have renounced but who do not become monastics.[64] Dharmapāla, along with Subhodānanda and others like him, continued to blur the distinction between laity and *saṅgha* throughout the final decade of the nineteenth century.

Dharmapāla's vision of a resuscitated Buddhism and thus a resuscitated Ceylon necessitated the involvement of socially active renunciants, or *anagārikas*, who were to be made members of a special order. According to Dharmapāla, he was the first to revive this canonical model of religious piety: "In 1891 I thought of forming the Order of *Anagārikas*, and in 1896 I became one. In the time of the Buddha there were the *Anāgāmi Brahmacāri Upāsakas*."[65] Drawing upon conventional, though ambiguous, models of piety found in the canonical literature, in this case, celibate laypeople who had attained *nibbāna*, Dharmapāla supported his new objective by proving its continuity with orthodoxy. However, the role Dharmapāla proclaimed for himself and others was not readily accepted by all; in January, 1898, Dharmapāla wrote that the "priest is willing to work with me provided that I show him by what authority I call myself an *anagārika*."[66] Nonetheless, in January, 1899, Dharmapāla wrote that "the *Brahmacāri* Order [of celibate laymen had been] started. They are to crop their hair and wear light yellow cloth, tunic and toga. Take *ata sil* [that is, the eight precepts] four times a month..."[67] Adopting a lifestyle which drew upon both that of the monk and the householder, Dharmapāla considered himself to be the rightful heir of both the monastic and lay tradition. Thus, like Subhodānanda, he was a champion of Protestant Buddhism.

One month after Dharmapāla became an *anagārika*, he wrote "the Priest at Buddhagaya [sic] to ordain [him] under the Bo Tree."[68] Dharmapāla eventually became a *sāmaṇera* (novice monk), and spent the last few months of his life as a fully ordained monk, a *bhikkhu*, and continued to be involved in social issues. Dharmapāla's own example suggests that he understood Buddhist practitioners to be of three types: (1) the pious *upāsikā/upāsaka* who observes the five precepts on a permanent basis and the eight precepts at the appropriate times;[69]

(2) the *brahmacāri*, or *anagārika*, who observes the eight precepts on a permanent basis, dons a robe, but remains "in-the-world;" (3) and the *sāmaṇera* who observes the ten precepts and eventually becomes a fully-ordained monk. For Dharmapāla, these categories were not simply categories of practice, but a trajectory for his own life. He had a similar plan in mind for the Countess who, in August, 1897, became the first woman to become a Buddhist on American soil. In fact, immediately after her public induction into the Buddhist faith, Dharmapāla commented in a New York interview that the Countess "... will enter the ancient *Anagārika* Order to which I belong now. This hermit order is 1000 years old." The interview concluded with a summary of the Countess's goals: "She is hoping to learn for several years, get promoted from grade to grade and finally to become a teacher in the religion, a *bhikkhunī*."[70] Thus, the Countess was to pass through the stages of pious devotee, socially active renunciant, or *anagārika*, and eventually become a nun.

Leading New York newspapers recorded the Countess's induction into Buddhism, which began the first stage of her life as a Buddhist. In August, 1897, several articles appeared describing Dharmapāla's activities, and included the culmination of his efforts – the conversion of the Countess. According to an article in a Sinhala newspaper, Dharmapāla had encouraged many American women to observe the eight precepts kept by devout Buddhist laity: "about 300 ladies observed the eight precepts and meditated with Mr. Dharmapāla in Chicago."[71] It appears, however, that the women who observed the precepts did not necessarily become Buddhists; according to Dharmapāla's diary accounts, only two people converted to Buddhism during his first two missions to the United States. The first person to publicly accept Buddhism was C. T. Strauss, who met Dharmapāla in 1893 at the World Congress of Religions in Chicago, while the Countess was the second.[72] As the first female initiate into the Buddhist faith in the United States, Dharmapāla considered the Countess to be unique and important: "She is the first woman in this country to accept the religion founded 2,486 years ago." Moreover, he called her the "pioneer of the religious movement which it is expected will unite the life of the Western people with the Spirituality of the East."[73] Because Dharmapāla had such high expectations for the American convert, the ceremony he planned had to be suitable for the woman who was "ready to sacrifice everything for the world and Buddha."[74] The anticipation of the event in the New York newspapers was high; reporters kept their readers upto date on the impending conversion of the Countess:

Invitations have been sent to several hundred persons in this city who are either full-fledged Buddhists or very much in sympathy with the principles of the faith. The exact character of the ceremony has not been explained. In fact, the disciples of the Buddha have only a vague idea of them, as it will be the first time in the history of the faith in this city that a student of the mysteries has been publicly accepted. Anagārika Dharmapāla will conduct the service.[75]

As tensions mounted in New York's New Century Hall on prestigous Fifth Avenue, Dharmapāla busied himself preparing the Countess for the ceremony, suggesting that a "white robe should be worn"[76] on the celebration day. The American accounts of the "picturesque ceremony" are lively and informative:

H. Dharmapāla, a Buddhist priest of the Order of Anagārika, took his place in front of the altar. He wore a flowing gown of yellow, the robe of the Order, and carried in his hand three white roses. Behind him came the Countess. She is of middle age, tall and slender, with a mass of black hair, making still more pale by contrast a colorless face. A scarf of white to represent the dress she will wear henceforth, was draped over one shoulder and across her bosom, partially concealing her dress of black silk and lace and the rose at her throat...[77]

Six vows were recited; the first five vows were the five precepts that the pious Buddhist is to observe on a permanent basis. They included: "abstaining from taking conscious life; from stealing; from sensual indulgences; from slander and untruth; and from alcohol and stupefying drugs." The sixth, "I will take truth for my guide," was Dharmapāla's innovation.[78] The newspapers, as well as Dharma-pāla's diaries, suggest that the Countess renounced her lay life completely – husband, child, and material comfort – in favor of her life of an *upāsikā*.[79] Traditionally, however, an *upāsikā/upāsaka* is one who observes the five precepts while maintaining the householder's lifestyle, which includes family responsibilties and the moral accumulation of wealth.[80] By renouncing lay life completely, but not changing formal status – she was still a laywoman (*upāsikā*) – the Countess helped Dharmapāla revive what he considered to be an ancient and traditional category in Theravāda Buddhist practice: the *anagārika*.

The conversion of the American Countess made a splash in the Sinhala and English newspapers of Ceylon. In an interview before the ceremony began, the Countess reflected upon her life:

It is true I intend to leave my husband, my child, my home. In order to work for Buddhism I must leave all these. It would seem a great thing to those who value the things of this world, but to me it is only the massing of a dream. I have been searching for peace all my life, and I now know I shall find it there in India (sic) trying to bring light to those women.[81]

Though the Countess was reticent to speak of her family, she did mention her husband. According to the Countess, her husband "sympathiz[ed] with [her] feelings, but [was] not of this faith and [did] not want to be discussed in connection with [her] resolve." The Countess added that they had "lived in San Francisco and had wealth, social position and all that is supposed to make life worth living." She also mentioned that she had an eighteen year old son, who was at college in California.[82] Having renounced all that, the Countess set sail for Ceylon two days after her induction into Buddhism.[83]

Before the Countess arrived in Ceylon, the Catholic newspapers in Colombo learned of her apostasy and took every opportunity to undermine her credentials as a Buddhist missionary, and Dharma-pāla's credentials as her teacher. An editor of a Catholic newspaper reduced the Countess to nothing less than a charlatan – an imposter who was not able to teach Buddhist children their own religion:

She informed her interviewer that she had deeply studied Theosophy for six years, but that it is only during the last six months that she has gone into a deep study of Buddhism, the true philosophy of which she did not understand, until her mind was enlightened by Dharmapāla. Before her conversion to Buddhism she was a Catholic. After deep scientific research into Buddhism, in which she understood nothing ... she at once gave up her religion ... So this clever woman, who after six months of study of Buddhism had understood nothing about it without the aid of Dharmapāla, is going now to teach the Buddhist girls their religion in its purity![84]

The Catholic newspaper editor claimed that the Countess was unqualified to teach Buddhism, and also argued that she had a very superficial appreciation of her new faith and may, at some point in the not so distant future, decide to become a Hindu, should the spirit move her.[85] Moreover, the editor warned that she should be careful and "not imitate a certain lady, a convert to Buddhism, who was found dead at the bottom of a well at Maradana."[86]

Despite these critics who condemned the Countess for her seeming lack of knowledge about Buddhism, and though by her own admission she had become a Buddhist after only a brief introduction to Buddhism, she did have friends who were Buddhist scholars. Among them were Dr. and Mrs. Rhys Davids, pioneers of Buddhist studies in England, who entertained Dharmapāla during a brief visit to London at the Countess's request.[87] According to her critics in Ceylon, however, such influences were not apparent.

Two years after the Countess arrived in Ceylon, another critique of her knowledge of Buddhism, as well as an insight into some of her activities in Ceylon, appeared in a Sinhala Catholic paper. According to the newspaper, the Countess needed a remedial course in Buddhism:

She has also said that she started an *upāsikārāmaya*, and there are lay keepers of the ten precepts and lay keepers of the eight precepts who could be referred to as *bhikkhunīs*...Though the knowledge of this lady is very valuable to Ceylonese Buddhists, what does a *pundit* know about Buddhism who says that there is no difference between a lay keeper of the ten precepts and a *bhikkhunī*?[88]

This Catholic writer spoke for many of his or her Catholic contemporaries and, as we have seen, a few Buddhists, who were uneasy about blurring the distinction between the lay keepers of the precepts and the ordained clergy. Like some of the laywomen of the period, the Countess eventually donned the ochre robe in spite of having no formal status, thereby adding to the late nineteenth-century conflation of lay and monastic traditions.[89]

Thus, the Countess argued that she had re-established the ancient order of nuns of Ceylon. Indeed, she aligned herself with Bhikkhunī Saṅghamittā, the nun who, tradition claims, had introduced the nuns' lineage to the island: the Countess changed her name to Sister Saṅghamittā soon after moving to Ceylon.[90] Moreover, the Countess alleged that she and the others in her Upāsikārāmaya were *bhikkhunīs*. I shall have more to say on this in chapter 4. Suffice it to say here that according to the sources, the Countess had not only rediscovered the lifestyle of the ancient nun of Ceylon and revived it, she had also reformed it; "the Order she was going to organise was to be a free, useful working society for the people, paying special attention to the education of the young."[91] Thus, her project to enhance the religious life of women, much like the forest monks of Sri Lanka whom

Carrithers has documented, provides another instance of the "rediscovery, revival and reform" of Buddhism in late nineteenth-century Ceylon.[92]

The Countess's tenure in Ceylon was riddled with problems from the day she arrived. She was stricken with various illnesses, most of which, according to Dharmapāla, were psychological.[93] Dharmapāla wrote that he often found her in "a state of anxiety," but felt that "when she finish[ed] her work she [would] be a liberator to the world."[94] Despite her illnesses, the Countess and Dharmapāla in November, 1897, set about negotiating for property that would satisfy the requirements needed for a lay nunnery. They looked at three pieces of land, all of which were located in prestigous areas of Colombo.[95] Finally, after careful consideration, they decided upon a location in the most prestigous area of Colombo – Cinnamon Gardens – where Higgins had established her school after withdrawing from the Saṅghamittā School for Girls.[96]

In the meantime, Dharmapāla maintained an interest in the Saṅghamittā School for Girls, which had been under the care of the Theosophical Society, but had never functioned properly.[97] He also visited the Museus School for Girls, which he called a "splendid success."[98] Dharmapāla developed an interest in reviving the Saṅghamittā School and researched the possiblities of developing a proper curriculum for young Buddhist women. He and his peers accomplished this task by moving the Saṅghamittā School to the premises of the Saṅghamittā Upāsikārāmaya, where it was envisioned that Buddhist "nuns" would teach the future generation of Buddhist women in Ceylon.[99]

In December, 1897, the project of organizing an Upāsikārāmaya became a local issue, and various members of the Theosophical Society contributed to the success of this historic event. Even Olcott was present in Ceylon during this period, though it is not clear from Dharmapāla's diaries how he responded to the lay nunnery work. However, the Countess did not admire Olcott, in spite of the fact that they were both in Ceylon with the same mission of reviving Buddhism. In a July, 1898 diary entry, Dharmapāla wrote that Olcott had visited the lay nunnery at least once and had remarked that the Countess "hates the Colonel [Olcott] like the devil."[100]

Nonetheless, it was Olcott's Theosophical Society, as well as Dharmapāla's Mahā Bodhi Society, which approved the selection of Gunter House on Darley Lane, in Cinnamon Gardens, to serve as the future Saṅghamittā Upāsikārāmaya.[101] The members of both societies decided that the Saṅghamittā School for Girls and the Upāsikārāmaya should merge in the hope of reviving the ill-fated school.[102] In other words, the students of the Saṅghamittā School for Girls were to begin tuition at the Upāsikārāmaya. Buildings for the housing of students and lay nuns – the teachers of the school – were quickly made ready for their new tenants.[103]

While architects remodeled Gunter House to accommodate a boarding school and a Buddhist lay nunnery, journalists interviewed the Countess who had an eye toward collecting donations for her project. In an interview with a newspaper reporter in January, 1898, the Countess described her plans for the Saṅghamittā School for Girls:

> The existing premises will be given up. As a boarding school the Saṅghamittā has not been a success ... The school will be under the guardianship of the Buddhist Nuns, which the Countess is organizing. Gunter House is practically to be converted into a nunnery and run on the same lines as a Roman Catholic convent. As far as possible these nuns would be the teachers ... All the primary work ... will be done by Buddhist nuns. The Countess expects to have European ladies shortly to join her. They would belong to the Order and be Buddhist teachers.[104]

The founding of the Buddhist convent was, therefore, quite a noteworthy and international project.

Not unlike other Protestant Buddhists in Ceylon, most prominent among them Olcott, the Countess drew upon Christian forms to rejuvenate Buddhism. For instance, in his attempts to revive Buddhism, Olcott had introduced a Buddhist Catechism, encouraged Buddhist Sunday Schools, and encouraged a Young Men's Buddhist Association, all of which were clearly modelled after Christian institutions, as Obeyesekere has pointed out.[105] Moreover, Dharmapāla himself, a staunch Buddhist and champion for the disentanglement of Ceylon from Christian influence, used Christian models to propagate Buddhism. On more than one occasion, he referred to the Countess, that is, Sister Saṅghamittā, as "Lady Mother Canavarro,"[106] and often mentioned in his diary his desire to start a Buddhist "Church."[107] Olcott, Dharmapāla, and Countess Canavarro all envisioned a type of Buddhism transformed upon

Christian lines. Paradoxically, the religion they publicly denounced served as the paradigm for their projects in Ceylon. In fact, Canavarro's descriptions of her school and upāsikārāmaya project were marked by Christian terms. When asked by a newspaper reporter if she had given a name to the new "Order" that she had been organizing, the Countess responded: "yes, I have given it a name; it will be 'The Saṅghamittā Buddhist Nuns.' I shall be the Mother Superior. There are two ladies coming from America and one lady is expected from India. She is an English lady and all are Buddhists."[108] The reporter then asked if the "nuns" at the Saṅghamittā Convent would wear a habit. The Countess answered: "yes, but I am not yet quite prepared to say what the distinctive garb or habit will be."[109] Indeed, in January, 1898, the date of this interview, though the Countess did not know the type of habit that would be worn by her nuns, she had already experimented with various forms of clothing deemed appropriate for her new vocation.[110] According to the photos, she eventually decided on a modified Catholic habit.[111]

The opening of the "nunnery" was an eagerly anticipated event in Colombo Buddhist social circles. Secular and religious newspapers announced the opening.[112] On April 30, 1898, Dharmapāla and the Countess declared the School and the Upāsikārāmaya open, and parents enrolled their daughters in the new institution of learning. The opening, by all accounts, was a success. According to one newspaper, "many Buddhist men and women attended and had friendly discussions with the lady-in-charge. All were served refreshments. Some students who attended played the piano and there was much merry-making. Those who participated dispersed in the evening in a very happy state." Moreover, several students "handed in their applications for residing at the school."[113] In short, the opening of the Saṅghamittā School was very auspicious. For a few months, the Saṅghamittā School and the Upāsikārāmaya functioned normally.[114] In fact, Dharmapāla and the Countess, the "mother superior" of the new Buddhist "convent," spent hours soliciting funds for the Saṅghamittā Upāsikārāmaya and School, despite tensions that were already becoming manifest in their relationship.[115] However, according to Dharmapāla's diaries and newspaper accounts, the two toured Ceylon together in a rickshaw collecting contributions to aid in the education of the Buddhist young women of the island.[116]

Dharmapāla's diaries suggest that the Countess wanted to assume full responsibility for the administration of the school and the Upāsikārāmaya even before it opened. "She does not want to be interfered with," wrote Dharmapāla. "Such is the world!"[117] Despite Dharmapāla's attempts to control the residents of the Upāsikārāmaya, that is, despite his attempts at "institutional subordination" (to use Sponberg's terms), the Countess was insubordinate. According to Dharmapāla himself, though they both established the convent, she did not want to be controlled by him. Nonetheless, Dharmapāla was pleased with the Upāsikārāmaya's success; by June, 1898, the Saṅghamittā Upāsikārāmaya, which had functioned for only two months, had already admitted "a few *upāsikās*" to the "Order."[118]

In July, 1898, while the Upāsikārāmaya and the School flourished, Dharmapāla wrote that he could no longer rely on the friendship of the Countess. His diary accounts reveal that her "impulsive" behavior could only serve to undermine their efforts to elevate the position of women in Buddhism.[119] By September, 1898, just four months after the school and the lay nunnery were declared open, Dharmapāla considered inviting another American woman to come to Ceylon to replace the Countess as mother superior. By October of the same year, her "strange behavior" had, according to Dharmapāla, begun to alienate the resident lay nuns of the Saṅghamittā Upāsikārāmaya. In fact, in mid-October Dharmapāla wrote that he and the Countess had debated whether or not to sell the Upāsikārāmaya due to the crisis created by her inability to live in harmony with the other renunciants.[120] While the two considered whether or not to close the school and the lay nunnery, a young Theosophist from Boston, Catherine Shearer, made arrangements to join Dharmapāla in Ceylon to help in his cause to educate Buddhist women. Shearer, who later became known as Sister Padmavatie (sic), was to play a significant role in the Upāsikārāmaya work.[121]

In spite of problems at the convent – Dharmapāla referred to the Countess as a "strange person" on more than one occasion – the two continued to work together to collect contributions for the School and the Upāsikārāmaya.[122] After Shearer arrived in Ceylon in October, 1898, to assist the Countess, the latter became free to travel around the island to solicit funds.[123] In November, 1898, Dharmapāla and the Countess prepared an itinerary for their highly publicized tour, despite the Countess's behavior which, according to

Dharmapāla, had become even more erratic.[124] On October 9, 1898, Dharmapāla while on tour with the Countess entered cryptic lines in his diary about an experience he had had with her: "I passed an emotional night," he wrote. "Two loving hearts met. In the bosom of my consciousness was a peace. Oh, what spiritual love. Received a rebuking letter from the *upāsikā*. Oh what changes! From the most loving to the most cruel letters received within 24 hours."[125] According to Dharmapāla's diary entries, however, the Countess had something other than "spiritual love" in mind; unlike Dharmapāla, she did not believe in chastity, even for people who had chosen a religious vocation.[126] While in Matara soliciting funds in October, the celibate Dharmapāla expressed his feelings for the Countess, as well as for women, in general:

The *Upāsikā* is extremely kind. She is willing to do anything for my sake. Even to sign her death warrant. I am determined to die for the *dhamma*. Nothing in the world attracts me. I must go to India ... "Better to embrace a red hot iron ball than to embrace a woman." I will remain pure. The *Upāsikā*[127] wrote a loving letter offering me the "highest sacrifice." I read it thrice, then burnt it ... May I become Buddha. I showed my power to the *Upāsikā*. I will shake the foundation of the world ...[128]

Dharmapāla's contradictory views of women frequently mirror the views of the Pāli Canon. On the one hand, Dharmapāla praised women such as the Countess because they were necessary for the propagation of Buddhism. On the other hand, women confine men to a cyclical existence and tempt them away from the Buddhist path. Thus, they should be avoided; for Dharmapāla, the Countess's behavior confirmed as much.

Nearly four years after the Matara incident, when Dharmapāla learned the news of the impending marriage of the Countess, he wrote a brief account of their stormy relationship:

Mr. Strauss writes that he heard of the report of the proposed marriage between Mme. Canavarro and Mr. Phelps. It would be a shame if such a thing happens. It's diabolical. The woman is a she devil. Unhappy is the man who falls into her clutches. She tempted me; but she failed in her diabolical efforts. I sincerely hope that there is no truth in the report.[129]

A few days later, he provided a synopsis of the history of the American Countess who, according to the sources, was the first to institutionalize female renunciation in Ceylon in recent history: "In 1897 an American woman followed me from California all the way to England, France, Ceylon and India spending her money to make me her victim. But I escaped the Devil."[130] The Countess and Dharmapāla's stormy relationship, however, does not undermine the fact that together they not only re-established the tradition of female renunciation in Ceylon, they helped to institutionalize it, as well. Moreover, the Countess's contribution to the changing face of education in Ceylon toward the turn of the twentieth century cannot be overstated; only three months after the opening of the lay nunnery, the Countess wrote that she had "established six [Buddhist] girls' schools" on the island.[131] Before her arrival, there was only one.[132]

In June, 1899, while in India reminiscing about his experiences with the Upāsikārāmaya work in Ceylon, Dharmapāla wrote that the Countess had made false claims about both his organization, and her status in the monastic community. "Today accidentally I happened to read a letter returned to the dead letter office addressed to Mr. Parson by Countess Canavarro," Dharmapāla wrote in his diary. "She has written that the [Mahā Bodhi] Society 'is about to terminate!' She has written deliberate untruths about the revival of the "*Bhikkhunī* Order in Ceylon" and about the educational work."[133] Dharmapāla had become uncomfortable with the claims of the Countess who, in his view, was a "member of the *Anagārika* Order" and not a member of the *bhikkhunī saṅgha*. Because he had studied the *Vinaya*, Dharmapāla understood the historical problems associated with the resuscitation of the nuns' lineage, albeit he had entertained hopes of its revival for many years.[134] From Dharmapāla's point of view, it was acceptable for the Countess to consider herself a Buddhist "nun;"[135] however, claims to formal status were unfounded.

A few days after reading the letter in which the Countess had made false claims, Dharmapāla wrote that his decision to go to India was a wise one, based on her erratic behavior. She vexed him even while he was in India: "received letter from M. Canavarro," Dharmapāla angrily mused. He added that "she writes about things which no pure person ought to write. I flung it into the W. P. Basket. It was my karma to have come in contact with her. I forgive her for all the harm she has done to me. If I suffer now it is all due to my foolishness. I look back with surprise at her past conduct. I am glad that I left Ceylon for India."[136] What had started as a project destined to elevate the position of women in Ceylonese Buddhist society had deteriorated into an embarrassment for the MBS, as well as for the entire Colombo Buddhist elite. The controversy surrounding the Saṅghamittā Upāsikārāmaya's Mother Superior, and her relationship with Dharmapāla, was apparently "buried with great difficulty."[137]

Members of the MBS, alleging immoral behavior, ousted the Countess from their organization and from the lay nunnery; they also accused her of attempting suicide,[138] and mismanaging the Upāsikārāmaya and School funds.[139] They did not permit her to return.[140] She took up residence in a section of Colombo close to Cinnamon Gardens, Dematagoda, where she made an attempt to establish another "nunnery" and school.[141] Within a few months, however, the woman who was once a socialite in California, and later the impoverished and disgraced "mother superior" of the first "lay nunnery" in Ceylon's modern period, made plans to leave the island and return to the United States.[142]

CONCLUSIONS

Though the Countess and Shearer were American, Ceylonese women renounced under Dharmapāla's tutelage. According to a printed account of the Saṅghamittā Upāsikārāmaya, which I explore in chapter 4, several Ceylonese women renounced and became lay nuns at the Saṅghamittā Upāsikārāmaya. The careers of women like the Countess, Shearer, and the Ceylonese women who donned the ochre robe in the 1890s reminded Ceylon Buddhists that women can be powerful vehicles for the spread of Buddhism.

Dharmapāla, by his own example, showed laypeople, including laywomen, that monks were not the sole conservators of Buddhism in the island. Though, as we have seen, he wrote that women were vile,[143] he also wrote that they were indispensable for the resuscitation of Buddhism in the island. Dharmapāla's contradictory thoughts on women reflect in many ways the attitudes of the monk editors of the Pāli Canon. Like them, Dharmapāla alleged that women could be good Buddhists and could attain *nirvāṇa*, an attitude of soteriological inclusiveness. He also argued that female world-renouncers were necessary for Buddhism's survival. In other words, he glorified the feminine. Yet, women needed guidance, and their supposed baser instincts needed taming; Dharmapāla could not escape ascetic misogyny. Once controlled, however, that is, once institutionally subordinated, women could be useful for the spread of Buddhism. I further explore this tendency in Dharmapāla's writings in chapter 4. Here it is worth reiterating that Dharmapāla and others, while drawing upon positive canonical attitudes toward laywomen *and* nuns, encouraged women to stimulate Buddhism by preaching, teaching, and acting as exemplars of piety through renouncing the world. This late nineteenth-century social reproduction was indeed successful. The Buddhist revival gained momentum in the early twentieth century and gave birth to other attempts to institutionalize female renunciation, thus producing a different set of concerns about women and renunciation. It is important to remember that the ideological work begun by Dharmapāla in the 1880s and 1890s, which took as its task the reconstruction of Buddhist civilization in Ceylon, has now become an established ideology for many Buddhists in contemporary Sri Lanka. Dharmapāla argued that Buddhism had always been the national religion of the island, an argument that has, to a large degree, shaped contemporary politics and recent ethnic strife.[144]

To sum up, his interest in the resuscitation of the tradition of female renunciation stemmed from his concern over the debased condition of the "national religion." After all, according to the texts themselves, nuns were one of the four communities of followers that the Buddha himself had envisaged for the world; Dharmapāla reiterated that claim for Ceylon. Before exploring other attempts to revive the tradition of Buddhist female renunciation, attempts that were similarly grounded in the new Sinhala identity that took shape toward the turn of the twentieth century, we will return briefly to the Countess's "Order of Saṅghamittā Nuns."

CHAPTER 4

The Saṅghamittā Sisterhood

INTRODUCTION

In July, 1899, Dharmapāla wrote that he had "Received a printed account of the Saṅghamittā Convent." Apparently, it contained "so many blunders" that he "returned it with a request not to send it out."[1] Though Dharmapāla did not specify the "blunders," there were many rules in the pamphlet that have no canonical precedent. As Dharmapāla had based his reformation of Buddhism upon ancient texts, any diversion from the texts would have been unacceptable to him. He never tired of preaching that Buddhists needed to read these texts, and that his country needed to re-establish Buddhism along the lines of the great Buddhist civilization immortalized in the *Mahā-vaṃsa*.[2] The Countess, too, read the *Mahāvaṃsa*. However, she interpreted differently than Dharmapāla at least one of the legends within the text, namely, the legends concerning the formation of the *bhikkhunī saṅgha*. In this chapter, I explore her interpretation of the ancient order of nuns and the ways in which the Countess sought to reform the rules that guided it. I base my study on what seems to be the only extant copy of the rules of the Saṅghamittā Order, which the Countess published in pamphlet form in 1899.[3] Study of the pamphlet affords us with an interesting example of the reformation of alleged traditional Buddhist values, ideals, and institutions that were a marked feature of late nineteenth-century Protestant Buddhism in Ceylon.

THE SAṄGHAMITTĀ ORDER OF NUNS

In addition to specifying the rules of the Saṅghamittā Order, the pamphlet outlined the daily routine of the lay nuns, and described their appearance and goals. It also describes the induction ceremony into the "order," and lists the names of the resident lay nuns. At the time of its publication, there were eleven "sisters" affiliated to the lay nunnery; among these, it is possible to piece together biographical data with reference to five of them. All the sisters took clerical names, it is not therefore possible to establish who among the remaining six were Ceylonese or foreign. Nor does the Countess provide this information in the pamphlet. However, she does give the clerical and lay names of three of the sisters who held the most responsible positions in the Sanghamittā. Of course, preeminent among them was the Countess herself.[4]

Though the Countess originally intended to create an order of nuns free from the restraints of the ancients, she later developed a code for behavior – a *vinaya* – which was to regulate life at the "nunnery." I have reproduced in full the contents of the pamphlet in the Appendix to this chapter; in this section, I discuss some of its more interesting features.

The first two pages of the pamphlet provided the reader with a brief biography of the organizer of the Sanghamittā, Countess Canavarro, as well as an account of the history and purpose of the order that she had created. According to the pamphlet, the Countess permitted several indulgences that were antithetical to the meaning of the ancient nun; these included "visiting ones' lady friends," and permissiveness, in general. For the newly created order of nuns in ancient India, such indulgences created scandal in the *sangha* and gossip in the lay community.[5] Such gossip concerning the indulgent behavior of nuns prompted the Buddha to provide laws designed to circumvent the controversy – to prohibit nuns from lapsing into lay behavior. For instance, when it was discovered that a group of nuns travelled in a vehicle, rather than by foot, "people spread it about saying: 'How can these nuns go in a vehicle, like women householders who enjoy sense pleasures?' They told this matter to the Buddha." According to the text, the Buddha exclaimed: "if a nun should go in a vehicle, it is a *pācittiya* offense."[6] Thus, indulgences such as "accepting invitations to breakfast" and "driving," both of which the Countess allowed, would have been an indication to the members of the ancient order of nuns that one among them was turning "back to the low life of the layperson."[7]

The pamphlet also revealed that the Countess allowed her nuns to be members of Olcott's Theosophical Society. Yet, within a few months of the publication date of the pamphlet, the Countess wrote to her American friend, Paul Carus, declaring that Olcott had condemned her activities. In fact, in a letter to Carus in 1900, soon after returning to the United States, the Countess mentioned that Olcott had defamed her in his publication, the *Theosophist*.[8] Many of the supporters of the Saṅghamittā were nonetheless members of the Theosophical Society and, therefore, it was prudent for the Countess to maintain good relations with them. Moreover, the decisions that the Countess made with regard to her Sisterhood had to receive the approbation of the Society which, for all intents and purposes controlled the activities and the management of the Upāsikārāmaya.

The account of the Saṅghamittā Sisterhood contains a discussion of the duration of the probationary period for novitiates. According to the rules the Countess drafted, the novice spent one year in white robes and her life was not as regulated as that of the fully fledged renouncer. Unlike the Countess, who required that her novitiates spend a relatively short period as a candidate and wear white – the color traditionally associated with the laity – the editors of the *Bhikkhunī Vibhanga* envisaged two stages of novicehood. The first stage required a two year probation period, in which the candidate was to wear the robes of the order,[9] thereby distinguishing her from the laity. During this time, the *sikkhamānā* – "the one who is learning" – kept the five precepts, as well as the sixth of the ten precepts that regulated mealtimes.[10] In other words, she was "to live in the six precepts." At the end of the two year probationary period, if the order of nuns agreed that the candidate was worthy, they inducted her into the monastic order as a *sāmaṇerī* (novice nun). Her induction commenced the second stage of her novicehood.[11] The *sāmaṇerī* was one who conformed to the ten rules of training, that is, to the ten precepts. Both the male and female novice kept the ten precepts.[12] The time of her final ordination (*upasampadā*) was left to the discretion of the order of nuns.[13]

Though the life of the novice at the Saṅghamittā Upāsikārāmaya was regulated, it is not possible to determine the degree to which the candidates were obliged to uphold the rules. Moreover, the Countess did not organize the sisters into an "order" until nine months after the Saṅghamittā Upāsikārāmaya had been established; this suggests that originally the life of the sisters – whether "novices" or "nuns" – was loosely regulated. Nonetheless, the fully initiated "nun" took vows and wore the color associated with the *saṅgha*.

The appearance, as well as the daily activities of the Saṅghamittā sisters, were similar to those of contemporary lay nuns. In fact, the schedules posted on the walls of contemporary village *upāsikārāmayas* in Sri Lanka that I visited in 1988 and 1989, and later in 1992, mirror in many ways the schedule at the Sanghamittā.[14] Like the lay nuns of the present, the Countess and her sisters meditated, ministered to the needs of the laity, and took counsel from learned teachers. In other words, like contemporary lay nuns, the Sanghamittā sisters were "this-worldly" ascetics.

According to Dharmapāla's diary, he often made special trips to the Sanghamittā – in his capacity as "teacher" – to advise the lay nuns. Though the Countess was the leader of the sisters, she and the sisters were ultimately under Dharmapāla's leadership, which suggests an attitude of institutional androcentrism. As Sponberg has argued in his review of ancient Buddhist texts, institutional androcentrism became prevalent in the monastic community once female renunciation was well-established in India.[15] This attitude also prevailed in the 1890s. Indeed, Dharmapāla echoed the Buddha by claiming that women are as capable as men of attaining *nibbana*, and that women can be instrumental in the propagation of Buddhism; yet, he reinforced the contemporary social standard of his day: male authority. Dharmapāla made frequent trips to the Sanghamittā, and often admonished the sisters to be "strict in their life."[16] He also involved himself in the affairs of the students; the final page of his 1898 diary included what he considered a proper "Curriculum of Studies in [the] Sanghamittā Convent" for the children whom the lay nuns educated.[17] From mat-making to meditation, Dharmapāla developed a course of study that he deemed appropriate for young Buddhist women. The Countess, as we saw in chapter 3, resented his involvement in the Upāsikārāmaya.

The Countess's own writings indicate that initially the daily routine at the Sanghamittā Upāsikārāmaya was not highly structured. In a letter written to Carus while on a lecture tour in December, 1898, eight months after the opening of the institution, the Countess wrote that she had established the "first Buddhist convent in Ceylon for 1400 years."[18] She continued with a description of her new order: "liberal views are entertained by the founders, there is freedom from dogmatism, and *no* vows are given by those who enter, but a desire to give."[19] Thus, the thoroughly regimented life at the Sanghamittā in the final days of its existence was in opposition to the Countess's original ideas of a Buddhist order of nuns and was doubtless a response to male authority.

According to the pamphlet, there was a formal initiation into the Saṅghamittā Sisterhood. The novice was to meditate on the "perishable nature of the body," and then ask the officiating monk to pardon her faults in language reminiscent of confession in Catholicism.[20] It is traditional for a novice monk to ask the officiating monk to pardon his misdeeds at the time of his induction. For instance, in ordinations of novices into the Amarapura Nikāya[21] in contemporary Sri Lanka, they repeat the Pāli "*sabbam aparādam khamathe me bhante,*" that is, "pardon all my faults, oh sir." However, the Buddhist notion of pardon is different from the Catholic sacrament of confession.

In addition to the general Protestant Buddhist trend of the day to reform Buddhism along Christian lines, the Countess maintained a very eclectic point of view throughout her career as a Buddhist "nun." In fact, as late as 1901, almost one year after she had returned to America, impoverished and humiliated,[22] the Countess continued to give interviews in which she praised Christ while describing her life as a Buddhist sister. In one of these interviews, when asked why she became a Buddhist nun, she answered: "Because I am a Buddhist; but when I became a Buddhist I did not renounce Christianity. I am a Christian and will remain a Christian; but my Christianity widened, and my faith has expanded. I have not lost Christ by understanding Buddha. The spirit is the same in Buddhism and in Christianity."[23] Though on occasion the Countess denounced Christianity, her non-sectarian point of view is evident in the early days of her tenure in Ceylon. In March, 1898, just prior to the opening of the convent, the Buddhist "nun" wrote to Carus that "Christ's teachings are but a repetition of Lord Buddha's."[24] Moreover, in January, 1899, the very month in which the Countess made the request to organize an order of nuns, she wrote to her American confidant that the "Buddha's gentle, loving precepts can only be equalled by the same teachings of Christ."[25] Thus, the Countess believed in a fundamental harmony between Buddhist and Christian doctrine. Therefore, given the Countess's convictions, together with the nature of the Buddhist revivial in Ceylon, it is not surprising that the Saṅghamittā sisters abided by Buddhist precepts that had been reinterpreted from the point of view of Christianity. Nor is it surprising that they wore "habits," held confessions, and were governed by a "diocese."[26] The Saṅghamittā Sisterhood, though a Protestant

Buddhist organization, was profoundly influenced by Catholic Christianity.

The "vows" that the lay nuns at the Sanghamittā Upāsikārāmaya took were not those of the ancient *bhikkhunī*, but rather were the ten precepts of the pious laity. We saw in the Introduction that occasionally very pious laity abide by the ten precepts. Although the ten precepts of the laity and the clergy each share the same number and order, the content is different, as the placement of the verb distinguishes the precepts of the clergy from those of the laity. Though this may seem an insignificant difference, it is extremely important and is a subtle, yet powerful, way of classifying lay nuns in contemporary society, as we shall see in chapter 8. Nineteenth-century sources suggest that the precepts have determined status for decades. According to late nineteenth-century newspapers, Buddhists at that time explored and appreciated the differences between the precepts, much like people today. For instance, in a representative newspaper article of the period, a Buddhist defined the differences between the two categories of precepts: "There are two types of *sil* [precepts]. *Sil* observed by laymen is called *gihi sil* [householder precepts], while the *sil* the *bhikkhus* observe is *pāvidi sil* ['going forth' precepts]."[27] In other words, people are defined by the precepts they keep.

In contemporary Sri Lanka, all members of the monastic order who undergo final initiation recite the ten precepts of the world-renouncer: the *pāvidi dasa sil*. In this process, the novice monk recites each precept, but rather than repeating the verb after each of the ten, he chants "*samādiyāmi*," or "I undertake to keep" *after* he has recited them *all*. Thus, though each of the ten precepts is chanted separately, they are regarded as one entity. Therefore, if one is "broken," *all* are so considered. On the other hand, with the inclusion of "*samādiyāmi*" after each precept of the householder, each of the ten remains a *separate* entity. If, for instance, a layperson breaks the precept concerned with stealing, none of the others is affected. Therefore, it is considered "easier" to maintain the "householder," as opposed to the "going forth," precepts.

Though the monk would never chant the precepts in the style of the householder, it is not unknown for the very pious householder to chant them in the style of the "going forth" precepts, albeit if only five are repeated. However, as it is the layperson who recites the five in this manner, they are not referred to as "going forth" precepts, but rather as "householder" precepts. The newspaper article explains further:

In the day to day life of the layman, it is natural to break the five precepts. But he can always renew them by observing them again. If he has observed *sil* by saying the five precepts as one – *pañca sīlā sikkhāpadaṅ samādiyāmi* – and breaks one precept, the other four also break. In the same way, if he has observed the five precepts separately and breaks one of them, he could renew his *sil* by observing that one only.[28]

Though the laity occasionally repeat the five precepts in the manner of the monk, the ten "going forth" precepts are only chanted by monks, and a few of the contemporary lay nuns of Sri Lanka.[29] As the wording of the ten precepts in the printed account of the Saṅghamittā Upāsikārāmaya suggests, the ten precepts that the Saṅghamittā sisters kept were those of the householder. Thus, the Countess does not seem to have known the difference between the precepts for those renouncing the world – the Countess's own description of what she had done – and those of the laity. If she did, the difference was thus an insignificant one.

When asked about the rules of her sisterhood, the Countess referred to the ancient order of nuns in Ceylon:

The Countess Canavarro ... explained that the Order of Buddhist Nuns which she was organising had never been known in Ceylon before. Saṅghamittā brought over with her many ladies and formed an Order of Priestesses simply to preach and teach the religion ... What the Countess proposes to do is not to reorganise that Order of Priestesses but to form a new Order. The former society was very strict. The Priestesses complied with the Ten Precepts which confined them to eating only at certain times and narrowed their lives ...[30]

The Countess was, therefore, unaware that there is a difference between the ten precepts and the strict 311 monastic rules of the ordained nun. Her ignorance on this point may account for many of the claims that she made for herself and the "nuns" at her convent; when later the Countess introduced a code of behavior by which to live – the ten precepts – she believed that it was the code of the ancient ordained nun. Thus, from her point of view, she and her flock were no different than the *bhikkhunīs* about whom she had read in the *Mahāvaṃsa*.[31] Though, as the interview suggests, the Countess initially considered the ten precepts to be too "narrow," she did eventually appropriate them, but only after she had reinterpreted them to suit the needs of her new order. Precisely when this occurred is not clear; yet, it is probable that Dharmapāla's controlling hand directed her. Within a few months of creating the rules for her order, however, the sisters dispersed and the Saṅghamittā closed its doors.

The pamphlet ends with a plea to those in sympathy with the work of the Saṅghamittā sisters to contribute to their general fund. In spite of this plea, the Countess and the members of her order were never able to raise the money needed to pay the mortgage for Gunter House – the Saṅghamittā Upāsikārāmaya and School. In fact, according to one newspaper, the Countess became so destitute that she and the sisters often had to beg for alms. "In brief, when funds get low this delicately nurtured woman, earthen bowl in hand, goes forth with her maidens into the highways and byways of the city, as church sisters do, and begs money to carry on her three-fold work among the poor; such begging bowls Buddhist disciples carried in ancient times."[32] The Countess's "begging rounds" were to no avail; she and the sisters were unable to collect the money they needed to make Gunter House their permanent home. Nor was she able to rally adequate support; the pamphlet, designed to inspire faith in the general Buddhist public, did not achieve its desired ends. These internal problems at the lay nunnery proved to be insurmountable and Gunter House was closed soon after the Countess published the pamphlet.[33] However, Shearer, who had travelled to Ceylon to assist the Countess, remained at Gunter House, while the Countess and her close associate, Sybil LaBrooy, established a rival "nunnery" and school in another section of Colombo.[34] In spite of the problems that Shearer faced in Ceylon, she seems to have devoted the remainder of her life to Buddhism.

CONFLICTING MODELS OF RENUNCIATION: SHEARER AND THE COUNTESS

The Theosophists who travelled to Ceylon to work for Olcott's cause, like the Countess, were sympathetic to the needs of the Buddhist public. Among them was the American Shearer, one of the four members of the Saṅghamittā Upāsikārāmaya who held important posts. According to the pamphlet, Shearer was the head sister and, as the Countess's correspondence indicates, she also served as the mother superior of the Saṅghamittā Upāsikārāmaya at various

periods in its history. For instance, writing in March, 1899, from the
MBS in Calcutta, where she had gone to assit Dharmapala though
he had discouraged her from making the trip, the Countess stated
that the work she had begun in Ceylon was "ably carried on by
Miss Shearer and does not demand much of my time."[35]

The Countess, who often requested her American friends to
encourage other women to travel to Ceylon to assist her, was
eventually joined by Shearer in late October, 1898.[36] Her appeals for
help also appeared in an American publication, which summarized
her needs and their solution thus:

> We have to add that although she had devoted all her own means to the
> enterprise, she still needs money and assistance. She has received help from
> various sources, but new needs produce new demands, and the burden of
> caring for everything grows too much for her shoulders. She wrote for help
> to America, and we are informed that Miss Shearer, an American lady who
> saved the money for the long journey from her scant salary as a governess,
> has now gone to join the Countess and share the burden of the work.[37]

Her American friends glorified her work in Ceylon and offered much
assistance; some Americans, such as Shearer, were indeed motivated
by her example.

Shearer, who arrived in Colombo in late 1898, just six months after
the opening of the Saṅghamittā Upāsikārāmaya, considered Dharmapāla to be her teacher. According to Dharmapāla, Shearer was
one of his "American students" who, not unlike the Countess,
seemed perfectly suited for the educational work in Ceylon. After
their initial meeting in America in 1897, he and Shearer maintained
their relationship by corresponding frequently. Dharmapāla decided
that Shearer, who was herself a Theosophist, a Buddhist, and a nurse
by profession, would join the Countess in Ceylon.[38]

In August, 1898, Dharmapāla began to mention Shearer in his
diaries. The first entry proclaimed that he had written a "letter to
Miss C. Shearer, 38 Commonwealth Avenue, Boston Mass. The
thought comes to me of reestablishing the *Bhikkhunī* Order."[39] This
entry echoed those of the period in which Dharmapāla developed a
relationship with the Countess; indeed, something about Shearer
reminded him of his early interest in reviving the order of nuns in
Ceylon.

Two weeks after the Countess's initial dissatisfaction with the
Upāsikārāmaya work, Shearer arrived in Colombo and was greeted

by a welcoming committee similar to that of the Countess. At first, the Countess seemed pleased with Shearer's contribution. She indicated as much in a letter to Carus with whom she had been corresponding on a regular basis since arriving in Colombo in 1897.[40] Yet, within months of their first encounter, the Countess's attitude toward her helper changed dramatically. At the same time, Dharmapāla increasingly began to question his affiliation with the Countess.

The day after Shearer's arrival, Dharmapāla indicated that the strain in his relationship with the Countess had manifested itself again. He wrote that he had "received letter from Upāsikā again showing her attitude towards [him]. How many times has she not done so." He added that "she wants that I should concentrate myself to her and forget others..."[41] Within one week, however, the Countess became the vice-president of the MBS, while Shearer was appointed joint secretary and Dharmapāla, the life president.[42] Thus, the relationship between the Countess, Shearer, and Dharmapāla was consolidated even further, in spite of its tensions and problems.

The day after the MBS elections, Dharmapāla wrote that the Countess was again "changing her attitude." He added that her odd behavior toward him was not his fault: "May the Gods know that my motives are pure."[43] In spite of the fact that the Countess proved to be a disappointment, this did not interfere with his attitude toward the other American convert to Buddhism. In the same diary entry in which he articulated his distaste for the Countess, he described Shearer's potential: "Miss Shearer is willing to go through anything for the sake of truth."[44] Such statements are reminiscent of the language he used to describe the Countess when they first met.

Within two weeks of her arrival in Ceylon, Shearer began travelling around the island in order to procure funds for the Saṅghamittā Upāsikārāmaya and School.[45] Beginning in November, 1898, Shearer was often left in charge of the Saṅghamittā School so that the Countess could spend her time soliciting contributions in Colombo and outstation areas, including Kandy, and Matara.[46]

In early January, 1899, Dharmapāla gave Shearer the name Padmavatī, a name that came to him in one of his meditations after she arrived in Colombo.[47] Not unlike the Countess, Shearer was often the subject of articles and commentaries in the newspapers of Ceylon. Indeed, even her new name was noteworthy. According to one newspaper, "American Madam Shearer, who has been appointed a teacher at the Saṅghamittā School and has read many books on Buddhism and has understood its truth, has become a Buddhist *upāsikā* by the name of Padmavatī."[48] I cannot determine whether Shearer was inducted into the Saṅghamittā Sisterhood by the method described in the printed account of the order. However, both the newspapers and Dharmapāla wrote much about her life. According to them, she seems to have occupied her time with meditation and the scholarly investigation of Buddhism. She even donned the ochre robe.[49] Yet, according to the Countess, Shearer was not a very good nun; in a letter to her American confidant, she mentioned that Shearer will "neither teach nor nurse. She is a dreamer."[50] Such statements suggest that Shearer, unlike the Countess, was not a proponent of "this-worldly" asceticism. Though Shearer was involved in the Upāsikārāmaya school, mental discipline rather than social work marked her career as a world-renouncer.

In the first few months of 1899 the frequency of arguments between the Countess and Shearer increased. Though Dharmapāla had travelled to Calcutta to continue the work of the MBS in India, he was fully aware of the situation at the Saṅghamittā Upāsikārāmaya. By October, 1899, the friction between the Countess and Shearer was such that the former moved out of the lay nunnery. She and LaBrooy transfered the students to a different location and the teaching continued as usual. According to a Sinhala newspaper, the new Upāsikārāmaya and school were destined to become a huge success:

The improvement of the Buddhist school, which was started by M. D. S. Canavarro recently is a great joy for the Buddhists ... 80 students attend this school and there are five hostel teachers. There are six teachers who teach the children. Three of them are from America ... The Buddhist people did not expect *Upāsikā* Canavarro would have courage to establish another school after the problems she faced during the past period. We wish all the best for *Upāsikā* Canavarro and Lady LaBrooy who also joined in this.[51]

The Catholic newspapers, however, were not as charitable as the secular papers and used the demise of the Saṅghamittā project as a powerful polemical tool.

According to a series of articles published in a Sinhala Catholic newspaper, the Buddhist "camp" had slowly but surely deteriorated, and the plight of the Countess became the central symbol of Buddhism's demise. At the height of the trouble, in November, 1899, a correspondent of a Catholic bi-weekly repeatedly interviewed the Countess, who lodged complaints against Shearer. In the same paper, Shearer defended herself and offered a different version than the Countess had of the demise of the Upāsikārāmaya:

Due to her [the Countess's] behavior, when the members of the Maha Bodhi Association realised that it was difficult to work with her harmoniously, they gave her the money to return to her own country, which she refused to accept. Because of that she faced difficulties. She gave up her work at Gunter House. It is all her fault. When she came back to the Sanghamitta forcibly, the other ladies too left as they did not want to share the responsibilities with her. Therefore, it is she who closed up the afternoon school. She says that what happened to her is a good lesson for other ladies who intend coming here, but I do not think the intelligent people will refrain from helping in the great service of teaching our Buddhist children just because one person was misled.[52]

Dharmapāla's diaries support Shearer's statements; yet according to the interviews with the Countess, as well as her correspondence to America, the trouble in the Sanghamittā was due to Shearer's divisive behavior.[53]

All of the leading newspapers in Ceylon mentioned the departure of the Countess Canavarro – Sister Sanghamittā, the mother superior – from the shores of Colombo.[54] It is not clear, however, how long Shearer remained in Ceylon after the demise of the Sanghamittā Upāsikārāmaya. She did remain in Ceylon for at least a short period; Dharmapāla in December, 1900, wrote about her work in Ceylon. Soon thereafter, she must have returned to Amerca. In April, 1901, only four months later, Dharmapāla mentioned her again; this time, it was not in regard to her life as a world-renouncer: "Received letters from Chicago. Miss Shearer writes to say that she is engaged to be married on her return to America. A few days ago she wrote and then she did not write me anything about this latest development. The law of change. Oh how true it is. The 'child of my bosom' is going to become the wife of another man."[55] She did not marry, however, for Dharmapāla mentioned her many times in the years to come, in relation to her work as a Buddhist "nun." In fact, from 1901 until her death in 1909, Shearer, or Padmavatī, as she was known, was involved in the study of Buddhism; much of that time was spent meditating in Japan and Burma while a lay nun.[56] According to Dharmapāla, "seeing the Burmese nuns and their self sacrificing lives, Miss Shearer expressed her desire to join their ranks, and with the consent of her friends she took up the *upāsikā* life [that is, the life of a lay nun] and lived in a cottage at the Upyatawya Kyoung, Boundary Road, Rangoon, studying the *Abhidhamma* in Pāli and learning the Burmese language."[57]

It is not remarkable that Shearer was drawn to the study of Burmese Buddhism, considering that there was much cultural exchange between Ceylon and the other countries of Southeast Asia during the period she was in Colombo. In fact, in the newspaper debates of the late 1890s that were reviewed in chapter 2, Buddhists often cited Burmese lay nuns to defend the laity's revolutionary appropriation of the monastic robe. In fact, the same writer who cited the Countess among those who appropriated the robe of the monk also mentioned that Burmese lay nuns had done the same. "While I write this letter, there are about twelve *dasa sil upāsikās* [lay nuns who keep the ten precepts] from Burma in front of me. They are all not only wearing the yellow robes but their heads are shaven ... If you visited the Temple of the Tooth during the last two years, you may have seen Burmese *Upāsikās* wearing yellow robes."[58] In addition to this, other articles written well after Shearer's arrival in Ceylon mentioned bands of Burmese nuns on pilgrimages to the Temple of the Tooth in Kandy.[59] In fact, one article mentioned the funeral of a Burmese lay nun who had been living in Kandy during the same period in which Shearer worked at a school there:[60] "On the twentieth of January [1899] in Kandy, the body of the Burmese *Upāsikā*, who had been living with *Upāsikā* Fernando[61] in her home in Katukelle in Kandy,[62] was taken to the burial grounds with much ceremony and cremated. More than 1,000 Buddhists from nearby areas accompanied the body. About 100 *mahā saṅgha* members [i.e., monks] travelled ahead of the body and lay white cloth ... "[63] This description of the funeral suggests that the Burmese lay nun was held in high esteem; the participation of the order of monks, in such large numbers, was (and is) a feature of the funerals of very important persons only. Thus, given their high visibility in Ceylon, Burmese nuns must have been familiar to Shearer, as well as to other Buddhists, even before she travelled to Rangoon. Even Dharmapāla was intrigued by them.

Writing in Burma in 1910, nearly ten years after his initial visit there, Dharmapāla again displayed an interest in Burmese lay nuns: "At Mandalay ... In the evening went to see the nun who talks in Pāli.[64] She is about 54 years old. Her husband had built a Kyoung

Pagoda and at his death she became a nun. She was also teacher to the Queen of Burma ... "[65] Impressed with the scholarly acumen of Burmese lay nuns, Dharmapāla hoped that the women of Ceylon would follow their lead, and study the Buddhist texts in the original Pāli.[66] Though Dharmapāla, by his own admission, had had a difficult time during the Countess's tenure in Ceylon, he wanted to begin a similar project in Burma. In spite of everything, the resuscitation of Buddhism, which necessitated the advancement of women through Buddhist education, was being achieved in Ceylon.

In April, 1907, prior to Shearer's arrival in Burma, Dharmapāla began a campaign there to educate Buddhist children. His diaries refer to his work among Buddhist lay nuns in Burma. "An *Upāsikā* came and talked with me and I learnt that there are 500 of them. I suggested that they should learn English and become teachers of girls and suggested getting Miss Shearer to open a school. Mrs. P. Nwai's daughter is Mah Khin Than and she has a Christian name, 'Noeline Nelson.' This was something startling and I spoke ardently about the want of a Girls' School."[67] The lay nuns of Burma heeded Dharmapāla's advice. As Dharmapāla suggested, they invited Shearer to Rangoon to help in their project to educate Buddhist girls. Shearer accepted the invitation and arrived on September 5, 1907. She immediately met with the lay nun Ohn Ghine, who was active in the Burmese branch of the MBS. Prior to her arrival, notice was given of her future plans in the journal published by Dharmapāla's MBS: "Miss C. Shearer, who has been studying the philosophy and methods of the Zen form of Japanese Buddhism in the Temple of Engakuji, Kamakura, Japan, has accepted the invitation of that esteemed Buddhist, Moung Ohn Ghine to visit Burma to take part in the establishment of a girls' school for Buddhist Burmese girls."[68] Buddhists rejoiced in the work she had started, which was intended to elevate Buddhist women in Burma. However, her tenure in Burma was short lived; she died of dysentery nearly two years after her arrival.[69]

While in Burma, Shearer published articles about her experiences, which included vivid descriptions of the religious life of lay nuns on a pilgrimage in Mandalay: "Mandalay has many temples. The Arakan Pagoda is the most popular, as early in the morning and late at night men, women, priests and nuns silently repeat their holy aspirations, '*Neban, Neban* [*nibbāna*], may I realize *Neban*,' being the theme of their thoughts to find salvation."[70] Inspired by the serious intent of the lay nuns of Burma, Shearer undertook the study of *vipassanā* meditation with monks and lay nuns of Rangoon, and corresponded with scholars, such as Mrs. Rhys Davids, about meditation techniques.[71] Unlike the Countess, Shearer eventually divorced herself from worldly involvement.

The Countess, by contrast, together with Dharmapāla and other Protestant Buddhists, maintained that active immersion in the world, rather than the passive spiritual progress that meditation alone delivers, is the most appropriate path for the world-renouncer and the Buddhist in general. Yet, Shearer, too, had Protestant Buddhist tendencies; the choices she made suggest that she did not believe that only through the *saṅgha* could one seek or find enlightenment. This very idea led laypeople to take up *vipassanā*, or insight meditation, the more rigorous meditation that is traditionally associated with the *saṅgha*. These themes are reiterated in the lives of Sinhala and western lay nuns who are the focus of Part II of this study.

CONCLUSIONS

Despite Dharmapāla's withdrawal from the Upāsikārāmaya project, his inclusive attitude toward women continued as he encouraged them to make the resuscitation of Buddhism their primary duty, rather than their family-centered work as householders. The Countess and Shearer, though American and formerly Christian, were at different points in their careers as lay nuns paradigms of Dharmapāla's vision of socially responsible women. It is likely that his interest in them had as much to do with his colonial mentality, as it had to do with their abilities to re-establish the order of nuns in the island. In other words, he may have valued them because in his period Sri Lankans valued westerners and their culture despite their criticisms of the west.

Nonetheless, as much as Dharmapāla wanted to revive the order of nuns in Ceylon, and as much as the Countess tried to fulfill his dreams, the order was not revived. Yet, because of their work, late nineteenth-century women entered a new phase in the history of Theravādin Buddhism. The Countess and her "sisters," by choosing to become world-renouncers, challenged the stereotype of the pious Buddhist woman as wife and mother; they helped to make renunciation a respectable choice for Buddhist women in Ceylon. Despite androcentrism, or even Dharmapāla's misogynous views as we saw in chapter 3, these women experimented with various forms of renunciation and introduced an insitutionalized form of female renunciation that was without precedent in their period.

APPENDIX TO THE SANGHAMITTA SISTERHOOD
Order
of the
Sanghamitta Buddhist Sisterhood
Sanghamitta Convent, No. 2, Darley Lane
Cinnamon Gardens, Colombo

Founded by
The Anagarika H. Dharmapala
Organised by
Madame de Souza Canavarro [the Countess]
Organised November 1897
Established April 1898

Object

To educate and elevate the Singhalese [sic] women and spread the doctrine of enlightenment. "Go ye Oh Bhikkhus, for the benefit of the many, for the welfare of mankind, out of compassion for the world. Preach the doctrine which is glorious in the beginning, glorious in the middle, glorious in the end, in the spirit as well as the letter. There are beings whose eyes are scarcely covered with dust, but if the doctrine is not preached to them they cannot attain salvation. Proclaim to them a life of holiness, so that they can understand the doctrine and accept it."[72]

Members of the Community

Sister Sanghamitta (Madame de Souza Canavarro)
Mother Superior

Sister Padmavatie [sic] (Miss C. Shearer)
Head Sister

Sister Dammadinna [sic] (Miss S. LaBrooy)

Manager of the Household

Sister Upalavathi (Dasa Sil Upasika)
Sinhalese Teacher of the Religion

Sisters: Sister Selevatie [sic]
Sister Saradavati
Lay Sisters: Sister Karnavtie [sic]
Sister Sunanda
Sister Ensina
Sister Chandravatie [sic]

Order of the
Sanghamitta Sisterhood
Founded by
Anagārika H. Dharmapala
˙ Organised by
Madame de Souza Canavarro

Madame de Souza Canavarro, an American Portugese lady, wife of a Portuguese gentleman of a noble family of Portugal and a member of the Diplomatic Core [sic].

Madame Canavarro is an American by birth, English and Spanish by descent, her English family name being Russell and her American family name Putnem, her forefathers Generals and Statesmen. Roman Catholic by education, early youth spent in Mexico, late years residence of San Francisco U.S.A.[73]

Renounced the Christian religion in 1893. Publicly declared a Buddhist, renouncing the world in New York City August 29th 1897; sailed for Ceylon September the 1st 1897 accompanied by the Anagārika H. Dharmapala Buddhist Missionary her Teacher and Spiritual guide. Arrived in Ceylon 14th October 1897.[74]

With the assistance of the Buddhist [sic] of Ceylon and under the auspices of the Mahā Bodhi Society, Madame Canavarro Organised the Order.

An appropriate building and grounds was purchased by the Mahā Bodhi Society, to found a Convent for the Sisterhood.

On the 30th day of April 1898 the Convent was formerly opened with a *Perit* [sic] which is a Buddhist ceremony.[75]

As an adjunct to the Convent, the "Sanghamitta School for Girls" founded by a board of Sinhalese ladies, established in 18—[sic] was taken charge of; in conjunction a boarding school for young ladies, a poor school, and an orphanage was established.

This order was established with the object of uniting Buddhist ladies in a community of Sisters to work for humanity in any way their abilities will permit them, preach the Good Law, spread the doctrine of Enlightenment, found and teach Buddhist Schools.

Sister Saṅghamitta Mother Superior and organiser (Madame Canavarro) with the help of her staff will give religious instructions under their teacher The Anagarika H. Dharmapala. All minor differences occurring in the Convent will be taken to the Mother and by her adjusted. Any important religious question will be referred to the Teacher.

The Community of Sisters will be supported by public contributions, income from the Schools and fancy bazaars; all necessaries will be furnished to the Sisters by the Mother. Every Sister is expected to help as far as it is in her power towards raising a general fund.[76]

Requisites for admission to the Sisterhood

A good character, upright life, willingness to obey the rules of the Order and to be guided by the Superior, a desire to do altruistic work for humanity, and aspirations to follow the good Law propounded by the Tatagatha [sic].[77]

Indulgences[78]

Travelling accompanied by another Sister, or sent out by the Teacher. Visiting ones' lady friends, driving, accepting invitations to breakfast by lady friends, corresponding, female callers, reading moral and scientific books, periodicals and papers approved by the teacher, walking acompanied by a lady friend or Sister, having one's own apartment, clothes, stationery, etc. to ones self, hours of reading in one's own room.

A Sister may be a member of the Theosophical Society, and an E.S.T.[79]

One year is given for the Novitiate, if at the expiration of that time the Candidate is not willing to unite with the fraternity [sic] she is free to retire. A Novitiate wears the white robe and has not quite such strict rules.

When the last vows are taken the Sister is given the Yellow Robe,[80] and if she has money will make it community money or give it over to her relatives.

At the taking of the last vows there is a simple and impressive ceremony; release may be given from all vows by the High Priest or the Diocese.[81]

Rules for the Sisters

Daily Routine

A.M.	5–6	Meditation
	6–7	Ablutions, dressing, offering of flowers and tea
	7:15–8	Gathas
	8–9	Preparing lessons or correspondence
	9–9:30	Recreation
	9:30–11:20	School (study of Pali and Sinhalese)
	11:30	Dinner (or breakfast)

AFTERNOON SESSION

P.M.	12–1	Meditation
	1–3	School
	3:30–5	Listening to sermons or studying the religion
	5–6	Exercise
	7–8	Preparing lessons
	8–9	Listening to a lecturer in social communion
	9–10	Meditation

Ordination of the Sister

The ordination may be in a Temple or at the Convent. The ceremony requires the presence of a High Priest and five deacons.[82]

Previous to the ordination the candidates are subject to an examination of the knowledge of the Buddhist Scriptures, and duties of a nun. Examinations and ordinations are held on full moon days in *Wesak* [sic], and on three succeeding *Poya* [sic] days, or quarters of the moon.[83]

The Ceremony

The candidate accompanied by the Mother Superior richly dressed in silks and jewels,[84] enters and makes obeisance to the Priest, and says "Grant me leave to speak. Lord graciously grant me admission to the Sanghamitta Order of Nuns," (three times repeated).

The priest rises and gives permission, the candidate is led out and dressed in the robes of the order, repeating the while, "I put on these robes as a protection against cold, heat, as a protection against insects, serpents wind, sun, rain, and for modesty; I shall wear them in all humility for use and not for ornament."[85] The candidate, having put on the robe, returns to the side of the Mother, both approaching the Priest, kneels while he places in her hands the Chaplet and kneeling cloth,[86] repeating all the while the *tacapanaka*, or formula of meditation on the perishable nature of the human body as follows; *kasa* [sic], *loma*, etc.[87] Then the candidate speaks and says "Lord[88] forgive me all my faults; let the merit that I have gained be shared by my Lord. It is fitting to give me a share gained by my Lord, it is good, it is good, I share it. Graciously give me Lord, the three refuges, the five precepts[89] and the vows of the Order. After the precepts are given, the Candidate still kneeling repeats the following formula.

I——do solemnly pledge my vows as a Sister of the Sanghamitta Order of Buddhist Nuns, under the following ten vows, and that I will to the best of my ability live up to them."

To the service of Lord Buddah [sic], I dedicate my life.

To the service of The Blessed Truth, I dedicate my life.

To the service of the Holy Ones, I dedicate my life.[90]

(I)   I promise to abstain from destruction of life or injure any living being.

(II)   I promise to abstain from stealing, and not to take anything not freely given.

(III)   I promise to live a life of chastity.[91]

(IV)   I promise not to lie, deceive or slander.

(V)   I promise to abstain from intoxicating means of enjoyment.

(VI)   I promise not to eat at improper times that is according to the rules laid down by the order.

(VII) I promise to abstain from dancing, the singing of worldly songs, the visiting places of amusement.

(VIII) I promise to avoid the use of perfumes of every kind, and to avoid worldly vanity.

(IX)   I promise to abstain from the use of luxurious beds,

(X)   I promise to always dwell in voluntary poverty. Of my own free will and for my salvation and the extinction of sorrow, I do this day take upon myself the vows of this order. May the "Blessed Ones" receive me in the order of the Sanctified. *Gatha*, all joining.[92] There is a balance of Rs. 6,000 to pay on a mortgage and the Sisters have to obtain the amount by soliciting, anyone in sympathy with the work far and near are kindly requested to contribute some small amount ever so small [sic], and the thanks and blessings of the inmates of the institution will follow them.

The Convent building is a spacious one, with nearly three acres of compound situated in the most desireable and healthy spot in Colombo. The cost of the Building and grounds, Rs. 25,000.

PART II

The institutionalization of tradition: the early twentieth century and the lay nun

INTRODUCTION

In the decades that followed the Countess's tenure in Ceylon, Ceylon Buddhists continued to provide women with a place in which they could renounce lay life. As projects to re-establish the tradition of female renunciation increased in the early decades of the twentieth century, the vocation of women who had renounced their lay identity became institutionalized, perhaps after a hiatus of several hundred years. In this chapter, I explore traditional notions of the pious laywoman, notions that have shaped the vocation of the lay nun, and draw a contrast with older patterns of thought concerning the laity. I hope to build a picture of the changes that have superseded traditional ideas about gender, on the one hand, and the laity, on the other. In chapters 3 and 4, I showed how Buddhists from other cultures, including Europeans and Southeast Asians, transformed late nineteenth-century Buddhism in Ceylon. In this chapter, I describe a project that was intended to resuscitate Buddhism by elevating women and providing them with a place to renounce. The project was the brain child solely of Ceylon Buddhists; however, British sympathizers called attention to the project, thus popularizing it, while Burmese Buddhists provided the guidelines for the project, which today is the most well-known upāsikārāmaya in the island.

Though, as we saw in chapter 3, the Saṅghamittā Upāsikārāmaya was a response to the specific changing social situation of late nineteenth-century Ceylon, Ceylon Buddhists, such as Dharmapāla, often invoked the Burmese lay nuns' example. Moreover, Burmese lay nuns were highly visible in Ceylon at that time;[1] their example doubtless influenced the changing role of Buddhist women in the island. This was also the case in the early 1900s,[2] when a Sinhala woman named Catherine de Alwis journeyed to Burma to become a lay nun. Her spiritual successors maintain that she was inspired to renounce having met some Burmese lay nuns at the Temple of the Tooth in Kandy. Much like the Countess, de Alwis captured the attention of the elite in Ceylon when she renounced and organized an upāsikārāmaya. Furthermore, de Alwis, later known as Sudharmācārī, was formerly a Christian who gave up material wealth and position in favor of the life of a Buddhist lay nun.

SINHALA, FEMALE RENUNCIATION: CONTEXT AND CREATION

Though both the Countess and de Alwis were converts to Buddhism,[3] there were many differences between the two former Christians. De Alwis's career as a lay nun began in Kandy and not in Colombo, the stronghold of the Theosophical Society. Therefore, she was not as influenced by people such as Dharmapāla, who fashioned the Buddhist revival in Ceylon along Christian lines. However, de Alwis was a product of the latter part of the nineteenth century; a period in which the Theosophical Society launched a campaign islandwide to educate Buddhist female children.

Because de Alwis's life was not directly influenced by Colombo Buddhist society, her upāsikārāmaya project did not have the western orientation of the other Buddhist ventures of the period. According to the published description of de Alwis's lay nunnery, each and every renunciant who lived there was Sinhala, as were its founders.[4] Accounts of the founding of the lay nunnery indicate that like the Saṅghamittā Upāsikārāmaya, the affluent and educated Buddhists of Ceylon were involved in its establishment. Among them was D. Baron Jayatilake,[5] who had previously played a leading role in the Saṅghamittā Upāsikārāmaya.

It is not surprising that urban, western-educated Buddhists were involved in the initial stages of the Kandy Upāsikārāmaya project. The precedent had been set for their contribution a decade earlier with the work of Dharmapāla and his Colombo-based, urban-elite Buddhist friends in the Saṅghamittā project. Tissa Fernando has suggested that the elite spearheaded such projects as a form of cultural resistance against the British.[6] Fernando argues that the growth of this westernized elite resulted in the formation of a group who were never considered equal to the British, whom they emulated. Further, the displacement of caste – the most important determinant of social status – with personal achievement and an English education, resulted in frustration for many in Ceylon. Tracing the rise of the new elite in the tumultuous late nineteenth century, Fernando suggests that: "While Westernized Ceylonese were emulating the life style of European officials, they were also being constantly reminded of the fact that there were second-class citizens in their own country ... As a Ceylon newspaper complained, 'every man who goes abroad for his education comes back here humiliated to find that in his own home he is the subject of a despotic administration. He is barely tolerated. His opinion is worth nothing. He has no voice in guiding the affairs of his own country'."[7] Frustration and deprivation of this sort linked the western-educated, urban-elite to the Buddhist revival of the late nineteenth and early twentieth century. According to Fernando, "Developments in the late nineteenth century brought about an unprecedented awareness that what the West could offer, including Christianity, was incompatible with the traditional Buddhist ethos of the country."[8] It was in this social milieu that de Alwis, from one of the most elite families of Ceylon, began her career as a renunciant at the turn of the twentieth century.

De Alwis was born in Bentara, in the southern region of Ceylon, to David and Louisa de Alwis in 1849.[9] Her mother died when she was young and impressionable, and her father passed away when she was aged twenty-five, leaving her "deeply distressed and disgusted with the nature of *saṃsāra*."[10] While grieving for her father, de Alwis met a Buddhist who counseled and consoled her, and eventually converted her to Buddhism. After becoming a Buddhist in Bentara, de Alwis moved to Kandy, where she came into contact with a few Burmese lay nuns and other Buddhists, among them the Fernando family on tour in Kandy who later helped accommodate Burmese female renunciants in 1898.[11]

After spending time in Kandy with various pillars of the Buddhist establishment, de Alwis made plans to travel to Burma. While there, she learned about Buddhism under the guidance of venerable monks and a female renunciant by the name of Mahā Upāsikā who ordained her (by asking her to recite the ten precepts), and then bestowed upon her the clerical name Sudharmācārī. The duration of Sudharmācārī's stay in Burma cannot be ascertained, nor can the year in which she arrived in Rangoon. However, the biographies agree that she returned to Kandy in 1905. Upon returning, she, the

Fernando family, and other interested parties acquired land and established the Sudharmā Upāsikārāmaya, which was later known as Lady Blake's.

While Sudharmācārī and the members of her newly formed organization – the Sudharmā Society – began to make plans for the Upāsikārāmaya in 1905, they considered their project a milestone in Ceylon's Buddhist history:

For a long period of time, there were virtually no *brahmacārī* [celibate devotee] *Upāsikārāmayas* in Ceylon. The great Sudharmācārī *Upāsikā* reintroduced this *brahmacārī* tradition and, by doing so, she helped the Sinhala ladies who were interested in the spiritual lifestyle. She also helped by ordaining those who wanted to become *brahmacārī upāsikās*.[12]

Despite the precedent set by the Saṅghamittā Upāsikārāmaya less than ten years earlier, Sudharmācārī was hailed as the first to organize *dasa sil upāsikās*, or laywomen who keep the ten precepts, that is, lay nuns, into a cloister.

According to one account, the recent convert to Buddhism intended to re-establish a tradition of cloisters for *laywomen* rather than *bhikkhunīs*; de Alwis's biographers contended that she was not interested in reviving the order of nuns, but rather in rejuvenating the community of female lay disciples. "After the enlightened *bhikkhunī*, Saṅghamittā, came to Ceylon, thousands of cloisters for laywomen fell into disrepair.[13] Nonetheless, Sudharmā Mother *Upāsikā* who began to keep the *dasasil* recently, formed an institution to follow certain principles with her students and to educate girls, and to erect the first cloister for laywomen,[14] with the aim of teaching Buddhism on behalf of Buddhist women."[15] Like the Theosophists of Ceylon, including the Countess, de Alwis was interested in the advancement of women through education. However, unlike the Countess, Sudharmācārī and her biographers recognized the difference between the *dasa sil upāsikā* of their day and the *bhikkhunī* of ancient days. Invoking a passage from one of the dialogues of the Buddha, Sudharmācārī's biographers further aligned her with pious laywomen, rather than with ordained nuns:

The Buddhist religion rests upon four beams: the monk, the nun, the pious layman, and the pious laywoman.[16] Among the four beams, the beam of the nun has completely collapsed, leaving the Buddhist religion shaking and unstable. It is proper to say that Śrī Sudharmācārī *Upāsikā Māniyan Vahansee*[17] helped greatly in restoring the beam of the pious laywoman which was on the verge of collapsing.[18]

Contemporary lay nuns who follow in Sudharmācārī's lineage confirmed that de Alwis did not intend to re-establish the order of nuns in Ceylon.[19]

Sudharmācārī's biographers harkened back to the time of King Devānampiyatissa, a time when Anulā and her retinue who abided by the ten precepts and lived in an *upāsikāvihāra*, eagerly awaited the arrival of the Bhikkhunī Saṅghamittā:

It is said that the birth of a great man or woman will bring about the resurrection of things in the world when they are destroyed as a result of time. During the reigns of great kings like King Devānampiyatissa and King Dutugemanu, the cloisters for lay women that were in the *thousands* became dilapidated and existed in name only. At a time such as this,[20] the great Sudharmācārī *Upāsikā* built the Śrī Sudharmācārī Upāsikārāmaya in Katukale, Kandy. By doing this, she restored the tradition of celibate laywomen's cloisters.[21]

Sudharmācārī, like Subhodānanda ten years earlier, subscribed to the Mahāvaṃsa-view of history. Both considered that the tradition of the cloistered laywoman continued for centuries after Anulā was ordained, even though there is no textual or epigraphical evidence to support such a theory. In fact, according to the *Mahāvaṃsa's* own evidence, the cloister for laywomen in which Anulā had been living was converted into a cloister for ordained nuns after Saṅghamittā had introduced the nuns' lineage to Ceylon.[22]

Though the opening of the Sudharmā Upāsikārāmaya was announced in the newspapers of Ceylon, it did not make the same splash that the Saṅghamittā Upāsikārāmaya had made nearly one decade earlier. Yet, it did not go unnoticed. A Sinhala newspaper from the period provided an account of the Sudharmā Upāsikā-rāmaya project prior to its inauguration: "A large house with a picturesque property of two acres situated on Katukale Street in Kandy has been bought by the Justice William Dunuwila of Kandy and M. Fernando ... for rupees 3400 and has been established as a place where aged *upasikas* can reside and where religion is taught under the leadership of C. D. A. Sudharmacari,[23] a Sinhalese *upasika* of a high ranking class."[24] Unlike Dharmapāla, who was often disgusted by the lack of youthful people actively involved in the

Buddhist life of Ceylon,[25] Sudharmācārī welcomed aged, pious lay devotees. However, eye-witness accounts of the Upāsikārāmaya suggest that younger women did become pupils of Sudharmācārī, don robes, and contribute to her project of enhancing women's education through Buddhist teachings.[26]

According to the English newspaper that was sent abroad to those interested in events in Ceylon, the British Governor's wife, Lady Blake, was the guest of honor at the opening of the convent: "A Buddhist *upasika aramaya*, a place for the accommodation and training of Buddhist *upasikas* (ladies), was opened yesterday by Her Excellency Lady Blake. This has been a long felt want of the the Buddhists of Kandy and much credit is due to Sister C. de Alwis Sudharmacari, under whose auspices the institution was established ... Lady Blake in declaring the institution open, expressed the wish that it would prosper as an *aramaya* for the pious nuns and the aged ... "[27] Lady Blake's interest in the Sudharmā Upāsikārāmaya was remarkable for many reasons. Unlike the wife of her husband's predecessors, Edith Blake involved herself in local issues, among which was the restoration of Buddhist culture in Ceylon. Dharmapāla had attempted to solicit the aid of Governor Ridgeway's wife in the late 1890s but to no avail. In fact, in 1897 and 1898, Dharmapāla recommended to the Countess that she involve the wife of the then governor, Sir Ridgeway. But as Lady Ridgeway was not inclined toward the work of the Theosophists, she declined.[28] Similarly, prior to the tenure of Governor Ridgeway, during the tenure of Governor Havelock, the WES had tried to persuade the governor's wife to become involved in the Saṅghamittā School. However, Lady Havelock was not interested in their project to educate Buddhist girls.[29] Unlike her predecessors, Lady Blake, however, did not have to be persuaded to become involved in local concerns, especially with regard to Sudharmācārī and her supporters. Rather, she donated her time, energy and money to their cause. Dharmapāla, who supported Lady Blake's role in the Buddhist revival, wrote that she contributed much to the new project to educate young women; he even "Wrote letters to Lady Blake offering RS 1000/- for the proposed girls' school."[30]

Lady Blake was so impressed with Sudharmācārī and her pupils that she continued to write about them long after leaving Ceylon. In an article that appeared in a London Buddhist publication, she offered impressions of the incumbent of the lay nunnery, as well as a description of the daily activities at the lay nunnery. In addition,

Lady Blake demonstrated that she understood the difference between a *dasa sil upāsikā* and a *bhikkhunī*:

But in the course of time either the eight regulations were deemed too weighty,[31] or religious zeal amongst Buddhist women must have grown faint [and] full ordination for women was allowed to die out... But though priestesses are no longer found in these countries, *upasikas* (which may be translated as Deaconesses)[32] are still an institution in Burmah [sic] and Ceylon, and are generally known as Buddhist nuns...[33]

According to Lady Blake, the duties of the Buddhist "nun" at the Sudharmā Upāsikārāmaya included: assisting in the charge of the Temple of the Tooth, sweeping the sacred precincts, decorating the shrines with flowers and tapers, spending time in meditation, and instructing women and children in the doctrines and practices of their religion.[34]

In addition to Lady Blake, other expatriates offered glimpses into the lives of the lay nuns at the Sudharmā Upāsikārāmaya during its formative years. Bella Sidney Woolf, in the guide to Ceylon that she wrote soon after the opening of the Upāsikārāmaya, provided a description of the lay nuns:

At this Nunnery, Sudhammachari [sic] houses a number of aged, destitute and blind women, who have become nuns – and she also has a school for children numbering nearly 200. Sister Sudhammachari has been the means of rescuing many children from undesirable surroundings. Sister Sudhammachari and her nuns have their heads shaved like the priests, and they wear a dress of apricot over an under-dress of white... Sister Sudhammachari is a most interesting personality, and she writes and also speaks English fluently.[35]

As in the other sources, references to old nuns appeared in this article, as did references to the education of children by the residents of the Upāsikārāmaya. Sudharmācārī thus provided a social service for two groups – the aged and the deprived – and she and her pupils became well-known as far away as Colombo and Anurādhapura.

Lady Blake was not a Theosophist;[36] the source of her interest in Buddhism, however, cannot be ascertained from the available source material. All that can be said with any certainty is that Lady Blake became enamoured of the people and culture of Ceylon. In an article written for an English journal when she had returned to England,[37] Lady Blake displayed a vast knowledge of Buddhism in Ceylon. She described many rituals and festivals, as well as the canonical Pāli verses which serve as their basis. Moreover, she recounted the story of

Bhikkhunī Saṅghamittā's arrival in Ceylon with the branch of the Bō tree and she used the *Mahāvaṃsa* as her source for Ceylon's history. She also offered an account of female religiosity in Ceylon:

Close by every Buddhist temple and monastery in Ceylon there will be found a sacred Bo tree; indeed, the act of dedication of a *vihara* or *arama* is the planting of a young Bo tree. An *arama* for *pansikas*[38] – i.e., nuns – was to be consecrated in the neighborhood of Kandy. A young Bo tree that had been raised by the priests of the Sri Mahabodhi of Anuradhapura was presented for the occasion, which was of special interest, as no *arama* for nuns had been consecrated in Ceylon for many hundreds of years.[39]

Like Sudharmācārī's biographers, and despite the Countess's project, Lady Blake believed that the Sudharmā Upāsikārāmaya was the first "nunnery" to be established in centuries.

Lady Blake continued her description of the consecration of the Sudharmā Upāsikārāmaya with a very vivid description of the female renunciants who participated:

The nuns stood in a double line, barefooted with shaven heads – the shaving of the hair being the act by which they dedicated themselves to the religious life; lay sisters and professed nuns, all were clad in a white robe, over which one of pale salmon colour was folded over the left shoulder; at one side stood a long line of grave sedate-faced priests, also shaven and barefooted, but wearing robes of a brilliant yellow...[40]

Many interesting points emerge from Lady Blake's account of the dedication of the Upāsikārāmaya. First of all, her description of "nuns...in a double line" suggests that in only a short time, Sudharmācārī had attracted quite a few women who were interested in renouncing lay life. In addition, Lady Blake alluded to two types of renunciants at the Sudharmā Upāsikārāmaya. On the one hand, there were the "lay sisters," and on the other, the "professed nuns," all of whom wore the same robes. Based on this evidence, it is safe to surmise that the lay sisters were the older pious laywomen who were descibed in the newspaper accounts as "the aged." The "professed nuns" must have been the younger "pious nuns" to whom the newspapers also referred.[41] By allowing aged women to retire into an *ārāmaya*, Sudharmācārī gave new meaning to the term "*upāsikā*."

THE UPĀSIKĀ IN THERAVĀDA BUDDHISM

It has remained a tradition for pious householders (*upāsikās/upāsakas*) toward the end of their lives to dress in white and keep either the eight (*ata sil*) or the ten precepts (*dasa sil*) on a permanent basis.[42] This partial renunciation, however, does not include donning an orange robe and becoming cloistered in an *ārāmaya*. This is a relatively new phenomenon and, in the case of elderly Buddhist women, its inception can be traced to the founding of the Sudharmā Upāsikārāmaya. The door had already been opened for women to actively participate in Buddhism. As we have seen, Dharmapāla and the Countess in 1898 provided women with a place to renounce the world. Both Dharmapāla and the Countess referred to such women as *upāsikās*, though the Countess preferred to call them nuns. It is with Sudharmācārī's project, however, that the term *upāsikā* took on new meaning. No longer was it reserved for women who retire to a life of meditation in their own homes after family responsibility ends, nor even for women who maintain the precepts on *pōya* days or for extended periods. At the Sudharmā Upāsikārāmaya, young women who considered themselves to be enlivening the tradition of female renunciation and elderly women, whose tradition it was to partially renounce the world toward the end of their lives, came together under one roof. Early twentieth-century Buddhists called both groups *upāsikās*. The merging of the two groups was symbolized by the colors Sudharmācārī and the other renunciants wore; as the newspaper articles, photographs and eye-witness accounts suggest,[43] their outer robes were ochre, the color of monastic attire, while their blouse robes were white, the color of the laity. Their robes were thus a metaphor for their dual, and somewhat paradoxical, status as lay monastics.[44]

LADY BLAKE'S UPĀSIKĀRĀMAYA: THE EARLY YEARS

In a Buddhist journal owned by the YMBA of Colombo, the editors devoted a considerable amount of space to Sudharmācārī's project to educate girls. Like the 1890s, the early decades of the twentieth century witnessed a campaign among Buddhists to provide a proper Buddhist education for their children. Buddhists built many schools for boys in the 1890s; yet schools for girls remained a concern of Buddhists islandwide. Despite the Countess and Dharmapāla's success in opening several girls' schools, early twentieth-century

Buddhists sorely lacked schools for girls. According to the printed accounts of the Upāsikārāmaya, Sudharmācārī was in charge of the education of 150 girls, most of whom were indigent. The newspapers lauded her efforts as well as those who assisted her. They were, indeed, exemplars:

Yesterday our good Sister, Dharmavati *Upasika* (of the Katukelle Buddhist Nunnery, Kandy) called on us on her usual monthly "begging" round: – and her visit is the immediate cause for this letter of mine ... A few years ago Sister Sudhammacariya, the Chief *Upasika* of the above mentioned "*arama*" got round a few poor, ragged children of her neighbourhood and started a "class" for them ... Her little school though unostentatiously carried on had attracted the attention of the outside world, and among her "helpers" there were Miss Sidney Woolfe the well-known authoress, Mrs. Locke, the wife of Dr. R. H. Locke, late of the Peradeniya Gardens, whose interest as evinced by her letter to the *Ceylon Observer*[45] popularised the institution a great deal, and Lady Edith Blake [the wife of the then governor] who proved a good friend and ready helper throughout ...[46]

The writer added a description of one of the renunciants who resided at the Sudharmā Upāsikārāmaya:

The Sister Dharmavatie [sic], (it is she who has all these years come on the monthly "begging" round for the school on behalf of her teacher and guide, the Sister Sudhammacariya), with whom I began my letter, like her superior, is a fine specimen of the Buddhist Sisterhood and is the possessor of a striking personality. Her smile and her voice ringing true and sincere draw your heart to her and animate you, as it were, by an infusion of some of her own "*metta.*"[47] Her brilliant face with the fully developed nose, the well-cut mouth and very intelligent eyes, that light up a complexion beautiful by nature peeping from under an intellectual forehead, would make her the "observed of all observers" in any crowd. Her shaven head which partly hides her three score and ten and the exceedingly pretty saffron-coloured robe, which partaking of the colour of her face, is thrown over one shoulder, thereby partly exposing to view a plain white jacket and which reaches down to her feet in loose, ample, folds greatly becomes her age, her sex and her mission, and to give a finishing touch, the Peace of homeless life (*pabbajja*), – that life of single blessedness, far from home and kindred lends a lustre to her whole being and reflects on every feature her spiritual life within.[48]

This eloquent and detailed description of Sister Dharmavatī suggests that at the time the article was written, female renunciation was considered a valuable vocation. Though the writer praised Sister Dharmavatī, his or her interest in Dharmavatī's beauty attests to the strength of stereotyping: even in renunciation, Dharmavatī was first of all a woman – a feminine beauty – and only secondarily a world-renunciant. Despite focusing on Dharmavatī's appearance, the writer also valued Dharmavatī's vocation. A plea from this period to the women of Ceylon further demonstrates the high esteem in which the residents of the Sudharmā Upāsikārāmaya were held: "Shall we not imitate our dear Sisters Sudharmacariya and Dharmawatie [sic]? Is their work not a sufficient incentive? If not then have we yet forgotten the life the Venerable Sanghamitta led or the work she did in making known the Way the Great One taught? Then let us do as she did always recalling to mind that 'the Gift of Truth exceeds all other Gifts.'"[49] This plea is an excellent illustration of the way in which the *Mahāvaṃsa* and *Dīpāvaṃsa*, especially the legends of Saṅghamittā, resonated in early twentieth-century Ceylon. Moreover, it attests to the model of Buddhist piety that Sudharmācārī and her pupils provided women, as well as men.

The contribution that Sudharmācārī made to the resuscitation of Buddhism in Ceylon is still discussed today.[50] Sudharmācārī not only provided a model for others who were similarly motivated, she also made the path of renunciation in Buddhism attractive for women. For ten years, from 1907 to 1917, Sudharmācārī and her assistants continued their campaign to provide a Buddhist education for girls in their Upāsikārāmaya. In addition to the educational work, Sudharmācārī made plans to open a lay nunnery in Anurādhapura, near the site of the sacred Bō tree where, according to the *Mahāvaṃsa*, the king had erected a cloister for ordained nuns in ancient days.[51] According to a Buddhist publication, the establishment of a lay nunnery in Anurādhapura was a necessity:

A residence for Buddhist nuns at Anuradhapura has been a long felt want. An institution of this nature exists in Kandy; presided over by the well-known Sister Sudharmachariya [sic]. Established during the require [sic] of His Excellency Sir Henry Blake, with the good Lady Blake as the prime supporter, this institution has proved to be a most useful one. Its activites are many-sided and Sister Sudharmachariya and her colleagues may well be proud of it. A visit will prove the want of more of its kind. As such Mr. Pedris's gift is the more welcome. In the quiet and sublime atmosphere of Anuradhapura, amidst the noble and sacred ruins, the nun, who as a woman has had the courage to bid farewell to the pleasures of the world, can lead a quieter life than perhaps in any other part of the Island.[52]

Aside from describing the establishment of Anurādhapura's first abode in centuries for female renunciants, thus satisfying a need of

Buddhists there, the writer encourages world-renunciation by women.

Appealing to Buddhists with similar arguments as those used by Dharmapāla in the 1890s, many monks were as vocal as laypeople in encouraging the participation of women in the Buddhist revival. One monk, feeling the threat of Christian missionaries in his country, explained that women were the foundation of Buddhism: "It is a good idea to establish girls' schools under Buddhist auspices. The mothers of the race make the race. If the mothers are impregnated with Christian ideas, the children of those mothers cannot help but be the same."[53] Along similar lines, a commentary of the period, echoing many of the late nineteenth- and early twentieth-century concerns of Buddhists, centered upon the education of Buddhist children: "If you send your children to Christian schools, or in any other way allow them to come under the influence of proselytising agencies, or if you help such agencies, you will be guilty of aiding and abetting those who are doing their very best to destroy all traces of Buddhism from this land."[54] Within a few years of this commentary, Sudharmācārī made a success of the Sudharmā School for Girls in Kandy, an important satellite of the Upāsikārāmaya. The Buddhist publications of the period contained articles listing the names of people who contributed to the school,[55] both financially and in other ways.[56]

Though during the first decade of the twentieth century many people rallied around Sudharmācārī and some women even renounced under her tutelage, other women assumed the renunciant lifestyle without Sudharmācārī's influence. For instance, a young woman became a lay nun under the guidance of Burmese lay nuns living in Colombo:

The only daughter of *Upāsaka*[57] Mr. Silva was ordained[58] as an *upāsikā* on the 16th of this month, Saturday, at 8:00 p.m. at the Borälla Burmese *āvāsaya* [dwelling for clergy]. She is his only daughter and is about 18 years old ... She took the ten precepts and joined the Burmese *upāsikā* group. They left on Sunday for a pilgrimage to Anurādhapura ...[59]

The young woman discussed in this article renounced in March of 1907, which suggests that four months before Sudharmācārī opened her Upāsikārāmaya, at least one female donned the robe independently of her. However, like Sudharmācārī, Mr. Silva's *upāsikā* daughter was certainly affected by Ceylon's changing social situation,[60] the course of which was controlled by the laity. The laity's contribution to the Buddhist revival were as important as the challenges the revival made to the traditional role of women in Ceylonese Buddhist society. Sudharmācārī and the other lay nuns at her Upāsikārāmaya vivified the image of women in the canonical literature as seekers of liberation, even though they might not have wanted to be aligned with *bhikkhunīs*. Yet, the positive valuation of female renunciation engendered by the residents of the Upāsikārāmaya did not outlive its founder. In the next section, I discuss the ambivalent attitude toward female renunciants that later ensued and compare the contemporary situation at the lay nunnery with its early years.

LADY BLAKE'S UPĀSIKĀRĀMAYA TODAY[61]

The present (and fifth) incumbent of Lady Blake's Upāsikārāmaya is Kotmalee Sudharmā.[62] Kotmalee Sudharmā was born Wimala Weeratunga in 1938 and attended school until the seventh standard.[63] At the age of fourteen, impressed with the female renunciants with whom she had come into contact in Kandy, she left home for Lady Blake's and, within two weeks – in September, 1952 – became a lay nun.

The charismatic Sudharmācārī had died in 1939. According to the lay nuns who at present live in the Upāsikārāmaya that Sudharmācārī established, the fortunes of the Upāsikārāmaya suffered after her death. As a result, Kotmalee Sudharmā's parents worried about their daughter's choice to become a renunciant and reside at Lady Blake's; they did everything in their power to detain her. However, she demonstrated to her parents in a series of hunger strikes that she would not be stopped. In the interviews, Kotmalee Sudharmā explained that she became a lay nun because she felt that she could do the work of the Buddha properly only in a lifestyle that was conducive to devoting one's life to the religious path. This, she claimed, could not be accomplished in lay life.

Kotmalee Sudharmā was ordained by a Burmese female renunciant, Māwicārī, the incumbent of the Upāsikārāmaya at the time. Kotmalee Sudharmā succeeded Māwicārī in 1978, when the latter became too ill to manage the Upāsikārāmaya's affairs. Māwicārī died in 1981.[64] Kotmalee Sudharmā's promotion did not go uncontested by the other renunciants. A schism occurred at Lady

Blake's at the time of Māwicārī's death, a schism that is still apparent by the proximity of the living quarters of the lay nuns who were students of Māwicārī, compared to those who are students of Kotmalee Sudharmā. Eight lay nuns spend their time "down," while four have little if any communion with them, and lead a separate existence "up."[65]

Unlike Sudharmācārī, the present residents of the Upāsikārāmaya do not have similar educational or social credentials. With the exception of two of the present residents, the renunciants are drawn from uneducated, farming families. The remaining residents are the children of mechanics. It was impossible to determine the caste affiliations of the lay nuns. Though some lay nuns I interviewed were quick to volunteer their caste affiliations,[66] most were adamant that such a question was an invalid one. Unlike lay nuns, Sri Lankan *bhikkhus* are divided upon caste lines. The lay nuns argue that such an arrangement goes against the spirit of the teachings of the Buddha who, according to one lay nun, believed that "caste has nothing to do with the *dhamma*."

In 1989, the oldest member of Lady Blake's was ninety,[67] while the youngest was in her late teens. Among the elderly group of lay nuns who claim lineage from Māwicārī, one, an "up" resident, is insane and poses a nuisance to the rest of the group. Though she often made my stays in Kandy miserable, from a sociological point of view her presence is of import to this study. Lady Blake's has maintained its tradition of housing elderly, as well as youthful renunciants, a tradition not prevalent in most of the other lay nunneries around the island.[68] In fact, the Ministry of Buddhist Affairs has proposed recently that only women between the ages of sixteen and sixty should be considered for "ordination."[69] The trend in Sri Lanka, therefore, is to discourage elderly women from donning the robe. In fact, the order of monks follows this rule very much, though it has no canonical precedent. Several lay nuns mentioned that monks who enter the order late in life have lower status than those who enter in their youth, even if they are ordained at the same time. Be that as it may, at Lady Blake's old women continue to live in robes and continue to be ordained under Kotmalee Sudharmā's tutelage.

The elderly insane renunciant spends her time screaming at people at the bus halts along the Peradeniya Road, while the younger group attends the *pirivena* (Buddhist schools that have traditionally been reserved solely for monks), where the government has organized a

Buddhist curriculum for them and the other lay nuns in the vicinity of Lady Blake's. The lay nuns abide by a schedule established by the founder herself; it is representative of most lay nunneries in contemporary Sri Lanka:

Morning

4:00	The day begins
4:00–5:00	Buddha *pūjā* and meditation
5:00–6:00	Preparing *dānaya*[70] and lessons
6:00–7:00	Buddha *pūjā* and *dānaya*
7:00–8:00	Bathing
8:00	Lessons begin
11:30	*Dānaya*

Afternoon

2:30	*Gilānpāsa*[71]
2:30–4:30	Lessons resume
4:30–5:30	Cleaning the compound
6:00–7:00	Worship
7:00	*Gilānpāsa*
7:15–8:00	*Pirit* recitation
8:00–9:00	Meditation
9:00–10:00	Review of lessons
10:00	Bedtime

The older group does not attend the *pirivena*, but rather accepts invitations to chant *pirit*, or visits patients, or assists in worship and other ceremonies at the Temple of the Tooth. Assistance at the Temple of the Tooth has symbolic significance: it is an assertion of the lay nuns' "rights" to participate in Buddhist ceremonies. On Sunday mornings, most of the residents of the Upāsikārāmaya teach neighborhood children, which amounts to their only source of religious education.

The accounts and the other mundane affairs of the Upāsikārāmaya continue to be administered by a group of lay people. According to Kotmalee Sudharmā, their intervention into the matters of the Upāsikārāmaya has caused as much harm as good, as the Fernando family's involvement suggests. As we have seen, the Fernando family helped to institutionalize the tradition of female renunciation by contributing to Sudharmācārī's project in the early 1900s. None-theless, one of the relatives of the family recently lodged a complaint against Kotmalee Sudharmā and claimed ownership of the Upāsi-kārāmaya compound. He also asserted that he had rights "over the buildings, the inhabitants, and the land." According to Kotmalee Sudharmā, he tried unsuccessfully to evict the renunciants.[72] Kotmalee Sudharmā won the court battle against him on August 2, 1988; however, his family continues to serve as overseers of the Upāsikārāmaya.

The attitudes of the Fernando family toward the tradition of female renunciation in the early 1900s, and those of their relatives eighty years later, represent all too well the shifting attitudes of the Buddhist public toward the revived tradition of female renunciation. Though the recent court battle against Kotmalee Sudharmā repre-sents an extreme case, the ambivalence toward the tradition is symbolically attested to by the very existence of legal proceedings against the female renunciants. The laity's involvement in the Upāsikārāmaya affairs has in many ways been responsible for the relatively good standard of living at Lady Blake's. However, many of the lay nuns there told me that they resent the laity's control over their lives.

Despite the recent difficulties that the Upāsikārāmaya has faced, the lay nuns at Lady Blake's enjoy a much higher standard of living than many of the other lay nunneries around the island; it is not, however, the same standard which Sudharmācārī enjoyed.[73] Yet, the Upāsikārāmaya's historicity keeps it in the public eye. Moreover, with the establishment in 1981 of *pirivena* education for lay nuns, its choice as a site for the Kandy district will keep it an active and vital resource for many women in Sri Lanka and elsewhere who desire to renounce the world.

Though the attitudes of the original benefactors toward the residents of Lady Blake's Upāsikārāmaya are not shared by con-temporary society, the lay nuns continue to counsel lay persons in need, teach Sunday school, conduct *pirit* ceremonies, minister to the ill, and meditate. Yet, unlike their analogues in the 1910s and earlier, as well as the members of the order of monks in Sri Lanka, they lack the financial and emotional support traditionally reaped from such a pious lifestyle.[74] In contemporary rural Sri Lanka – from where the vast majority of lay nuns are drawn – there is an understanding that women's primary work is reproductive work, which includes the care of children and other associated tasks.[75] Essentially, the domestic sphere is assumed to be the female sphere, rather than the public religious arena. Thus, having defied the traditional stereotype of nurturing mother, lay nuns very rarely secure the support they need.

CONCLUSIONS

The positive valuation of female renunciation during the first decades of the twentieth century was related to the elite status of the women who donned the robe. Not unlike the women who renounced the home life during the time of the Buddha,[76] or when the nuns' lineage was introduced to Sri Lanka,[77] or during the 1890s, the women who renounced the world under Sudharmācārī's tutelage were drawn from the upper echelons of society.[78] This positive valuation was also quite possibly related to the involvement of the Europeans who, in the British period, were a powerful source of prestige. Though Lady Blake and the other British people did not actually help in establishing the Upāsikārāmaya, they were very instrumental in founding the school associated with the Upāsikārāmaya and in calling attention to the lay nuns.

As the sources of the period suggest, not only did Buddhists encourage women to renounce, they valorized the feminine. In fact, the early history of Lady Blake's Upāsikārāmaya reflects a particular attitude toward women and world-renunciation, namely, soteriological androgyny. In other words, the "socially defined gender characterization" of women as mothers, even in renunciation, continued to be valorized,[79] as it had been to some degree during the early phases of the Countess's Saṅghamittā project. Today, however, Buddhists for the most part "relegate women to a lower capacity for pursuing the spiritual path."[80] The most dramatic example of this new ideology about women and world-renunciation is the court case against Kotmalee Sudharmā. The message of the case is loud and clear: lay nuns are no longer considered necessary for the survival of Buddhism. Sudharmācārī may have redefined the role of the *upāsikā*, but according to contemporary wisdom *upāsikās* should remain lay householders – they should not renounce the world.

What accounts for these changes? Firstly, we have seen that a different set of concerns about women arose once they entered lay nunneries. That is, Buddhists in the early phases of both the Saṅghamittā project and Lady Blake's valorized women, thereby providing the conditions for women to renounce; however, a problem arose concerning their maintenance once they had renounced. I shall have more to say about this in chapter 6. Secondly, as a result of independence in 1948, the need for the elite's mobilization of support for Buddhism began to diminish. As a consequence, *dāyakas* became ambivalent about the female renunciants that they had enthusiastically sponsored. In the next chapter, I explore a similar trend in the history of a lay nunnery much like Sudharmācārī's. It, too, was established prior to independence and lost much of its support once Buddhism had been restored in post-independent Ceylon.

CHAPTER 6

The lay nun in transitional Ceylon

INTRODUCTION

Buddhists in the decades prior to independence in 1948 continued to hail lay nuns as exemplars of Buddhist piety, much as they had done since the 1890s. However, we must recognize a bias even in the elaboration of the feminine and its concomitant: widescale interest in female renunciation. As we shall see below, Ceylon Buddhists rallied support for lay nuns primarily for the benefit of the country. Moreover, the laity's strict control over the female renunciants attested to in the sources of the period, suggests a preoccupation with regularizing the lay nunnneries. In this period, the laity continued to experiment with ways to deal with the "social unacceptablity (indeed unimaginability) of an autonomous group of women not under the direct regulation and control of some male authority."[1] The history of the Vihāra Mahā Devī Upāsikārāmaya (VMD) is an example of such experimentation. Despite institutional androcentrism, the sources of the period suggest that the elite perceived that a *bhikkhunī sangha*, or something like it, was necessary for the survival of Buddhism in Ceylon.

Just as the destiny of Buddhism was in the hands of the Colombo-based, western intelligentsia, so too was the political scenario.[2] The Colombo-based VMD project to re-establish the tradition of female renunciation during the 1930s – organized and fueled by Colombo politicians – reflects this phenomenon. In fact, the very people who determined the course of the politics of the island in the post-independence period sponsored the VMD project. The history of the VMD Upāsikārāmaya, like the histories of the other upāsikārāmayas explored thus far, suggests that during periods in which the Sinhala elite have helped to determine the future of the island, it was western-educated women who renounced and the westernized who supported

them. After independence, however, women from all walks of life
began to don the robe and lead the renunciant lifestyle; at the same
time, the elite's patronage began to diminish. In this chapter, I ferret
out reasons for changes in attitudes toward female renunciation after
independence. I provide an account of the views of elite Buddhists
toward women and renunciation in the 1920s, the 1940s, and in post-
independent Ceylon. These views represent a variety of concerns
about women and renunciation, all of which have to do with the
perception of Ceylon as caretaker of Buddhism. Such study provides
an interesting example of the changing face of Buddhism in Ceylon in
the mid-twentieth century.

WOMEN, BUDDHISM, AND LAY NUNS IN THE EARLY TWENTIETH CENTURY

English-speaking Buddhists in the first few decades of the twentieth
century took great interest in Bhikkhunī Saṅghamittā. In 1923, the
editor of a bilingual magazine for women helped to resume a festival
in honor of Bhikkhunī Saṅghamittā.[3] According to the reports, the
attempt at reinstituting the celebration was a success. Sponsored by
the Srī Puśpadāna Society in Ambalangoda,[4] the celebration
included a large Buddha *pūjā*, a parade of Buddhist laity, monks,
tom-tom beating and yellow flags, which symbolized Saṅghamittā's
clerical affiliations. Moreover, "eight nuns, or *Dasa Sil Upāsikās*, head
shaven and in yellow tinted robes," participated.[5] According to a
1932 editorial, at least one Buddhist considered Bhikkhunī Saṅghamittā responsible for "raising ... womanhood to the highest stage of
moral perfection and mental development;"[6] she was a paradigm for
womanly behavior. The writer referred to Saṅghamittā and her
brother, Mahinda, as the "spiritual parents" of Ceylon Buddhists;
they were to be emulated so that the "moral well-being" of Ceylon
might be raised.[7] As the editorial suggests, the idea of an inextricable
relationship between Buddhism and nationalism had become firmly
entrenched by the 1930s. Moreover, renunciation of the world was
equated with patriotism.

During the years when interest in the tradition of female
renunciation increased in Ceylon, the dilemma over the proper
education of Buddhist children, especially girls, continued to occupy
the minds of English-speaking Buddhists. In a manner reminiscent of

the 1880s, socially conscious Buddhists appealed to their brethren to educate the mothers of their nation. In one example, a Buddhist made an emotional plea in his discussion of the methods used by Christian missionaries to convert all Buddhists in Ceylon:

It remains only to make a final appeal to you to your sense of patriotism as Buddhist Sinhalese, as the proud inheritors of a great past, into whose hands through the passage of long and eventful centuries has descended the priceless heritage of your glorious Faith, a faith which teaches "a salvation by emancipation of the mind through knowledge," to put forth your best efforts to found this College for Girls, – the future mothers of your race,[8] – which would make your daughters worthier, your sons better, yourselves glad at heart, your homes happier and more inviting and your beautiful land, your hills and valleys, rich with a richness beyond your deeming.[9]

Implicit in this appeal to educate the Buddhist daughters of Ceylon is a political awareness of the role of Buddhists in shaping the destiny of Ceylon. By making Buddhists of Sinhalese girls, patriotic Buddhists could benefit their country. In this way, Ceylonese Buddhists continued to rediscover their Buddhist heritage, including the tradition of female renunciation, much like Dharmapāla and his colleagues had a few decades earlier. Moreover, they continued to mobilize themselves for the sake of their country well into the 1940s and 1950s. This pattern is repeated in the history of the VMD elite enterprise to organize lay nuns into an upāsikārāmaya near Colombo in the 1930s and 1940s.

THE VIHĀRA MAHĀ DEVĪ UPĀSIKĀRĀMAYA: THE EARLY YEARS

Sudharmācārī died in 1939. Her career spanned nearly thirty years, during which time political power in Ceylon was gradually transferred to the Ceylonese. Though Buddhists continued to perceive Buddhism as moribund, great strides had been taken to resuscitate it. Concomitantly, constitutional reforms and the devolution of power resulted in the empowerment of the Ceylonese. This was a slow process, and resulted in universal suffrage for all in 1931. As the British groomed the elite minority for the complete transfer of power in 1948, the masses remained virtually unaffected by the reforms.

The upper echelons of Ceylonese society, who had resisted the British by securing more power for themselves in the governance of the nation, continued to resist them through a religious idiom. Three years before Sudharmācārī died, various members of the Sinhala community who had been active in politics, as well as their wives, formed a committee – the Vihāra Mahā Devī Samitiya (VMD committee). Their intentions were to "train and maintain *Dasa Sil Upāsikās* in an *ārāmaya* established at Biyagama [Kalaniya, near Colombo] and at similar institutions controlled by the *Samitiya*."[10] On June 27, 1936, J. R. Jayewardene and his wife,[11] together with one of the catalysts in the reforms under the British in 1920, D. B. Jayatilake,[12] who had played a large role in both the Saṅghamittā project and Lady Blake's, met to discuss the formation of the VMD committee. They were joined by Mrs. A. M. de Silva, whose husband was a notable lawyer in Colombo, and Mrs. Justin Kotalawala, whose brother-in-law would later serve as prime minister. Sri Nissanka, who eventually became a leading member of the Marxist Party, the LSSP (Lankā Sama Samāj Party), hosted the gathering at his home in the most prestigious neighborhood in Colombo.[13]

The result of their efforts is a lay nunnery that continues to function today. It was ceremonially opened on October 25, 1936, by Mrs. D. S. Senanayake,[14] whose husband, the Minister of Agriculture and Lands, served as the first prime minister of independent Ceylon. The beginnings of the VMD lay nunnery were indeed auspicious. Colombo's most notable citizens, whose life revolved around Ceylonese politics, were its founders. The rich donated land, the elite promised to build rooms, politicians and their families dedicated a library, while applications poured in.[15]

The Sinhala elite's affirmation of Ceylon's Buddhist heritage not only contributed to changes in the political scenario, but also it helped to firmly re-establish the tradition of female renunciation in Ceylon. At the first meeting of the committee, they decided that the lay nunnery would be called Vihāra Mahā Devī, in honor of Dutugamunu's mother, an important figure of the *Mahāvaṃsa*:[16] "the nunnery, while perpetuating the name of Lanka's noblest woman and mother, will aid all women who desire to follow the Noble Eightfold Path."[17] An article from 1940 further reflects the sentiments of the period concerning women and nationalism. "'Women must take their place by the side of men in national work,' said Sir Baron Jayatilake at a public meeting held under the auspices of the Vihāra Mahā Devī Samitiya at the *Upāsikā Ārāmaya*, Biyagama recently. 'The *Samitiya* and its *Ārāmaya* show that the co-operation is not lacking'."[18] In Buddhist Ceylon "national work" was religious work and the VMD lay nunnery project epitomises the way that women were considered to be as responsible as men in such work.

After Mrs. Senanayake conducted the traditional ceremonies associated with house-warmings, two women took the vows of the *dasa sil upāsikā*, or lay nun. The account of their rite of passage is reminiscent of the ordination of the novice into the Saṅghamittā Upāsikārāmaya: "Sisters Visākhā and Sujātā, next took their oaths of renunciation kneeling before the priests. The oath was to the effect that they solemnly and truly renounced the world of their own choice; that they would faithfully observe the ten precepts of the '*Dasa Sil Upāsikā*'; and that they would emulate with all their strength those extinct '*Āriyas*' to the best of their abilities."[19] The women were then "admitted" to the "nunnery," but not without swearing to abide by the strict guidelines of the VMD committee: "After they were admitted the two nuns signed a document, which the Nayake Thero [leading monk] of Vidyalankara Pirivena, the President and members of the Society managing the Nunnery also signed as witnesses."[20] The VMD committee legislated all aspects of the lay nuns' lives in the lay nunnery: the times that they were to rise in the morning and the time they would retire at night, and the selection of worthy candidates. Not unlike the overseers of the Saṅghamittā Upāsikārāmaya until its demise in 1900, the VMD committee remained very active in the affairs of their lay nunnery. According to the "Rules for *Upāsikās*," the lay nuns had to agree to honor and abide by many guidelines at the Upāsikārāmaya:

1 Admission is restricted to those selected by a Selection Board of the Vihāra Mahā Devī *Samitiya*.
2 Applications shall be made on the prescribed form to the Secretary.
3 The Selection Committee may require new entrants to serve a probationary period of at least six months.
4 New entrants shall not be less than 25 years nor more than 50 years of age. The Selection Board may waive this rule at its discretion.
5 All *Upāsikās* on being enrolled as resident *Upāsikās* must take the prescribed oath consenting to abide by the rules of the *Samitiya* and the *Upāsikās*.[21]

Thus, applicants were scrutinized and controlled by the laity. And like the lay nuns at the Saṅghamittā Upāsikārāmaya and Lady Blake's, they had to abide by a timetable:[22]

Morning

5:00	The day begins
5:30–6:00	Buddha *Pūjā*[23]
6:00–6:30	Worshiping the Buddha by all
6:30–7:30	Morning *dānaya* [alms]
7:30–8:30	Free time
8:30–10:30	Study
10:30–11:00	Bathing
11:00–12:00	Buddha *Pūjā* and *dānaya*

Afternoon

12:00–1:00	Worshiping the Buddha, free time
1:00–2:00	Study
2:00–3:00	Reading
3:00–4:00	Teaching
4:30–5:00	Exercise and *gilānpāsa*
5:00–6:30	Teaching visitors
6:30–7:30	Worshiping Buddha
7:30–8:00	*Dhamma* study
8:00–9:00	Meditation and retiring
9:00–10:00	Lights out

Though Sister Visākhā, the first head nun of the Upāsikārāmaya, devised the time table,[24] the VMD committe approved it. The time table therefore reflects the VMD committee members' vision of the appropriate monastic regime for female renunciants. As the table suggests, the committee stressed worship, study and service in the daily routines of their lay nuns.

As we saw in chapter 2, the incursion of the laity in the monastic affairs of the island was one of the ramifications of the "disestablishment of Buddhism" in the 1840s. At the VMD lay nunnery, the incursion consisted of: "two patrons, one lay and the other belonging to the *Sangha*, a President, five Vice Presidents, two Joint Secretaries, a Treasurer and a Working Committee… the Working Committee shall consist of fifteen members exclusive of the office bearers, elected annually at the General Meeting."[25] Thus, in the early years of the VMD lay nunnery, twenty-five people had committed themselves to regulating the lives of only two lay nuns.

Moreover, the lay nuns were controlled by Buddhists who observed fewer precepts than they. The "Rules for *Upāsikās*" continued with a section entitled "Control of *Upāsikās*:"

1 All *Upāsikās* must obey the Chief *Upāsikā*, who must herself obey the rules governing the *Samitiya* and the Upāsikārāmaya.
2 The President with the sanction of the Committee, or any other person authorised by the Committee, shall have the power to exercise any authority of the *ārāmaya* premises and any inmates therein.
3 On admission all movable property except necessary clothing and books shall be handed over and shall be in charge of the matron. The Chief *Upāsikā* can exercise her discretion with regard to the enforcing of this rule. The matron shall hand over such property to the Society after making an inventory.
4 No Resident *Upāsikā* shall be entitled to receive personal gifts without the sanction of the Chief *Upāsikā*.
5 No resident *Upāsikā* shall leave the *ārāmaya* premises without the written permission of the President of the *Samitiya*. If the President is not available in Colombo, one of the Secretaries may give such permission if the Chief *Upāsikā* so recommends. In urgent cases, the Chief *Upāsikā* may give leave; which fact must be immediately communicated to the President.
6 The Maximum period of leave so granted shall be three days excepting in cases of illness.[26]

According to these rules, even the chief lay nun was subordinate to the VMD committee. Any one of its members had the authority to intervene in the affairs of the lay nunnery, while the chief lay nun herself had to communicate all activities to the president of the committee. Control of the lay nuns became one of the VMD's preeminent concerns. Though their concerns echo Dharmapāla's, the life of the lay nun at the VMD Upāsikārāmaya was much more highly regulated than at the Saṅghamittā Upāsikārāmaya. Yet, as we shall see, the goal of the VMD committee, much like the Countess's, was to provide a structured environment for women trained in useful social services.

Sri Nissanka best articulated the goals of the VMD committee; he related their project to Ceylon's role as defender of Buddhism. In his address to the Annual Meeting of the VMD committee in 1936, attended by a representative of the British government, Nissanka made conciliable allusions to the past and linked the committee's work to state patronage of Buddhism:

With the advent of the British the tide of events changed and the famous clause in the Kandyan Convention of 1815 entered into between the representatives of His Britannic Majesty's Government and the chief representatives of this country restored the waning confidence of a stricken people ... Buddhism has steadily advanced since this time and although it has gained much of the lost ground, the condition of some of the Priesthood and of the Nuns leaves much to be desired ...[27]

In other words, the role of the committee was to elevate the monastic community, which had been one responsibility of the state prior to the disestablishment of Buddhism. Sri Nissanka continued with an affirmation of his and his colleagues' role *vis-a-vis* the disestablishment of Buddhism:

Throughout the Island great advances have been made and thousands of societies have taken upon themselves the well-nigh impossible responsibility of shouldering the onerous burden which at one time weighed heavily on the Crowned Heads of the Rulers of the Island.[28]

Due to the disestablishment of Buddhism nearly one century earlier, it had become incumbent upon the laity to purify Buddhism. Though this trend had been evident in the nineteenth century, by the 1930s the laity had clearly replaced the state in matters pertaining to Buddhism. Continuing his address, Sri Nissanka summarized the goals of the committee:

The *Bhikkhuni* (Priestesses) Order, now being totally extinct by reason of the causes adumbrated above, there still exists in the country an Order of *Upasikas* (Nuns); but without proper control and protection. To meet this deficiency, a Society ... was formed.[29]

The lay nuns had indeed made great strides in re-establishing a tradition of female renunciation; however, according to Sri Nissanka, they were in need of "control," which became the main purpose of the VMD committee.

Within the first year of Upāsikārāmaya's foundation, the very large VMD committee had initiated only a handful into the lay nunnery:

The number of resident *upasikas* has now increased to five, and though it is hoped to accommodate a considerable number in the near future, the Society has had to refuse many applicants. The Selection Committee is very careful with regard to new entrants, as the Society intends to establish a new

Order willing to abide by the stringent rules of the Society. The Society wishes to discourage the idea that the *Aramaya* is meant to be an asylum for the aged and the decrepit.[30]

The VMD committee members were not the first to attempt the resuscitation of the tradition of female renunciation; they were, therefore, able to examine the situation of other lay nunneries and learn from their strengths and weaknesses. For instance, Lady Blake's was known in the early years as an old folks' home due to the number of "old nuns" who resided there.[31] The VMD committee, on the other hand, was eager to revive a tradition in which women could actively serve their community, as in days gone by:

At the annual meeting of the Vihara Maha Devi *Samitiya*, Sir Baron Jayatilake who presided said that from the time Buddhism had been introduced to Ceylon, the *Bhikkhu* as well as the *Bhikkhuni* had worked jointly for the welfare of the country. But since the *Bhikkhuni* section ceased to exist 700 or 800 years ago, the country had disintegrated. Therefore, for the real revival of the people the restoration of the *Bhikkhuni Sasana* was essential.[32]

Resounding in Jayatilake's sentiments is one of the points of this chapter: namely, that the existence of a *bhikkhunī* order in Ceylon has been perceived as a necessity for the welfare of Buddhism and Buddhist people.

At the opening of the VMD lay nunnery, D. S. Senanayake reminded Buddhists of the true mission of women:

... after emphasising the significance and value of such an institution, [he] deplored the fact that Buddhists who spoke so much of "*ahimsa*" should not have taken steps to educate their women in the art of succouring the sick. Such work in Ceylon was being mostly done by Christian Sisters, and it was time that the women of the country should stir themselves and work for the welfare of their fellow-beings in a selfless way.[33]

Though they harkened back to the era when the order of nuns ministered to the laity, the image of Christian sisters weighed heavily on the minds of the founders of the VMD. As in the 1890s, Buddhism in Ceylon continued to be influenced by Christianity well into the twentieth century. According to the committee, the lay nuns' role in society could best be fulfilled by tending to the infirm, something they had seen Christian nuns doing:

We must find some useful work for our *Upasikas* to do in the neighbouring villages. Today besides their duties and meditations and teaching, no work of value to the residents of the vicinity is being done ... We have written to

the Honorable Minister of Health asking him to erect a hospital close to the
Aramaya, where our *Upasikas* can learn nursing and afford to help the sick.
Arrangements are being made to conduct a First Aid class among the
Upasikas.[34]

The committee's attitude about the appropriate vocation for lay
nuns was further expressed in Sri Nissanka's closing remarks at the
inaugural proceedings of the VMD lay nunnery:

Those Buddhist Sisters who wished to enter that *Ashram* should live an
exemplary religious life. They should do selfless service to their sisters in the
teaching of *Dhamma*, and were also expected to teach in their spare hours
spinning and weaving, domestic science and hygiene.[35]

Sri Nissanka and the other VMD committee members' choices for
topics that the lay nuns should teach testifies to the power of
stereotyping. They suggested that though female renunciants had
renounced lay life, a division of labor should permeate their vocation:
female renunciants were to teach gender determined "female" work
to the women of their community.[36] While they modelled the lay
nuns' vocation along Christian lines, the committee members hoped
that "the noble example of selfless service, set by the distinguished
Bhikkhunis of the *Buddhasasana* in suffering and in silence, [would]
inspire [the] *Upasikas* in their future work."[37] The aim of the
committee was not to house those *upāsikās* who traditionally retire to
a life of meditation after fulfilling their family responsibilities, but
rather to train lay nuns in "selfless service;" thus encouraging a
"this-worldly" asceticism for women.   In fact, the committee,
articulating Protestant Buddhist concerns, wished to redirect the
course that the nascent tradition of female renunciation in Ceylon
was taking. According to the VMD, renunciation was meant for
those who were willing to dedicate their lives to social service rather
than for old women who spent their time meditating. To achieve
these aims, the committee "decided to open a child welfare centre for
the benefit of the neighbouring village of the *aramaya*" in 1941, to
provide the lay nuns with useful work.[38] Thus, the lay nuns never
relinquished their nurturing, motherly role even though they had
renounced lay life.

   Prior to opening the orphanage, the members of the committee
agreed to affiliate with the All Ceylon Buddhist Congress (ACBC),
which eventually took control of the VMD's Children's Welfare
Centre. Founded in 1919, with Sir D. Baron Jayatilake in the

Chair,[39] the object of the ACBC was "to promote, foster and protect the interest of Buddhism and of the Buddhists and to safeguard the rights and privileges of the Buddhists."[40] Established to protect Buddhist interests in Ceylon, according to Jayatilake the ACBC in its early years "provided education, the organizational support, motivation and the techniques appropriate for the Buddhists to voice their grievances and work collectively for their legitimate rights without resorting to violence."[41] In other words, Jayatilake argued that the function of the ACBC was a continuation of the state's before Buddhism was disestablished. In short, echoing Sri Nissanka Jayatilake claimed that if Buddhism had not been disestablished, committees such as the ACBC would not have been necessary. According to the ACBC, "It is the Sinhala Buddhist population that has no organization other than the ACBC to look after their interests unless the democratically elected government takes up that responsibility."[42] The VMD committe and the ACBC thus shared the same agenda, namely, the protection and control of Buddhism in Ceylon.

In 1945, the VMD committee handed over nearly all of its responsibilities to the ACBC. The latter had already been given control of the VMD Children's Home located on the premises of the lay nunnery. The committee decided that the four lay nuns who had renounced at the VMD lay nunnery would be controlled by the ACBC.[43] Thus, within only ten years of establishing the lay nunnery, the committee transferred control to the ACBC. They decided that "The Buddhist Congress [ACBC] shall be responsible for looking after the *Upasikas* resident now in the *Aramaya* and for any other *Upasikas* who may be admitted."[44] For all intents and purposes, the committee had relinquished its control of the lay nunnery project.

In many ways, the committee's relinquishment of power reflected the transitional nature of Ceylonese politics in the late 1940s and throughout the 1950s. The establishment of the VMD lay nunnery was one medium through which the elite members of society protested against the British government's neglect of Buddhism and Sinhala culture. In December, 1945, with independence looming on the horizon, Buddhism seemed similarly liberated. Thus, the Senanayakes, Jayewardenes, Jayatilakes, and Sri Nissankas turned their attention completely toward the governance of the island.

PORTRAITS OF TWO LAY NUNS IN PRE-INDEPENDENT CEYLON

Before continuing with the narrative of the political situation in Ceylon in the 1940s and its relationship to the tradition of the female renunciant, I will turn my attention toward two of the most well-known lay nuns of the period, the German Sister Uppalavaṇṇā and the Sinhala Sister Sudharmā.[45] Their biographies afford us an insight into the aspirations of the women who renounced in the years immediately prior to independence.

I have chosen to focus upon Sister Uppalavaṇṇā and Sister Sudharmā for two reasons. First of all, because they are both discussed in the Minutes of the VMD committee, their life stories reflect the nature of the tradition of female renunciation during the decades under review. Secondly, I am able to offer fairly reliable information about them both. Moreover, their attitudes toward their own tradition reflect the different ways that lay nuns – both western and Sinhala – have perceived their vocation.

In September, 1938, the woman who had been selected to act as the chief lay nun, Sister Visākhā, ordained another woman without the consent of the committee. In addition, she "left the *Aramaya* premises" without the committee's permission.[46] She thus lost the committee's favor. It is not surprising that there were problems between the lay nuns and the committee. When a secular body holds authority over those committed to spirituality, there is an inherent tension. The power that the VMD committee held over the residents of the Vihāra Mahā Devī Upāsikārāmaya recalls the tension between the king and the *saṅgha* until the British took control of the island. Despite similar tensions at the Upāsikārāmaya, by December, 1938, the committee had begun to search for a replacement for Sister Visākhā. That same month, they selected two members from among themselves to meet Upāsikā Uppalavaṇṇā, "and to invite her to be the chief Upasika at Biyagama."[47] However, within a few days, "Upasika Uppalavanna ... regretted her inability to join the *Aramaya*."[48]

Sister Uppalavaṇṇā, formerly Else Buchholz, was born in The Tiergarten quarter of Berlin.[49] According to her biographer, she came from an elite family and was a musician.[50] While living in the Black Forest, Buchholz became acquainted with Buddhism. At the time, the German Buddhist monk, Bhikkhu Ñāṇatiloka (Anton

Gueth),[51] who had been living in Ceylon as a monk since 1904, was also visiting the Black Forest. Formerly a virtuoso of the violin, the monk shared Buchholz's musical background: "Common musical interest led to Buddhist conversation, and Else Buchholz resolved to seek her salvation in the Order of Buddhist nuns."[52] Gueth was the first German man to "don the *bhikkhu's* robes," in Ceylon, while Buchholz was the first German woman to renounce the world there.[53] The nature of Buchholz's former religious affiliations, if any, are not clear from the available source materials. She became committed to Buddhism in 1920, however, after her meetings with Bhikkhu Ñānatiloka, and decided to renounce the world in Ceylon.

When Buchholz became a Buddhist, Ceylon was still a British colony. Thus, as a German, Buchholz was considered a foreign enemy and was not permitted to land. Therefore, she travelled on to Japan, where she studied for six years. Finally, in 1926, she was permitted to enter Ceylon, where she began her life as a renunciant. According to Buchholz's biographer, she chose Ceylon as the perfect place to renounce the world because Ceylonese Buddhism "represented the original teachings of the Buddha." Though it cannot be ascertained who conducted her "ordination," it is most probable that Bhikkhu Ñānatiloka, her teacher, conducted the rite of passage. Her biographer provides a description of her metamorphosis from German socialite to renunciant:

Here Miss Buchholz, as a nun, was transformed almost to unrecognisability. The hair was shorn from her head, her eyebrows were shaven off. Bareheaded and barefooted, with the iron bowl of the begging monk on her arm, she must go from door to door in the hot tropical sun and wait, without speaking a word, till someone may come out and give her something.[54]

A photograph of Buchholz, that is, Sister Uppalavaṇṇā, taken in 1982 just prior to her death, reveals that unlike Sudharmācārī, Uppalavaṇṇā wore an orange robe *and* an orange blouse. Indeed, the color of both pieces of clothing was symbolic of her complete renunciation of lay life. In short, her clothes symbolized her commitment to the *bhikkhunī's* vocation.

According to Sister Uppalavaṇṇā's biographer, as well as her chief patron,[55] "she strictly adhered to the *Vinaya* ... she never accepted any food offered to her after twelve noon. She followed all the precepts and used to say that if any of the Buddhist clergy handled cash or enjoyed worldly pleasures it would be better for them to give up the robes."⁵⁶ Sister Uppalavaṇṇā also abided by the Buddhist liturgical calendar; she seems to have confessed her misdoings to a community of renunciants, in the style of the ancient order of monks and nuns:

On the days of the four quarters of the moon, like every member of the Order, she keeps the appointed holy day on which certain excerpts out of the Book of Discipline are read, and the ascetics, male and female,⁵⁷ from the neighbouring hermitages, in a sort of general confession, mutually reveal to one another their misdeeds and sins.⁵⁸

Unlike the lay nuns at the Saṅghamittā Upāsikārāmaya, Lady Blake's, and the VMD lay nunnery, Uppalavaṇṇā adhered to the ten precepts, as well as to the additional 311 rules of the ordained nun. Moreover, she lived in a "little hut made of palm-leaf matting," rather than revelling in the relative luxuries of the late eighteenth- and early nineteenth-century lay nunneries. Her abode and lifestyle, thus, were in stark contrast to those of the renunciants whom we have met so far, except perhaps Catherine Shearer. According to her biographer, Uppalavaṇṇā was influenced by these lay nuns; Sister Uppalavaṇṇā lived as "a hermit because the lax life of the ordinary nun's cloister [did] not appeal to her."⁵⁹ It is no surprise, then, that she refused to act as chief lay nun of the Vihāra Mahā Devī Upāsikārāmaya.

The sources indicate that Sister Uppalavaṇṇā was very familiar with the *Vinaya* texts. Her insistence on purity of practice, in accord with the books of discipline, attested to her knowledge of the Buddhist monastic code. As many early western Buddhists were inclined to do,⁶⁰ Uppalavaṇṇā stressed a return to the pristine life of renunciation envisaged by the texts, rather than as they had been interpreted by contemporary Buddhist culture. Whether or not this life was followed became Sister Uppalavaṇṇā's yardstick for evaluating her own life, as well as the the lifestyle of other renunciants in Ceylon. Thus, in spite of the fact that the order of nuns had not existed in Sri Lanka since the eleventh century, Sister Uppalavaṇṇā followed in the footsteps of the ancient *bhikkhunī*, rather than the lay renunciants who had preceded her. Sister Uppalavaṇṇā's ideal of renunciation was represented by an austere lifestyle and insistence upon the main- tenance of all the 311 rules of the *Vinaya*, solitary meditations, a begging bowl, and a patched robe.⁶¹ Her life was in stark contrast to the ideal of renunciation advocated by the members of the VMD committee, represented by their focus upon worship, on the one hand, and service, on the other.

Sister Sudharmā, educated at Museus College in Colombo, and later at the University of Ceylon, was the paradigmatic example of the VMD committee's vision of female renunciation.[62] The seventy year-old (in 1989) Sudharmā, who speaks English fluently, related her life-history to me at the VMD Upāsikārāmaya in May, 1989. Extremely humble and gracious, Sudharmā told me that many scholars had come to interview her, but that she would rather teach Buddhism than relate her autobiography. I began the interview by asking her about her parents and her childhood.

Sudharmā's father was a farmer, and her family owned rice fields. She recalled that she was not "an ordinary child:"

I was very pious as a child and observed the eight precepts as often as possible. I loved to wear white, and would not wear the jewelry and pretty frocks which my mother wanted me to wear. My mother noticed that I was a very caring child who always wanted to help old and poor people. Even now, I have donated two *läkhs*[63] of my own money from my pension to build an *ārāmaya* which will house pilgrims who are old and poor in Anurādha-pura. I have given about five or six *läkhs* to the Vihāra Mahā Devī Upāsikārāmaya.[64]

Reflecting upon her life, Sudharmā thus considers those who dedicate their lives to service to be "ideal" Buddhists. In my second interview with Sudharmā, I asked her why she became a renunciant:

When I was eight or nine, my friend Jane and I met a nun on the road. This was my first encounter with a nun. In those days, they were called *meheni*, or *bhikkhunī*. I used to chat with her and pleaded with her to take me to her temple. As a child, from very early on (four of five years of age), I expressed a desire to my mother, after observing the eight precepts with my parents and my grandparents on the *pōya* days, that I wanted to become a monk. My mother could not understand what such a young child could gain from observing the eight precepts. I did not know that only men become monks, but I kept on begging my mother to let me become one. At age ten or so, after having spent two years reading about meditation and the Buddhist doctrine, I clipped my own hair very close to my head and when my parents saw me, they began to wail. My brother, too, begged me not to become a nun. After some time, my hair grew back, and I carried on with school. At age twelve, a nun named Dhammawatī came to my village to learn Pāli.[65] She was living very close by. After many chats with her, and after having been impressed by the graphic pictures of the various hells depicted in the

Botale temple constructed by the Senanayake family[66] (I knew that if a stayed at home, I would have to lie unavoidably, and did not want to wind up in hell), combined with my predilection for the ascetic lifestyle attained in previous births, I once again clipped, and then shaved, my hair.[67]

Sister Sudharmā's narrative is interesting for a variety of reasons. First of all, she relates that at the age of eight, that is, in 1927, female renunciants were a feature of the Ceylonese landscape in the country as well as in the city.[68] Moreover, they were not known as *dasa sil mātāvo*, or "Mothers of the Ten Precepts" (as they are today), but rather as *bhikkhunīs*. This suggests that they were either held in high esteem, or that they were such a rare phenomenon in the country that people were not sure what to call them. Secondly, that Sudharmā was self-ordained is of import to this study. It suggests that there may have been more self-styled female renunciants in Ceylon when she was a child and earlier. Not having been influenced by the movements in Kandy and Colombo to reinstitute the tradition of female renunciation, Sudharmā nonetheless renounced the world. Her narrative continued with comments about her early affiliation with the VMD lay nunnery:

My mother was now convinced of my sincerity and agreed that I could become a nun but that I would have to stay in the area until I grew up. For about three months, I studied with Dhammawatī, and continued to live at home in a special room which my mother allocated. My mother agreed that only under these conditions could I live as a nun. Three months later, Dhammawatī returned to her village, and I continued to meditate and study at home. At this time, the Senanayake family took me to Biyagama, where I have been ever since. Of the original nuns at Biyagama, being the youngest, I am one of the only surviving members.

Sudharmā's dedication to Buddhism and service impressed the VMD committee so much so that in December, 1938, the members "decided to discuss at the next meeting whether the Warakapola Upasika should be sent to a Buddhist Girls' School in Colombo."[69] Two months later, they "decided … to send Upasika Sudharma to Museus Girls' School for her education."[70] Sudharmā furthered her education at the University of Ceylon, where she received a BA in Oriental Language and Culture. Sudharmā is today the most highly-educated lay nun in Sri Lanka.

Though Sudharmā was self-ordained,[71] she referred to Māwicārī of Burma, who served as the incumbent at Lady Blake's for a short period after Sudharmācārī's death, as her teacher. According to the Minutes of the VMD committee, Māwicārī became the chief lay nun at the VMD Upāsikārāmaya for a while: "Upasika Visakha who was functioning as chief Upasika for some time left us ... She has written in asking for permission to come back and the *Samitiya* has agreed her request. Upasika Mawicari of Burma who took her place has also left us and established an *aramaya* at Moratunduwa."[72] Thus, given Visākhā and Māwicārī's affiliation with Lady Blake's, the lay nuns of the VMD are also part of the lineage established by Sudharmācārī at Lady Blake's in 1907. However, unlike the residents at Lady Blake's, known as an old folks' home in its early years, all the lay nuns at the VMD lay nunnery were expected to devote their lives to enhancing the Buddhist community. This was a standard considered too high by many of the residents of the lay nunnery. The VMD committee summed up the problem thus: "the difficulty is in the training of the *Upasikas*. Few of them seem to appreciate the ideals we seek to establish to provide an *aramaya* for those women who seek to follow the Buddha's way of renunciation and service. Some of the *Upasikas* are rather reluctant to adhere to the strict disicipline the *Samitiya* enforces."[73] Sister Sudharmā, on the other hand, fulfilled the vision of the members of the committee by conforming for the most part to their Protestant Buddhist ideals of a "this-worldly" asceticism. Though from a rural area rather than Colombo, Sudharmā had a city girl's education, and dedicated her life to social service.

Sister Uppalavaṇṇā dedicated her life to treading the path of renunciation that she considered the members of the ancient order of nuns to have traversed; this path included retreating from social relationships. By contrast, Sudharmā's interpretation of renunciation demanded involvement "in the world," and her goal was a life devoted to the betterment of society, her childhood dream. The emphases in their careers reflect the contemporary scene; as we shall see in chapters 7 and 8, present-day Sinhala lay nuns are for the most part aligned with social service, while the foreign female renunciants resident in Sri Lanka are aligned with the contemplative tradition.[74]

There are marked differences between the ideals of renunciation between Sister Uppalavaṇṇā and Sister Sudharmā; however, there are striking similarities, as well. They were both patronized by the elite; though Sister Uppalavaṇṇā was supported by the village community near her humble dwelling, she, like Sudharmā, attracted the attention of elite members of Colombo society. Moreover, they both "renounced the world" in the pre-independence period, a period that valued the contribution female renunciants made to the Buddhist revival.

In the decades immediately following independence, interest in the tradition of female renunciation continued, although with a few notable changes. In the next section, I explore these differences and relate them to the political climate of Ceylon.

THE FEMALE RENUNCIANT IN POST-INDEPENDENT CEYLON

The elite Sinhala Buddhist faction continued to govern after independence, albeit only for one decade.[75] During the 1940s, Ceylon began to adjust to its independence, while the elite competed among themselves for power. They had displaced the British, and though they had articulated Buddhist concerns prior to independence, they continued with the policies of the British toward Buddhism. In fact, the elite United National Party (UNP) government of post-indpendent Ceylon (1948–56) "extended a measure of patronage to Buddhism but were unwilling to move against Christian agencies."[76] The opposition criticized them for not making Buddhism a part of their party's political agenda but they defended their stance: "at the general election of 1952, the UNP under Dudley Senanayake's leadership, in countering the [Sri Lanka Freedom Party] SLFPs call for the state to provide greater facilities for the propagation of Buddhism, declared in the manifesto that there was no need to render any special assistance to 'the great religion of the Buddha'."[77] At first glance, it seems paradoxical that those who participated in the Buddhist renaissance by founding the VMD lay nunnery were not compelled to support Buddhism further. Yet, Senanayake, Jaye-wardene, and other politicians had worked successfully toward liberating their country from the control of the British. In short, because Sinhala Buddhist politicians had helped to purify Buddhism, they could maintain the policies of the colonial government toward Buddhism with a clear conscience. The secretaries of the VMD committee, in their second anniversary report, made this connection between the committee's work and the "purification"[78] of Buddhism: "Our work has been heralded in the press and by the public as an attempt to regenerate the Buddha *Dharma* as it exists in Lanka today. If we accomplish our object we may well merit such praise."[79] Having helped to resuscitate Buddhism and convinced that a policy of separation between church and state was best for Ceylon,[80] the elite assumed the task of governing their nation without changing many of the policies of the British.

While the elite had spearheaded the campaign to resuscitate Buddhism in the late 1800s, the masses began to join the bandwagon in the decade following independence. The elite had successfully dislodged the British, yet because many Buddhists perceived the UNP's stance toward Buddhism as unsympathetic, the UNP itself was dislodged from power soon after independence. With the celebration of Buddha Jayanti[81] in 1956 approaching, the question of Buddhist loyalties became a powerful political weapon in the years immediately following independence. A politician from one of the most aristocratic families in Ceylon, S. W. R. D. Bandaranaike, was among the first to articulate the government's neglect of Buddhism and Sinhala culture.[82] Sinhala language became an important issue in the early 1950s, while Buddhism began to play a major role in politics. Bandaranaike's program attracted a large following from the rural populace from whom the elite had become more and more alienated throughout centuries of colonial rule in Ceylon.[83] As over seventy percent of Ceylon's population lived in rural areas and as most of these people were sympathetic to Bandaranaike's Buddhist platform, the UNP suffered a smashing defeat in 1956.[84] Essentially, the UNP's unsympathetic stance toward Buddhism would no longer be tolerated by rural Buddhists whom Bandaranaike's pro-Buddhist, pro-Sinhala platform had reached. From its aristocratic roots in the late 1800s, to its rural, fundamentalist reaction to the city's worldly and secular culture in the 1950s, the Buddhist revival in Ceylon had radically changed its face in many ways. Moreover, by 1972 for all practical purposes Buddhism had become the state religion; the republican constitution of 1972 accorded Buddhism "the foremost place" and enjoined the state to "protect and foster" the religion.[85] The proletarianization of the Buddhist revival had now become integrated into mainstream political structures.

At the same time that politics was proletarianized, so was the vocation of female renunciation. In short, when the masses began to play a larger part in the governance of the island and when they began to contribute to the Buddhist revivalism of their day, rural women began to enter lay nunneries. In fact, rural women continue to dominate the lay nunneries, thus indicating that the past forty years have shown no deviation from this trend that began in the

1950s. The following list illustrates the metamorphosis that politics, the Buddhist revival and one of its most notable expressions – female renunciation – have undergone since the late 1800s:

1880s–1940s	Colonial Ceylon/elite politics Elite Buddhist revival gathers momentum Elite women renounce
	————————
1950s–1960s	Post-independence Ceylon/varied participation in politics Mass Buddhist revival gathers momentum Varied participation of elite and rural women in the lay nunneries
	————————
1970s–present	The Ceylon government once again "protects" Buddhism Goal of Buddhist revival is achieved Rural women characterize the tradition of female world-renunciation

CONCLUSIONS

There are many differences between the women who renounced the world from the end of the nineteenth century until post-independence Ceylon, and the women who renounce today. Despite these differences, there are some striking similarities. In both periods Buddhists perceived lay nuns as being necessary for the welfare of Buddhism and ultimately for the welfare of Ceylon. Yet, once the women had renounced, the problem of how to cope with female world-renouncers became of paramount importance for many, just as the history of the Vihāra Mahā Devī Upāsikārāmaya suggests. As in the early monastic community in India, it was socially unthinkable for women to regulate themselves[86] and thus structures were imposed to protect and control them.

Much like late nineteenth-century Buddhists, the VMD committee fashioned its project along Christian lines. Their model was the Ceylon community of Christian nuns. Yet, they also borrowed heavily from traditional Buddhism and echoed early Buddhist attitudes about women and world-renunciation. Indeed, from the late nineteenth century when women once again donned the ochre robe and cloistered themselves, female renunciants have only been quasi-autonomous, much like their (ordained) counterparts in ancient India.[87] These anomolous groups of quasi-autonomous women continue to punctuate the island's landscape. In the contemporary scene, the lay nun is referred to as "mother" (*mātā*; *mäniyo*) by those who support her, and she maintains many female tasks even after her renunciation, much like the women who have preceded her. It is now time to meet some of these contemporary lay nuns, or "Mothers of the Ten Precepts," with whom I worked and lived while conducting research in Sri Lanka.

CHAPTER 7

The dasa sil mātā in contemporary Sri Lanka

INTRODUCTION

In this chapter, I explore the contemporary practice of female renunciation in Sri Lanka.[1] Though the laity continue to support female renunciants as many have done since the 1890s, a vast majority of lay nuns at present are impoverished; they find it difficult to ensure the laity's patronage. Moreover, women are no longer encouraged to renounce as they had been in the past; instead, they are expected to fulfill the role society has determined for them as wife and mother.

For many Buddhists in Sri Lanka, the conflict between social and religious obligations is a recurring phenomenon. For women, the conflict is usually resolved by giving priority to social demands, and conforming to female stereotypes. This is certainly the case with the contemporary lay nuns: the *dasa sil mātāvo*. That lay nuns never lose their association with their lay role as nurturers is perhaps best illustrated in a typical obituary of a lay nun:

Embuldeniya – Nanso Hamine Upāsikā Mathawa [sic],[2] beloved wife of late Mr. D. S. Embuldeniya, loving mother of late Grace, Charlotte, Piyadassi Dayasena, Karunalatha, late Chandradasa, expired ...[3]

It is striking that no mention is made of Embuldeniya Sil Mātā's lay nunnery connections, such as her teacher, and students. In other words, she is first and foremost a wife and mother, despite her renunciation of lay life. By comparison, the death announcement of a monk connects him to his monastery rather than to his blood relatives:

Ven. Dedigama Sri Saranankara Maha Thera – (Chief Incumbent of Sri Jayawardhanarama Purana Raja Maha Viharaya, Renagala, Nunga-muwa, Yatigaloluwa and Sri Pujjyawardhanaramaya, Rangellepola).

Beloved teacher of Ven. Kuragamuwe Dhammaransi Thera, Ven. Aule-
gama Seelawimala Thera, Ven. Paramaulle Medhalankara Thera and Ven
Pelawatte Saṅgharakkhitha Thera, passed away ...[4]

Unlike the lay nun, the monk is survived by other world-renouncers
rather than his family; unlike the lay nun, he has completely severed
his lay identity.

One consequence of this type of stereotyping is that the lay nuns'
activities are centered in the domestic realm and are related to gender
determined work, even though they are world-renouncers. In the
majority of lay nunneries I visited, the renunciants spent hours baby
sitting for those who support them,[5] devoted much time and energy
to sewing and stitching their own robes, and cooked their own meals.
In the monasteries I visited, however, monks received robes rather
than sew them, and accepted prepared rice and food rather than cook
their own meals. Nonetheless, it can be argued that contemporary
lay nuns are the analogues of monks in society – they preach, teach,
receive alms, and spend much of their time conducting pūjās for their
dāyakas. However, much of their religious service is confined to
maintenance and support roles. These roles, such as preserving
religious sites and supporting monks, are indeed essential to the
operation of the religion. However, they do not require clerical
status. Yet by virtue of their public role as preachers, teachers, and
ritual specialists, contemporary lay nuns demonstrate that Buddhism
is able to create a space for women in public, religious life.

In the sections below, I offer an account of contemporary Buddhist
female renunciation based on biographies of Sinhala lay nuns and the
attitudes of Sri Lankan Buddhist society toward the nuns. Moreover,
I describe the lay nuns' attitudes toward contemporary Buddhism.
The account links the classical tradition of female renunciation
immortalized in the texts, with the living practice of contemporary
lay nuns of Sri Lanka. In the process of this illustration, I highlight
innovations and differences among the lay nuns and compare their
vocation to that of the ancient *bhikkhunī*. Though the lay nuns are not
members of the *saṅgha*, they provide many of the functions of the
defunct Theravādin order of nuns, albeit with important differences.
Essentially, this study of the contemporary lay nuns of Sri Lanka is a
study of continuity and change in Theravāda Buddhism.

I also offer lay nuns' own critique of the amount of power they
have vis-a-vis Buddhist laywomen. Contemporary rural women do
not have the support of their families if they choose to renounce the

world, even though most continue many traditional female roles even after renouncing, because they do not completely comply with society's demands. The lay nuns take vows that are often costly, vows that can sever ties with their families forever. Yet by renouncing the world, they are offered options that were severly circumvented in lay life. Though the laity continue to regulate the lives of most lay nuns, the laity no longer control the lay nunneries in the manner that was customary in the formative period of renewed interest in female renunciation. Buddhist women who renounce in the present have far more control over their lives than they had in the past. Moreover, by virtue of their renunciation of the world, these rural women gain control over their own destinies.

WOMEN, RENUNCIATION, AND POWER

The position of women in rural Sri Lanka differs from that of their Buddhist sisters in the metropolitan areas where western ideals have influenced the status of women.[6] By comparing the status of women in rural areas with that in the cities, I do not suggest that village women are the downtrodden, subordinated creatures they are commonly assumed to be. The elements of culture and society in rural Sri Lanka that lead most observers to consider it strongly male-centered do exist, but they may mislead the observer to a distorted view of the relative power of men and women.[7] However, women who come from rural backgrounds have far fewer choices than the daughters and sisters of the Colombo elite.[8] By comparison, metropolitan women are freer than other Sinhala women to chart their own destinies. It is not uncommon for the elite woman to become highly trained in a professional occupation, postpone marriage, or choose to forego marriage altogether and devote her life to career goals, rather than to family.[9] In short, such a woman has power over the choices she makes.

The rural woman, on the other hand, is expected to marry, and if for some reason she does not, she becomes a burden to her family. In other words, whether she marries or not, the rural woman's life is chartered for her. In one of my earliest conversations with Kotmalee Dhīrā Sudharmā of Madivala, the incumbent of the lay nunnery that was my primary research site, she told me that the choice to renounce the world can be very liberating for rural women:

Women and men are forced to marry. Sometimes these marriages are satisfactory, but often they are not. When women get married, they cannot spend time meditating because they have to raise children. When women from the village do not marry, they have to live a life that their family sees fit. I did not want to marry, and I did not want to stay at home. By renouncing, I do not have to keep having babies like most women; I can spend the rest of my life dedicated to Buddhism.[10]

Kotmalee Dhīrā Sudharmā and other lay nuns around the island implied that renunciation, and especially celibacy, is related to female power. When I asked Kotmalee Dhīrā Sudharmā why she became a lay nun, she touched upon the themes of power, celibacy, and renunciation:

I did not want to marry; I never married. From early in my childhood, I never wanted to marry. If I had married, I would have had to have had children, and I would have had no independence. Some men are not good; they drink *ärräk* and neglect their wives and children.[11] *Dukkha*. By becoming a *sil mātā*, I do not have to worry about these things; I can do what I please.[12]

By highlighting Kotmalee Dhīrā Sudharmā's explanation that in becoming celibate she avoided a predictably unfulfilling life, I do not intend to undermine what are perhaps best described as her "religious reasons" for renouncing the world. In Kotmalee Dhīrā Sudharmā's world-view, the village woman's life is tainted by *dukkha*: one of the three marks of existence the Buddha described in the early discourses. *Dukkha* and lack of independence motivated Kotmalee Dhīrā Sudharmā to become a renunciant.[13] In his study of the forest monks of Sri Lanka, Carrithers relates how they made a similar observation concerning the relationship between *dukkha* and renunciation:

In the traditional explanation individuals leave the world because of *dukkha*, and *dukkha* may be explained as old age, sickness, or death; or sorrow, lamentation, sadness and so forth ... In a kind of shorthand forest monks today frequently say that they took the robes because of "disillusionment with the world." When pressed more closely they may enumerate a number of factors: family catastrophe, quarrelling in the family, poverty ...[14]

Thus, it is not uncommon for renunciants – both male and female – to cite domestic disharmony as a motivating factor in choosing their vocation. For one lay nun, Sunandā Sil Mātā, a difficult domestic problem provided the impetus to renounce the world:

I married when I was quite young. It was a love marriage. I had three children. We were very happy. Then one day to my horror, I found my husband with our servant girl in bed and was dumb struck. After that incident... I hated men. I wanted to do everything that men could do. I even started to consume liquor. I used to drink about two bottles of *ärräk* and smoke about three packets of cigarettes a day... One day an elderly carpenter asked me whther it was not better for me to become a *Dasa Sil Mātā* than waste my life this way... The day I stepped foot in this *ārāmaya* ... I stopped my liquor and smoking... The *Dhamma* helped me to overcome every obstacle...[15]

From Sunandā Sil Mātā's point of view, the fundamental un-satisfactory human condition (*dukkha*) could best be alleviated by becoming a celibate nun.

Other lay nuns offered reasons similar to Kotmalee Dhīrā Sudharmā's and Sunandā Sil Mātā's for renouncing the house-holders' life. In interviews with the younger generation of lay nuns at Lady Blake's in Kandy, one of the teenage members of the group clenched her teeth, squinted, and exclaimed:

Sister, marriage is *dukkha*. Who wants to marry? When girls marry, they have many children. It is too much work for us. As soon as they rise in the morning until they go to sleep at night, women are working for their children and husband. They have no freedom to meditate. We have a better life. Their lives are not good.[16]

Though this young lay nun has never married, both formerly married and unmarried lay nuns invoked unfulfilling marriage scenarios when discussing their reasons for renouncing the home life.[17] I interviewed many formerly married female renunciants who regard an unhappy home life as the catalyst for donning the ochre robe; it is striking how much their stories echo Sunandā Sil Mātā's. For instance, Kotagoda Dhammādinnā explained that disharmony in her home life was the impetus for renouncing the world:[18]

My marriage was not arranged; it was a love marriage. I was married for twenty two years. I have six children – three boys and three girls. My husband has been paralyzed for fifteen years, he is a drinker. I wanted to die during most of my married life. I was miserable. I was always busy taking abuse from my husband. He is not a good man. I loved my children, but I wanted to die. Without telling anyone, I went to Anurādhapura to worship the eight holy places and decided to become a *dasa sil mātā*.[19]

Kotmalee Dhīrā Sudharmā, Sunandā Sil Mātā, the young renunci-ant at Lady Blake's, and Kotagoda Dhammādinnā each suggested that powerlessness over her future, or the desire to chart her own destiny, was the reason for renouncing the householder's life. These stories are paralleled in the biographies of each lay nun I interviewed. Moreover, each lay nun related how she was resisted by a family member when she renounced.

Unlike Buddhist society of the late 1890s that supported the renunciation of the world by women, contemporary society does not support the *dasa sil mātā's* decision to renounce her lay identity. This is especially evident in the negative attitudes of families whose daughters and sisters have opted to lead the renunciant's celibate lifestyle, instead of the roles traditionally associated with rural women: wife and mother. In the case of one lay nun, Dharmeśvarī Sil Mātā, her family's reluctance to permit her to renounce led to her forced confinement:

... I wanted to become a *dasa sil mātā*. My father would not hear of it, nor my brother. After the death of my father, my brother took us over. He wanted to give me in marriage. Several suitors came to see me. I spoke to them and told them the truth. I was locked up in a room for days ... I was not allowed to do what I wanted.[20]

In other words, Dharmeśvarī Sil Mātā was powerless to make her own choices. Dharmeśvarī's forced confinement is related to issues of celibacy and power. As Lawrence Babb's study of the Brahma Kumaris suggests, celibacy and power are recurring themes in many South Asian religious traditions. Indeed, study of the Brahma Kumaris, a celibate Hindu sect, provides many clues for understanding Sri Lankan rural families' initial reluctance to allow their women to renounce the world.

As Babb explains, on the surface the symbols of the Brahma Kumaris are familiar ones in Indian society, and "are surrounded by a halo of highly conventional legtitimacy." For instance, "The Brahma Kumaris are advocates of yoga, which they say will bring peace of mind. They urge vegetarianism, abstinence from tobacco and alcohol, and celibacy. In none of this is there anything truly novel or objectionable."[21] Indeed, vegetarianism, yoga, and celibacy are highly respected in Hindu society. However, celibacy for women is highly suspect:

The source of the tension ... has to do with women. From its earliest days the movement has been mainly associated with women. This in itself raises no problems. In many ways women have always been the true custodians of what is called "popular Hinduism." However, the involvement of women

in a movement that advocates celibacy is quite another matter... this
constitutes a direct challenge to the prevailing imagery of who women are
and what they should be in the social order...[22]

For the Brahma Kumaris of India, as well as for the lay nuns of Sri
Lanka, celibacy is tantamount to autonomy. In both cases, the
women express a will to be free as women by using traditional
concepts. In practicing yoga, maintaing a vegetarian diet, and
abstaining from intoxicants, the Brahma Kumaris legitimate their
activities. The lay nuns similarly legitimate their vocation by
practicing meditation and teaching others to meditate, adhering to
the ten precepts, and cloistering themselves. However, one of the
most potent concepts of renunciation in Hinduism and Buddhism –
celibacy – is not traditionally associated with women, but with men.
Thus, for a woman to renounce her sexuality is not only a radical
break from tradition, but is also a radical movement toward
autonomy. In the case of rural women who become lay nuns in Sri
Lanka, their show of autonomy meets the resistance of those whose
world-view is traditionally Buddhist. As we saw in chapter 6,
autonomous female world-renouncers are not socially acceptable in
Buddhist Sri Lanka.

By renouncing the world and thus becoming liberated from the
oppressive regime of rural Buddhist society as one lay nun stressed,
women provide themselves with optimum conditions for achieving
the liberating goal of the Buddhist path.[23] Thus, by becoming
renunciants, rural women have access to power. This spirit of
autonomy and power is further enhanced by the informal relationship
the lay nuns have with the monastic order.

Only eight of the Sinhala lay nuns I interviewed would accept
ordination into the monastic order. The majority would not accept
entrance into the *saṅgha*, even if it were possible, for initiation would
mean institutionalized subordination to the monks. Mahāgoda
Sumettā, echoing many of the lay nuns I interviewed, explained why
so many of her peers are against ordination into the *saṅgha*:

I do not wish to see the reintroduction of the nuns' lineage in Sri Lanka. The
Vinaya is so strict and it would be impossible to observe all 311 rules. It is
difficult enough for many lay nuns to observe only ten, but I observe them
carefully.[24] I would wind up in hell if I tried to observe the rules of the
bhikkhunī; their life was more difficult than mine. More importantly,
however, if the nuns' lineage is reintroduced, then we would have to live by
the Eight Rules which Lord Buddha gave to his foster mother when she

became a member of the monastic order.[25] I do not wish for this to happen; I do not want monks to be involved in my life.[26]

Sumettā argued that if lay nuns were ordained, they would fall under the controlling hands of monks, the fate of the Buddha's foster mother, Mahāpajāpatī Gotamī, who tradition alleges was the first Buddhist nun. In conversations I had with Sumettā and other lay nuns around the island, I learned that the majority of lay nuns are extremely familiar with the traditional account of the establishment of the order of nuns by the Buddha and his foster mother. According to the account in the *Vinaya* texts, the Buddha was reluctant to admit women into his order. When he finally agreed, he asked Mahāpajāpatī Gotamī to accept Eight Rules as part of her ordination, rules that subordinated the order of nuns to the order of monks.[27] In fact, the first rule requires that a senior nun pay respect to a monk who has only been ordained for a day. In one of my group discussions with the lay nuns who would prefer to enter the *sangha*, I learned that though they believe most of the account, they do not accept that an omniscient and benevolent being such as the Buddha could have been capable of subordinating learned nuns to novice monks. Though a few lay nuns would accept ordination if it were possible, like Mahāgoda Sumettā they are aware that the Eight Rules subordinated the order of nuns to the order of monks. In short, like Sponberg they argued that the story exemplifies the institutional androcentrism of the early *sangha*, that is, the view that nuns need to be controlled by monks.[28] The lay nuns speculate that because most monks accept the account as factual, if the nuns' lineage were reintroduced to Sri Lanka, their situation of relative independence would change. As Sumanā Māniyo argued:

the traditional relationship between the monks and the nuns would be re-established, and the autonomy which we presently enjoy would therefore be relinquished. Though I wish that there were a nuns' lineage in Sri Lanka and though I want to become a *bhikkhunī*, I do not want to be subordinate to the order of monks. I do not believe that the Eight Weighty Rules are good or that the Buddha gave them. The first one is not good because if a nun has been ordained for one hundred years, she could be an *arahant*. Why should an *arahant* bow to a novice monk?[29]

Whether for or against initiation into the *sangha*, all the lay nuns I interviewed agreed that if the nuns' lineage were reintroduced, the power which has become available to them as a result of their renunciation would be lost. In other words, instead of having their destinies chartered by their husbands, brothers, or fathers, their lives would be determined by the order of monks. Inevitably the lay nuns view the male institution of the contemporary *saṅgha* very differently from monks. The lay nuns see it as inaccessible, restricted, censuring, and above all, irrelevant to the pursuit of *nibbāna*. However, they all agreed that their lack of status in the monastic order has negative, as well as positive, consequences.

THE STATUS OF LAY NUNS IN CONTEMPORARY SRI LANKA

While women are empowered by virtue of their renunciation, their status is lower today that it was one hundred years ago, and is lower than that of monks. One reason for their low status today is that they are drawn from rural classes, and rural women who defy the traditional social order are instantly suspect. In contemporary Sri Lankan rural society:

aggressiveness, dissent and refusal to obey the rules laid down by men – as fathers, husbands, and employers or rulers – are regarded as undesirable characteristics in a woman. This dichotomy of good and bad as synonymous with a woman's acceptance or rejection of the prevailing system, at home, at work and in society, pervades the ideology relating to women.[30]

The role of women in rural society is to maintain the cohesion of the family, while one of the *many* roles of men is to teach the *dhamma*. Indeed, women can don the ochre robe and become cloistered, thus lending legitimacy to their vocation. However, as it is the male who is traditionally considered the purveyor of the *dhamma*, it is the male whose religious message is considered authoritative in contemporary Sri Lanka.[31]

I conducted interviews with over a hundred laymen and laywomen in Sri Lanka. Whether members of a university faculty or laborers, all responded negatively when asked if the lay nuns are members of the monastic order. Several, however, added that though female renunciants are not really members of the order, they do provide a similar function, and thus are not laywomen either. Yet, not one of my respondents answered in the affirmative when asked if lay nuns provide the same "field of merit" as monks.

As we saw in chapter 2, Theravādin Buddhists have traditionally believed that by providing alms to the the order of monks, the donor gains merit. According to the texts, the *saṅgha* is the "best field of merit." This does not mean that donations to others, such as lay nuns, provide no merit. It means, rather, that field of merit is a traditional form that refers exclusively to the monastic order; because the lay nuns are outside the *saṅgha*, they are not the *best* field of merit. Thus, in spite of the fact that lay Buddhists are aware of the canonical vision concerning the field of merit, they give to female renunciants and expect to receive merit.

On more than one occasion, I was fortunate enough to be invited by Kotmalee Dhīrā Sudharmā and her pupils on their formal alms-rounds in the tiny village near their lay nunnery.[32] The village, with a population of approximately two hundred people,[33] is comprised of carpenters, merchants, farmers and other economically depressed peoples. There are two fairly large and well established monasteries within a two mile radius of the lay nunnery. On my first outing with Kotmalee Dhīrā Sudharmā, I learned that the members of the Madivala community consider the lay nuns to be worthy recipients of alms. Kotmalee Dhīrā Sudharmā and her pupils were invited to chant *pirit* at the home of a young woman who was about to be married. Lay nuns, unlike monks,[34] are regularly invited to chant *pirit* at wedding ceremonies; although according to Gombrich and Obeyesekere,[35] once in a while a monk officiates at a wedding, but this is a rare departure from traditional Theravādin Buddhism. As is partially the case with lay nuns, monks' involvement in weddings is doubtless a response to the needs of lay Buddhists. Be that as it may, unlike lay nuns, monks are normally associated solely with death rituals: they are invited to chant *pirit* on the death anniversaries of their supporters. Their association with death makes them in-auspicious; indeed to cast one's eyes on a monk first thing in the morning is considered to bring bad luck. This does not seem to be the case with the lay nuns. While lay nuns, like monks, chant *pirit* at death anniversaries, they are mostly associated with life-affirming rituals, such as marriage. In short, lay nuns are aligned with life while monks are aligned with death. Though lay nuns have renounced the world, they continue to be associated with "the world." Their association with the life-affirming ritual of marriage is thus another example of their ambiguous status as lay monastics.

The laity responsible for arranging auspicious ceremonies such as marriages give alms to lay nuns and expect to receive merit. On the occasion I witnessed, there were no monks present, but rather seven lay nuns who were welcomed in the same way as monks might have been, albeit with important differences. We were all greeted warmly:

when we arrived at the house of the young woman who was about to be married, all the lay nuns' feet were washed, even mine. Then the lay nuns were seated and fed (I too was seated and fed along with the lay nuns). We were given jäk fruit curry,[36] rice, and lentil curry. Like all the nuns I interviewed or observed, the Madivala lay nuns are vegetarian. Lay nuns, unlike monks, do not eat meat of any kind (except for Maldive fish, which is considered a type of spice in Ceylonese cuisine). Though there is nothing in the monastic code which calls for *bhikkhus* or *bhikkhunīs* to be vegetarian,[37] the lay nuns, unlike the monks, are adamant about their vegetarianism.

One way the lay nuns define themselves as being separate from the world, is through a very rigorous control of the food they eat and when they eat it. Like monks, they do not eat solid foods after midday. Yet, unlike monks, the lay nuns' diet is austere. The laity are sensitive to this issue and only offer vegetarian *dānaya* to the lay nuns. It is thus less costly to offer *dānaya* to lay nuns than to monks. Nonetheless, those who offer expect to receive merit.

Shortly after participating in the alms-giving with the lay nuns, I witnessed a similar occasion in which monks had been invited to chant *pirit* on the occasion of the death anniversary of one of their *dāyakas* in a community similar to Madivala. The monks arrived by car and marched single file into the house. They were greeted at the door by a young woman who washed their feet. The family sponsoring the *pirit* then provided the traditional menu reserved for distinguished guests: king coconut milk, rice, peppers stuffed with Maldive fish, curried eggplant, fried potatoes, lentil curry, fish curry, beef curry, curd and treacle, and various fruits. The area where the monks were seated was well away from the laity, and it was clear that they were honored guests. The laity began their meal well after the monks. The monks' menu, as well as their reception, was fit for nobility.

Important conclusions can be drawn from this description of the lay nuns' interaction with their *dāyakas* and the traditional procedure for giving alms to the monastic order. First of all, that the laity were segregated from the lay nuns during the alms-giving is symbolic of the lay nuns' elevated position. On the other hand, that I, a layperson, was seated with those in robes, muddles the picture that such spatial segregation provides.[38] Moreover, my presence violated the traditional temporal separation between clergy and laity: I was fed at the same time as the lay nuns, rather than after, which is the form when offering alms to monks. When the laity offer alms to the monks, satiate them, and *then* begin their meals, they express their high regard for the *saṅgha*.[39] My inclusion with the lay nuns, on the other hand, suggests that they do not have the same status as Buddhist monks. Nonetheless, lay nuns play an important role in Sri Lankan Buddhist society. The lay nuns provide an alternative in reaping merit; because they are not monks and are vegetarian, they can be given simple foods. However, because they are monastics, they can provide an attenuated field of merit.[40]

Indeed, by representing a field of merit, chanting *pirit*, and preaching the Buddhist doctrine, the lay nuns function as ordained nuns must have done centuries ago. Moreover, at the request of their *dāyakas*, they minister to the needs of the people; this until recently, had been the hegemony of the monk. Echoing Protestant Buddhist concerns, *dāyakas* and lay nuns alike argue that the clergy should be more involved in the lives of the laity. Thus, even though the status of the lay nun is perhaps lower than her analogue in ancient India and Sri Lanka, and even though it is certainly lower than the monks', the lay nun is more closely identified with the clerical, rather than the lay, tradition.

According to Carrithers, it is not ordination that determines who is worthy of alms in rural areas, but rather "the real principle which determines who is a monk in the Sinhalese countryside [is] namely, that he [is] treated as such by laymen. This is not envisaged at all by the canon and commentaries."[41] This is true for the lay nuns, as well. I asked Kotmalee Dhīrā Sudharmā if the people who offer them alms realize that lay nuns are not ordained into the *saṅgha*. She said that because she and her pupils wear the robe, act in a clerical capacity toward the laity, and are more virtuous than the monks,[42] not being a member of the *saṅgha* is not an issue. She added that laymen and laywomen are not concerned with the subtleties of doctrine; rather, they give to whoever they believe are worthy of alms. Like some of the unordained male ascetics whom Carrithers has documented, the lay nuns present themselves as clergy, rather than as laity; a presentation that much of the laity I observed accept and encourage.

The lay nuns' assessment of their status also finds expression in words, especially when they refer to lay nuns and their novitiates. For instance, according to the *Vinaya*, the female who observes the ten precepts (*dasa sil*), rather than the 311 rules of the ancient nun, is an "*upāsikā*."[43] However, when lay nuns address one another or discuss each other verbally,[44] the lay nuns do not use the term *upāsikā*;

instead, *upāsikā*, or the Sinhala *upāsikāva*, is a term that they reserve for female pupils training to don the robe.[45] As we saw in chapter 5, Sudharmācārī and other early twentieth-century Buddhists used *upāsikā* to refer to women who had renounced. In the present, the preferred designation among lay nuns is *dasa sil mātā* or *dasa sil mäniyo*, though I have not been able to trace with any accuracy the origin of these designations. In short, contemporary lay nuns view their vocation as being distinct from that of the *upāsikā*, the traditional meaning of which is pious laywoman. This is also true of most lay Buddhists. Some Buddhists refer to lay nuns as *upāsikās*, but most of the laity use the same religious vocabulary for all renunciants, whether male or female.[46] Indeed, as the lay nuns convincingly argued, they are not laywomen; rather, they are monastics who are excluded from the monastic order.

THE LAY NUNS: THEIR PAST, PRESENT, AND FUTURE

The conditions under which I conducted my field study of 1988–89 were less than favorable; during my year in Sri Lanka, "an estimated 50 people a day died in skirmishes, kidnappings, and ambuscade between pro-government death squads and JVP [Janatha Vimukti Peramuna] gangs."[47] In many ways, the civil strife facilitated fieldwork; I often remained longer with groups of lay nuns than I intended, due to curfews or breakdowns in the transportation system. This created a situation in which I had to rely on the lay nuns for sustenance and lodging. I conducted interviews with lay nuns who ranged in age from four to ninety in various areas throughout the island, which included Anurādhapura in the north, and the Ruhunu National Forest, a wildlife reserve in the south.

Indrāni Mäniyo, who renounced in 1965 at the age of eleven, was perhaps the most candid renunciant I interviewed. Indrāni's story suggests that she, like other lay nuns, was powerless to control her destiny before donning the robes. Paradoxically, she remained powerless after renouncing:

I was born to Charles Samaranāyaka. My parents were not married. My father gave me over to the custody of Hewavitarane Mäniyo's *loku mäniyo's* son.[48] At the time Hewavitarane Mäniyo was looking after the lay nun who ordained her, and as I was always with that lay nun, Hewavitarane Mäniyo practically raised me. The man who adopted me became a monk, and I therefore spent all my time with Hewavitarane Mäniyo. When I was eleven, she decided that it was time for me to leave lay life. I was not particularly interested in that; however, because I did not want to offend Hewavitarane Mäniyo, I agreed.

By the time I was eleven, the man who adopted me had given up the robes. When I told him that I was going to become a *sil mātā*, he objected because he knew how difficult the life of the renunciant can be. But he fell ill, and when he was in the hospital, Hewavitarane Mäniyo ordained me. I did not want to defy the wishes of the woman who was like a mother to me. Now I care for Hewavitarane Mäniyo just like she cared for her teacher. That's all I do; living in this nunnery is just like living in a family. Isn't that right, Mäniyo?[49]

That Indrāni feels as domesticated as she might have been had she not renounced, is symbolized by the use of her lay name; though her ordination name is Ñānasīrī, she is known by the name given to her at birth. Indrāni told me that she has no time to meditate, but she does have time to participate in worship services (*pūjās*); in fact, she spends much of her time performing *pūjās* for her *dāyakas*.

As Indrāni's story suggests, though she has renounced the world, she has not renounced many aspects of her lay identity. She is a renunciant who maintains much of her traditional role even though she has donned the ochre robe. However, like the majority of lay nuns I interviewed, she maintained that renouncing the world is more empowering than marrying and having children.

In each lay nunnery I visited, except Lady Blake's in Kandy,[50] the lay nuns do their own cooking and cleaning. This was not the case in the monasteries I visited; in the monks' quarters, the lay community took turns supplying the morning and afternoon alms-giving. According to the *Vinaya*, neither the *bhikkhu* nor the *bhikkhunī* is supposed to cook. Lay nuns, however, spend hours before sunrise and again in the mid-morning preparing their own meals over a hearth because they do not have the support of the laity.

In my primary research site, and in the majority of the other lay nunneries I visited, the female renunciants continue to play an active role in the lives of their own families. Economic uncertainty, due in part to lack of affiliation with the monastic order, means that lay nuns usually remain in or near their village; more often than not, they find a teacher, or establish a lay nunnery, in their own neighborhood. Such close contact with their lay identity perpetuates many of the functions of a female sibling or child. Though they live in cloisters, lay nuns often continue to tend to the needs of their younger brothers and sisters, nieces, nephews, and cousins. This is also true of renunciants who were formerly married; each of the divorced or widowed lay nuns I met was visited almost daily by her children.[51] Sometimes the children came bringing alms and had a formal "religious" visit. At other times, however, they came seeking maternal affection. Paradoxically, while the female renunciant has renounced her lay connections – which she considers a source of *dukkha* – her family has not renounced her.[52]

This is especially striking in the life history of Mahāgoda Sumettā, the founder of the Yaśodarādevī Upāsikārāmaya, who renounced in 1957. Sumettā is from Mahāgoda,[53] Bentota, a south-eastern coastal town, but moved with her family to Ratmalana, where she continues to reside:

My father died when I was seven. I was very attached to him; I made the final decision to become a lay nun not long after his death. I had always observed the eight precepts during the appropriate times when I was small, and I was very religious.

When I decided to become a *sil mātā*, my family objected strongly. I was ten years old. Even my mother objected, but later she accepted my choice. When I left home, I had to pretend that I was going to stay in a hostel, but instead, I went to an *upāsikārāmaya* in Pānadura to become a lay nun ... I became very ill there, and my mother took me home for two months. At twelve, my mother permitted me to go to Lady Blake's in Kandy. I stayed there, studying with the Burmese *sil mātā*, for five years. After five years, I decided that I wanted to continue my studies elsewhere, and as my family was relocating to Ratmalana, I also went with them. My mother built me a *kuṭi*[54] near their house, and supplied me with all my food, books, etc. Except for my family, I was all alone; I was sixteen years old.[55]

Though Sumettā's family did not accept her decision to renounce, they have been an indispensable component of her survival as a lay nun. With her family's help, Sumettā has set up a school to teach other lay nuns. Ten women have renounced under her tutelage.

In the Madivala Upāsikārāmaya, the situation is somewhat different. Kotmalee Dhīrā Sudharmā, the fifty year-old (in 1989) founder of the lay nunnery, grew up in Kotmalee, in the hill-country of Sri Lanka, far away from Madivala. Unlike many lay nuns, Kotmalee Dhīrā Sudharmā established a lay nunnery many miles from her village. However, three of her ten siblings and their families followed her to Madivala and bought land. Her brother, his wife, and their young daughter live fifty feet away from the lay nunnery, while an elder and younger sister live within a mile.

During periods of heightened unrest while I was in Sri Lanka, Kotmalee Dhīrā Sudharmā's family provided her and her pupils (and often, me) with food. Though there were days when no one was sure who would provide the next meal, the proximity of Kotmalee Dhīrā Sudharmā's family to the lay nunnery meant that the lay nuns did not go hungry, if at all possible. Kotmalee Dhīrā Sudharmā intimated that if it were not for her family, she does not know how she and her pupils would have been able to survive the economic crises that have recently affected their *dāyakas*.

Kotmalee Dhīrā Sudharmā's relationship with her family has not always been so convivial. On the contrary, her father, an auto-mechanic, and her mother, a housewife, both protested when she decided to renounce:

I was ordained[56] even though my parents tried to stop me in every way possible. After spending days, and then weeks, crying and moping and not doing much of anything else, my father permitted me to leave home. I was twenty-two years old and it was time for me to think about marriage... Having put only a few things into my suitcase, I went to the temple in my village.

The day I left home, I had an inexplicable feeling of joy, even though I was leaving my ten brothers and sisters, and my property. I have had many experiences in past lives which have prepared me for the difficult life which I lead now. The training is a long process and it is carried over from one life to another. Not just anybody can become a *sil mātā* and maintain the lifestyle without acquiring the proper dispostion from previous births.

The monk who ordained me knew that I would be a good *sil mātā*. In the ordination service for the monk, the senior monk asks the initiates to say the Three Refuges in the following way: "*Buddhaṃ saranaṃ gacchāmi, dhammaṃ saranaṃ gacchāmi, saṅghaṃ saranaṃ gacchāmi.*"[57] I, too, recited the refuges this way. When lay people recite the Three Refuges, they say "*Buddhañ saranañ gacchāmi, dhammañ saranañ gacchāmi, saṅghañ saranañ gacchāmi.*"[58] That priest considered me to be no different from a *sāmaṇera*.[59] In fact, the day I was ordained, I preached *bana* and loads of people came to listen. My family all came, too; there were so many of them it took a mini-van and a car to transport them all![60]

Kotmalee Dhīrā Sudharmā renounced in 1960, while Sumettā renounced home life in 1957, soon after the Buddha Jayanti. At this time, people from every community in Buddhist Sri Lanka had been swept along by the tide of change, which included independence in 1948, and the overhaul of the political armature in the mid-1950s. "Pressures to reduce inequalities increased with the entry of the rural lower-middle class into the political power structure from 1956."[61] This resulted in egalitarian tendencies in every institution in Sri Lanka, including the tradition of the female renunciant, as we saw in chapter 6.[62] Kotmalee Dhīrā Sudharmā's background is different from those women who renounced in increased numbers prior to independence. Instead, she received a limited education in a rural school, and comes from a very large and economically depressed Buddhist family; indeed, Kotmalee Dhīrā Sudharmā's rural background typifies the new generation of lay nuns. Like every lay nun I met, Kotmalee Dhīrā Sudharmā had to fight against the prejudices of her rural community for the life-altering choices she has made.

Kotmalee Dhīrā Sudharmā stayed in a lay nunnery in Gampaha for a few years after her ordination. Eventually, she migrated to Madivala, Kotte, where the government in 1972 allocated her the plot of land on which she continues to reside, preach, teach, perform *pūjās*, and counsel her supporters. A committee was formed that same year – which consisted of laypeople from nearby Nugegoda – to monitor her and her pupils, and to see to their material needs.[63] The members raised enough money to enable Kotmalee Dhīrā Sudharmā to construct the main living quarters of the Upāsikārāmaya. According to Kotmalee Dhīrā Sudharmā, they attracted the attention of Ayyā Khemā, a German-born, American lay nun.[64] She and Kotmalee Dhīrā Sudharmā approached the government and asked them to sponsor an international training center for female renunciants on the same land. Together they made plans to create an important center of learning for lay nuns from all over the island. Later, as Kotmalee Sudharmā recounted, when she realized that one building would house Sinhala renunciants, and the other, foreigners, she told Ayyā Khemā that such a separation would be unacceptable. Ayyā Khemā then handed over all the funds that she had received from the government and left Madivala for Parappaduwa, where she was able to fulfill her dream of enabling foreign and local women to meditate in retreat, and if desirous, to don the ochre robe. Kotmalee Dhīrā Sudharmā suggested that Ayyā Khemā's involvement doubtless lent prestige to the project because "the government is less inclined to give money to a Sinhala *sil mātā* than a foreign one." In other words, European participation is still a source of prestige, even though Sri Lanka has been independent since 1948.

The early 1970s, the formative years of the Madivala Upāsikārāmaya, witnessed some interest in female renunciation, though not to the same degree as in the pre-independence period. The revival of Buddhism continued well into this decade; indeed the centrality of religion in the self-perception of the Sinhalese intensified to such a degree that Buddhism was given a preeminent place in the constitution of 1972.[65] In 1974, William Gopallawa, the then president of Sri Lanka, opened Madivala Upāsikārāmaya and declared that his government would support women who renounce the world. He also indicated that one of the main objectives of the Madivala Upāsikārāmaya was the re-establishment of the Theravādin order of nuns:

"If the *dasa sil matas* in Sri Lanka take a keen interest to reestablish the *Meheni Sasana* (Order of Buddhist nuns) here, I have no doubt it will receive the support of the Government," said the President, Mr. William Gopallawa, when speaking at the foundation stone laying ceremony for an ... Upasikaramaya and Educational Centre at Madivala, Kotte on Saturday.[66]

Though there was interest in the revival of the nuns' lineage among many in the early seventies, it decreased dramatically in the eighties. Not only did support diminish, but women no longer found renunciation as attractive as they had in the preceding decades. According to Kotmalee Dhīrā Sudharmā, "if you ask a group of young boys to raise their hands if they want to become a monk when they grow up, many hands will go up. But if you ask a group of girls, not one hand will be raised."[67]

According to the lay nuns, this is due to many factors. One lay nun suggested that Ayyā Khemā's visibility in the early seventies, as well as her outspoken support for the re-establishment of the *bhikkhunī* lineage, legitimated the vocation. According to Kotmalee Dhīrā Sudharmā, because Ayyā Khemā eventually alienated many people who had originally supported her by becoming a "Mahāyāna *bhikṣuṇī*," people lost interest in the lay nun movement. In short they argue that when Ayyā Khemā became an ordained nun in a Mahāyāna ordination ceremony in California in 1988, she offended many Buddhists. The Buddhist lay nuns and monks I interviewed intimated that Ayyā Khemā's Mahāyāna ordination poses a threat to the integrity of Theravādin Buddhism in Sri Lanka.

According to the lay nuns, when women began to enter lay nunneries who did not have "special qualities," many women lost interest in renouncing. Kotmalee Dhīrā Sudharmā, as well as

Kotmalee Sudharmā of Lady Blake's,[68] explained that over the past
few decades, many women have renounced who are not qualified to
teach or serve, a Protestant Buddhist concern. They both related to
me that renouncing often serves as a safety-valve for women who
have no other options. Thus, as more and more women become
economically disenfranchised and displaced, the number of "undesirables" in robes increases.[69] These leading lay nuns believe that
among the undesirables are "insane" renunciants,[70] or those looking
for an easier life than the rural setting can offer. As a result, these
women cannot live up to Kotmalee Dhīrā Sudharmā's and Kotmalee
Sudharmā's ideal of Buddhist renunciation.

   In my journeys around the island, I had the opportunity to
interview some of the women characterized as insane by Kotmalee
Dhīrā Sudharmā and Kotmalee Sudharmā. They are highly visible
at the sacred pilgrimage sites, which include Kataragama in the
south, Adam's Peak in the hill country, and Anurādhapura in the
north.[71] Perhaps the best way to describe them is to compare them
with bag ladies in America. I saw them carrying their belongings
over their shoulders, looking completely unkempt and in need of
sustenance. Some of these women were obviously disturbed: on one
particular occasion, I witnessed a robed woman who must have been
in her late seventies screaming at traffic in Anurādhapura. She
attracted the attention of many while she mumbled and yelled insults
at pedestrians. As a consequence of these outbursts, the government
has proposed rules designed to curtail the activities of such "undesirable" women.

THE GOVERNMENT AND THE LAY NUNS

That renunciation serves as a type of safety valve for displaced
women is as apparent to the Ministry of Buddhist Affairs as it is to
Kotmalee Dhīrā Sudharmā and Kotmalee Sudharmā. The displaced
women to whom they refer evoke stories about women who had
renounced centuries earlier. According to the *Cūlavaṃsa*, in the
formative period of Buddhism in Sri Lanka nunneries served as a way
out of unpleasant situations for many women.[72] In the 1980s, the
government made attempts to circumvent such cases. To effect this,
according to Mr. Abhaya Weerakoon, the Secretary to the Minister
of Buddhist Affairs, the Ministry decided to begin to register the lay
nuns in January, 1984.[73] This plan was implemented to bring all the

lay nuns under one umbrella; the government hoped that registration would both legitimate the lay nuns and determine who is "really a *dasa sil mātā*."[74] Moreover, the Ministry planned to use the registration as a way to determine where schools should be established for the lay nuns in need of a proper religious education. By 1987, the Ministry had set up seventeen educational centers, which amounted to nearly one per district.[75]

In addition to establishing schools for the lay nuns, the government in 1987 made a special provision in the budget of the Ministry of Buddhist Affairs that was designed to care for those who are particularly destitute. Though the Ministry became involved in the activities of the lay nuns in 1984 and continues to be in the present, they took the most dramatic steps recently. In 1988, Weerakoon proposed rules designed to unify female renunciants, on the one hand, and to create an order of nuns, on the other.[76] This action amounts to a purification of the tradition of female renunciation; it is, perhaps, the first instance of such purification in the history of Buddhist female renunciation in Sri Lanka.[77]

Weerakoon's advice to the lay nuns is sweeping: he hopes to change popular opinion concerning female renunciants by implementing various rules and regulations, which would upgrade their position in society.[78] The guidelines Weerakoon offers as a framework to create uniformity among the lay nuns are based loosely on the regulations that governed the ancient order of nuns. According to Weerakoon, if a female wants to become a *sil mātā*:

(1) She should not be physically disabled or deformed.
(2) She should not be mentally ill.
(3) She should not have an incurable illness.
(4) Her character must be pure.
(5) She should not be suffering from any social disease.
(6) She should not have earned disrespect from the people in the area in which she lives.
(7) She should not be below sixteen years of age or above sixty.
(8) She should be one who has completed the GCE O level.
(9) She should be one who has obtained the permission of her parents or her guardian to observe religious duties.
(10) She should live in the *ārāmaya* she expects to join under the guidance of the leading *sil mātā* and understand and become accustomed to the proceedings of the *ārāmaya*.

(11) It should be clear to the applicant that she is suited for the life in an *ārāmaya* and that she can adapt her pattern of living accordingly.

(12) The *guru mātā* must be convinced that the applicant is suited for life in an *ārāmaya*.

(13) She should know by heart the *sutras* used in the Buddha *pūjā*.

(14) She should obtain at least one month's training at a meditation center.

(15) She should accept responsibilities and share one's duties at the *ārāmaya*.

(16) She should have the ability to conduct a Buddha *pūjā* and obtain merit in a pleasing manner for those *dāyaka's* visting the *ārāmaya*.[79]

There is no consensus among the lay nuns concerning Weerakoon's proposals. Kotmalee Dhīrā Sudharmā has accepted his proposals and has agreed with the most controversial among them, proposal number seven. She holds that by the age of sixteen, a young woman is in a position to know if she prefers the renunciant's life to the householder's. Moreover, Kotmalee Dhīrā Sudharmā added that if an age limit of sixty is imposed, this will discourage poor old women from becoming renunciants simply because they have no other options. Women should be able to meditate properly and lead a life of social service, both of which are difficult to do after the age of sixty, or during childhood.[80]

Mahāgoda Sumettā, on the other hand, has not accepted the proposals of the Ministry. She argues that the younger the initiates are, the more likely they are to become good lay nuns:

When candidates are very young, I can train them to be very good nuns. I know this is true because I have ordained old and young people alike. Too many people become nuns after becoming fed up with the world. In my view, if a young person becomes a nun, it is purely for religious reasons. By the age of twelve, most children have already gone the wrong way; Buddhism is too good to be tarnished by the world.[81]

At the time of my field study, Sumettā had in her custody a five year-old lay nun named Sudāsikā. I met Sudāsikā, who renounced lay life aged four. When I met her, she was out playing in the lay nunnery compound, all bound up and burdened with her robes. She was a tiny little thing, with round dark eyes peering out from a freshly shaved head, grinning from ear to ear, but was very shy. Sumettā told me that Sudāsikā is from Anurādhapura and that she was born near a lay nunnery that Sudāsikā and her mother used to visit when Sudāsikā was a baby. When I asked Sumettā how such a young person can make a decision to renounce the world, she told me that it was the result of a disposition which Sudāsikā had developed over the course of her past lives. According to Sumettā, Sudāsikā's mother is unwed and does not have the means to support her, but she added that Sudāsikā asked to renounce under her own volition.

Mahāgoda Sumettā also has in her custody other children who have renounced the world. In addition to caring for these young lay nuns, Sumettā has organized an orphanage on her property, where children victimized by ethnic strife are "mothered" by the older renunciants.[82] When I first approached Sumettā's Yaśodarādevī Ārāmaya, I was struck by the sight of little girls and young renunciants all playing together. Whether tiny lay nuns or orphans, they all behaved like children. At the appropriate times, however, the lay nuns would be called in from playing and solemnly assume their vocation as religious specialists.[83]

Though the Ministry of Buddhist Affairs has proposed that "if a *sil mātā* wants to ordain a pupil she must send the appropriate letters to the Ministry,"[84] Mahāgoda Sumettā does not comply with this proposition. While I was doing research at her lay nunnery, she made no attempts to notify the Ministry that she had decided to ordain one of her pupils; she does not feel that it is necessary to report the choices that she makes in her lay nunnery either to the Ministry, or to anybody else. This is not surprising. Sumettā does not want to see the re-establishment of the nuns' lineage because this would mean relinquishing her independence. For the same reason, she does not condone the incursion of the state into her affairs.

Mahāgoda Sumettā's opinions about the proposals of the Ministry are shared by many lay nuns. For instance, Kotagoda Dhammādinnā's words echo Sumettā's; she believes that it is the responsibility of the female renunciants themselves to create an environment that would attract a qualified younger generation of female renunciants. According to Dhammādinnā, there is no sense of unity among lay nuns: "young nuns are crooked and against us; our young nuns are nothing like the Catholic sisters."[85] She added that a crisis in her tradition can be averted by learning from the example of Christian nuns, rather than from the imposition of rules and regulations by the state. While she agrees with the Ministry that female renunciants are in need of reform, she does not believe that this reform should be imposed from outside. However, in spite of the lay nuns' over-whelming dissatisfaction with government intervention, the Ministry of Buddhist Affairs continues with its campaign to "purify" the contemporary "order" of lay nuns.

CONTEMPORARY BUDDHISM FROM THE POINT OF VIEW OF LAY NUNS

The lay nuns that I interviewed, whether or not they agreed with the Ministry's proposals, all argued that the monastic fraternities, rather than lay nuns, are in need of purification. Though lay nuns are critical of the contemporary *sangha* and, in particular, a few individual monks, they also respect and support it. In fact, when both monks and lay nuns take part in a *pirit* ceremony or in a *dānaya*, the lay nuns see to the needs of the monks. Thus, if the laity has gathered together both monks and nuns for an alms-giving, the lay nuns help the laity (usually women) distribute the alms to monks. In other words, the women serve and the men eat. Put differently, "the stereotyped reception of nurture as male activity and provision of nurture as a female one" finds expression among monks and lay nuns in contemporary Sri Lanka.[86] Only when the monks are fed, do the lay nuns receive *dānaya* from the laity. In this way, they become receivers, rather than nurturers and feeders of others. Monks, on the other hand, play no role in offering *dānaya* to the lay nuns. In short, the lay nuns themselves reinforce male superiority. As we have seen, most lay nuns do not like being institutionally subordinated to the order of monks. However, the lay nuns argue that it is appropriate for them to support the *bhikkhu sangha*. They argue that such was the role of the ancient *bhikkhunī sangha*.

Much of the lay nuns' criticisms of monks has to do with the latter's involvement in politics. I conducted research in Sri Lanka during the tumultuous events of 1988–89; I was able, therefore, to witness at first hand the involvement of monks in the political life of the island, as well as discuss with lay nuns the monks' unprecedented immersion in the political arena. Without exception, each lay nun I interviewed remarked that monks should not take part in governing at any level, either as activists who incite people to take up arms, or as passive supporters who voice partisan views. They maintained that monks who engage in violence, or support it in any way, should be purged from the *saṅgha*. However, because many lay nuns' roots are rural like most of the people who were involved in the revolt against the Jayewardene government, they were sympathetic to the values of the opposition that were articulated by monks and laity alike. Lay nuns always seemed to know when the JVP was planning to disrupt life on the island, and they referred to them affectionately as the *podi anduwa*, or little government. However, they did not condone the JVP's violence and were certainly opposed to the violent nature of some of the monks, who have been identified as JVP sympathizers.[87] Lay nuns primarily subscribe to the Mahāvaṃsa view of history, and thus believe that Buddhism in Sri Lanka should be protected from threats posed by Hindu-Tamil culture. Nonetheless, they related that they do not believe that violence is the best weapon. In fact, they urged people to meditate and pray for peace to prevail in the country.

In a trip I made to the island in the summer of 1992, I was able to witness the first of many "Samādhi Walks" made by over a hundred *dasa sil mātāvo*, which were aimed at bringing unity to the various ethnic groups in the country. They walked 160 miles, meditating, preaching peace, and conducting *Bodhi pūjās* along the way.[88] In my conversations with Buddhists around the island, I discovered that many viewed the lay nuns' walk as political in nature. Some implied that the lay nuns were pawns of former President Premadasa and that they had been exploited by the government run media to drum up sympathy for his government. Others remarked that at least they were not engaging in violence as some monks have been known to do. The lay nuns themselves argued that it is the role of the the clergy to preach the Buddhist message of non-violence; as they are clergy, it is their role, as well.

Unlike monks, few lay nuns enter universities. Many lay nuns in 1988-89 told me that as university life is similar to lay life, it is thus inappropriate for them. They mentioned that they do not enter universities because they have seen that university life is not conducive to the monks' spiritual development. Referring to monks who enter the *saṅgha*, attain a free university diploma, and then leave the robes, or take up politics while studying, the lay nuns argue that renunciation is a life-long commitment, and not something one does lightly to obtain a degree, or to become further immersed in lay life. According to one lay nun, the goal of Buddhism is to attain *nibbāna*, and not to acquire "fat bellies, money, a secular education, and fancy cars, as many monks are prone to do." Implicit in this statement is a general critique of the *saṅgha*, a critique that is shared by many among the laity in contemporary Sri Lanka.

Unlike the monks that Gombrich[89] and Bond interviewed,[90] the vast majority of lay nuns with whom I conducted research all said that it is possible to attain *nibbāna* in this lifetime.[91] Much like the lay meditators that Bond describes,[92] the majority of lay nuns I interviewed are hopeful that their meditation practices can result in the highest attainment. In this respect, their practice is aligned with the laity, rather than the monks; paradoxically, many lay meditators, unlike the majority of the *saṅgha*, believe that *nibbāna* is a possible goal in this lifetime. But like the monks, one of their primary roles is to perform *pūjās* for their *dāyakas*, which the lay nuns claim, is part and parcel of the *nibbāna* quest.

CONCLUSIONS

On balance, the Sinhala lay nuns' attitudes toward gender and institutionalized religion – as expressed by their own spiritual lives and teachings – are both radical and conservative. Many of their assumptions about the nature of women are derived from stereotypes and belong to the conventional wisdom of their day, including the ease with which they reassert many traditional female roles after renouncing. Despite such stereotyping, or perhaps because of it, their sense of religious self is continuous with their sense of social and biological self: they are nurturers, they are mothers, *and* they are world-renouncers. They are not male-defined even though in their culture men, rather than women, are considered spiritually advanced; rather, they affirm their gender in the symbols they have appropriated, such as the statues and paintings of Saṅghamittā with which they decorate their *upāsikārāmayas*. Indeed, by maintaining the same relationship with the *saṅgha* that they had before they renounced, the lay nuns affirm both their quasi-lay status and cultural notions of gender. In short, they do not abandon their femaleness when they abandon their home life,[93] even though by renouncing they violate cultural norms of gender.

Moreover, much of what they believe about their own vocation is in large part shaped by their readings of the Pāli texts, the very texts that reinforce stereotypes. Yet the conclusions female renunciants draw from those stereotypes are not commonplace, especially as they relate to autonomy, celibacy, and power. Their activities in the public sphere, including their peace marches and their *pūjās*, are a radical break from the traditional role of the female as passive supporter of religion; a role which, because they are village women, is ascribed for them. Though they patronize monks, they too are patronized; and though they listen to monks' sermons, they too teach the *dhamma*. Despite this, as we shall see in chapter 8, the *saṅgha* has tried to control lay nuns by campaigning against attempts to ordain women and preaching that lay nuns are lower in status than monks. Nonetheless, lay nuns have created semi-autonomous communities that for all intents and purposes remain outside monks' control. By renouncing the world, these women create conditions that both affirm *dukkha* and assuage it: their lives are difficult as lay nuns, but they structure their lives so that they might attain the peace of *nibbāna*. It is only in renunciation, they argue, that they can hope to attain *nibbāna*, the prerogative, they add, of both men and women.

CHAPTER 8

Novitiates, western lay nuns, and cave dwellers

INTRODUCTION

Lay nuns who represent the contemporary mainstream tradition of female Buddhist renunciation in Sri Lanka, such as Sumettā and Dhammādinnā, live in groups and village settings. As we have seen, they devote their lives to study and *pūjā*, as well as to service. In this chapter, I offer an account of lay nuns whose interpretation of female renunciation sets them apart from most women who have donned the ochre robe. While they do not typify contemporary female renunciation, their contribution and impact is influential. I also explore both the attitudes of monks toward lay nuns and lay nuns' opinions of their own tradition. All the lay nuns I interviewed,[1] whether they conform to the mainstream tradition of female renunciation or not, see themselves as Theravādins whose destiny it is to embody true Buddhism and protect its integrity.

Foremost among the renunciants I introduce in this chapter are Americans, Europeans, and an Australian who have all converted to Buddhism and donned the ochre robe. Their biographies suggest that their background and outlook are radically different from the Sinhala lay nuns we met in chapter 7. Though there are only a handful of western lay nuns in Sri Lanka, they are very prominent in the cities and villages around the island. Such women are often vociferous in their support of the tradition of Theravādin female renunciation and they, rather than Sinhala lay nuns, have become its spokespersons.

Others who do not typify the contemporary tradition of female renunciation in Sri Lanka are the cave-dwelling lay nuns of the Ruhuṇu National Forest. Unlike lay nuns who live in village settings throughout the island, those who live in the caves of the southern forests have limited contact with people. Instead of counseling the laity, they spend hours in meditative silence, much like the western lay nuns. These lay nuns represent the contemplative monastic tradition, which is as old as Buddhism itself; yet it is not traditionally associated with women. Though it is unusual for women who renounce lay life to opt for the hardships of living in the forest, the women who retreat to caves offer a viable alternative to the domesticated life of the village lay nun.

Whether they live in a village or in a cave, most female renunciants have been initiated by a teacher in a ceremony marking her passage from laity to monastic. However, there is no standardized training for novitiates, be they in the village or forest. Although the Ministry of Buddhist Affairs has encouraged lay nuns to conform to a specific program of training, each lay nunnery leader, or *loku mäniyo*, has a different vision of what the training of her pupils should be. Moreover, though most ordinations are similar to each other, there are important differences. In the next sections, I explore two separate ordination rituals for lay nuns. Moreover, I provide the attitudes of contemporary village lay nuns, monks, and laity toward women and world-renunciation that these rituals reflect.

NOVITIATES AND FEMALE RENUNCIANTS: THEIR RITE OF PASSAGE

I asked Indrāṇi about her ordination.[2] She told me that the lay nuns she knows imitate the initiation of the *sāmaṇerī* given in the *Vinaya* when they ordain a novice. However, unlike the *sāmaṇerī*, the lay nuns "take" the householder's ten precepts (*gihi*) rather than the precepts of the monk/nun (*pabbajjā*). This distinction between the two ways of taking the ten precepts is appreciated by lay nuns and laity alike; that the laity and the female renunciants take the precepts of the householder, while novice monks take the renunciant's, has far-reaching ramifications.

Though it is customary for lay nuns to take the householder's ten precepts, there are exceptions to this rule. For instance, Kotagoda Dhammādinnā told me that a monk gave her the renunciant's precepts when she renounced lay life.[3] Kotmalee Dhīrā Sudharmā, as we have seen, also chanted the renunciant's precepts when she became a lay nun. However, others, such as Sumanāsīlī Mäniyo, explained that it is not proper for female renunciants to take the ten precepts of the monastic order.

Sumanāsīlī was born in 1954 and renounced in 1971. She is a pupil of Sister Sudharmā of the Vihāra Mahā Devī Upāsikārāmaya in Anurādhapura,[4] but when I met her in 1989, she was living in Colombo in order to attend the Maligakanda Pirivena.[5] In our conversations, Sumanāsīlī told me that it is the duty of lay nuns, rather than the government, to provide the conditions that will attract worthy women to her vocation. Sumanāsīlī's account of her life reveals her attitudes about the contemporary practice of lay nuns, as well as her role in its future:

I was the twelfth child in my family; I was the baby. My father died when I was seventeen and his death left me in an absolute daze. He was in the army and was a very good man. During a trip to Kurunāgalla with my mother, I met two *dasa sil mātāvo* who impressed me quite a bit. They invited us to keep visiting them, and eventually the *loku mäniyo* asked me to renounce. My mother protested. She said that my father would not approve of such a thing; I had already taken my O Level exams and was studying for my A Levels[6] and my mother told me that I had to finish my education; this was my father's wish. However, my father's death made me realize the impermanent nature of things – that things in the world really mean nothing. Because I was attracted to the *sil mātā's* life, I decided to leave home. Before I left home, I had my horoscope read.[7] It said that I would not leave home but would enjoy a prosperous life as a wife. I did not let this stop me; I was determined to become a *sil mātā*. I did not go back to school either; I do not believe that it is appropriate for *sil mātāvo* to go to university, to become nurses or to have too many activities in the lay world which we have given up. Instead, we should meditate and devote our lives to Buddhism.[8]

Brave to renounce though her horoscope suggested a different life for her, Sumanāsīlī is proud of the life that she has created for herself as a lay nun. Though she sees continuity between her vocation and that of the ancient *bhikkhunī*, she argued forcefully in our conversations that lay nuns have no right to assume the privileges of the members of the defunct order of nuns: "It is not proper for *dasa sil mātāvo* to go on alms rounds, or to use the robe of the *bhikkhu* or *bhikkhunī*;[9] bowls and robes are handed down from *bhikkhunī* to *bhikkhunī*, and there is no such tradition like this in Sri Lanka today."[10] Sumanāsīlī sees herself walking in the footsteps of the *bhikkhunī*, but she does not think that she and those who share her vocation should "pretend to be *bhikkhunīs*, which could bring the downfall of Buddhism." I also asked Sumanāsīlī about the differences between the householder's and the renunciant's ten precepts. She answered by explaining to me the differences between *bhikkhunīs* and lay nuns: "The reason that we should not wear the robe of the *bhikkhunī* is that we have taken the householder's precepts, which anyone, even you, can take. There is no order of nuns in Sri Lanka, therefore women should not take the renunciant's precepts."[11] For Sumanāsīlī, purity of practice and preservation of tradition are more important than the precepts she has taken.

Other lay nuns challenge Sumanāsīlī's point of view. In my discussions with Mahāgoda Sumettā, she told me that she does not agree that only those entering the *saṅgha* have the right to take the renunciant's precepts. In the ordination ceremony of Sumettā's student that I attended, Sumettā instructed the novitiate to ask the monk for the renunciant's precepts.[12] Though lay nuns can give the five and the eight precepts to their own pupils and patrons, as far as I can tell they never give the ten. All the lay nuns I interviewed agreed on this point.

S. K. Līlāwatī, the novitiate, was born in 1934 in Nuwara Eliya and has suffered from epilepsy since childhood. Due to her condition and her age, she is not the type of candidate the Ministry wishes to see donning the ochre robe. Even Sumettā intimated that Līlāwatī was not fit to renounce; she told me that she was only ordaining Līlāwatī because "the *upāsikāva* seems so eager to become a lay nun." Under normal conditions Sumettā (following the *Vinaya* rules) only ordains those who are completely healthy: "she should be strong enough to meditate and to provide social services." Despite Sumettā's ambivalent attitude, I found Līlāwatī to be very serious about her intentions, as well as extremely pious and devoted to her new vocation. Unlike many candidates, Līlāwatī trained for a relatively long period of time; she kept the nine precepts for two years.[13] Before Līlāwatī's ordination, the other lay nuns, as is customary, referred to her as the "*upāsikāva*." In keeping with her lay status, Līlāwatī always wore white before her ordination; the color symbolizes Buddhist laity in Sri Lanka.

Sumettā commissioned a reading of Līlāwatī's astrological chart before the ordination to determine both the most auspicious time for the event, and the letter that would serve as the initial of her new name.[14] The reading did not suggest that Līlāwatī would be a bad female renunciant. Moreover, Līlāwatī's family had finally agreed to permit her to renounce. Thus, Sumettā agreed to ordain her.

Sumettā told me that she always asks permission from a candidate's parents before she ordains anyone.[15] If the parents are dead and the candidate is unknown to her, she asks for a letter from the candidate's principal, monk, or village headman attesting to the worthiness of her intentions.[16] Līlāwatī's parents are both dead, and her only living relatives, her brothers, initially opposed the ordination. Līlāwatī told me that her brothers tried to arrange marriages for her, and that they believed that women should become mothers of children and not "mothers" of the ten precepts. Not one member of her family, nor any friends, attended the ceremony.

Based on his horoscope reading, the astrologer decided that the most auspicious time for the ordination ceremony would be 6:50 a.m. on Vesak, the anniversary of the birth, enlightenment, and death of the Buddha.[17] I arrived at 6:30 a.m. and found Līlāwatī sitting away from the normal hustle and bustle of the morning activities at the lay nunnery; the orphans were having their breakfast, while the lay nuns busied themselves with preparations for the ceremony. At 6:45 a.m., Sumettā, two other senior lay nuns, and Līlāwatī approached the altar where they venerate the Buddha image daily.[18] Sumettā carried in her hand a watch which she kept consulting; it was important that Līlāwatī's first lock of hair be cut precisely at 6:50 a.m. The ceremony began when Līlāwatī, clad in white, venerated her teacher and the other two lay nuns, who had acted as her advisors during her training. All the while Līlāwatī followed Sumettā's instructions, which were sharp, clear imperatives. Līlāwatī offered the three elder lay nuns the traditional betel leaves in the order of their seniority and then sat down on a mat in preparation for the cutting of her long, shiny black hair with silver highlights. The other lay nuns began to chant *pirit*. Though there is no tradition of chanting *pirit* at the ordination of male novitiates into the *saṅgha*, *pirit* is chanted at the ordination of lay nuns. *Pirit* is associated with "this world;" the *saṅgha* members, at least theoretically, are "in the world" but not "of the world" and thus they do not chant *pirit* – symbolic of the laity – at their ordinations. *Pirit* chanting is thus a determinant of the lay nuns' status in Buddhism; it symbolizes one aspect of their dual status as lay monastics.

At exactly 6:50 a.m., Sumettā cut one of Līlāwatī's tresses, which the latter accepted and pondered for about one minute; here, hair served as a metaphor for the Buddhist idea of impermanence. In the background, the children played, while the other lay nuns chanted *pirit* and tried to keep the flies at bay. The odor of curried potatoes, which were being prepared by the neighborhood sponsors for the midday almsgiving, lingered in the air.

Sumettā resumed clipping Līlāwatī's hair, all of which was placed in front of the latter for her to contemplate. After she had clipped off every strand, Sumettā began to shave Līlāwatī's head. In spite of the nicks, the blood, and the discomfort, Līlāwatī sat patiently. At the conclusion of this process, Sumettā wrapped Līlāwatī's head in a white towel. Līlāwatī then venerated Sumettā three times, and was escorted by the other lay nuns to the bathing area. No other lay people, except for me, were allowed to view the bathing.

The lay nuns poured cold water over Līlāwatī's naked body, and all the hair that had fallen down around her shoulders was washed away by the splashes. Līlāwatī soaped her head and body, and the lay nuns in attendance then rinsed her off. They then draped her in a white sārī, and covered her head and eyes with part of the sārī cloth.[19] In the meantime, Sumettā sat outside waiting for Līlāwatī to return.

Līlāwatī's advisors escorted her back outside and instructed her to carry a set of robes. They directed her to sit in front of Sumettā, which she did, and then they removed her head covering. Līlāwatī offered Sumettā the robes, which the latter ceremoniously touched but did not accept. Instead, she instructed Līlāwatī to hold the robes close to her chest. Sumettā took the ochre-colored string that held the robes intact, and draped it around Līlāwatī's neck – a symbolic, and public act of the private decking of the novitiate in the raiment of the renunciant. Sumettā then escorted Līlāwatī to the library where Līlāwatī's attire was transformed.

When Līlāwatī emerged, she looked utterly different; no remnants of her lay identity were apparent. She seemed very comfortable in her new robes and her bright smile exclaimed that her decision to renounce was the correct one. She returned to the altar, where she conducted a *pūjā* by herself; she then worshipped Sumettā in the same way as she had at the beginning of the ceremony. Shortly thereafter, all the lay nuns, including Līlāwatī, entered the dining hall where neighborhood families offered them alms. Though Līlāwatī had exchanged her white sārī for the ochre robes of the lay nun, Sumettā kept referring to her as "*upāsikāva;*" she had not yet taken the ten precepts and was, therefore, still a novitiate. After the almsgiving, Līlāwatī worshipped each resident lay nun in order of seniority. All present giggled when Līlāwatī venerated five year-old Sudāsikā. A man who does volunteer work for the lay nunnery then drove

Sumettā, Līlāwatī, and me to a nearby monastery; here Līlāwatī could take the ten precepts from a monk. Though the lay nuns give the five precepts to each other and to their *dāyakas*, they never give the ten. Like *pirit* chanting at their ordinations, the lay nuns' reluctance to give the ten precepts symbolizes their ambiguous status.

The monk whom Sumettā had asked to administer the precepts had never officiated at the ordination of a lay nun. Līlāwatī approached him; she had been coached by Sumettā to bow in respect, to sit on her hauches in a posture of entreaty, and to request in Pāli the renunciant's ten precepts. Sumettā then chanted the appropriate request, which Līlāwatī repeated with serious intent. Līlāwatī made the request for the renunciant's precepts three times, which is traditional at the initiation of a male novice into the monastic order.[20]

Sumettā continued to direct Līlāwatī; she told her to chant the *namaskāraya*,[21] that is, the traditional salutation which precedes most Buddhist rituals in Sri Lanka. The monk then instructed Līlāwatī to repeat each of the Three Refuges, which he began to chant. After reciting the first one, using the nasal "ň" ending of the nouns, considered appropriate for the laity, he interrupted and said to Līlāwatī: "use the 'ṃ' letter, okay?" In other words, the monk asked Līlāwatī to follow the process whereby a male novitiate is bestowed admission into the monastic order. However, I was surprised by the next phase of the ceremony: even though Līlāwatī had asked for the renunciant's precepts, she was given the householder's. That Līlāwatī repeated the Three Refuges in the manner that male novitiates repeat them, but was only given the householder's precepts, suggests that the officiating monk, like most rural Buddhist people, is not clear about the formal status of the lay nun in Sri Lankan society.

The monk then preached that good fortune would certainly befall Līlāwatī and her teacher as a result of this meritorious activity. The tone of the *bana* was very optimistic:

Now, on this Vesak Day, a *sil mātā* has been ordained; much merit will accrue from this. The head nun of Yaśodāradevī Ārāmaya, Mahāgoda Sumettā Mäniyo, is one with whom we associate very closely and with friendship. I am among those who are rejoicing on this auspicious occasion in that *upāsikārāmaya*.

It is a highly valuable and worthwhile act of merit that was carried out by Sumettā Mäniyo, of giving *dasa sil* and ordaining this *sil mātā*. Now our Buddhists will worship this new *sil mātā*. Similarly elders, scholars, the very rich, and even royalty and ministers of the government will fall on their knees and worship the state that this lay nun has attained on this *pōya* day.

At this time, we must think of the highly valuable religious precepts that were taken ... Your behavior from today must be more virtuous than usual. The use of words must be more virtuous than is considered normal. Also your duties must be carried out in a manner which brings honor to your teacher.

... When we become ordained to the state of renunciation, we must tolerate all things. Lord Buddha told us that sometimes we may not have alms or robes or facilities, but that we should conduct religious rites and ceremonies anyway. All this must be tolerated because we did not become ordained to enjoy luxury but to suffer for others; to live off their alms, to receive their robes.

At this time, this *sil mātā* who has taken these ten precepts should see that her conduct is unquestionable. That is a word of advice I offer to you on behalf of the order of monks.

... This *sil mātā* who received the ten precepts today and received its merit should carry out her duties in a manner in which her parents who reared her, her brothers, sisters, and relatives will recieve merit. Similarly, your behavior and actions should be such that you would cause your teacher to attain *nibbāna*, yourself to attain *nibbāna*, and your family. Thus, this idea should be firmly embedded in your mind. We bless this *sil mātā* who received today the ten precepts and wish that she may be free of sorrow and illness.[22]

The ordination ended when the monk bestowed a new name upon Līlāwatī.[23] Thus, in this way – in a matter of two hours and forty minutes – the "*upāsikāva*" was transformed into Śāntā Sil Mātā.

Śāntā's rite of passage from lay life to renunciant was very different from the ordination of a female novice I witnessed a few days later.[24] I met the novitiate, Somā Ranasinghe, one week prior to her initiation. When I met her, the Susilārāmaya in which she was training was beginning to show the signs of an impending celebration; the resident lay nuns were busy decorating the *pūjā* room that contained large statues of the Buddha and Bhikkhunī Saṅghamittā. It was clear that an auspicious event was about to take place.

Somā Ranasinghe grew up near the Susilārāmaya and explained that, from an early age, she had been drawn toward the lifestyle of the female renunciant. She is one of eleven children and comes from an economically depressed, rural family. Unlike Līlāwatī, who spent two years observing the nine precepts, Somā spent only a few months observing the eight precepts. As part of her training, Somā, or "*upāsikāva*" as she was called, was in charge of making tea for the resident lay nuns and other domestic duties. Her teacher instructed her how to meditate and encouraged her to memorize various *sutras* chanted at *pirit* ceremonies.[25] Somā, who was unmarried, was in her late twenties at the time of her ordination.

Like many lay nuns, Somā had had her astrological chart read before her initiation. The astrologer decided that the most auspicious time for the event would be 8:54 a.m. on May 25, 1989. When I arrived at the lay nunnery on the morning of her ordination, Somā was dressed in a clean, white sārī and her long, black hair glistened with coconut oil.

The *pūjā* room was crowded with the members of the Susilārāmaya committee, interested neighbors and the novitiate's large family who had agreed after much struggle to allow Somā to renounce. The lay nuns instructed Somā to sit in front of her teacher's head nun, Sudāsī Mäniyo, who was joined by seven other lay nuns. At 8:30 a.m., Sudāsī gave a *bana*, the theme of which was the tradition of female renunciation in Sri Lanka. According to Sudāsī, "though there is not a nuns' ordination lineage in Sri Lanka today, and will not be until Maitreya Buddha comes,[26] the *dasa sil mātāvo* can perform a similar function in society. Therefore, this is a very serious ceremony, and when one becomes a *sil mātā*, it is not to be taken lightly." According to Theravāda Buddhist eschatology, Maitreya Buddha is to succeed Siddhartha Gautama, this historical founder of Buddhism, at the end of this *buddha*-age. Many Buddhists believe that only a *buddha* can establish an order of monks and an order of nuns. Thus, those who subscribe to this belief feel that it is impossible to re-establish the order of nuns in Sri Lanka until the advent of Maitreya Buddha, which is expected in nearly 2,500 years.

At precisely 8:53 a.m., the sermon ended, the *pirit* began, and Sudāsī began to prepare to cut Somā's hair as the audience looked on with tense anticipation. With a lock of Somā's hair and a watch in one hand, and a pair of scissors in the other, Sudāsī kept inquiring if her watch was synchronized with the clock in the main hall. Chants of efficacious *sutras* filled the room which, by this time, was crowded to capacity. At 8:54 a.m., Sudāsī snipped, then caught, the first lock of hair, gave it to Somā to contemplate and continued to cut the rest. She was joined by Somā's teacher, who helped wrap Somā's head with a white towel, when the last piece of hair had been cut. They then escorted Somā to the living quarters of the lay nunnery; we did not witness the shaving of the head, which was done in the privacy of another room. Somā returned and worshipped her parents and the congregation of lay nuns with betel.[27] She again took her seat by her teacher in front of Sudāsī Mäniyo and received a set of new robes. The robes were symbolically passed to Sudāsī, who touched them and gave them back to Somā. Sudāsī removed the jacket and the waist string from the neatly folded pile of robes and placed the jacket on Somā's back. She then tied the string loosely around Somā's neck, asked her to stand up, and escorted her out of the room. The other lay nuns constantly chanted *pirit* and instructed me to stand here and there to photograph the event. Somā finally returned fully robed. All eyes turned toward her, and exclamations of "*sādhu, sādhu, sādhu, sāāā*" echoed throughout the room.[28] Somā sat down and patiently awaited the arrival of the monk who had been invited to give her the ten precepts.

Though there were many similarities between the two ordinations I witnessed, there were also a few striking differences. The atmosphere of Līlāwatī's ordination was very different to Somā's. During the part of the ceremony over which Sumettā presided, I was under the impression that she and the other lay nuns would have preferred to have been tending the orphans in their care. However, when Līlāwatī went before the monk, who proceeded to elevate us with his words, Sumettā became a proud advisor. The opposite was true of Somā's initiation. The lay nuns who officiated at her rite of passage were enthusiastic and excited. Yet, when the monk, invited to give the precepts to Somā, gave the *bana*, the atmosphere became sombre.

The monk who officiated at Somā's ordination, the Venerable Madihee Paññāsīha, is unquestionably one of the most powerful members of the monastic community in Sri Lanka today. As the leader of the Amarapura Nikāya,[29] the Venerable Paññāsīha speaks for many monks who are opposed to the re-establishment of the order of nuns. In the next section, I explore his and other monks' attitudes toward women and world-renunciation and link them to the perceived role of Sri Lanka as the caretaker of Buddhism.

MONKS, LAY NUNS, AND ORDINATION

On July 23, 1988, a convention was held in the Venerable Paññāsīha's monastery (in Mahāragama) to discuss reforms to the order of monks. One of the items on the agenda was the restoration of the order of nuns. It was summarily quashed by the officiating monk, the Venerable Paññāsīha. According to the order's most strident critic, the Venerable Paññāsīha's views concerning the re-establishment of the Theravādin order of nuns were not convincing:

...The paper submitted on the call for the Restoration of the *Bhikkhuni* Order is none other than a copy of the article by Ven. M. Pannaseeha [sic], published some time ago in most newspapers, both English and Sinhala, rejecting the call and closing the door to even the possibility of Restoring the Order of Nuns.

All the dogmatic and obscurantist arguments known to him are cited, and no place or consideration has been given to the advocates for the Restoration. This paper may have taken about half an hour to read. So within the next half an hour the convention has to adopt a resolution endorsing this very conservative, and anti-feminist stand which closes the door of freedom open to women in the *Bhikkhuni Sasana* by the Lord Buddha.

...The *Sangha* may lead the Sinhalese Buddhists to keep to the caste-system, with the Buddhist sects exclusive to the various castes, and refusing to restore the *Bhikkhuni* Order to women, so that they can never challenge the superiority of the male-dominated *Sangha*, which was originally "an *Ubhato Sangha*," the two-fold *Sangha* of *Bhikkhus* and *Bhikkhunis*.[30]

Having read this critique of the Venerable Paññāsīha's attitudes toward the order of nuns, I was not surprised when the Venerable Paññāsīha administered the householder's, rather than renunciant's, precepts at Somā's initiation. Nor was I surprised by the tone of his *bana*. It began, however, on a very positive note:

Today is a special day because we have ordained a new *sil mātā* among the rest. Normally a person observes the ten precepts privately, and now we are observing it publicly. We should keep in mind that by doing so, a person should first practice and then serve as an example for others. That is the reason we are making a public ceremony.[31]

Now that she has forgone the householder lifestyle and put on the robes, she is now ordained (*pävidi*). When you were in lay life, you observed the five precepts, but now you have "established yourself in a higher discipline."[32] Next we need a name that is different from what you had.[33] Yesterday when we discussed this, you suggested the name "Sumedhā." [Sighs of "*sādhu, sādhu, sādhu, sāāā!*" echo throughout the room.] Now you have changed your status and have changed the five precepts into the ten. You have started a new life with a new name...

After describing Somā's change in status, the Venerable Paññāsīha explained that though Somā was no longer a layperson, her new status was not equal to those monks who belong to the order because it is less rigorous:

...Now the order of nuns no longer exists, but the beams of the *upāsaka* [pious layman] and the *upāsikā* [pious laywoman] are still strong.[34] People ask questions concerning the ten precepts taken by the *sil mātāvos*: "Is there a special set of precepts for the novices and the monks, and for the *sil mātāvos?*" There is a difference. According to the Buddha, what he meant by ordination was to abide by the Three Refuges. In the beginning, he said, "*ehi bhikṣu bhava*,"[35] this was ordination. Then, when the Buddha went on tour and later when the disciples went out, if someone wanted to become a monk, he had to appear in the presence of the Buddha. At that time, he allowed that if a person abide with certain qualities and in a certain way, then he could become ordained by reciting the Three Refuges. Since they have to be abided by perfectly, when ordination was done, there were two ways to observe the Three Refuges. The first way is with the "ṅ," and the second way is with the "ṃ." By saying it like that [with the ṃ], they said the Three Refuges and were automatically ordained as a novice monk. These ten precepts belong to novice monks and are called renunciant's precepts. The difference between these precepts and the other is that with the renunciant's, the verses are spoken first and then at the end "*samādiyāmi*" is proclaimed. All the verses are connected with "*imāni pabbajjā dasa sil samādiyāmi*."[36] These ten precepts we just observed today, if you fail to observe one, you have only broken one.[37] But in the renunciant's ten precepts, if you break one, then all are broken. In the renunciant's, if only one precept is broken, still all ten have to be recited again; in other words, all are broken. The *sil mātās*' precepts are the lay precepts.[38]

At the conclusion of the initiation, the Venerable Paññāsīha's chauffer drove him to another appointment and those assembled enthusiastically offered alms to the lay nuns.

The origins of the Venerable Paññāsīha's conservative views about lay nuns' "real" status are not difficult to trace. He was one of the members of the committee convened in 1954, to investigate the condition of Buddhism in Sri Lanka; Paññāsīha argued then that Buddhism needed to be strengthened. He has also "reiterated the 'truths' about the destiny of Buddhism and the Sinhalese enshrined in monkish chronicles like the *Mahavamsa*,"[39] and has "sounded the apocalyptic note that the Sinhalese have declined in every sphere of activity."[40] The Venerable Paññāsīha is thus heir to an orthodox tradition that protests against changes, which are perceived to threaten the integrity of that tradition; changes that question the very identity of Theravāda Buddhism in Sri Lanka. The possibility of women undertaking the precepts in the manner of monks raises the specter of change for monks like the Venerable Paññāsīha. Some of my informants also argued that monks would not like to see women ordained because then the *saṅgha* would have to compete with them for donations, including temple property and lands.

That such an important monk accepted the invitation to officiate at Somā's initiation, suggests that the *saṅgha* recognizes her vocation as a viable alternative to domesticity for religiously motivated women. However, that the tone of the *bana* by one of the most highly-respected spokesmen for the monastic order was cautious, suggests that the lay nuns are not considered by at least a few monks to be their counterpart in Sinhala Buddhist society. Yet, in my interviews with many monks around the island, I learned that the younger generation had a more favorable impression of lay nuns and would agree to their ordination into the *saṅgha*.[41] Some junior monks believe that women are just as deserving as men to enter the Buddha's monastic order; this, after all, was the vision of the Buddha himself.[42] It is senior monks, such as the Venerable Paññāsīha, who quell attempts to re-establish the order of nuns in Sri Lanka. Elder monks cite various reasons for their inability to resuscitate the order of nuns. Among these, the most often cited are the lack of the consecrated boundary needed to induct a woman into the monastic order[43] and the lack of the proper quorum of Theravāda nuns required to preside over such an ordination, as we saw in chapter 1.

Another leading member of the Amarapura Nikāya, the Venerable Piyadassi of the Vajirārāmaya in Bambalapitiya, Colombo, told me that the nuns' lineage cannot be restored until Maitreya Buddha appears thousands of years from now.[44] Though the Venerable Piyadassi has ordained many lay nuns, he warns against women who go to Mahāyāna ordinations and return calling themselves *bhikkhunīs*, because he believes that it creates dissention in Sri Lanka.[45]

Balangoda Ānanda Maitreya, the ninety year-old (in 1989) former leader of the Amarapura Nikāya, is also opposed to movements to re-establish the order of nuns.[46] A confidant and religious adivsor of former President Premadasa,[47] the Venerable Ānanda Maitreya told me that it is impossible to re-establish the Theravādin order of nuns because a woman must receive ordination from "both sides," that is, from the order of monks and the order of nuns. He added, however, that though it is impossible to re-establish a formal order of nuns, women can "enter" as lay nuns and keep all the 311 rules of the *bhikkhunī*.[48] The Venerable Balangoda Ānanda Maitreya volunteered that the female renunciants' low status in Sri Lankan Buddhist society is a result of their lax behavior. If they abided by the 311 *Vinaya* rules, the Venerable Ānanda Maitreya argued, their status would be much higher:

> Practice is what is important. If the lay nuns keep the nuns' [*bhikkhunī*] precepts, then they will become nuns. Of course, not in the traditional sense, but this should not matter to them. The point is this: if they conduct their practice like nuns used to, then they will be regarded as nuns [*bhikkhunīs*]. They should also become more learned. In Burma, the *upāsikās* [lay nuns] are very learned, and though they also are not ordained into the order, monks go to them for advice. This could be the case in this country, but because our *sil mātāvo* do not abide by the *bhikkhunī* precepts and because they are not learned, their status is low.[49]

Thus the most powerful monks in Sri Lanka – the older generation – are not in favor of re-establishing the Theravādin order of nuns.[50] Most Sinhala lay nuns, as we have seen, are not bothered by this resistance, for they themselves are not in favor of the changes that affiliation with the monastic order would bring. Like some monks, many lay nuns do not even believe that re-establishing the order of nuns is necessary for proper monastic practice. In addition, some agree with the monks who argue that it is not possible to resuscitate the order of nuns anyway, given the lack of a Buddha in this present age to do so. While Sinhala lay nuns are not, for the most part, in favor of re-establishing the order of nuns, there are those in Sri Lanka who have rallied for its immediate revival. A few lay nuns, as we have seen, urge that the Theravādin order of nuns must be resuscitated.[51] This group of lay nuns is mostly comprised of western women; in fact, it is these women and the laity who keep the issue alive.

WESTERN WOMEN AND THE PATH OF THE BUDDHA

Sri Lanka and India have been host to many western women who have renounced the world under the tutelage of South Asian, as well as foreign, monks.[52] In 1937, Evelyn Grant Robinson became one of the first English woman to "recite the Ten Precepts and change her name and identity to become Sister Vajirā, a Buddhist nun,"[53] in Saranath, India. Though she was ordained in India, she began residing in Sri Lanka in 1935, where she passed her life with a great reputation for Buddhist meditation. Alone in her living quarters in Kandy, Sister Vajirā devoted her life to Buddhism. Even though she lived as a recluse, she befriended an American female renunciant

named Sister Dhammādinnā, who had also sought refuge in
Buddhism; like Sister Vajirā, Sister Dhammādinnā lived "alone in a
cottage of her own, leading a life of strict seclusion."[54]

Western female renunciants continue to follow in the footsteps of
Sister Vajirā and Sister Dhammādinnā, choosing the path of
meditation, rather than that of service and devotion. Like Sister
Vajirā and Sister Dhammādinnā, these western proclaimers of the
Buddha's message – there were only five in Sri Lanka in 1989 –
usually attract a large following. Though they are in Sri Lanka to
learn from the great Sinhala and foreign meditation masters, they
have contributed much to Sri Lankan religiosity themselves. Their
most important contribution has been their influence in helping to
popularize meditation among the laity.[55]

Gombrich has remarked that Europeans who travel to Sri Lanka
and don the ochre robe often contribute "the results of their own
western education to the current of Buddhist ideas."[56] This is
certainly the case with two German women who journeyed to Sri
Lanka in 1986 to become Theravādin nuns; their textual interpe-
tation of Buddhism led them to believe that they had every right to
enter the *saṅgha*. Their demands to enter provoked many debates
about the initiation of women, debates that hinged upon the proper
role of women in Buddhism.[57] Though Gombrich refered to
European monks who had "passed their lives there with great
reputations for holiness,"[58] other foreigners, including the two
German women, are not remembered as favorably.

Bridget Jarcord and Ingrid Heck decided to become Theravādin
nuns when they were aged thirty and twenty-eight, respectively.[59]
For fifteen months, the former social worker and business consultant
studied with the German monk, the Venerable Ñānaponika.
However, their relationship with the German monk deteriorated,
and he eventually had the two committed to the Angoda Mental
Hospital. Their relentless pursuit of ordination, which included
sleeping in the jungle, as well as on the monk's veranda – without
having been invited – resulted in their arrest and forced commitment
to an institution. Feeling dissatisfied with the tradition of the lay nun,
which they claimed was "not rooted in Buddhist teaching,"[60] the
two German women, who called themselves Bhadrā and Dhammā,
tried to live according to the *Vinaya*. Their interpretation of the
Buddha's monastic code included living near their teacher and
immersing themselves in meditation. In fact, "From waking up to

going to sleep at night [they] spent almost eighteen hours in meditation, in reading and writing."[61]

Though Bhadrā and Dhammā's pursuit for ordination was frought with controversy, their interpretation of Buddhist practice is similar to that of most western Buddhists who have similarly donned the ochre robe in Sri Lanka.[62] While conducting research, I had the opportunity to interview every foreign lay nun in Sri Lanka. Their interpretation of the ideal path for the renunciant is radically different from most Sinhala lay nuns'. Like the German lay nun, Sister Uppalavaṇṇā, whom we met in chapter 6, Bhadrā and Dhammā spent most of their time meditating, rather than performing *pūjās* or ministering to *dāyakas*.

In my interviews with the foreign lay nuns, each one discussed her vision of Buddhist renunciation with me and compared her vision to the Sinhala lay nuns'. When I asked one of them about the practices of the Sinhala lay nuns,[63] she said that their lifestyle deviates from the Buddha's vision of renunciation. She said that very few Sinhala nuns know how to meditate and would rather spend hours "feeding Buddha statues."[64] In fact, most of the western lay nuns I interviewed implied that the practice of their Sinhala counterparts is too lax, and thus inappropriate for the life of a world-renouncer. An American lay nun, Ayyā Ñāṇasirī,[65] even organized a convocation of lay nuns – local and foreign – from various parts of the island with the express purpose of teaching the Sinhala lay nuns how to meditate.

Approximately fifty Sinhala lay nuns and most of the foreign lay nuns participated in the convocation.[66] In addition, many Sri Lankan laywomen attended the week-long session held in a hotel in Beruwala, on the south-eastern coast of the island. Some came from as far away as Kandy, in the hill country, to receive religious instruction from the lay nuns. The majority, however, came from Colombo; yet, both groups of laywomen represented the most affluent echelons of society and all these women had been educated in English-medium schools. They also congregated around the western lay nuns. One of the laywomen informed me that because she and her friends were more comfortable communicating in English than Sinhala, they naturally sought guidance from the western renunciants. Unlike their western counterparts who taught meditation for most of the day, the Sinhala lay nuns spent the greater part of each day performing *pūjās*.

Bond offers an explanation that may account for the popularity of western lay nuns among the elite. It can be argued that the women who attended the convocation "represent examples of lay Buddhists who have been alienated from traditional Theravāda Buddhism ... The foreign meditation teachers who understand the modern context have provided reinterpretations of the Buddhist cosmology and practical methods for addressing one's situation through meditation."[67] Thus, English-speaking, urban elite laywomen, alienated from the traditional village interpretation of Buddhism, find refuge in foreigners whose education and experience is more like their own than the rural lay nuns'. Rather than the path of devotion taught by Sinhala lay nuns, which includes merit-making, observing the ten pecepts, the hope of heaven and with difficulty, *nibbāna*, westernized Sri Lankan women prefer the path of meditation, a path they consider to be a useful response to Sri Lanka's social problems.[68] Though these elite women preferred the path of meditation, they intimated that western lay nuns understimate the efficacy of *pūjā* for creating a calmness in one's mind as well as faith in Buddhism.

Each of the western female renunciants told me that she considers the path and teachings of the Sinhala lay nuns to be in accord with the Buddha's vision of the appropriate lifestyle for laity. Unlike the Sinhala lay nuns, western lay nuns refer to themselves as "Ayyā," the Pāli honorific for *bhikkhunī*;[69] they use the begging bowl associated with the monastic order,[70] and spend hours meditating. Their interpretation of the proper path for the world-renouncer usually excludes contact with the laity which is, as we have seen, a marked feature of the activities of Sinhala lay nuns. Instead, the western lay nuns devote their attention to their own mental development.

Ayyā Vāyāmā, an Australian Buddhist lay nun, is perhaps more closely associated with the Sinhala laity than any of the other western lay nuns I interviewed. At the time of my interview with Ayyā Vāyāmā, she was thirty-six years old. Formerly an Anglican who taught Sunday School in Sydney for eight years, Ayyā Vāyāmā holds a Bachelors Degree in Sociology from a leading Australian University. In 1977, she went to Sri Lanka on a chartered tour and, while there, bought some books about Buddhism. She became so intrigued by Buddhism that she investigated whether or not she could actively pursue Buddhist Studies in Australia. While in lay life, in 1982, Ayyā Vāyāmā discovered that Wat Buddha Dhamma near Sydney conducted week-end meditation retreats of which she availed herself frequently. Her first teacher was the famous Bhikkhu Khāntipālo,[71] who is renowned in Sri Lanka and America.

Ayyā Vāyāmā's initial introduction to meditation was very satisfactory. On her second retreat, having been convinced that Buddhism "spoke to her needs and her own situation," she took refuge in the five precepts. Things then began to rapidly change in her life. In 1983, the young Australian woman met Ayyā Khemā, who was teaching meditation at Wat Buddha Dhamma. In July of 1984, having decided that the renunciant lifestyle suited her needs, she travelled again to Sri Lanka; unlike her initial trip in 1977, which was purely for pleasure, her 1984 sojourn changed her life. From July until November, the young Australian kept the eight precepts – a commitment which very ardent lay Buddhists make for extended periods of time. Having kept the eight precepts for five months, she returned to Australia to explain to her family, friends, and former boyfriend that she had made a commitment to Buddhism. She remained in Australia until March, 1985.

Ayyā Vāyāmā explained to me why she renounced her lay identity: "constant loss kept showing me that there is nothing to hang on to; that everything is impermanent. In a period of only four years, my father died, my relationship with my boyfriend ended, my mother died, and then my grandfather. It was a personal period of *dukkha.*" I inquired whether one can have this knowledge of the true nature of reality without renouncing. Ayyā Vāyāmā answered that: "it is possible to know that life is marked by *dukkha* without becoming a monk or a nun. But by becoming a nun, the framework for serious practice is provided. Only as a nun could I have been able to direct my mind toward one-pointedness.[72] The rules which I keep give support to my daily activities – there is now no need to consider whether or not I should do this or that; the rules determine my choices. By becoming a nun, I am also identified publicly – now shame and dread enter into whether or not I practice properly."

Ayyā Vāyāmā was ordained at Parappaduwa, Ayyā Khemā's refuge for Buddhist female renunciants and other women who desire the solitude of a remote island for meditation.[73] She was the third of Ayyā Khemā's pupils to be initiated. Eight monks, including Piyaratna Mahā Thera[74] and four lay nuns, including Ayyā Khemā, officiated at the ceremony. Three and a half years after donning the ochre robe, Ayyā Vāyāmā returned to Australia for a brief visit.

Ayyā Vāyāmā is no longer affiliated with Ayyā Khemā but instead lives in Ambalangoda with a Sinhala lay nun.[75] She holds a small meditation class twice each week for the neighborhood laity and gives six religious talks each month. Like all the western lay nuns I interviewed, Ayyā Vāyāmā meditates for at least four hours each day.[76] Moreover, echoing the other western and Sinhala lay nuns, she believes that *nibbāna* is a possibility in this lifetime. To that end, she has dedicated her life to Buddhism.

Thus, unlike the Sinhala lay nuns I have introduced thus far, the western lay nuns spend very little time, if any at all, engaged in Buddha *pūjā*. However, there is not a completely clear-cut dichotomy between Sinhala female renunciants and their western counterparts. Though none of the western lay nuns have chosen the path of devotion, there are many Sinhala lay nuns who have also eschewed that path. Like the western renunciants, such Sinhala lay nuns have dedicated their time to the pursuit of *nibbāna* – by way of meditation. In the next section, I introduce a Sinhala woman who lived as a lay nun and then returned to lay life. Her life in robes approximated that of the western, rather than the local, lay nuns we have met thus far.

A SINHALA LAY NUN AND HIGH SOCIETY

During the course of my field study, I met only one woman, Ayoma Wikramasinghe, who had renounced her renunciation. According to my informants, this is an extremely rare event among the lay nuns, because women, as we have seen, must fight against prejudice to renounce. Yet even though Wikramasinghe is no longer a lay nun, she spends much of her time in meditation and in solitude. It is no surprise that Wikramasinghe became a lay nun; the daughter of the Kotalawalas,[77] and the grand-daughter of the de Silvas, all of whom were the primary movers of the Vihāra Mahā Devī Upāsikārāmaya in the 1930s, she has always been involved in lay nunnery projects.[78] As a child, her parents and her grandparents supported many lay nuns – both foreign and local – and she developed a fascination for world renunciation. Wikramasinghe's childhood years marked the height of the Buddhist revival among the elite of Colombo and, as we have seen, it was not unusual for women from her social and economic class to don the ochre robe. However, as we saw in chapter 6, the frequency with which elite women renounced the homelife after independence decreased dramatically. Thus, Wikramasinghe does not typify the type of woman who has opted for the renunciant's lifestyle since the 1950s.

I interviewed Wikramasinghe at her palatial residence and family home in the prestigious Cinnamon Gardens area of Colombo,[79] the site for most of the meetings of the Vihāra Mahā Devī committee. Though her parents were extremely wealthy, she informed me that no amount of wealth could assuage the suffering of a young girl who suffered from chronic gynecological problems. Wikramasinghe's father, Justin Kotalawala, was an avid Buddhist and meditator. Aged fourteen, she began to observe the eight precepts on *pōya* days, and by the age of eighteen, she began to meditate with her father. In the earliest phase of her meditation practices, Wikramasinghe travelled with her father to a meditation retreat in Mandalay. While in Burma, she met an American female renunciant, whose example influenced the choices that the young Sinhala Buddhist woman would make later in her life.[80] She recounted her life in the following way:

During my first trip to Burma, it became clear to me that I did not want to marry. However, I was working in a firm after completing my studies, and there I met a man who was also interested in Buddhism and meditation. I was very interested in him, but because he was not of the same caste and social standing, my parents forbade me to marry him. They introduced me to my husband, and though he was not my choice, we have been very happy together.

When we were courting, I told him that I was much more interested in spirituality than in marriage. He did not seem to mind. I conceived on my wedding night, and in spite of the fact that I became a mother soon after my wedding, I continued to meditate. I now have three grown-up children.

Not too long ago, I met a German monk by the name of Ñānawimala who encouraged me to become a nun. In the meantime, I came in contact with the Australian monk, Khāntipālo, and learned about a German woman who was interested in becoming a nun. This German woman came and stayed with me, and it was in my house that her head was shaved; I shaved her head myself. This woman is now known as Ayyā Khemā.

I, too, became more and more interested in becoming a nun. For two years, I wore a brown *sarong* and jacket.[81] The day after my daughter's wedding, I went with a friend to my farm in Homagama to meditate for a while. Before leaving, I told my family that I wanted to become a nun and they were not pleased. I had even worn the sarong and jacket during the celebrations for my daughter – but I do not think that anyone thought that I would actually become a nun. Two days after I left home, I shaved my own head and put on the robe. When I emerged, my friend was startled to see the transformation.

I asked Wikramasinghe whether she had had a formal initiation, as is customary with most lay nuns:

During the two years in which I dressed in the brown *sarong*, I observed the eight precepts. I never ate past midday and, as far as possible, I maintained all eight. After donning the robe, I again took the eight precepts at the Vajirārāmaya Temple in Bambalapitiya[82] where Ayyā Khemā had originally taken the ten precepts. Because I own land and have other worldly possessions, I did not think that it was appropriate to take the ten precepts, for I would be violating the tenth, the one concerned with possessions and money.[83]

Two of Wikramasinghe's children and her husband accepted her decision to renounce and visited her weekly, bringing alms with them on each visit. Even the child who was confused by her behavior eventually began to visit on a weekly basis. Wikramasinghe spent many hours each day in meditation and continued to live as a recluse for fourteen months. However, while Wikramasinghe meditated, her husband's health began to fail and she decided that she was needed at home. Her duty as a wife and mother weighed heavily on her conscience. Moreover, after a conversation with the Venerable Ñānawimala, in which he disclosed that he had meditated for twenty years before reaching the first *dhyāna*,[84] the discouraged lay nun decided to leave the robes. Though Wikramasinghe is back at home, she has the opportunity to meditate and has enouraged her husband to join her. According to Wikramasinghe, she and her husband still maintain a very warm relationship, but she misses her life of meditation on the farm in Homagama.

In the next section, I introduce other Sinhala female renunciants who, like Wikramasinghe, have opted for the meditative life. Unlike the lay nuns we met in chapter 7, who spend most of their time serving their *dāyakas*, the lay nuns we meet below spend most of their time meditating.

THE CAVE DWELLERS OF THE FOREST

It is recorded that the Buddha warned *bhikkhunīs* against living in isolated areas. According to the *Vinaya*, during the time of the Buddha, "*Bhikkhunīs* dwelt in the forest, and men of bad character violated them. They told this matter to the Buddha. 'A *Bhikkhunī* is not, *bhikkhus*, to adopt the forest life. Whosoever does so, shall be guilty of a *dukkaṭa*'."[85] However, because contemporary female monastics are not regulated by the monastic code, those who are attracted to the secluded life of the forest are free to reside there. I met three such renunciants who live in caves deep in the jungle, in one of the most remote areas of the island. Though they live in isolation, they are pupils of a lay nun whose abode is much more traditional. Their teacher, Kegalle Uttarā Mäniyo, who lives at Kataragama,[86] sees them once or twice each month and arrives laden with supplies. In addition, they are visited, infrequently, by pilgrims who seek out the ancient and historic caves that the lay nuns have made their monastery; they too provide the lay nuns with some items necessary for their material comfort.

At Kataragama, I interviewed Kegalle Uttarā Mäniyo, the most well-known lay nun of the area: she has a reputation, as far away as Colombo, for being gifted with prophetic vision. The lay nunnery over which she presides, Mahāsena Sänāsuma, is located immediately outside the sacred precinct of the Kataragama god and faces the most imposing structure in the entire compound, the Kiri Vihāraya Dāgoba. A long narrow path, extending from the Kiri Vihāraya, eventually arrives at Mahāsena Sänāsuma, settled within a quiet area of lush greenery. It is not noticeable from the Kataragama precinct. As I approached the lay nunnery, two of Uttarā Mäniyo's students were sweeping the area in preparation for the evening *pūjā* and the impending *pōya* celebration of the following day.

Though diminutive in stature, Uttarā Mäniyo has a giant personality and commands much respect from the twelve lay nuns who live at Mahāsena Sänāsuma, and from those who travel hundreds of miles to receive her advice. A whole array of people, including former President Premadasa, her most famous patron,[87] have visited her Upāsikārāmaya. When I visited her Upāsikārāmaya in 1989, a large photograph of President Premadasa hung in the greeting room, as did a portrait of his daughter and a photograph of his entire family.

Like most of the lay nuns I interviewed, Uttarā Mäniyo does not wish to see the re-establishment of the order of nuns in Sri Lanka.[88] Claiming that it is impossible to revive because it would mean introducing a Mahāyāna lineage into a Theravādin country, she teaches her students to preserve tradition and not fill their minds with such controversial issues; instead they should meditate. Uttarā

Mäniyo told me that she spends much time engaged in conducting
pūjās and meditates five to six hours each day.

Meditation has played a pivotal role in Uttarā Mäniyo's life.
Fifteen years before I met Uttarā Mäniyo, she had travelled from her
home village of Kegalle all the way to the edges of the Ruhunu
National Forest, where she had a vision of the god Kataragama while
in a meditative trance. Without a preceptor, the mother of seven
shaved her own head, donned the robe, and henceforth was known as
Uttarā Mäniyo.[89] She then divorced her husband who later died.

Uttarā Mäniyo's life in many ways evokes the biographies of some
of the women Obeyesekere has presented in his essay on Hindu
female ascetics in Sri Lanka, particularly Juliet Nona.[90] Like Juliet
Nona, Uttarā Mäniyo grew up in an extremely pious Buddhist family
and married even though she did not want to. Moreover, the lives of
both women have been marked by ecstatic experiences: Juliet Nona
had experienced fits of possession before becoming an ascetic; Uttarā
Mäniyo had been a mouthpiece for the gods before "going forth."
Both visionaries were told while in trance to go to Kataragama and
both went: Juliet eventually became a Hindu priestess and returned
to Colombo; Uttarā Mäniyo became a Buddhist "nun" and
continues to reside at Kataragama. Uttarā Mäniyo to this day has a
reputation as a visionary.

Uttarā Mäniyo's visions usually have religious, as well as political,
overtones. Kataragama, who appeared in her first prophetic vision,
is considered the national god of Sri Lanka and is known for his war-
like demeanor.[91] After moving to Kataragama, Uttarā Mäniyo had
another vision in which Dutugamenu, a hero of the *Mahāvamsa*,
rather than Kataragama, appeared to her. With the aid of former
President Premadasa, she has erected a statue in front of her lay
nunnery in honor of Dutugamenu.[92]

It was the god Kataragama himself who asked Uttarā Mäniyo to
establish a residence at Dutugamenu's legendary childhood home,
Situlpavvihāra, forged over two thousand years ago from a series of
caves in the Ruhunu National Forest. There, among the ancient
statues that transport the onlooker to another era, and among the
bats that unabashedly fly at eye level, three of Uttarā Mäniyo's
pupils, who were all in their thirties in 1989, as well as a novice, live
without the distractions of village life. All of Uttarā Mäniyo's
students are expected to experience life in the caves.

The lay nunnery consists of two small caves, one of which serves as a sleeping area, and the other, a kitchen. The sleeping area is also used as a sitting room and in 1989 was decorated with pictures of Uttarā Mäniyo and the Buddha. There is also a cave that has been transformed into a shrine room (*Budugee*) that houses what appears to be a very old statue of the Buddha.[93] In front of the caves, and slightly to the left, is an ancient relic chamber (*dāgoba*) considered to house the remains of Vihāra Mahā Devī, the mother of Dutugamenu.[94]

Though the lay nuns perform *pūjās* in the *Budugee*, they spend most of their time meditating. They rise at 4:00 a.m., offer alms to the Buddha image and then begin their day of meditation. Because there are many tasks associated with living in a cave – gathering water and cooking fuel – they devote much time attending such tasks. Yet even their daily tasks are imbued with a special significance; they practice walking, or "working," meditation as they see to their own material needs. These women told me that their quiet environment, rather than the hustle and bustle of village life, is more suitable for the attainment of *nibbāna*. Moreover, they added that by living in such ancient caves, caves that have been inhabited by meditators on and off for over 2,000 years, they carry on a time-honored Buddhist tradition. They thus claim to represent an ancient practice, despite the Buddha's injunctions against women living in isolated regions.

CONCLUSIONS

Like the ancient *bhikkhunī saṅgha*, the contemporary female world-renouncers of Sri Lanka are the objects of ascetic misogyny, as many monks' attitudes toward lay nuns suggest. Their misogyny undoubtebly stems from a fear of the feminine, inasmuch as the feminine can prove a threat to monks' celibacy. Yet, these monks' attitudes toward women and world-renunciation also have much to do with their concern about the welfare of Sri Lanka as a Buddhist country. Essentially, they condemn anti-Theravādin practices, such as women taking the monks' precepts, that may potentially corrupt Sri Lankan Buddhism. Though their style of ascetic misogyny is counterbalanced by monks who have favorable impressions of lay nuns, their misogynous views resonate throughout the *saṅgha*.

Because the revived tradition of female renunciation is still relatively new in Sri Lanka, there is little consensus among lay nuns on many issues, including: the appropriate rite of passage for the novice; whether or not the *bhikkhunī* lineage should be reinstated, or even, if it can be; or the proper vocation of the female world-renouncers. It is not surprising that Ayyā Ñāṇasirī, an American, Ayyā Khemindā, from Holland,[95] and Ayyā Vāyāmā, an Australian – the three western renunciants who attended the convocation – emphasized the importance of meditation in their interviews with me. Western renunciants who have resided in Sri Lanka – male and female – have historically eschewed the path of devotion in favor of the contemplative life. As we saw in chapter 6, westerners' interpretations of Buddhism have usually leaned toward its theoretical side. In many ways, their orientation reflects Protestant Buddhist ideology, in which "religion is privatized and internalized: the truly significant is not what takes place at a public celebration or in ritual, but what happens inside one's own mind or soul."[96] *Pūjā*, and other outward expressions of piety are considered insignificant; rather, what might be deemed the more "rational" aspect of Buddhism – meditation – is considered the only useful practice for salvation. Though in the texts, "no need had been felt to justify the rationality of Buddhism, let alone to posit a contrast between religion and philosophy: the Dhamma was both,"[97] western lay nuns approach the religion as a rational philosophy.

Yet, unlike Dharmapāla and other champions of Protestant Buddhism, western lay nuns do not argue for a "this-worldly" asceticism either for monks, or female renunciants. Rather, they insist that world-renouncers should disavow worldly connections. The majority of Sinhala lay nuns, on the other hand, argue that all renunciants should devote their lives to selfless service; a notion that Dharmapāla would have found acceptable. Thus, Protestant Buddhism, from its creation in the late nineteenth century to its manifestations in the present, is an ideology with many possible variations. Despite differences, both western and Sinhala lay nuns reflect Protestant Buddhist concerns in their thoughts on their vocation. All the lay nuns, whether Sinhala or western, regardless of how they were ordained, or the path they tread, view their practices as traditional; like other Protestant Buddhists, they have returned to the texts to legitimate their behavior and practices. Moreover, whether they champion the re-establishment of the order, or whether they agree with many monks that such is an impossibility, they find their justification in tradition. In the next chaper, I provide other instances of innovation, which are nonetheless derived from tradition.

CHAPTER 9

The Sri Lankan Bhikkunī Saṅgha: trends and reflections

INTRODUCTION

A few interested parties, laity and lay nuns alike, have taken steps to legitimate the lay nuns' vocation by changing their status from lay to ordained. With the support of the Korean government and interested Sri Lankan Buddhists, several Sri Lankan lay nuns travelled in 1988 to America where five accepted ordination into the monastic order from a dual saṅgha; Ayyā Khemā took the vows of the bhikṣuṇī at the same time. According to the Vinaya, as we have seen, a dual saṅgha is needed to initiate a woman into the order. The monks who participated in the ordination were from Theravāda and Mahāyāna communities in America, while the ordained nuns were drawn from the latter. This ordination of the Sri Lankan lay nuns did not go uncontested; most older monks living in Sri Lanka, who argue that the Buddha never wanted to establish an order of nuns in the first place, echoing the ascetic misogyny of the texts,[1] argue that the lay nuns have not changed status. They have predictably declared that Mahāyāna intervention in Sri Lankan Buddhist affairs destroys the integrity of the Theravādin tradition. They are not alone; the majority of the Sinhala lay nuns I interviewed also regard the Mahāyāna ordination of their peers as illegitimate from the point of view of proper Theravādin practice. Like conservative monks, they claim that Mahāyāna Buddhism is a corrupt version of Theravāda and thus has no place in Sri Lanka.

In addition to those who have received ordination abroad, are other women who claim to be members of the monastic community without having been granted the dual ordination. Though their numbers are relatively small, they receive attention from the media and other lay nuns. Interviews with one of them – Theranā – were among some of my most interesting experiences in Sri Lanka. Like

other lay nuns, she claims to have relinquished fully the role
determined for her by society: the role of nurturer, of private
supporter of Buddhism. Among the contemporary female renunciants, Theranā's vision of Buddhism is the most radical; she argues
that women, too, should have access to the public sphere that has
been male-controlled and dominated. Yet, she considers herself to be
more legitimate than lay nuns. Her views are in many ways echoed
by some Sri Lankan monks living in the United States; they claim
that women, as well as men, are rightful heirs to the monastic
tradition. Before exploring these monks' attitudes toward women,
renunciation, and the steps they have taken to open the *saṅgha* to
women, we return to Sri Lanka where some women claim to be
ordained nuns.

THE CONTEMPORARY BHIKKHUNĪS OF SRI LANKA

In December, 1988, eleven lay nuns, accompanied by Anulā
Rājāpaksa, an English-speaking laywoman, journeyed to California
to participate in an historic Mahāyāna ordination. Six members of
the original group returned to Sri Lanka before they were ordained,
complaining of being home sick and uncomfortable; however, five
remained. At the end of their stay, ordained Mahāyāna nuns
together with Theravāda and Mahāyāna monks bestowed the title of
bhikṣuṇī upon them.[2] The two I met were very eager to discuss their
experiences of America and show me their certificates and photographs. Despite now being members of the monastic order, Dhammāsīlā[3] and Visākhā Dhammāsīlā[4] have not changed their style of life
since becoming ordained nuns. They wear an ochre robe, but not the
robe of the *saṅgha*; nor do they follow the *Vinaya*, the monastic rules.
In light of this, I asked them why they took the vows. Dhammāsīlā
answered: "We were chosen by our teacher to go to California, so we
went. We took the vows of Mahāyāna *bhikṣuṇīs*. We were able to visit
places that we had never been able to see and never dreamed that we
would see. People spent so much money on us. It was a wonderful
experience and we met many nice people. We knew that the monks
in Sri Lanka would not accept our new status before we took the
vows, so that is why we have not changed our lifestyle. Ayyā Khemā
was also there." Dhammāsīlā and Visākhā Dhammāsīlā, though
srāmaṇerīs,[5] are content with their former status. Unlike their
compatriot, Theranā, whom we meet next, they believe that they can

walk in the footsteps of the Buddha without being recognized as members of the monastic order. In other words, the *saṅgha* is irrelevant to their vocation.

I met Theranā on two occasions. I had already heard about her teacher, Uttama Sādhu, a self-ordained, controversial "monk," from a number of informants. I had also learned that he had served as a teacher to women who claim to be *bhikkhunīs*. I was, therefore, very interested to meet him and his pupils.[6] When I told the lay nuns at my primary research site, the Madivala Upāsikārāmaya, that I was interested in meeting Uttama Sādhu and his female disciples, they told me that "they are very strange; sometimes the police are called to go there." Though this was meant as a warning, it made me even more curious to meet them. Indeed, because they were so nervous about my safety, one of the lay nuns, Dhammāpālī Mäniyo, insisted on accompanying me.

It was difficult to find Sasuna Sänāsuma, the hermitage over which Uttama Sādhu presides. It is located at the end of a winding road, on a steep gradient, in the little village of Rattanapitiya in Nugegoda. All those who enter the compound are questioned by its owners, who also live on the property in a house adjacent to the religious edifices.

When we approached Uttama Sādhu, who presides over the monastery, I told him that I was conducting a study of *dasa sil mātāvo*, and he immediately began to scold us in Sinhala:

There is no such thing as a *dasa sil mātā*. The Buddha never ordained women to be *sil mātāvo*. My pupils are *bhikkhunīs*. You (pointing to Dhammāpālī) are not doing the Buddha's work. The Buddha never told us to go and work in hospitals, to chant *pirit*, to minister to our supporters, or to touch money; he told us to meditate – to try to attain *nibbāna*. This cannot be done in hospitals or by accompanying laywomen on trips.[7]

Generally accepting the Protestant Buddhist notion that all can attain *nibbāna*, he does not, however, advocate a "this-worldly" asceticism.

"How is it that your pupils are *bhikkhunīs*, Sādhu? Didn't the nuns' lineage end years ago," I asked. He gave a heated reply:

When Mahāpajāpatī renounced, the Buddha asked her to recite the Eight Weighty Rules. This served as her *upasampadā*. Therefore, I ordain my pupils in the same way. Twice each month, they recite these rules – on the *pōya* day and on the new moon day. There is no such thing as *sil mātāvo* – only *bhikkhunīs*.[8]

Thus, like the Buddha, Uttama Sādhu has established an order of nuns.[9] I was struck by the way he invoked the ordination of Mahāpajāpatī Gotamī as the precedent for ordaining women today; many monks use the story of her ordination to *prohibit* women's entrance into the *saṅgha*.[10] Unlike most monks I interviewed, Uttama Sādhu's attitude toward women and renunciation bespeaks soteriological inclusiveness. "Are there any *bhikkhunīs* here now," I asked. He called to one of his two female pupils.[11]

Śāntinī, or Theranā, as she later referred to herself, appeared, cloaked in a dark-brown, patched robe without a blouse underneath.[12] She spent about two minutes clearing her throat; it seemed that she had been meditating and had not talked for quite sometime. After explaining to her that I was conducting a study of the tradition of female renunciation in Sri Lanka, I asked her if she considered herself to be a *bhikkhunī*. She nodded. She also informed me that she keeps the 311 rules of the *Bhikkhunī Vinaya*.[13]

At the time of the interview, Theranā had been a *bhikkhunī* for fifteen years. Like all the *dasa sil mātāvo* that I interviewed, Theranā told me that she is a vegetarian. However, her insistence on a total vegetarian diet, unlike the female renunciants we have met thus far, stems from spiritual issues of healing and health. Uttama Sādhu and his monks and nuns are well-known for their healing powers; not only are people in Nugegoda familiar with their curative abilities, but their powers have also been featured in a Colombo, English-medium newspaper article.[14] In Sri Lanka, as is the case with most Hindu and Buddhist cultures, strict asceticism, including vegetarianism, is aligned with healing and magical powers.[15] Thus vegetarianism not only empowers Uttama Sādhu and his pupils, it also legitimates their vocation. Foremost among their powers is the reception of messages about Buddhism and world issues that float through the atmosphere; moreover, they claim to be receiving through radio waves the entire Pāli Canon in the original Magadha.

As I mentioned above, the Sinhala lay nuns at my primary research site warned me not to go alone to interview Uttama Sādhu. Much of their uneasiness about his form of Buddhism stems from his practices, such as healing, which the lay nuns regard as non-Buddhist. The lay nuns in Madivala claimed, as do most Buddhists, that possession and illness can be healed by Hindu priests and priestesses. Yet, as one lay nun succinctly stated, "*sil mātāvo* meditate, not heal."[16] Priestesses and *dasa sil mātāvo* achieve higher status when they assume their new vocations, both of which represent protest movements within traditional Sri Lankan culture.[17] All the *dasa sil mātāvo* at my primary research site, however, viewed their vocation as distinct from that of the priestess. Theranā's association with the priestess vocation thus calls into question this distinction.[18]

Traditional lay nuns are also suspicious of Uttama Sādhu because he is self-ordained and claims to ordain others.[19] This is surprising, since these lay nuns have not been ordained by the *saṅgha*, it seems paradoxical that they should be critical of others who renounce without the traditional rite of passage. Yet, as we have seen, most lay nuns do not consider themselves to be *bhikkhunīs*, even though they have assumed the *bhikkhunī's* vocation. As one lay nun told me, men, unlike women, do not have to *assume* a monastic vocation; men can legitimately enter the *saṅgha*. In short, monks like Uttama Sādhu pose a threat to traditional monasticism.[20] Thus, while lay nuns, as we have seen, are critical of the contemporary *saṅgha*, they hold its ideal in high regard and feel duty-bound to protect it.

For the lay nuns at my primary research site, as well as others, Uttama Sādhu and his nuns' imposter behavior involves not only wearing the robe of the ordained clergy, but also using the traditional bowl to collect alms. As far as I know, with the exception of the wandering "bag-lady" lay nuns, the nuns affiliated with Uttama Sādhu's hermitage are the only nuns in Sri Lanka who beg for alms; they, along with the monks, go on daily alms tours through Rattanapitiya. This, too, made the lay nuns in Madivala uncomfortable. From their traditional point of view, Theranā and the other nun who live at Uttama Sādhu's hermitage are not *bhikkhunīs*; they, therefore, have no right to assume the robe and bowl of the ancient order.[21]

When I asked Theranā about her ordination, she told me that she shaved her own head and does not have a female preceptor; Uttama Sādhu is her only teacher. She observes no time table, which she claims is "for people in lay life." Instead, she meditates most of the day. Theranā added that she does not "go about shopping in the villages and talking to lay people like the lay nuns; the lay nuns are no different from you [meaning me]."[22]

I also asked Theranā about the monks who live at Sasuna Sänasuma. She told me that the monks are segregated from the nuns: "There is a tall wall which separates our living quarters – it goes right through to the end. We never see the monks, except when we meet in the *bana* hall to recite the *Vinaya* rules. We spend all of our time meditating." To my knowledge, Sasuna Sänasuma is the only monastery in Sri Lanka to house both male and female renunciants. In traditional Theravādin practice, the living quarters of male and female renunciants have been separate from one another. The lay nuns at my primary research site, however, intimated that there is much more going on at Sasuna Sänasuma than meditation. I frequently heard allegations of immorality from lay nuns about their peers throughout the island. The lay nuns' ambiguous status is a powerful source of suspicion for clergy, laity, and the lay nuns themselves.

Like the western lay nuns we met in chapter 8, Uttama Sādhu and his monks and nuns follow the path of meditation, rather than that of service and devotion, which is the path of the majority of Sinhala lay nuns. Yet, like most Sinhala and western lay nuns, Theranā and her teacher hope to attain *nibbāna*. According to Theranā, her entire life is structured to facilitate the attainment of that goal.

CONCLUSIONS

As this study thus far suggests, the Buddha's vision of a two-fold order (*sangha*), or a four-fold community, is not important to many monks in Sri Lanka today; yet it has been important to the laity from time to time, since the late nineteenth century. However, Sri Lankan monks living in America have taken steps to re-establish the order of nuns – to re-establish the four-fold community alleged in the texts – albeit on American soil. Like Uttama Sādhu, their attitudes toward women and renunciation suggest that they believe women are also heir to the monastic tradition; they argue that all Buddhists have the right to enter the *sangha*.[23] The first steps were taken by monks in Los Angeles in 1988, while the second steps were taken in 1989 in West Virginia.

On May 29, 1988, the Venerable Ratanasāra of the Los Angeles Buddhist Vihāra ordained a woman into the *sangha*. With the help of Theravādin monks and Mahāyāna monks and nuns, a woman gained entrance into the Theravādin order for the first time in hundreds and hundreds of years:

In a bold step taken in Los Angeles by Ratanasara and colleagues, Dhammamitta, a Thai woman following the Theravādin Buddhist tradition was ordained in a rite that started her on a one- to two-year path toward ordination as a *bhikkhuni*. The order of fully ordained *bhikkhunis* has been maintained through the centuries in the Mahayana Buddhist countries, ... but in Theravadin circles the practice of ordaining women inexplicably died out several centuries ago. Theravadins, often the conservative traditionalists of Buddhism, have been reluctant to reinstate the order.[24]

In interviews with one of the officiating Sri Lankan monks, the Venerable Walpola Piyānanda, I learned that all the monks who reside at the Los Angeles Buddhist Vihāra share the Venerable Ratanasāra's views. According to a letter written by the Venerable Piyānanda, rallying support for the ordination, his interest in the re-establishment of the order of nuns in part derives from his experiences in the West:

Since the very inception of Buddhism in the U.S.A., American women have taken a keen interest in Buddhism and have been requesting ordination. This issue came up at the World Buddhism Conference held in Ann Arbor, Michigan, last summer, and it became quite obvious that American men support the quest of women for full ordination. Strong criticism is being made against the Theravada form of Buddhism because of the denial of women into the order. Some female devotees have abandoned Theravada temples and joined Mahayana temples and entered the *Bhikkhuni* Order. This number is ever on the rise ... If we are going to continue the spread of Theravada in this country [America], we need to reexamine our position on the ordination of women.[25]

In other words, the monk perceived women to be necessary for the propagation of Theravādin Buddhism in America, much as they have been in Sri Lanka.

To that end, the California based Sri Lankan monks ordained at Vesak, in 1988, a Thai woman lawyer; they were helped by Korean, Vietnamese, and Chinese monastic communities in America. The novitiate asked for the renunciant's precepts and was ceremoniously inducted into the monastic order as a *sāmaṇerī*. After her ordination, the Venerable Ratanasāra remarked on the historical significance of the event:

This is the first time in several hundred years that a woman has been given ordination in Theravāda Buddhism. The Buddha was egalitarian; we should be, too ... No one should have the right to interfere with a woman's right to follow the religious path ... The status of women in Buddhism must be viewed afresh. We find no reason to deny ordination to women, and decided to open the door for the restoration of the *bhikkhuni* order in America.[26]

Citing historical precedence for the inclusion of Mahāyāna monastics at Dhammāmittā's ordination, the Venerable Piyānanda argued that the participation of Mahāyāna nuns – a quorum of nuns is demanded by the *Vinaya* – was justified:

It is believed by some that the Theravada Order of Nuns cannot be re-established because Theravada *Bhikkhunis* no longer exist. However, it is well-known that the *Bhikkhuni* Order was brought to China from Sri Lanka by a *Bhikkhuni* known as Devasara. This Order of *Bhikkhunis* is still alive in China and is also well established in Los Angeles. Also, during the Buddha's time, ordination was just the ordination of *Bhikkhunis* into Buddhism, without any consideration of sectarian issues, such as Theravada or Mahayana. Therefore, I consider it proper to open the door for women to enter the Order in our Theravada tradition in America. What we would be doing is not a new practice, but the restoration of the Sri Lanka *Bhikkhuni* Order through an unbroken line which originated from Sri Lanka.[27]

In short, Sri Lankan monks in Los Angeles argued that by ordaining women, they were contributing to Buddhism's preservation. As we have seen, and as the expatriate monks told me, the texts allege that the Buddha himself envisaged a four-fold community of monks, nuns, laymen, and laywomen. Consequently, they believe that they have done Buddhism a great service by calling upon Chinese nuns – the spiritual descendants of Sri Lankan nuns – to recreate that four-fold community.

A similar spirit motivated the expatriate Sri Lankan monk, the Venerable Gunaratana of the Bhāvanā Society of West Virginia, to ordain an American woman as a novice (*sāmaṇerī*) in July, 1989.[28] Having ordained male novices into the monastic order, the Venerable Gunaratana ordained Misha Cowan, aged thirty-two and a computer operator from Los Angeles. Her reasons for renouncing echo Ayyā Vāyāmā's: "Now called Sāmā, Cowan said in an interview about a week before that she became serious about Buddhism after her fiance was killed in a car accident several years ago … She said that the Buddhist meditation technique *vipassanā* (insight) helped her to deal with her grief."[29] Cowan was ordained in the same fashion as male novices.[30] She continues to live as a novice in the Theravādin tradition.

The steps taken by expatriate Sri Lankan monks in America to restore the order of nuns were both radical and traditional. From their point of view, the ordination of women into the *saṅgha* is in keeping with traditional practice; they claim that by ordaining women, they preserve the Theravādin tradition. Though these monks now live in the United States, they continue to subscribe to the Mahāvaṃsa-view of history. Whether or not more Theravādin women will gain entrance into the monastic order, become *bhikkhunīs*, and establish the quorum needed to ordain women without the aid of the Mahāyāna Buddhist community, remains an open question.

The attitudes of Sri Lankan monks living in America toward women and world-renunciation are not new, as my own study has frequently suggested. In the preceding chapters, I have endeavored to show that Sri Lankan Buddhism has repeatedly accommodated female renunciants during periods of great social change. In such periods of Sri Lankan history, which include the 1890s, the 1930s–40s, and quite arguably, the formative years of Buddhism in Sri Lanka, Buddhists have encouraged women to actively engage in the propagation of Buddhism, by invoking the canon's inclusive attitudes toward women. Among these Buddhists are expatriate Sri Lankan monks in California and Virginia, who echo Dharmapāla and others, and argue that women are indispensable for the future of Buddhism.

Despite these negative views about women and world-renunciation that have appeared throughout the periods under review, Buddhist female renunciants made significant contributions to the spread of Buddhism in Sri Lanka, to its maintenance, and later to its resuscitation. The history of female renunciants in Buddhist Sri Lanka, therefore, confirms Jane Smith's thesis that women "often play vital and significant roles in times of profound religious change, change accompanied by some form of social upheaval."[31] Moreover, as fluctuation of interest in female renunciation attests, "normally these roles are substantially diminshed when the upheaval has ceased and social change is gradual rather than dramatic."[32] Indeed, at the present time, Buddhists no longer encourage the late nineteenth- and early twentieth-century role of the lay nun to revitalize Buddhism. Thus, one critical question remains: what is the future of the tradition of female renunciation in Sri Lanka?

My conclusions are several. Despite subordination, androcentrism, and even misogyny, contemporary Buddhist female renunciants find fulfilment in their renunciation: in the counter-culture that they have been forced to create. Though critical of the contemporary *saṅgha*, lay nuns agree with monks on many issues. First, they agree for the most part that it is impossible to re-establish the order of nuns.

Second, they exalt the role of Sri Lanka as the protector of the *dhamma*. However, they do not share most monks' misogynist views. Unsurprisingly, what most monks believe about women is not what most lay nuns believe about themselves. In my interviews with lay nuns, they always commented on their supposed inferiority and the monks' negative impressions of them. Yet, they have not internalized the idea of their gender as inferior; indeed, they see themselves as equal to monks in all aspects of the monastic vocation. As we saw in chapter 7, lay nuns often argue that their practice is superior to that of the monks.

Generally, lay nuns are not male-defined even though monks tend to set the standard;[33] rather, lay nuns affirm their gender in the roles that they have created for themselves, such as patronizing the order of monks and nurturing children. Society ascribes these roles to the lay nuns, and the lay nuns simultaneously ascribe them for themselves. Moreover, it is significant that the laity refer to lay nuns as "mothers." "Mother" is a common honorific throughout South Asia; the Buddha himself is referred to as "mother."[34] Indeed, despite the laity's lack of enthusiasm in patronizing lay nuns, when compared to the laity's patronage of the *saṅgha*, the laity values the *dasa sil mātāvo*: the Mothers of the Ten Precepts.

Though the roles that the lay nuns play in contemporary Buddhist society may seem subordinate to the roles of monks, the lay nuns believe that they are essential and necessary for the proper maintenance of Buddhism. I speculate that as long as lay nuns find fulfilment in these roles, Buddhist women will continue to renounce the world in Sri Lanka. Moroever, we cannot help but wonder: what "might [the *sangha's*] possibly transformed shape be, when the present generation of more 'orthodox' monk-elders and *mahanayakes* pass away,"[35] and how will this transformation affect the lay nuns' movement? However, lay nuns rarely speculate about these issues. For them, these are no longer relevant matters. They have committed themselves to renunciation and have in most cases turned their attentions toward *nibbāna*.

Epilogue
Women under the Bō tree

In May, 1992, nearly three years after completing my field study, I returned to Sri Lanka for three months. Though I was in Sri Lanka to explore an entirely new dimension of my research,[1] I visited many of the lay nunneries where I had lived in 1988–89.

When I left the island in September, 1989, I thought that fewer women would renounce the world in the years to come, based on the trends since the 1890s that I had documented. Much to my surprise, however, the lay nunneries were far more crowded in 1992 than they were in 1989. In 1992 Lady Blake's had twenty-five lay nuns and three women who were training to don the ochre robe; in 1989 it housed eight lay nuns. The Madivala Upāsikārāmaya in 1992 had fifteen lay nuns; in 1989 there were eight.[2] Kotmalee Dhīrā Sudharmā had died of throat cancer in April, 1991; Dhammāpālī Mäniyo had replaced her as the loku mäniyo.

In addition to the swelling populations in the lay nunneries throughout the island, there was a disturbing increase in the number of homeless lay nuns around the country, especially in the Anurādhapura area. In fact, in 1988–89, little did I know how prophetic the title of my book was: in 1992, I witnessed and interviewed lay nuns who were actually living in the gnarled and tangled roots of Bō trees in and around Anurādhapura. This was in stark contrast to the situation three years earlier; at that time, I noticed only one homeless lay nun in that area.[3]

While in Anurādhapura, I chatted informally with many of the homeless lay nuns who have made sleeping quarters for themselves in innovative ways. One lay nun, whom I shall call Dharmāsīlā,[4] had sewn old robes and rags together to make a three-foot square tarp, under which she slept. She had fastened the tarp to two corners on one side of two very large roots – each roughly four feet in diameter – of a very old and majestic Bō tree. The roots served as the rear of her makeshift lay nunnery. The other two corners had been fastened to two long sticks, each about six feet tall. Dharmāsīlā kept her few belongings at the rear of her shelter, nestled in the tree's roots. As Dharmāsīlā had no privacy in her tree, she used the public toilet facilities located approximately one mile away. Like the other lay nuns who have "squatted" in Anurādhapura, she bathes in the ancient tank adjacent to the sacred precinct of the city.

I asked the approximately forty-five year-old Dharmāsīlā how she ended up in Anurādhapura, living under a Bō tree. She told me that her husband was a drunk and that he used to abuse her. She enrolled her only child in boarding school in Colombo and left her old life behind, including her money. That was about two years before this interview. She had a teacher when she renounced, yet they have not maintained their relationship. Dharmāsīlā does not shave her head; rather, she wears it in a bun. When I asked her why she does not shave her head, she told me that she keeps it long to avoid upsetting her daughter, when she visits her in boarding school in Colombo. Apparently, the daughter has been somewhat traumatized by her mother's renunciation. Dharmāsīlā's hair is thus a concession to her daughter's feelings.

Dharmāsīlā told me that monks often tell her that she has no right to take up residence at the foot of the tree.[5] The lay nuns living in more traditional settings in the Anurādhapura area echoed the monks; they, too, have told her to move. When I asked the lay nuns living at the Saṅghamittā Upāsikārāmaya in Anurādhapura what they thought about the homeless lay nuns, they immediately responded by claiming that such lay nuns bring disrepute to their vocation.[6] They would like to see Dharmāsīlā, and the other lay nuns like her, set up residence elsewhere.

Dharmāsīlā's Bō tree is located across the street from the mound which tradition alleges is the tomb of the *bhikkhunī* who established the nun's lineage in Sri Lanka, Saṅghamittā. Near Dharmāsīlā, yet much closer to the Bō tree, which Saṅghamittā is said to have carried with her from north India, six lay nuns have laid claim to a concrete slab. They store their belongings on one side of the roughly three foot by five foot cement floor that has no ceiling or walls, and thus no privacy; like Dharmāsīlā, they use the public facilities because they, too, are unsecluded. One of the six, whom I shall call Prajāpatī, is the *loku mäniyo*; she is in her sixties, while the others range in age from thirty-five to seventy. They have a small kerosene stove upon which they cook and make tea; they also have tins of rice and lentils. I asked them what they do when it rains. Prajāpatī informed me that they run to the small, enclosed Buddha shrine nearby and wait for the inclement weather to pass. While I was talking to Prajāpatī and the lay nuns that share her slab, a young man who oversees the comings and goings of people to and from Prajāpatī's concrete slab began to interrogate me. He told me that he protects the lay nuns from "bad men;" he helps them when they need help.

I inquired from Prajāpatī why she and her pupils do not enter a lay nunnery. She replied that many lay nunneries require entrants to "donate" one thousand or more *rupees*;[7] as they have very little money, she has no hope of finding permanent residence in an *upāsikārāmaya*. Like Dharmāsīlā, Prajāpatī told me that monks have ordered them to leave the area, and have claimed that lay nuns have no right to appropriate pieces of land randomly. She counters that monks have no right to tell them what to do. "We meditate; we are good Buddhists," she remarked. "We are like Saṅghamittā."

The Bō tree, because it is associated with Saṅghamittā, has perhaps always attracted renunciant women. During my visit to Anurādhapura in 1992, I spoke to many of the lay nuns who were meditating under the Bō tree. Some of them had come from the southern-most regions of the island and had no money to make the return trip; others had arrived, thinking that they would find their way back, yet decided to stay in Anurādhapura to meditate and perform *pūjās* under the Bō tree. They, too, have found makeshift living quarters near the Bō tree. I counted eighteen homeless lay nuns living in the sacred compound of Anurādhapura.

What accounts for the increased numbers of women in robes in the early nineties? From what I can tell, there are two reasons. First of all, former President Premadasa, who was in office from 1989 until his assassination in May, 1993, supported the lay nuns in a way that his predecessor, President Jayewardene, does not. We have seen that before Jayewardene became president, he helped in the 1940s to establish the VMD Upāsikārāmaya. However, as President of Sri Lanka, he did not call upon lay nuns to perform *pūjās* at official functions as did Premadasa. In fact, Buddhists criticized Jayewardene precisely because he did not legitimate his presidency with Buddhist symbols. Conversely, both monks and lay nuns were highly visible in most of Premadasa's official *pūjās* and, as we have seen, he even sought the counsel of at least one lay nun, Uttarā Mäniyo. With his rural roots and low-caste affiliations, Premadasa appealed to many lay nuns, who in turn received his support. In short, he glorified their role and made them visible symbols of Sri Lankan Buddhism. Nontheless, even though more women entered lay nunneries during his presidency, the families of women who renounce still resist their daughter's and sister's wishes to don the ochre robe. Yet, the Buddhist fundamentalism that Premadasa helped architect from the day he became president might still change prevailing attitudes about women and world-renunciation.

The second reason for the increased number of women in robes has to do with ethnic violence, and the world-wide recession. Both have created massive unemployment and social upheaval in Sri Lanka, making the prospects of many quite grim. Several of the lay nuns I interviewed in Anurādhapura told me that their husbands had lost their jobs and had begun to drink heavily as a result of the island's problems. It was during such difficult times that eight of the twelve lay nuns I interviewed in Anurādhapura in 1992 had renounced the world. Of the remaining four, two were widows and the other two had never married. The vocation of the lay nun thus serves as a safety-valve for many women who have been adversely affected by the present condition of the island's economy and social strife. They said that, in spite of the hardships they face, they prefer the life they now lead to their lives as laywomen. "It is all *dukkha*," one lay nun added.

While the Ministry of Buddhist Affairs would like to prohibit women who have not been properly trained under the tutelage of a recognized *loku mäniyo*[8] from donning the robes, many women, as the homeless lay nuns in Anurādhapura suggest, are completely free from the Ministry's control. They do not seem to mind living exposed to the elements, though each one pointed out how difficult her life is. Moreover, they remain unconvinced by monks who urge them to leave the area. In defiance of monks, other lay nuns, and the Ministry of Buddhist Affairs, these women plan to remain living under the Bō trees of Anurādhapura.

The life of Dhammāwatī Hewavitarane Sil Mātāvo

I have included here the translation of a published account of the life of Dhammāwatī Hewavitarane:[1]

GOOD WISHES ON HER BIRTHDAY
HITHTHATIYA DHAMMĀWATĪ HEWAVITARANE SIL MĀTĀVA

We bestow our respectable gratitude upon Dhammāwatī Hewavitarane Sil Mātā of the Srī Rahula Mātā Ārāmaya situated in Grandpass, Colombo 14, founder of the Helen Ranawake Ārāmaya of Kottawa, Pannipitiya, and founder member of Dhammāwatī Hewavitarane Home for aged lay nuns, who is celebrating her seventy-fifth birthday and sixty-fifth year of observing *sil*.

In 1906, on December 20, the head of our lay nunnery, Rosalin Hewavitarane, was born. Her father and mother were Don Charles Hewavitarane and Glisa Hamy Hewavitarane, respectively. In 1916, Miss Hewavitarane left her parents and observed *sil* under the guidance of Saddhammācārī Sīlavatī at the Srī Rahula Mātā Ārāmaya. From that day onwards, she learned the religion, devoting her life to pious activities and attending to her aged teacher. When her teacher passed away, she took over as the head lay nun of the Srī Rahula Mātā Ārāmaya and continued to render great service to the Buddhist religion. We would like to put into writing a little of the great service done by her:

(1) For the welfare of the ladies of the Colombo area, a "Kulangana Samitiya" was formed to help in wedding and funeral expenses.
(2) Publishing of Srī Rahula Mātā Magazine once every three months.
(3) Organizing and running of the lay nunnery for over 20 years.
(4) Conducting the Srī Yāśodārā Dānasāla[2] in front of the Lankārāma at Anurādhapura for 12 years.

(5) Building a hall for the Jetavanārāmaya at Anurādhapura and erecting a statue of Maitri Buddha in this temple.

(6) Offering alms for monks during the Sambuddha Jayanti Festival.

(7) Offering alms to about 15,000 monks who were involved in the placing of the pinnacle for the Ruwanavelisaya.

(8) Fixing two pipe lines and a motor to the Lankārāma temple at Anurādhapura and offering alms with presents to 100 Buddhist monks to honor the occasion.

(9) Helping the orphans and all those who came for help, as much as possible.

(10) Helping the temples around our lay nunnery in their *kaṭhina*[3] offerings and other religious activities, as much as possible.

(11) She has ordained a large number of lay nuns.

(12) Chief Justice and Mrs. Ranawake offered her the residence at Rukmale Road, Pannipitiya, for the use of lay nuns in 1961.

(13) In 1962, a foundation stone was laid for building the Helen Ranawake Ārāmaya.

(14) She planted a Bō tree there in 1965.

(15) For the first time in the history of the island, she formed an all island *sil mātāvo* association.

(16) In 1969, she laid a foundation stone to build a home for the aged lay nuns.

(17) In 1970, the All Island Sil Mātāvo organization conducted its first and second anniversary at the Kettārāmaya, Colombo 14.

(18) She opened the Ranawake Ārāmaya and organized a 33 hour *bana* preaching and distributed alms to more than 75 monks.

(19) In 1974, she handed over the home for aged lay nuns to the social services department.

(20) In 1979, on December 12, Mrs. N. Fernando and Mrs. M. Perera who reside in England paid all the expenses of Hewavitarane Mäniyo to go on a pilgrimage to India and worship at the holy Buddhist shrines there. Two lay nuns went with her, Walpola Sumanawatī and Nikaweratiya Dhammikā Ñānasirī.[4] We took off from the Katunayake airport with the guidance of the Dharmaduta Society of the Maradana Srī Lanka Vidyālaya. We reached Buddha Gaya on December 20 and spent time doing religious activities like giving alms, observing *sil*, meditating, offering *gilānpāsa* to Lord Buddha, and making offerings to the sacred Bō tree. Then we started our

pilgrimage and worshipped in Lumbini, Kusinara, Banaras and a number of other sacred places. We reached Sri Lanka on January 16 after spending one month, touring and acquiring merit.

We wish happiness, good health, and long life to Hewavitarane Mäniyo on her seventy-fifth birthday and the sixty-fifth anniversary of her ordination as a lay nun; we hope that she continues her activities and furthers the Buddhist religion. Though she was born in a respectable, educated family,[5] she left all of them during her childhood and dedicated her whole life to the Buddhist religion in order to observe *sil* in solitude.[6]

May you be blessed with good health and attain *nibbāna*, banishing the sorrows of life with the merit your have obtained since renouncing the world, with the help of the residential and scholarly lay nuns, Buddhist and non-Buddhist villagers and other Sri Lankans, over the past sixty-five years.

The life of Sil Mātā Wadduwa Dhammācārī

THE BIOGRAPHY OF THE VENERABLE SIL MĀTĀ WADDUWA
DHAMMĀCĀRĪ
MEDITATION CENTER OF GALTHUDA, PELAWATTE,
PĀNADURA[1]

Dhammācārī Sil Mātā was born in 1922, on May 13 to K. H. Perera and the former Miss A. P. Athauda. Her family consisted of ten members; she had six brothers and three sisters. Unlike her siblings, she was very attracted to the religious activities of her father who was very pious.

On her fifteenth birthday, she got permission from her father to become ordained and from that day onwards, she began to improve her education by learning from her father, who was well-versed in Sinhala and Buddhism.[2] According to her father's advice, she maintained the five precepts most of the time, and the eight precepts on *pōya* days.

Her father passed away in 1945, on May 5, and she realized that the whole world is filled with sorrow. Under the advice of her father, she began to search for a suitable teacher and to maintain the ten precepts.

In 1957, she attended meditation lessons of Burmese monks and realized that she could not remain as a laywoman any longer. She therefore decided to help the orphans in the Biyagama Children's Home and worked there for a short period.[3] There, in 1958 with the backing of the lay nun, Vajirā Mäniyo, she was able to fulfil her wishes. She had the opportunity to improve her religious knowledge through the Buddhist books sent to her by a German Buddhist monk, the Venerable Ñānaponika.

In 1962, when her mother passed away, she gave up all the worldly activities and spent her time engaged in meditation. In 1978, she was ordained and became the second pupil of Nawala Dhammikā Mäniyo of Anurādhapura.

In 1980, she founed the Pānadura Vipassanā Meditation Society and in 1983 a Bō tree was planted there. Afterwards, she built a small meditation hut. One aim of Dhammācārī Mäniyo is to devote her life fully to Buddhism. She has no wish to do worldly things. If someone helps her to complete the meditation center, she will be able to impart to the world the knowledge of the doctrine that she has learned.[4]

The life of Sārāwatī Sil Mātā[1]

In the ancient kingdom of Dambadeniya, there was a place called Dambadeni Rock, where Sinhala royal princes hid themselves from enemies. There is an ancient village called Athuruwela (earlier, Hathuruwela) which is situated in the Western Province in a place called Dambadeni Udukaha.[2] There lived a coupled named Kalawitagoda Pathirannahalage Kirinelis Appuhamy and W. Punchinona whose loving daughter was born in 1922, on February 5. She was named Kalawita Pathirannahalage Lilinona. She was brought up by her parents and was educated up to the sixth standard along with her elder sister, Somawati. They attended Paranagama Vidyalaya. These two sisters spent time organizing religious activities in the village temple, giving assistance to the people who observed *sil* on *pōya* days, and taking part in Bodhi Pūjā. Both came to listen to *bana* preachings frequently. They jointly took part in *kaṭhina* offerings. The sister who was close to her like a shadow became ill and passed away. From then onwards, the pious child Lilinona found it difficult to take part in religious activities alone. The untimely death of her sister was of great sorrow to her. So the child Lilinona decided to become a Buddhist nun even though her parents objected.[3] However, she finally received permission from her parents.[4]

Lilinona went to Anurādhapura, where she began to reside at the Mallikārāmaya. While there, she was greatly influenced by some Burmese lay nuns who had taken up residence in Anurādhapura. One of their pupils was Sumanāwatī, who shaved Lilinona's head and gave her the robes. A Burmese monk gave her the eight precepts and the name Sārāwatī. According to her father's wishes, Sārāwatī went to the Madagampola Upāsikārāmaya at Alawwa. Later, her relations and devotees built an *upāsikārāmaya* at Hunupola, Kurunegala, and she went to live there during this period. She eventually returned to Anurādhapura, after a devotee named Walidu Upāsikā built a lay nunnery for her with facilities like a well, a lavatory, etc.

In 1966, she began to make improvements on the lay nunnery. She had a shrine room built and later established a Sunday School for the Tissawewa area of Anurādhapura. In 1974, with the permission of the chief incumbent of the Srī Mahā Bodhi Tree, she planted a sapling of the Bō tree on her compound and celebrated with a *dānaya* to the monks.[5]

Since returning to Anurādhapura, she has continued to build places for lay nuns to meditate and live, while offering alms to the Buddha, and seeing to the well-being of other lay nuns. Today is her sixty-eighth birthday. To commemorate the great service she has done for Buddhism over the past fifty years, today there is an alms giving for fifty monks and eighteen lay nuns. With all this merit, may she have good health and long life while invoking the blessings of the Triple Gem to serve the people. I conclude this small book dedicated to the services done by her.[6]

Notes

INTRODUCTION: THE TRADITION OF BUDDHIST FEMALE
RENUNCIATION IN SRI LANKA

1 This is the stock phrase for renunciation in the Pāli texts. I will refer to both lay and ordained women who have renounced the world as "world-renouncers," "world-renunciants," or simply "renunciants." Those who do not renounce remain "in-the-world."

2 R. A. L. H. Gunawardena has argued that women's contribution to the spread of Buddhism in Sri Lanka was significant. According to Gunawardena, inscriptions dating between the third and the first centuries, BCE, allege that women supported Buddhism in many ways during its formative years in Sri Lanka. In fact, according to Gunawardena, twenty-one of the fifty-eight inscriptions discovered at Mahintale, while fourteen of the twenty uncovered at Kottadamuhela, record donations made by women. That women patronized Buddhism in Mahintale, as well in Kottadamuhela, testifies that they were also instrumental in the expansion of Buddhism throughout the northern and southernmost areas of Sri Lanka. The fourth century *Dīpavaṃsa* and the fifth century *Mahāvaṃsa* also allege that women played significant roles in the spread of Buddhism. Among the women who supported the new religion were *bhikkhunīs*, attesting that both nuns and laywomen played important roles in the early history of Buddhism in Sri Lanka. For more on women's patronage of Buddhism in Sri Lanka, see R. A. L. H. Gunawardena's insightful "Subtile Silks of Ferreous Firmness: Buddhist Nuns in Ancient and Early Medieval Sri Lanka and Their Role in the Propagation of Buddhism," *The Sri Lankan Journal of the Humanities*, 14, nos. 1 and 2 (1988), 1–59.

3 See *The Dīpavaṃsa*. Trans. Hermann Oldenberg (New Delhi: Asia Educational Services, 1982), pp. 205–207; for the Pāli text, see pp. 98–99. For more on *The Dīpavaṃsa* and its importance to this study, see chapter 1. The *Dīpavaṃsa* is a post-canonical work.

4 *The Mahāvaṃsa*. Trans. Wilhelm Geiger (Colombo: Government Press, 1986), p. 197. The *Mahāvaṃsa* is a post-canonical work.

5 See *The Mahāvaṃsa*. Trans. Geiger, pp. 243–245. It might be argued that

the term *bhikkhu*, or monk, is used generically in the texts as the monastic recipients of alms. Yet the *Mahāvaṃsa* makes explicit in several places that monks *and* nuns received gifts. For instance, both nuns and monks are mentioned in an example of one king's benificence: "... the ruler of the earth ... appointed great almsgiving to the brotherhood of *bhikkhus*. He bestowed clothing on thirty thousand *bhikkhus* and the same on twelve thousand *bhikkhunīs*," p. 238.

6 Gunawardena, "Subtile Silks," 1–17.
7 The Theravāda Buddhist texts, for the most part, are preserved in Pāli, while most Mahāyāna Buddhist texts are preserved in Sanskrit.
8 Leon M. Feer, ed., *Samyutta Nikāya*, vol. 1 (London: Routledge and Kegan Paul Ltd., 1973), p. 33. Unless otherwise stated, all translations in this work are mine.
9 That is, *nibbāna*.
10 E. Hardy, ed., *Anguttara Nikāya*, vol. 3 (London: Luzac and Company, Ltd., 1958), pp. 67–68. Māra is the Buddhist personification of evil.
11 Allan Sponberg, "Attitudes toward Women and the Feminine in Early Buddhism," in Jose Ignacio Cabezon, ed., *Buddhism, Sexuality, and Gender* (New York: State University of New York Press, 1992), pp. 3–4.
12 Ibid., p. 8.
13 Ibid., p. 18.
14 Ibid., p. 20.
15 Ibid., p. 25. Though soteriological androgyny is a later development (after the sixth or seventh century, CE), it is important from the point of view of this study.
16 Like "renounce the world," this is another traditional description in the texts of the renunciation of lay identity.
17 For a similar explanation of women, renunciation and the reproduction of believers, see Josephine Reynell, "Women and the Reproduction of the Jain Community," in Michael Carrithers and Caroline Humphrey, eds., *The Assembly of Listeners: Jains in Society* (Cambridge University Press, 1991), pp. 41–65.
18 According to the *Vinaya*, the Buddha praised Visākhā for nurturing the order of monks; she was held up as an exemplar for all: "She who is very much delighted and endowed with virtue, gives to a disciple of the Buddha, overcoming selfishness her gift is heavenly and without grief, filled with happiness. She gains a long, heavenly life, due to her meritorious ways. She is at ease and healthy, and will delight for a long time with the gods in heaven." For the Pāli text, see Hermann Oldenberg, ed., *Vinaya Piṭakam*, vol. 1 (London: Luzac and Company, Ltd., 1964), p. 294.
19 According to the "Mahāparinibbāna Suttanta," the Buddha proclaimed to Māra that he would not die "until the monks and nuns, and the male lay disciples and the female lay disciples, having themselves learned the doctrine, teach it." In other words, the Buddha envisioned

a four-fold community. For the complete Pāli text, see T. W. Rhys Davids and J. Estlin Carpenter, eds., *The Dīgha Nikāya*, vol. 2 (London: Luzac and Company Ltd., 1966), pp. 112–114.

20 See especially Richard Gombrich and Gananath Obeyesekere, *Buddhism Transformed: Religious Change in Sri Lanka* (Princeton University Press, 1988), and Stanley Jeyaraja Tambiah, *Buddhism Betrayed?: Religion, Politics, and Violence in Sri Lanka* (University of Chicago Press, 1992).

21 Gombrich and Obeyesekere, *Buddhism Transformed*, p. 7. Though the concept of Protestant Buddhism has come under fire, it is a useful tool for understanding the changes that took place in Buddhism in late nineteenth-century Sri Lanka. For a critique of the concept, see H. L. Seneviratne's review of *Buddhism Transformed* in *Journal of Ritual Studies*, 4/2 (Summer 1990), 398–402.

22 For more on the lay meditation movement in Sri Lanka, see George Bond, *The Buddhist Revival in Sri Lanka: Religious Tradition, Reinterpretation and Response* (Columbia: University of South Carolina Press, 1988), pp. 76–241.

23 Estimates differ as to the number of female renunciants in Sri Lanka. According to the Ministry of Buddhist Affairs' most recent statistics, in 1989 there were 1,260. This figure is based on the number of questionnaires returned, which the Ministry of Buddhist Affairs had sent to all registered cloisters. The All Ceylon Buddhist Congress (ACBC) estimates that there are roughly 5,000 female renunciants in Sri Lanka. Interviews with the Ministry and the ACBC were conducted on November 28, 1989, and January 30, 1989, respectively. The population of Sri Lanka is approximately eighteen million.

24 As many of the nineteenth-century sources I have consulted refer to the island as Ceylon, I have followed that usage when necessary to maintain consistency.

25 For more on this period of experimentation, see Bond, *The Buddhist Revival in Sri Lanka*, throughout.

26 Michael Carrithers, *The Forest Monks of Sri Lanka: An Anthropological and Historical Study* (Delhi: Oxford University Press, 1983).

27 That is, since the demise of the order of nuns in the eleventh century. For more on the demise, see chapter 1 of this study.

28 For more on the Countess and her contribution to the spread of Buddhism in America, see Thomas Tweed, *The American Encounter with Buddhism* (Bloomington: Indiana University Press, 1992).

29 The Mahā Bodhi Society (MBS) of Colombo houses Dharmapāla's diaries. Much of the material in chapters 3 and 4 is based on those diaries, passages of which have been published in the *Journal of the Mahābodhi Society*.

30 For instance, Richard Gombrich and Gananath Obeyesekere in their fascinating book on the contemporary scene in Sri Lanka speculate that renewed interest in female renunciation is an import from Burma. See Gombrich and Obeyesekere, *Buddhism Transformed*, p. 276.

31 Richard Gombrich, *Theravada Buddhism: A Social History from Ancient Benares to Modern Colombo* (London: Routledge and Kegan Paul, 1988), p. 17.

32 Tradition alleges that Buddhism and the monks' and nuns' lineages were introduced to Sri Lanka in the third century, BCE.

33 In Buddhist Studies, men have been viewed for the most part as the true representatives of their societies, while women's lives emerge only in reference to men. For instance, in his classic study of Buddhism in Sri Lanka, Walpola Rahula relegates to a footnote in his opus the contribution of Bhikkhunī Saṅghamittā, alleged to have established the order of nuns in Sri Lanka. After describing in full Saṅghamittā's brother's contribution to ancient Sri Lankan society, Rahula states that "Saṅghamittā's influence over the women of Ceylon in moulding their life and character was equally great." See, *The History of Buddhism in Ceylon* (Colombo: M. D. Gunasena, 1966), p. 60. Because the monastic experience of women in Buddhist Sri Lanka is glossed over, the uninformed reader is left with the distorted impression that the religious virtuoso in early Sri Lankan Buddhism was always male. In Walpola's study, nuns are implicitly defined as insignificant.

34 I. B. Horner, *Women Under Primitive Buddhism*, 2nd edn. (Delhi: Motilal Banarsidass, 1975).

35 See Mabel Bode, "The Women Leaders of the Buddhist Reformation," in *Transactions of the 9th International Congress of Orientalists* (London: n.p., 1892), pp. 341–343. The *Manoratha Pūraṇī* is Buddhagosa's (fifth century, CE) commentary on the *Anguttara Nikāya*; and Caroline A. Foley, "The Women Leaders of the Buddhist Reformation," in Ibid., pp. 344–361. The *Paramattha Dipānī* is Dhammapāla's (sixth century, CE) translation of Buddhaghosa's commentary on the *Udāna*, the *Vimāna Vatthu*, the *Peta Vatthu*, the *Theragāthā* and the *Therīgāthā*.

36 D. N. Bhagavat, *Early Buddhist Jurisprudence* (Poona: Oriental Book Agency, 1939). See in particular "Women Under the Vinaya," pp. 158–190.

37 Meena V. Talim, "Buddhist Nuns and Disciplinary Rules," *Journal of the University of Bombay*, 34, no. 2 (September 1965), 98–137.

38 Other writers who have focused upon the tradition of Buddhist female renunciation include Jothiya Dhirasekera, "Women and the Religious Order of the Buddha," *Journal of the Mahābodhi Society*, 75, nos. 5–6, (May–June 1967), 156–171. See also Dhirasekera's *Buddhist Monastic Discipline* (Colombo: M. D. Gunasena, 1982), which contains a chapter on "Women and the Religious Life of the Order;" Amarasiri D. Weeraratne, "The *Bhikkhunī* Order in Ceylon," *Journal of the Mahābodhi Society*, 78, nos. 10–11 (October–November 1970), 333–337; Arvind Sharma, "How and Why did the Women in Ancient India Become Buddhist Nuns?" *Sociological Analysis*, 38–39 (Spring 1977–Winter 1978), 239–251; Nancy Auer Falk, "The Case of the Vanishing Nuns: The Fruits of Ambivalence in Ancient Buddhism," in Nancy Auer Falk

and Rita Gross, eds., *Unspoken Worlds: Women's Religious Lives in Non-western Cultures* (New York: Harper and Row, 1980), pp. 206–224; Diana Paul, *Women in Buddhism* (Berkeley: University of California Press, 1979); Paula Richman, *Women, Branch Stories, and Religious Rhetoric in a Tamil Buddhist Text* (Syracuse: Foreign and Comparative Studies Publications, 1988). See also Richman's "The Portrayal of a Female Renouncer in a Tamil Buddhist Text," in Caroline Walker Bynum, Stevan Harrell, and Paula Richman, eds., *Gender and Religion: On the Complexity of Symbols* (Boston: Beacon Press, 1986), pp. 143–165; and Sulak Sivaraksa, "Buddhist Women: Past and Present," *Kahawai: Journal of Women and Zen*, 1, no. 3 (Summer 1979), 3–11. Sivaraksa's study provides a bridge between the ancient and contemporary traditions of the female renunciant in Buddhist South Asia. Also of importance is Patrick G. Henry and Donald K. Swearer, *For the Sake of the World: The Spirit of Buddhist and Christian Monasticism* (Minneapolis: Fortress Press, 1989), pp. 113–121. Henry and Swearer provide a brief account of the ancient Buddhist order of nuns and suggest that the female, as well as the male, can be exemplars of Buddhist monasticism. In addition are studies that have incorporated field experiences in Sri Lanka into their analysis of the female renunciant in Buddhism. Most notable among these are by Lowell Bloss, "The Female Renunciants of Sri Lanka: The *Dasasilmattawa*," *The Journal of the International Association of Buddhist Studies*, 10, no. 1 (1987), 7–32; and Elizabeth Nissan, "Recovering Practice: Buddhist Nuns in Sri Lanka," *South Asia Research*, 4, no. 1 (May 1984), 32–49. Nissan's is an excellent, ground-breaking study of the contemporary tradition of female renunciants in Sri Lanka. See in addition Gombrich and Obeyesekere, *Buddhism Transformed*, especially chapter 8, "The Contemporary Resurgence of Nuns," for an interesting perspective on the rise of the "nun" in the modern period. See also Nirmala S. Salgado, "Custom and Tradition in Buddhist Society: A Look at Some *Dasa Sil Matas* from Sri Lanka in Relation to the Concept of Women in Buddhism" (Colombo: International Institute for Ethnic Studies, n.d.), cyclostyled; and K. M. Lilly Thamel, "A Study of the *Dasa Sil Mata* in the Buddhist Society of Sri Lanka" (Colombo: International Institute of Ethnic Studies, n.d.), cyclostyled. See also Thamel's "The Religious Woman in A Buddhist Society: The Case of the Dasa-Sil Maniyo in Sri Lanka," Dialogue (Colombo), vol. 11, nos. 1–3 (1984), 53–68. Also noteworthy is Kusuma Devendra, "The *Dasa Sil Matavo* of Sri Lanka" M. A. thesis, Sri Jayewardene Pura University, Sri Lanka (1986). Devendra served as Bloss's field assistant while he conducted research in Sri Lanka in 1983. See also my "The Female Mendicant in Buddhist Sri Lanka," in Cabezon, ed. pp. 37–61. For an insightful study of Buddhism and gender, see Rita M. Gross, *Buddhism After Patriarchy: A Feminist History, Analysis, and Reconstruction of Budddhism* (Albany: State University of New York Press, 1993).

39 Mi Mi Khaing, *The World of Burmese Women* (London: Zed Books Limited, 1984).

40 Chatsumarn Kabilsingh, *Thai Women in Buddhism* (Berkeley: Parallax Press, 1991).

41 Susan Murcott, *The First Buddhist Women* (Berkeley: Parallax Press, 1991).

42 Mohan Wijayaratna, *Les Moniales bouddhistes, naissance et developpement du monachisme feminin* (Paris: Editions du Cerf, 1991).

43 As the contributors to Jonathan Spencer's anthology on ethnic strife in Sri Lanka warn us, this "sacred mission" ideology is in part a post-independence construction. See Jonathan Spencer, ed., *Sri Lanka: History and the Roots of Conflict* (London: Routledge and Kegan Paul, 1990).

44 Whether or not their perceptions are historically accurate is outside the scope of this study. The point that I wish to make here, and that I develop later in this study, is that the attitude of contemporary Buddhists in Sri Lanka to the tradition of female renunciation is in large part shaped by this view.

45 The *Dīpavaṃsa* claims that "twenty thousand *bhikkhunīs*" were able to assemble in one place. Though this number does not inspire confidence, it suggests that many women renounced lay life. See *The Dīpavaṃsa*. Trans. Oldenberg, p. 205.

46 H. L. Seneviratne, "Identity and the Conflation of Past and Present," in H. L. Seneviratne, ed., *Identity, Consciousness, and the Past* (University of Adelaide Press, 1989), p. 5.

47 Ibid., pp. 5–6.

48 The *Vinaya* rules governing ordination require a quorum of nuns and monks to initiate a female into the *saṅgha*: "When a *Bhikkhunī*, as novice, has been trained for two years ... she is to ask leave for *upasampadā* [higher initiation] from both *saṅghas*." *Vinaya Texts: Sacred Books of the East*, part 3. Trans. T. W. Rhys Davids and Hermann Oldenberg (Delhi: Motilal Banarsidass, 1984), p. 324. According to the texts, the Buddha required that at least ten *saṅgha* members (of both the nuns' and monks' communities) officiate at an initiation for women: "I allow, oh monks, that you should ordain by a group of ten, or by a group exceeding ten, or by a crowd." For the Pāli text of this rule, see Hermann Oldenberg, ed., *Vinaya Piṭakam*, vol. 1 (London: Luzac and Company, Ltd., 1964), p. 58 (1.30.2). For the Pāli text of the ordination procedure for nuns, see Hermann Oldenberg, ed., *Vinaya Piṭakam*, vol. 2 (London: Luzac and Company, Ltd., 1964), pp. 271–274.

49 According to Kabilsingh, there never was a *bhikkhunī saṅgha* in Thailand. For more on women and world-renunciation in Thailand, see Kabilsingh, *Thai Women in Buddhism*.

50 See Khaing, *The World of Burmese Women*, p. 78.

51 In the "Mahāparinibbāna Suttanta" (see Rhys Davids and Carpenter, eds., *Dīgha Nikāya*, vol. 2, p. 154) and the monastic code (see Oldenberg,

ed., *Vinaya Piṭakam*, vol. 2, p. 287), another view is endorsed. In the former, the Buddha says to Ānanda: "Ānanda, after my death, the *saṅgha*, if it wishes, can change the minor rules;" according to the *Vinaya*, however, the elders who participated at the First Buddhist Council were not able to decide which among the rules were minor. When asked what rules the Buddha permitted to be changed, Ānanda said "I did not ask the Buddha, 'which rules are minor rules?'" Nonetheless, there are a plethora of "rules" that the contemporary monks of Sri Lanka observe that are not a manner of canonical law. For instance, only a monk can sit on the same level as a monk. In addition, the contemporary controversy over how the robe should be worn was not forseen by the *Vinaya*. Moreover, there are accepted practices that are clearly in violation of the *Vinaya*. For example "though monks were not expected to practice medicine," many monks are renowned in Sri Lanka today for their curative abilities. For more on the evolution of these monastic "rules," see Rahula, *The History of Buddhism in Ceylon*, pp. 156–172. Perhaps the most striking change has been the introduction of fraternities determined by caste-affiliation.

52 I do not mean to suggest that all monks in Sri Lanka are conservative. One does not have to look too far back in history to see that there have been many monks, such as those who are the focus of Carrither's 1983 work, or Uttama Sādhu, whom we meet in chapter 9 of this study, or monks involved in the revolutionary JVP, whose responses to social change cannot be deemed conservative.

53 For exceptions, see my discussion of the cave-dwelling renunciants in Part II below.

54 Lawrence C. Watson and Maria-Barbara Watson-Franke offer a model for interpreting life history called the ideal self, "which consists of a series of interrelated statements about the bases, structure, and functional implications of self-appraisal." In other words, the informant appraises his or her own life via normative statements about *ideal* behavior in the community. This is the approach I have taken in this work; in Part II below, the female renunciants I interviewed appraise their own behavior *vis-à-vis* other renunciants in their tradition. For more on the ideal-self approach to understanding biography, see Lawrence C. Watson and Maria-Barbara Watson-Franke, eds., *Interpreting Life Histories: An Anthropological Inquiry* (New Brunswick, New Jersey: Rutgers University Press, 1985), especially pp. 161–188.

I THE ANCIENT ORDER OF NUNS IN SRI LANKA

1 The *Cūlavaṃsa* is an ongoing continuation of the *Mahāvaṃsa*.

2 See Oldenberg, ed., *The Dīpavaṃsa*, pp. 62–113 for the Pāli text of the saga of the inception of Buddhism in Sri Lanka; for the translation, see pp. 167–221. See also *The Mahāvaṃsa*. Trans. Geiger, pp. 51–61.

3 It records that nuns came from Rohana to Anurādhapura. See *The Dīpavaṃsa*. Trans. Oldenberg, p. 205.

4 Ibid., p. 209: "Having heard the well spoken speech of the *Bhikkhunīs*, which had been delivered..., the royal lord gave to the *Bhikkhunīs* whatever they desired."

5 Gunawardena, "Subtile Silks," 15.

6 For instance, Hugh Neville, drawing attention to the unique consequence given to the nun, states that "It can scarcely be a record of the Theravāda fraternity of the Mahāvihāra... It certainly is not a record of the Dhammaruci sect of the Abhayagiri community... But it dilates on a third society, the community of Theravādin nuns. It would seem that Mahānama was jealous of their fame..."(Hugh Neville quoted in G. P. Malalasekera, *The Pāli Literature of Ceylon* [Colombo: M. D. Gunasena, 1928], p. 136.) Though the renowned Pāli scholar, G. P. Malalasekera, pointed out errors in Neville's emphatic suggestion that the order of nuns, rather than the order of monks, was responsible for the *Dīpavaṃsa*, he was nonetheless swayed by him. Malalasekera wrote that "This suggestion about the authorship of the *Dīpavaṃsa* is very ingenious and deserves careful consideration. I am not aware of its being published anywhere yet, and hence I have quoted it in full... There are certain minor points – which do not affect the main argument at all – in Neville's statements which are not strictly correct..." (Malalasekera, *The Pāli Literature of Ceylon*, p. 137). Though the issue cannot be resolved here, the *Dīpavaṃsa* remains one of the most valuable resources for gaining an insight into the lives of the ancient nuns of Sri Lanka.

7 Oldenberg, ed., *The Dīpavaṃsa*, p. 68.

8 According to the *Vinaya*, an order of monks and an order of nuns are needed to ordain a female into the *saṅgha*. In contrast, the *Vinaya* only requires an order of monks at the ordination of a male into the monastic community.

9 Oldenberg, ed., *The Dīpavaṃsa*, p. 84.

10 Ibid., p. 85. For a description of the precepts, see the Introduction to this study.

11 Geiger, ed., *The Mahāvaṃsa*, p. 141. A *vihāra* is a monastery.

12 The *Dīpavaṃsa* suggests that five hundred women followed Anulā, while the *Mahāvaṃsa* suggests that one thousand emulated her. It is likely that both numbers are entirely symbolic; in other words, the message of the texts is that many women renounced lay life in the early period.

13 The fully ordained nun is to abide by the ten precepts as well as 311 *Vinaya* rules. Prior to her ordination the novice nun is to abide by the ten precepts. The chronicles thus allege that Anulā and the other women kept the precepts of the novice nun.

14 They remained in this liminal period for six months. The *Mahāvaṃsa* alleges that the branch of the sacred Bō tree arrived in December and that the Upāsikāvihāra was built in June.

15 For more on liminality, see Victor Turner, "The Center Out There: Pilgrim's Goal," *History of Religions*, 12, no. 3 (February 1973), 191–230.

16 These fascinating figures are the subject of chapter 2.

17 Oldenberg, ed., *The Dīpavaṃsa*, p. 88.

18 That is, worship.

19 Geiger, ed., *The Mahāvaṃsa*, p. 163.

20 China and Sri Lanka shared a relationship which seems to have begun in 97, CE, when the king sent an embassy to China "bearing presents of ivory, water buffaloes and humped oxen." This friendship continued well into the fifth century and beyond. According to the references, there were at least five formal exchanges between the king of Sri Lanka and the emperor of China prior to the arrival of Sri Lankan nuns in China. It is conceivable, therefore, that their reputation preceeded their arrival in China. See John M. Senaveratne, "Some Notes on the Chinese References," *The Journal of the Royal Asiatic Society* (Ceylon Branch), 24, no. 68 (1915–1916), 106–111, for a detailed summary of cultural exchange between Sri Lanka and China.

21 The transliterated Chinese title is *Pi-chiu-ni-chuan*; it was compiled by Pao Chang in 526, CE.

22 W. Pachow, "Ancient Cultural Relations between Ceylon and China," *University of Ceylon Review*, 7, no. 3 (July 1954), 183.

23 As we have seen, ten nuns are needed to confer *upasampadā*, the higher ordination. The Chinese sources suggest that at least nineteen nuns were involved in the mission to China. See Pachow, "Ancient Cultural Relations," 184, and Senaveratne, "Some Notes on the Chinese References," 107, in which it is quoted that eight nuns arrived on the first visit and eleven nuns followed. The story of the establishment of the Chinese order of nuns by Sinhala nuns seems to be widely known in China. Ravi Pandit, a reporter, interviewed Chinese nuns who related the same story as the *Biography of the Nuns* ("Buddhist Nuns in China Today," *Sunday Observer* (Colombo), 15 February 1981).

24 Pachow, "Ancient Cultural Relations," 184.

25 "In respect to its numerical growth, however, the order of nuns probably lagged very much behind the order of monks." Gunawardena, "Subtile Silks," 26.

26 See the translations of the Kukurumahan Damana Pillar inscription and the Ayitigevava Pillar inscription in *Epigraphia Zeylanica*. Trans. Don Martino de Zilva Wickremasinghe in Don Martino de Zilva Wickremasinghe, ed., *Epigraphia Zeylanica*, 2 (Colombo: Government Press, 1985), pp. 19–25.

27 C. E. Godakumbura, "Sinhalese Festivals: Their Symbolism, Origins and Proceedings," *Journal of the Royal Asiatic Society* (Ceylon Branch), 14, n.s. (1970), 107. Godakumbura quotes from the Mahākalavatta pillar inscription, *Epigraphia Zeylanica*, 5, p. 334.

28 Hettiaratchi, S. B., *Social and Cultural History of Ancient Sri Lanka* (Delhi: Sri Satguru Publications, 1988), p. 104.

29 Wilhelm Geiger, ed., *The Cūlavaṃsa* (London: Luzac and Company, Ltd., 1980), p. 154. For a translation of this passage, see *The Cūlavaṃsa*. Trans. Wilhelm Geiger (London: Luzac and Company, Ltd., 1973), p. 183: "He built a home called Mahāmallak and made it over to the *bhikkhunīs* proceeding from the Thera School."

30 However, the *Cūlavaṃsa*, like the *Mahāvaṃsa*, alleges that they were never patronized to the extent of the order of monks. The sagas of kings contained within the *Cūlavaṃsa*, for instance, suggest that kings were far more beneficent toward monks. See, for example, chapter LIV, which recounts how Mahinda IV refurbished monastic properties, gave alms to monks and provided them with robes in good faith. In this long account, the order of nuns is mentioned only once (See *The Cūlavaṃsa*. Trans. Geiger, pp. 181–183).

31 R. A. L. H. Gunawardena, *Robe and Plough: Monasticism and Economic Interest in Early Medieval Sri Lanka* (Tucson: University of Arizona Press, 1979), p. 39.

32 Quoted in D. Amarasiri Weeraratne, "*Bhikkhunī* Order," *Daily News* (Colombo), 14 September 1989.

33 D. Amarasiri Weeraratne, "A Welcome Move Towards Reviving *Bhikkhunī* Order," *The Island* (Colombo), 7 June 1987; and D. Amarasiri Weeraratne, "Demoting the *Dasa Sil Matas*," *Sunday Observer* (Colombo), 11 August 1991. Other articles in favor of the restoration of the order with the aid of the Chinese include Dr. T. Kariyawasam, "Case for a Buddhist Order of Nuns," *Daily News* (Colombo), 14 July 1986; Romesh Fernando, "*Bhikkhunī* Order – Questions Again," *The Island* (Colombo), 18 September 1988; K. Don Buddhadasa, "Equal Rights for Buddhist Nuns, *Weekend* (Colombo), 7 June 1987.

34 Venerable Madihee Paññāsīha Mahā Nayaka Thera, "The *Bhikkhunī* Order – Can it Be Re-established," *Daily News* (Colombo), 19 June 1986. For more on the Venerable Paññāsīha, see chapter 8 below.

35 Charles Keyes, in his (1984) study of popular Theravādin Thai texts, has argued a similar point for contemporary Thailand. However, Keyes argues that "Thai Buddhist culture does not relegate women to a religiously inferior status relative to men" (223). He concludes that in terms of their ability to provide sons for the monastic community, perhaps the greatest contribution that anyone can make, Thai women are considered superior. According to Keyes' interpretation of Thai Buddhism, women are more naturally suited than men to sustain the religion: "While a man must reject his "nature" (that is, his sexuality) in order to pursue the path, a woman must first realize her "nature" (becoming a mother) as a prerequisite to her traversing the path" (229). See "Mother or Mistress but Never a Monk: Buddhist Notions of Female Gender in Rural Thailand," *American Ethnologist*, 11, no. 2 (May 1984), 223–241. For a criticism of this article, see A. Thomas Kirsch, "Text and Context: Buddhist Sex Roles/Culture of Gender Revisited," *American Ethnologist*, 12, no. 2 (May, 1985), 302–320.

36 For more on recent attempts to re-establish the *bhikkhunī saṅgha* in Sri Lanka, see Part II of this work.

37 *Saṃsāra* is the cycle of birth, death, and rebirth. See the Introduction to this book for a specific example of this type of ascetic misogyny.

38 The interview with this elderly monk was conducted at a bus stop in Battaramulla on May 15, 1989.

2 NINETEENTH-CENTURY CEYLON: THE EMERGENCE OF THE LAY NUN

1 As Gombrich and Obeyesekere explain, Buddhists "still do not articulate Protestant Buddhism as a separate phenomenon, let alone agree that it can be contrasted with traditional Sinhala Buddhism" (*Buddhism Transformed*, p. 7). Nonetheless, it is a useful tool for understanding the types of changes that occurred in late nineteenth-century Sri Lankan Buddhism.

2 Richard Gombrich, "From Monastery to Meditation Centre: Lay Meditation in Modern Sri Lanka," in Philip Denwood and Alexander Piatigorsky, eds., *Buddhist Studies: Ancient and Modern* (London: Curzon Press, 1983), p. 26.

3 Gombrich and Obeyesekere, *Buddhism Transformed*, p. 215.

4 Ibid., pp. 215–216.

5 Ibid., p. 7.

6 They had made these claims since the mid-eighteenth century. See Carrithers, *The Forest Monks*, p. 70: "In 1753 ... ordination in the Siyam Nikāya was limited, by royal decree, to the highest caste, the Goyigama." I am indebted to H. L. Seneviratne for this summary of trends in the *saṅgha* in the nineteenth century.

7 Kitsiri Malalgoda, *Buddhism in Sinhalese Society 1750–1900: A Study of Religious Revival and Change* (Berkeley: University of California Press, 1976), pp. 109ff. Following Malalgoda (pp. 66–69), when I refer to the "establishment" of Buddhism, I mean the formal organization of monasteries linked to each other "through ties of pupil-teacher relationships" that were monitored, patronized and protected by kings.

8 For instance, by the late nineteenth century, there were 806 Christian schools and only twelve Buddhist schools in the island. There were not, however, "Buddhist schools" before the British period; they were established in reaction to the Christianizing campaigns of the British. For more on the distribution of schools in the British period, see H. R. Perera, *Buddhism in Sri Lanka: A Short History* (Kandy: Buddhist Publication Society 1988), p. 76. Though it can be argued that the Buddhist revival began in the 1870s with the Pānadura debates, or perhaps, much earlier, scholars generally agree that it did not take shape until the 1880s.

9 "Reformation of the Priesthood," *The Buddhist*, 3, no. 26 (June 19, 1891), 206.

10 Ibid.
11 Carrithers, *The Forest Monks*, p. 75.
12 Ibid., pp. 79–80. Establishing a purity of practice by introducing a new ordination lineage is a Theravāda tradition. See Malalgoda, *Buddhism in Sinhalese Society*, pp. 97–105.
13 Gombrich and Obeyesekere, *Buddhism Transformed*, p. 7.
14 Helen Ford, *Notes of a Tour in India and Ceylon* (London: Women's Printing Society, 1889), pp. 144–146.
15 M. Bremer, *Ceylon Planter's Travels*, 1851 (London: Rivingtons, 1930), pp. 45–77.
16 Captain Basil Hall, *Travels in India, Ceylon and Borneo* (London: George Routledge and Sons, 1931). Though the book was published in 1931, Hall lived from 1761–1832 (p. 1).
17 William Knighton, *History of Ceylon* (London: Longman, Brown and Longmans, 1845), pp. 22–24.
18 Ibid.
19 See especially pp. 73–81 for Knighton's discussion of the history of the *Vinaya* rules. Knighton's book suggests that he was very well aware of all facets of Buddhism, including the philosophy, the rituals, and the history.
20 W. Osborn Allen, *A Parson's Holiday: Being an Account of a Tour in India, Burma and Ceylon in the Winter of 1882–83* (Tenby, England: F. B. Mason, 1885), p. 214. Allen, much like the other writers reviewed here, was heir to the Mahāvaṃsa-view of history. For more on the Mahāvaṃsa-view, see the Introduction to this study.
21 Ibid., pp. 114–115. The "nuns" whom Allen witnessed were lay nuns.
22 Bishop Reginald Stephen Copleston, *Buddhism Primitive and Present in Magadha and Ceylon* (London: Longmans, 1892), p. 391.
23 Ibid., p. 255. The emphasis is mine.
24 John Ferguson, *Ceylon in 1893* (London: John Haddon and Co., 1893), p. 395.
25 Ibid., p. 391.
26 Cited in Tennakoon Vimalananda, *The State and Religion in Ceylon Since 1815* (Colombo: M. D. Gunasena and Co., 1970), p. 202.
27 Ibid., p. 74.
28 Tambiah, *World Conqueror, World Renouncer*, pp. 162–178.
29 Ibid.
30 Ibid.
31 Ibid.
32 Quoted in Vimalananda, *The State and Religion*, p. 89.
33 Quoted in Ibid., p. 94.
34 Ananda Guruge, *Anagārika Dharmapāla* (Colombo: The Department of Cultural Affairs, 1967), p. 8.
35 Malalgoda, *Buddhism in Sinhalese Society*, p. 125.
36 Bartholomeusz, "The Female Mendicant in Buddhist Sri Lanka," 43.
37 By literature, I mean not only the texts which record the purifications,

but the scholarship which has interpreted them (see Tambiah, *World Conqueror, World Renouncer*, pp. 162–178).

38 For purification as a type of revitalization, see Ibid., p. 164, wherein one of the kings discussed is said to have asked the following: "Whom should I employ in order to restore the *Sāsana*?"

39 See Kitsiri Malalgoda, "Buddhism in Post-Indpendence Sri Lanka," in G. A. Oddie, ed., *Religion in South Asia* (New Delhi: Manohar, 1977), pp. 183–189 for an interesting discussion of the ways the disestablishment of Buddhism also affected the leaders of the post-independence period.

40 Gombrich and Obeyesekere, *Buddhism Transformed*, p. 7.

41 Dharmapāla was the most vocal on this topic. See chapter 3 for more on Dharmapāla's view of late nineteenth-century Buddhism.

42 Among these is the post-canonical work, the *Upāsakajanālankāra*.

43 T. W. and C. A. F. Rhys Davids, "Introduction to the Sigālovāda Suttanta," in *Dialogues of the Buddha*, part 3. Trans. T. W. and C. A. F. Rhys Davids (London: Luzac and Company, Ltd., 1957), p. 169.

44 For the Pāli text, see J. Estlin Carpenter, ed., "Sigālovāda Suttanta," in *The Dīgha Nikāya*, vol. 3 (London: Luzac and Company, Ltd., 1960), pp. 117–174.

45 Ibid., p. 118. For another translation of this *suttanta*, see Manric Walshe's in *Thus Have I Heard: The Long Discourses of the Buddha* (London: Wisdom Publications, 1987), pp. 461–462.

46 For more on the *Milindapañho*, see K. R. Norman, *Pāli Literature* (Leiden: E. J. Brill, 1972), pp. 110–112.

47 For the Pāli text, see V. Trenckner, ed., *Milindapañho* (London: Luzac and Company, ltd., 1962), p. 348.

48 Ibid.

49 Ibid., p. 351.

50 For another discussion of the capabilities of the laity in attaining *nibbāna*, see Stanley Tambiah, *The Buddhist Saints of the Forest and the Cult of Amulets* (Cambridge University Press, 1984), pp. 14–16.

51 The canonical *Kathāvatthu* records a similar conversation concerning the ability of the laity to attain *nibbāna*. See Arnold C. Taylor, ed., *The Kathāvatthu* (London: Routledge and Kegan Paul Ltd., 1979), p. 267.

52 A pious layman.

53 Subhodānanda's Mahāvaṃsa-view of history is striking.

54 For more on the differences in the way the ten precepts are observed, see chapter 4 of this study.

55 White is the color associated with the laity.

56 That is, the lay (*upāsaka*) monastery (*vihāra*) located at Poore.

57 "Letter to the Editor," *Lakminipāhana*, 6 August 1898; Anagārika Dharmapāla, who advocated a similar status for laypeople, mentions Subhodānanda's letter on the final page of his 1898 diary.

58 Carrithers, *The Forest Monks*, pp. 104–116.

59 For instance, other than offering that Anulā was cloistered while she

observed the ten precepts, the *Mahāvaṃsa* does not specify what sort of life she led.

60 Though Subhodānanda, according to his own account, had given up his status as a monk, he nonetheless had a forum – the lay cloister – and continued to preach. In fact, while he was resident at Poore Upāsakā-rāmaya (Poore is modern-day Talangama near Colombo), Sub-hodānanda warned the laity against various evils, including the evils of liquor, in language reminiscent of the Buddhist clergy. The *Lakmini-pāhana*, 13 August 1898, featured one of his sermons.

61 "Dasa Sil Upāsikāvak," *Sarasavisandaresa*, 14 July 1899.

62 "A Dasasil Upāsikāvak Who Dons Yellow Robes," *Sarasavisandaresa*, 15 September 1899.

63 "Upāsakas, Upāsikās Through Buddhist Schools," *Sarasavisandaresa*, 13 December 1899.

64 "Letter to the Editor," *Lakminipāhana*, 8 January 1898.

65 Ibid.

66 "Letter to the Editor," *Lakminipāhana*, 19 February 1898.

67 The tradition of leaving a male child in the care of a monastery when his horoscope suggests that he might be a threat to society continues to the present. Sri Lankan Buddhists generally believe that the child's fate will change for the better, while pursuing religious goals. It is interesting to note that contemporary lay nuns also follow this tradition, albeit with one major difference. When a female child has a "bad" horoscope, she is taken to a lay nunnery and left for a day, whereas a male child is given over to a monastery for his entire lifetime. This symbolic handing over of the female child suggests that contemporary Buddhist culture is not willing to permit their daughters to renounce the world, no matter what the circumstances may be. For more on the attitudes of the laity toward the status of the lay nun in contemporary Sri Lankan society, see part II of this work.

68 "Leaving the Robes of the Priesthood," *Lakminipāhana*, 10 September 1898.

69 *Lakminipāhana*, 19 June 1897.

70 "A Question to be Looked Into," *Sarasavisandaresa*, 13 December 1898.

71 "Questions Which Should be Addressed," *Sarasavisandaresa*, 23 December 1898.

72 Anagārika Dharmapāla, whom we encounter in chapters 3 and 4, advocated a similar status. See below.

73 Such persons are marginal in terms of the traditional distinction in Theravādin Buddhism between the path of the monk/nun and the path of the laity.

74 Malalgoda, *Buddhism in Sinhalese Society*, p. 290.

75 Ibid., p. 58.

76 Ibid., p. 54.

77 Ibid., pp. 49–65.

78 For more on the *saṅgha* and monastic property, see Gunawardena, *Robe and Plough*, pp. 53–94.
79 Malalgoda, *Buddhism in Sinhalese Society*, p. 57.
80 Stephen Kemper, "Buddhism Without Bhikkhus: The Sri Lankan Vinaya Vardena Society," in Bardwell Smith, ed., *Religion and the Legitimation of Power in Sri Lanka* (Chambersburg, Pennsylvania: Anima Books, 1978), p. 220.
81 Ibid.
82 Ibid., p. 221. The parenthetical glosses are Kemper's.
83 It can also be argued that the moral state of many of these figures, including some *gaṇinnānses*, approximated that of the "ideal" clergy rather than laity; not all the *gaṇinnānses* aspired to land control. For some, being a *gaṇinnānse* was the only alternative to lay life because the *saṅgha* was, for all intents and purposes, defunct.
84 For the Pāli text, see Oldenberg, ed., *Vinaya Piṭakam*, vol. 1, p. 307. The Pāli term is *theyyasaṃvāsaka*.
85 Ibid. See also p. 86, for another instance of one who "steals the signs of a monk," in this case, communion with monks.
86 According to the texts, this was the Buddha's refrain upon hearing that there were those who stole the attributes of the monk. See Oldenberg, ed., *Vinaya Piṭakam*, vol. 1, p. 307.
87 Trenckner, ed., *Milindapañho*, pp. 264–265.
88 Ibid.
89 Ibid.

3 THEOSOPHISTS, EDUCATORS, AND NUNS

1 For a brief history of the establishment of the Theosophical Society in Colombo and America, see Emma McCloy Layman, *Buddhism in America* (Chicago: Nelson Hall, 1978), pp. 171–174.
2 Dharmapāla wrote often that Saṅghamittā, who introduced the order of nuns to Sri Lanka (see chapter 1 above), was a powerful role model for Buddhist women. For references to Saṅghamittā in Dharmapāla's writings, see Ananda Guruge, ed., *Return to Righteousness: Return to Righteousness* (Colombo: The Department of Cultural Affairs, 1967), pp. 206, 214, 234, 339, 344, 443, 487, 692, 782, 786, and 788. In the last entry cited, Dharmapāla lauds Buddhist women and Buddhism and asks, "What other religion has had women missionaries but Buddhism?"
3 Dharmapāla's views were very passionate. In his diary entry for December 19, 1897, he wrote that he addressed a crowd, and "Spoke to them to be patriotic, that the Sinhalese should be united, that they were a great and unique people …"
4 For more on Dharmapāla and the renewed role of the *upāsaka*, see Donald K. Swearer, "Lay Buddhism and the Buddhist Revival in Ceylon," *Journal of the American Academy of Religion*, 38, no. 3 (September 1970), 255–275.

5 Guruge, ed., *Return to Righteousness*, pp. 341–346.
6 Ibid., pp. 142–143.
7 This emerges in his writings about gods in Buddhism. See, for instance, Ibid., pp. 144–148; and p. 78: "Happiness could be realised here not by sacrificing to the gods, and praying to get possessions, but in ceaseless activity in doing good in helping the sick…" This is a Protestant Buddhist notion inasmuch as his version of Buddhism, much like Protestantism, downplayed the importance of divine intervention. In other words, Dharmapāla stressed the "rational" aspects of Buddhism.
8 He implies this in his reflections on Europe and America. See Ibid., p. 717.
9 Tambiah, *Buddhism Betrayed?*, p. 59. Tambiah speaks here of Buddhists in the 1960s and 1970s. However, what he says applies to Dharmapāla and his associates.
10 See especially Bond, *The Buddhist Revival in Sri Lanka*, and Gombrich and Obeyesekere, *Buddhism Transformed*.
11 B. G. Gokhale, "Anagārika Dharmapāla: Toward Modernity Through Tradition in Ceylon," in Bardwell L. Smith, ed., *Tradition in Theravada Buddhism* (Leiden: E. J. Brill, 1973), p. 34. Also quoted in "The Mahā Bodhi Society," *The Buddhist* (June 10, 1892), 180.
12 Quoted from Dharmapāla's diary entry for December 5, 1899.
13 That is, *Jātakas*, the stories of the Buddha's previous incarnations.
14 H. Dharmapāla, "Burma and Buddhism," *The Buddhist* (June 26, 1891), 210.
15 H. Dharmapāla, "Burma and Buddhism (cont.)," *The Buddhist* (July 3, 1891), 217. In contemporary Burma, the lay nuns wear pink and orange robes rather than white robes that Dharmapāla witnessed. The "order" about which Dharmapāla wrote was an informal group of lay nuns.
16 His diaries are replete with statements concerning his fear of women. Among the most striking is the diary entry for December 11, 1898: "A feeling of inexpressible emotion came to me when the Upāsikā [Countess Canavarro] wanted to express that there are things which I don't understand and I stopped her." In his September 17, 1902 diary entry he discussed his struggle with celibacy in a third person narrative: "In his 19th year he offered himself to lead the holy life and he perservered til this year. This year in Japan he allowed his body to be rubbed by a woman and contaminated."
17 However, I have located an 1894 article that refers to "nuns" accompanying several monks and laywomen, among them, Dharmapāla's mother, on a pilgrimage to Bodh Gaya ("Pilgrims to Buddha Gaya," *The Buddhist*, 6, no. 50 (December 28, 1894), 400). Dharmapāla does not refer to this trip in his writings.
18 *Bhikṣuṇī* is Sanskrit and Sinhala, while *bhikkhunī* is Pāli.
19 Quoted from Dharmapāla's diary entry for July 13, 1897.
20 There are numerous examples of this attitude. See, for instance, Guruge, ed., *Return to Righteousness*, p. 106.

21 Ibid., p. 207.
22 She became nobility through marriage to Count Canavarro.
23 Robert S. Elwood, *Eastern Spirituality in America* (New York: Paulist Press, 1987), p. 19.
24 Ibid., quoted in Carl T. Jackson, *Oriental Religions and American Thought: Nineteenth Century Explorations* (Westport, Connecticut: Greenwood, 1981), p. 141. Though this is, perhaps, an overstatement, it attests to the interest of Americans in Asian religions during the period under review.
25 Gregory Tillet, *A Biography of Charles Webster Leadbeater* (London: Routledge and Kegan Paul, 1982), p. 49.
26 "Quarter Mile Clause," *The Buddhist*, 6, no. 26 (July 13, 1894), 207.
27 Tambiah, *Buddhism Betrayed?*, pp. 31–37.
28 Jill Roe, *Beyond Belief: Theosophy in Australia, 1879–1930* (Sydney: New South Wales University Press, 1986), p. 188.
29 Ibid., p. 188; also "History of the Women's Educational Society," *The Buddhist* (February 2, 1894), 25. Kate's mother, the Russian-born Buddhist, Elise Pickett, had arrived in Melbourne from New Zealand earlier in the same year, where she called a meeting to discuss Theosophy (Roe, *Beyond Belief*, p. 76). Due to Mrs. Pickett, the defunct Theosophical Society of Melbourne was revived, and she remained one of the pillars of the Theosophical community in Australia for many years. It is no wonder, then, that when Olcott requested the Australian Theosophical Society to send teachers to Ceylon – to help educate the demoralised Buddhists – the Picketts were eager to comply. They decided that Kate was well-equipped to help the Buddhist Educational Society in Colombo in their mission to educate Buddhist girls.
30 "History of the W. E. S.," *The Buddhist* (February 2, 1894), 25.
31 "A Retrospect and An Appeal," *The Buddhist* (1889), 247.
32 "The Work of Women," *The Buddhist* (1889), 295.
33 "The Work of Women," *The Buddhist* (January 16, 1891), 32.
34 "A Noble Project," *The Buddhist* (June 1889), 224. However, it will be recalled there were no Buddhist schools in Sri Lanka prior to the British; they were a reaction to christianizing campaigns.
35 "The Saṅghamittā School," *The Buddhist* (February 2, 1894), 25.
36 Ibid.
37 "A Retrospect and an Appeal," *The Buddhist* (1889), 246.
38 "The Wesleyan Mission Report," quoted in *The Buddhist* (1889), 295.
39 "Female Education," *The Buddhist* (July 10, 1891), 229.
40 "The Drowning of Miss Pickett," *The Buddhist* (December 11, 1891), 408. However, according to a fellow Theosophist employed in a Madras school, Pickett's death was accidental: "She was in the habit of walking in her sleep, and it seems probable that she fell into the well in a state of somnambulism." Quoted in "The Late Miss Pickett," *The Buddhist* (July 24, 1891), 246.
41 "The Cremation of Miss Pickett," *The Buddhist* (July 3, 1891), 223.

42 Ibid. The parenthetical remark is in the original.
43 Buddhadasa Kirthisinghe, "Marie Museus Higgins: American Mother of Ceylon's Buddhist Womanhood," *The Mahā Bodhi Journal*, 76, nos. 11–12 (November–December 1968), 327.
44 "The Women's Educational Society and the Sanghamitta Girls' School," *The Buddhist* (December 22, 1893), 388–390.
45 "The Sanghamitta Girls' School," *The Buddhist* (June 22, 1894), 182.
46 Roe, however, does not mention this in her opus on the Theosophical Society in Australia (1986).
47 Quoted from Dharmapāla's diary of October 31, 1897.
48 "Saṇghamittā Upāsikārāmaya," *Ganartha Pradīpaya*, 18 October 1897.
49 "Interesting to Buddhists," *Ceylon Examiner*, 30 October 1897.
50 "Madam Miranda Upāsikā," *Sarasavisandaresa*, 8 October 1897.
51 "Lady Miranda Upāsikā," *Sarasavisandaresa*, 12 October 1897.
52 In June, 1898, Dharmapāla while in India wrote that "The Upāsikārāmaya has a few *Upāsikās*. May it flourish." Prior to this, on April 7, 1898, he wrote, "May the Upāsikārāmaya flourish! Go ahead and do the Upāsikārāmaya work. The Saṇghamittā Upāsikārāmaya is the next work!"
53 As Gombrich and Obeyesekere point out, the late nineteenth-century Buddhist revival was fuelled by the elite. See *Buddhism Transformed*, pp. 6–8.
54 I have extracted from Dharmapāla's diaries over twenty typed pages of references to the Countess and their work together. The biographer commissioned by the Mahā Bodhi Society in Colombo to document Dharmapāla's life does not treat this period of his career, despite the abundance of material in the diaries. For that study, see K. B. Sugatadasa, *Anagārika Dharmapāla Apadānaya* (Vallamapitiya, Sri Lanka: Somarasiri Kasturi Aracci, 1986).
55 Quoted from Dharmapāla's diary entry of March 8, 1897.
56 Ibid., April 21, 1897.
57 Ibid., June 3, 1897.
58 Ibid., June 21, 1897 and June 30, 1897.
59 Ibid., June 14, 1897.
60 "Buddha's Fair Pale Convert," *New York Journal*, 31 August 1897.
61 Quoted from Dharmapāla's diary entry of July 6, 1897. HPB (Madame Blavatsky) and Annie Besant were both leaders of the Theosophical Society. He justified this recommendation by stating "That she should [show] her own individuality and not make anybody think that she had been hypnotised" (Ibid.) Shortly thereafter, Dharmapāla wrote to the Countess "to be made a Buddhist" (Quoted from Dharmapāla's diary entry of July 14, 1897).
62 Ibid., August 7, 1897.
63 Ibid., August 30, 1897.
64 Ibid., September 6, 1897.

65 Ibid.
66 Ibid., December 3, 1897.
67 Ibid., January 1, 1899.
68 Ibid., February 8, 1899.
69 For the duties of the householder, see the *Sutta Nipāta*. Trans. Bhikkhu H. Saddhatissa. (London: Curzon Press, 1985), 45 (verses 25–27). The *Sutta Nipāta* is a canonical work.
70 "Miranda de Souza Canavarro," *Ganartha Pradīpaya*, 26 April 1900. The interview in the Sinhala Catholic newspaper also appeared in the *New York Herald* immediately after the Countess's conversion to Buddhism.
71 "American Ladies Observing Ata Sil," *Sarasavisandaresa*, 21 September 1897.
72 "Buddha's Fair Pale Convert," *New York Journal*, 31 August 1897.
73 Ibid.
74 Quoted from Dharmapāla's diary of June 16, 1897.
75 "Buddha Gains a Convert," *New York Journal*, 30 August 1897.
76 Quoted from Dharmapāla's diary of August 28, 1897.
77 "Woman Vows to Follow Buddha," *New York Herald*, 31 August 1897.
78 "Buddha's Fair Pale Convert," *New York Journal*.
79 The subtitle of "Buddha's Fair Pale Convert" is "To Dharmapāla, High Priest, She Renounces Every Earthly Tie."
80 For more on the text that addresses the laity, the "Sigālovāda Suttanta," see chapter 2. For a translation, see "Sigālovāda Suttanta," in *Dialogues of the Buddha*. Part 2. Trans. T. W. and C. A. F. Rhys Davids (London: Luzac and Company Ltd., 1957), pp. 184 ff.
81 "Madam Miranda Upāsikā," *Sarasavisandaresa*, 5 October 1897.
82 "Buddha's Fair Pale Convert," *New York Journal*.
83 "She is now a Buddhist: The Countess de Canavarro Received into the Faith with Impressive Ceremonies," *New York Tribune*, 31 August 1897; also, Dharmapāla's diary entry for August 31, 1897.
84 "A Buddhist Countess in Ceylon," *Ceylon Catholic Messenger*, 19 October 1897.
85 "Correspondence," *Ganartha Pradīpaya*, 11 October 1897. The Countess eventually became a disciple of Swami Paramananda and dedicated her 1925 reminiscence of her life to him. See M. de S. Canavarro, *Insight into the Far East* (Hollywood, California: Strickland Publishing Company, 1925), pp. 183–187.
86 "A Countess Vows to Follow Buddha," *Ceylon Catholic Messenger*, 12 October 1897. The reference was to Kate Pickett.
87 Dharmapāla's diary entry for September 8, 1897.
88 "Countess Canavarro," *Ganartha Pradīpaya*, 29 May 1899.
89 "A Modern Instance of World Renunciation," in *The Open Court*, 13, no. 2 (February 1899), 110–115. The Countess Canavarro and the other Buddhist lay nuns are featured in this American publication. The article is complete with photographs of the robed lay nuns.

90 Among the collection of the Countess's letters in "The Open Court Publishing Company Archives" I found a notice, "To the Public," in which the Countess informed her friends in both Ceylon and America that she had changed her name: "When I came to Ceylon I took the vows of the Buddhist nun and as such I wish to be considered. According to the rites of Buddhism, when one leaves the household life and becomes homeless they take a religious name which I did and call myself Saṅghamittā." It is not clear when she took the name, though the notice is dated June 22, 1900.

91 "The Buddhist Countess and Her Work: Formation of a Sisterhood, Acquisition of a Convent, A Progressive Educational Scheme," *The Ceylon Independent*, quoted in full in *The Buddhist* (January 21, 1898), 3–4.

92 See Carrithers, *The Forest Monks*.

93 Dharmapāla's February 7, 1898, diary entry, as well as February 16, 1898 entry reflect that, from Dharmapāla's point of view, the Countess was emotionally unstable. On February 16, he wrote that the Countess "is a strange person ... " On February 1, two weeks earlier, Dharmapāla wrote that "M. Canavarro was obstinate and I had to calm her down. She is suffering mentally and physically ... "

94 Quoted from Dharmapāla's diary entry of October 30, 1897.

95 Ibid., November 1, and November 12, 1897; and December 14, 1897.

96 Ibid., November 12, 1897.

97 Ibid., November 29, 1897.

98 Ibid., October 30, 1897.

99 "The Buddhist Countess and Her Work," *Ceylon Independent*, 3–4.

100 Quoted from Dharmapāla's diary entry of July 8, 1898. In his April 12, 1898, diary entry, he wrote that he had told the Countess that "the Saṅghamittā Convent should not go under the Theosophical category. I will not have anything to do with those who forget the Buddha."

101 Darly Lane is now Foster Lane and the Upāsikārāmaya property now houses a factory.

102 A short history of the Saṅghamittā Upāsikārāmaya entitled "Countess Canavarro and the Lanka Mahā Bodhi Society: Why the Countess has left the Saṅghamittā Upāsikārāmaya, Full Details," *Standard*, 19 October 1899 refers to this event.

103 "The Buddhist Countess and Her Work," *Ceylon Independent*, 3–4.

104 Ibid.; the capital letters appear in the original. The frequency in which the Countess's name is mentioned in the newspapers of Ceylon – Buddhist, Christian and secular – attests to the fact that the Upāsikārāmaya work attracted much attention.

105 Gananath Obeyesekere's "Religious Symbolism and Political Change in Ceylon," in Gananath Obeyesekere, Frank Reynolds, and Bardwell L. Smith, eds., *The Two Wheels of the Dhamma: Essays on the Theravāda Tradition in India and Ceylon* (Chambersburg, Pennsylvania: American Academy of Religion, 1972), pp. 58–78. In this provocative work,

Obeyesekere addresses late nineteenth-century Buddhists' reinterpretation of Buddhism through Christian idioms.

106 Dharmapāla's diary entry for January 1, 1899.

107 Ibid., November 2, 1897.

108 "The Buddhist Countess and Her Work," *Ceylon Independent*, 3–4.

109 Ibid. The Catholic terminology is striking.

110 Just six months before the interview, that is, in August, 1897, when Dharmapāla formally inducted the Countess into Buddhism, she wore a black dress and draped one shoulder with a white piece of cloth "toga fashion" ("Buddha's Fair Pale Convert," *New York Journal*). As records of the interviews after the induction ceremony indicate, Dharmapāla hoped that the Countess would eventually pass through three stages of Buddhist practice, the third stage being ordination as an ordained nun (*bhikkhunī*), as we have seen. He suggested that the clothes worn symbolically defined each of the stages ("She is Now a Buddhist: The Countess de Canavarro Received into the Faith with Impressive Ceremonies," *New York Tribune*, 31 August 1897).

111 See the dust cover photograph of the Countess on Tweed's 1992 work, *The American Encouter with Buddhism*.

112 *Diṇamina*, 27 April 1898, and "Saṅghamittā Shastra Shālawa," *Sarasavisandaresa*, 29 April 1898.

113 "The Opening of the House of the Saṅghamittā," *Sarasavisandaresa*, 3 May 1898.

114 The article, "Saṅghamittā Shastra Shālawa," *Sarasavisandaresa*, 29 July 1898 gives an account of the curriculum at the school and the students who resided there. "The Saṅghamittā Upāsikārāmaya of Colombo," *Sarasavisandaresa*, 9 August 1898 attests to the school and the convent's success. At that time "There [were] 152 day scholars, 21 students, 7 *upāsikās* [lay nuns], orphans, and the Lady-in-charge..."

115 Dharmapāla's diary entry for July 11, 1898 alludes to these tensions.

116 "The Saṅghamittā Upāsikārāmaya of Colombo," *Sarasavisandaresa*, 9 August 1898; "Mahā Bodhi Talks," *Sarasavisandaresa*, 23 August 1898; and "Mr. Dharmapāla," *Sarasavisandaresa*, 9 August 1898. Dharmapāla's diaries also describe their tours.

117 Quoted from Dharmapāla's diary entry of April 10, 1898.

118 Ibid., June 23, 1898.

119 Ibid., July 11, 1898.

120 Ibid., October 9, 1898.

121 See chapter 4 for more on Shearer.

122 Dharmapāla's diary entry for February 16, 1898.

123 "This and That," *Ganartha Pradīpaya*, 24 July 1899. The article, which treats the subject of those who give up their religion, criticizes Shearer's conversion to Buddhism.

124 On November 3, 1898, Dharmapāla wrote that "the *Upāsikā* (Madam Canavarro) has given up all her individuality. She is willing to follow

me blindly." On November 8, only one week later, he stated that he went to see "the Upāsikā, and told her of the incident that I was going to India. She was furious, she began to weep, she fell at my feet, I consoled her."

125 Quoted from Dharmapāla's diary entry of October 9, 1898.

126 In her May 7, 1902 letter to Paul Carus, the Countess exclaimed "I am not an advocate of celibacy for anyone." See "The Open Court Publishing Archives" for the entire letter.

127 That is, the Countess.

128 Quoted from Dharmapāla's diary entry of October 22, 1898.

129 Ibid., July 31, 1902. However, the marriage never took place. It will be recalled that Strauss was the first American male to become a Buddhist on American soil, while the Countess was the first female.

130 Ibid., August 8, 1902.

131 "The Open Court Publishing Archives," the Countess Canavarro to Paul Carus, 9 June 1898.

132 "Education in Ceylon," in *The Mahā Bodhi and the United Buddhist World*, 10, no. 3 (November 1898), 34.

133 Quoted from Dharmapāla's diary of June 15, 1899.

134 On July 13, 1897, Dharmapāla wrote that he "first thought of resuscitating the *Bhikhuni Sangha* in 1890. Mrs. Canavarro will, I hope succeed in her efforts."

135 Dharmapāla, however, never referred to the Countess as a "nun" in his diaries, but rather as "Mother Superior," "Dasa Sil Upāsikā," or as "Sister Saṅghamittā." Yet, he is quoted as referring to the Countess as a "nun" in the English medium *Ceylon Examiner* ("Countess Canavarro to Go to India," 11 February 1899).

136 Quoted from Dharmapāla's diary entry of June 15, 1899. According to Dharmapāla himself, he perhaps would not have spent so much time in the late 1890s fighting in India for Bodh Gaya had he not wanted to escape from the Countess and the scandal.

137 "Mahā Bodhi Sangamāya," *Ganartha Pradīpaya*, 23 October 1899. In the Countess's reflections upon her life in Ceylon, she mentions the scandal and the way in which the monks of the Maligakanda Vihāra forced her to "remove her robe ..." Canavarro, *Insight into the Far East*, p. 141.

138 Dharmapāla's diary entry for November 4, 1899.

139 Ibid., December 9, 1899.

140 Ibid., November 22, 1899.

141 Ibid., February 6, 1900, refers to the new residence, as does "The Perishing of the Buddhist Camp," *Ganartha Pradīpaya*, 26 October 1899.

142 "Madame Canavarro," *Dinakara Prakāsaya*, 13 October 1900.

143 To further illustrate, Dharmapāla on board ship to Japan in 1902 wrote that "Whenever [women] get the opportunity they sin. So far I have kept myself free from their impurities. Now I have passed my

youth and I am now a full grown man. I hope in this life that I will not fall into sin" (Quoted from Dharmapāla's diary entry for April 21, 1902).

144 See Tambiah, *Buddhism Betrayed?*, pp., 19, 21, 25.

4 THE SAŅGHAMITTĀ SISTERHOOD

1 Dharmapāla's diary entry for July 26, 1899.

2 According to Dharmapāla, "Lanka, the pearl of the Indian Ocean, the resplendent jewel, became the future repository of the pure religion of the Tathagato [the Buddha]." His assumptions are based on his reading of the *Mahāvaṃsa*. See Guruge, ed., *Return to Righteousness*, pp. 481–484.

3 I found it in the Colombo Museum Library. *List of Books Printed in Ceylon: 1899* (July 19, entry number 4334). According to the *List*, two hundred copies of the pamphlet were printed at Clifton Press, Colombo. The particulars of the author are given as follows: "The name and residence of the Proprietor of the Copyright or of any portion of the copyright, Madame de Souza Canavarro, Saṅghamittā Convent, Colombo."

4 The Countess, who wrote the pamphlet, included a short autobiographical account, complete with her genealogy. She did not provide a biographical account of the other leaders of her community of lay nuns. According to the pamphlet, two of the four leaders of the Sisterhood were Ceylonese women: one was a Burgher, while the other was Sinhala. Sister Dammadinna [sic] formerly known as Sybil LaBrooy, was a Burgher which suggests that she, not unlike Sister Saṅghamittā, was formerly a Christian. Dharmapāla refers to LaBrooy often (c.f., his diary entries for November 30, 1898; December 8, 1898; December 19, 1898; January 16, 1898; and February 27, 1900), as do the newspaper accounts of the Saṅghamittā Upāsikārāmaya project (c.f., *Dinamina*, 19 November 1898, and 22 December 1898; and also *Dinakara Prakāsaya*, 17 November 1898). LaBrooy's printed genealogy also provides some biographical information (see the "Genealogy of the Family of LaBrooy of Ceylon," *Journal of the Dutch Burgher Union*, 24, no. 1 (July 1934), 73). According to the genealogy, LaBrooy was one of thirteen children. She was born on April 13, 1878, into an Anglican family and died aged forty-one on January 16, 1919. She became involved in the project of the Countess in 1897 aged nineteen and held the title of "Manager of the Household" at the Saṅghamittā Upāsikārāmaya. LaBrooy never married. Throughout the Countess's three year career in Ceylon, LaBrooy remained her loyal friend. In fact, according to the diary and newspaper accounts of the period, she became her only friend after Dharmapāla divorced himself from the Upāsikārāmaya project. In 1899, when the Countess was virtually evicted from the Upāsikārāmaya by the members of the MBS ostensibly for causing dissention in the lay

nunnery, only LaBrooy remained her ally ("The Lady Canavarro Upāsikārāmaya," *Diṇamina*, 13 February 1900 described the renewed efforts of the Countess and LaBrooy to continue the Upāsikārāmaya work). Dharmapāla's diary entries, too, suggest this. For instance, in his diary entry for November 3, 1899, Dharmapāla wrote that LaBrooy had "returned to the Convent, in spite of the fact that M. Canavarro had been prohibited access."

In November, 1899, a Catholic Sinhala newspaper ran a series of articles and letters which focused upon the demise of the Saṅghamittā Upāsikārāmaya and the School. Among those who wrote in support of the Countess's efforts were a European woman, and two Ceylonese women, Miss E. de Silva and Miss Grace Block, and Sybil LaBrooy ("Madame Canavarro and Buddhists in Ceylon: Reaching Great Poverty," *Ganartha Pradīpaya*, 27 November 1899; Dharmapāla's diary entry for November 30, 1899). By the spring of 1899, the rift between the Countess and Dharmapāla had become irreparable and the latter retreated to India. While in India, Dharmapāla received many letters from the Countess and LaBrooy. According to Dharmapāla, they were confrontational in nature. In his diary entry for May 10, 1899, Dharmapāla described the letters received from the Upāsikārāmaya.

Another lay nun about whom some information is known, like LaBrooy, was Ceylonese. However, LaBrooy was a Burgher, while Sister Upalavathi, according to the pamphlet, was the "Sinhalese Teacher of the Religion." While the lay names are given for the three other sisters who held responsible posts in the Saṅghamittā Upāsikārāmaya, that is, the Countess, Shearer, and LaBrooy, Sister Upalavathi is simply called the *Dasa Sil Upāsikā*.

In her reminiscences of her life in Asia, the Countess wrote that another one of the sisters, Karanawati, was a "fifteen year old ... low caste ... Sinhala girl" who "came accompanied by her mother to ask to enter the Hermitage." See Canavarro, *Insight into the Far East*, pp. 73–81. In the pamphlet, Karanawati is mentioned as a "lay sister."

5 For the Pāli text of the rules which governed the ancient order of nuns, see Hermann Oldenberg, ed., *Vinaya Piṭakam*, vol. 4 (London: Luzac and Company, Ltd., 1964), pp. 211–351. For the translation, see *The Book of the Discipline*, part 3. Trans. I. B. Horner (London: Luzac and Company, Ltd., 1964), pp. 156–426.

6 Oldenberg, ed., *Vinaya Piṭakam*, vol. 4, p. 338 (*pācittiya*, LXXXV). A *pācittiya* is a minor offense.

7 For more on this concept, see "Translator's Introduction," in *The Book of the Discipline, Sacred Books of the Buddhists*, Part 1. Trans. I. B. Horner (London: Luzac and Company, Ltd, 1970), p. XLVII. The Pāli term for this lapse in behavior is *hīnāyāvattati*.

8 In the May 28, 1901 letter to Paul Carus, the Countess wrote that Olcott "is labouring under a mistake as regards my character; there is an

article (in the *Theosophist*) wherein they had predicted my work in Ceylon would be a failure on account of my eccentric and sensational disposition and further stating that their predictions had been verified in my hysterical and impractical methods having broken up the work ... " Dharmapāla also mentioned the statements in the *Theosophist*: It "contains a para [sic] wherein Colonel Olcott maliciously and deliberately tells an untruth and misleads many against me regarding Countess Canavarro. He is trying wherever an opportunity is found to attack me ... " (December 9, 1900). According to the December 1900 issue of the *Theosophist*, the lay nunnery was "foredoomed to failure from the start ... the poor Countess ... was of a supersensitive, hysterical temperament, romantic and idealistic. She ought never to have been asked to come to Ceylon; and the blame of this disaster rests upon her equally impulsive, impracticable 'spiritual Guru' – as she styled him – H. Dharmapāla."

As early as April 1899, the *Theosophist* ran articles about the ill-fated project and its founders. In one article, "The "Wail" of Dharmapāla," Olcott wrote "So in the case of the good Countess whom, with a dramatic public ceremony in America he accepted as a Buddhist nun, and called to Ceylon to revive the Order of *Bhikkhunīs*, without calculating the chances of success in advance ... " Dharmapāla had failed (vol. 22, 1899, p. xxix). I would like to thank Colin Coster of the Melbourne (Australia) Theosophical Society for granting me permission to use their library.

9 The same Pāli word is used for the robe of the *sikkhamānā*, the *sāmaṇerī*, and the *bhikkhunī*. According to the description of the ordination of a woman as a *sikkhamānā* in the *Vinaya* literature, she was to approach "the Order, having arranged her upper robe (*uttārasaṅga*) over one shoulder." She was then to ask for permission to observe the six rules for training. For the Pāli text, see Oldenberg, ed., *Vinaya Piṭakam*, vol. 4, pp. 318–319 (*pācittiya* LXIII). The account suggests that a novice required the direction of an ordained nun; having been trained, the novice is to say, "Noble ladies, I (so and so), a probationer who has trained for two years in the six rules under the teacher (so and so), request the order for the agreement as to ordination." For the Pāli text, see *pācittiya* LXIV.

10 Ibid.

11 Though the *Vibhanga* proclaims that the novice is to first spend time maintaining the six precepts, and then later the ten, the *Cullavagga*, similarly a *Vinaya* text, proclaims that the novitiate is to maintain the six while no mention is made of a period in which the ten precepts are to be observed. For a translation of the *Cullavagga* rule, see *Vinaya Texts*, part 3. Trans. T. W. Rhys Davids and Hermann Oldenberg (Varanasi: Motilal Banarsidass, 1984), p. 324.

12 "A female novice means one conforming to the ten rules of training (*sāmaṇerī nāma dasasikkhapādikā*)." For the Pāli text, see Oldenberg, ed., *Vinaya Piṭakam*, vol. 4, p. 343. This rule is the content of *pācittiya*, XCI-XCII.

13 This is apparent from the description of the novice who seeks higher

ordination; one requirement was that she had to be agreed upon by the order of nuns, that is, deemed worthy by the *saṅgha*. See Oldenberg, ed., *Vinaya Piṭakam*, vol. 2, pp. 273–274.

14 See chapter 8 below.

15 Sponberg, "Attitudes toward Women and the Feminine in Early Buddhism," p. 13.

16 Dharmapāla's diary entries for September 10, and September 13, 1898.

17 Though the schedule is listed on the final page of the diary for the 1898 calendar year, it is not clear when it was written.

18 "The Open Court Publishing Company Archives," Countess Canavarro to Paul Carus, December 1898, Matara, Ceylon.

19 In the same letter, she describes Catherine Shearer who later joined the Countess in the Ceylon project as having a "beautiful character" and being a very "helpful" addition to the lay nunnery.

20 The participation of monks in the ceremony is reminiscent of the initiation of novices found in the monastic texts. Much like those initiations, the participation of monks in the ancient order, as well as in the Saṅghamittā Sisterhood, further suggests institutional androcentrism.

21 I did not witness ordinations of novices into the other fraternities but was told that all novices in Sri Lanka repeat this Pāli phrase.

22 See her letters to Paul Carus for 1900. They suggest that she was humiliated after the Upāsikārāmaya closed its doors for the last time.

23 Carus, Paul, "Sister Sanghamitta," *The Open Court*, 15, no. 4 (April 1901). The Countess maintained her early Theosophical ideas throughout her career as a lay nun in Ceylon and later.

24 Quoted from the March 28, 1898 letter to Paul Carus, just one month prior to the opening of the Buddhist convent.

25 Quoted from the January 3, 1899 letter the Countess wrote to Carus the day after she had received permission to establish the Saṅghamittā Order of Upāsikās.

26 The diocese included monks, laymen, and Dharmapāla.

27 "Sil," *Dinamina*, 22 February 1900; *gihi* is Sinhala for the Pāli *gihini* – "householder," while *pävidi* is Sinhala for the Pāli *pabbajjā* – "going forth."

28 "Sil," *Dinamina*, 22 February 1900; *Pañca sīla sikkhāpadaṅ samādiyāmi* is the Pāli refrain for the one taking the precepts. Translated, it means "I undertake to keep the five precepts."

29 For more on the precepts of contemporary lay nuns and their implication in ascertaining their status, see chapter 8 below.

30 "The Buddhist Countess and Her Work," *Ceylon Independent*, 3–4.

31 Ibid. "The Countess Canavarro, refreshing her memory with a copy of the *Mahāvamsa*," described the ancient nuns of Ceylon. Like Dharmapāla and other Buddhists in Ceylon at that time, the Countess subscribed to a Mahāvaṃsa-view of history.

32 Canavarro, *Insight into the Far East*, p. 91.

33 The pamphlet was published in July, 1899. Sister Saṅghamittā wrote to Paul Carus four months later, on November 6, 1899, saying that "you will be sorry to hear that the convent is no more. I will soon be homeless …"

34 *Diṇamina*, 13 February 1900, describes the new convent. Also, Dharmapāla mentioned visiting the Countess there in his February 6, 1900 diary entry.

35 Quoted from the March 20, 1899 letter to Paul Carus. However, Catherine Shearer was hired as the Head Mistress of the school.

36 Dharmapāla's diary entry for October 20, 1898.

37 Paul Carus, "A Modern Instance of World Renunciation," *Open Court*, 13, no. 2 (February 1899).

38 See the September letter from Catherine Shearer to Dharmapāla, included in the collection of Dharmapāla's letters to Paul Carus, "The Open Court Publishing Company Archives."

39 Quoted from Dharmapāla's diary entry of August 9, 1898.

40 See "The Open Court Publishing Company Archives." One-hundred and fifty of the Countess's letters to Carus have been preserved on microfilm.

41 Quoted from Dharmapāla's diary entry for October 21, 1898. Though the Countess did not want Dharmapāla to interfere with her Upāsikārāmaya work, she wanted his attention.

42 Ibid., November 1, 1898.

43 Ibid., November 2, 1898.

44 Ibid.

45 Dharmapāla mentioned this in his November 5, 1898 diary entry. Shearer made a trip to Kagalla, situated on the Kandy-Colombo Road.

46 See the letters from Sister Saṅghamittā (Countess Canavarro) to Paul Carus, from November 1898 to January 1899, "The Open Court Publishing Company Archives."

47 Dharmapāla's diary entry for January 6, 1899; and the entry for August 12, 1903.

48 "Shearer Upāsikāva," *Sarasavisandaresa*, 18 July 1899. In the Pāli literature, Padmavatī was a courtesan of King Bimbisara who had a child by him. The child, Abhaya, eventually became a monk, and later, an *arahant*. One day, after hearing him preach, Padmavatī, too, became an *arahant*. See Bimala Churn Law, *Women in Buddhist Literature* (Varanasi: Indological Book House, 1981), p. 29. See also G. P. Malalasekera, ed., *The Dictionary of Pāli Proper Names* (London: Luzac and Company, Ltd., 1960).

49 See Canavarro, *Insight into the Far East*, p. 139. Canavarro, quoting from her diary, reflected that during one of her absences in India, Shearer "had embraced Buddhism and had taken the yellow robe."

50 Moreover, "She does not find the work congenial … She is not useful for practical work." See the letter to Paul Carus dated September 9, 1899.

51 "The Lady Canavarro Upāsikārāmaya," *Diṇamina*, 13 February 1900; "Saṅghamittā Upasikava," *Diṇamina*, 25 November 1899, stated that the Countess would not return to America as was rumoured, but would reopen the Saṅghamittā School in a different location.

52 "Letter to the Editor," *Ganartha Pradīpaya*, 30 November 1899.

53 According to her November 22, 1899, letter to Carus, "Miss Shearer turns out to be a scheming adventurer who in some subtle way has wound Dharmapāla around her finger."

54 c.f., *Ceylon Examiner*, 9 October 1900; *The Dinakara Prakāsaya*, 13 October 1900; "Miranda de Souza Canavarro," *The Ganartha Pradīpaya*, 15 October 1900; *The Sarasavisandaresa*, 12 October 1900; *Diṇamina*, 10 October 1900. The poor condition of other leading newspapers prohibited further search for similar articles.

55 Quoted from Dharmapāla's diary entry of April 4, 1901.

56 Though Shearer meditated in Japan, she did not become a member of the order of nuns there.

57 "The Late Miss Catherine Shearer," *The Mahā Bodhi and the United Buddhist World*, 17, nos. 4 & 5 (April-May 1909), 131.

58 "Donning of the Yellow Robe by Upāsikās," *Sarasavisandaresa*, 3 January 1899. It is interesting that in Dharmapāla's descriptions of lay nuns in Burma, he suggested that they wore white. See chapter 2.

59 "Burmese Pilgrims in Ceylon Still," *Ceylon Examiner*, 13 March 1899; also *Ceylon Examiner*, 3 January 1899, and "Burmese Upāsikās," *Sarasavisandaresa*, 20 January 1899 contain further references to Burmese "nuns" in Ceylon.

60 Dharmapāla's diary entry of February 20, 1900. Shearer often assisted the Countess at the Saṅghamittā Upāsikārāmaya in Kandy throughout her stay in Ceylon. The complete history and demise of the Kandy lay nunnery cannot be fully documented from the extant resources. However, the Countess's 1925 book supplies some details. Reflecting on her work in Kandy, the Countess gave a brief history of its origins: "I conceived the idea of founding a home for *Upasikas*, who should feed the poor and care for orphan children ... I had drawn up rules by which I hoped to introduce new and elevating ideas... On my first visit to Kandy I had met a lady of high caste, unmarried, and of a very strong personality. She was an *Upasika*, the second whom I had met that was not old and ugly ... I wanted her for the head of the Upāsikārāmaya and finally she consented. This lady and myself opened the *Arama* (retreat) in the bungalow rented for the school where we expected to remain till the lady from India should arrive, when we would find other quarters ... To begin with, there were six *Upasikas*: this lady, myself and others. We formally opened the institution with a banquet to the priests who gave prayerful blessings for the success of our work." (Canavarro, *Insight into the Far East*, pp. 63–64). Her Protestant Buddhist concerns of "this-worldly" involvement are striking in her account of the Kandy lay

nunnery. In a letter to Paul Carus written in Kandy on March 28, 1898, three days prior to the opening of the Saṅghamittā Upāsikārāmaya in Colombo, the Countess wrote that she was in that town to "organize a body of nuns" for social work. The *Sarasavisandaresa* refers to the Kandy Upāsikārmaya only once, on July 5, 1898. In a notice, M de Souza Canavarro Upāsikā [sic; i.e., the Countess] proclaimed that "This is to say I have no connection with the Kandy Girls School although I wish it success. Although this school first began under the Colombo Saṅghamittā Upāsikārāmaya as an extension, for some reason it has been moved from under its wing. The *Upāsikā* section that I began I wanted to extend to Kandy. The money I have received for the Kandy Upāsikārāmaya has been spent as follows ... "

According to Dharmapāla's diaries, though the Saṅghamittā School in Kandy eventually became independent of the Countess's control, her *upāsikās*, especially Shearer, made frequent trips there.

61 She and her husband were instrumental in establishing Lady Blake's Upāsikārāmaya, the subject of chapter 5.

62 The section of Kandy where Lady Blake's Upāsikārāmaya is situated.

63 *Sarasavisandaresa*, 20 January 1899.

64 This is the first instance in Dharmapāla's diary in which her refers to a female renunciant who kept the ten precepts as a "nun." He never referred to the *upāsikās* at the Saṅghamittā Upāsikārāmaya as "nuns" in his diaries.

65 Quoted from Dharmapāla's diary entry of April 16, 1900.

66 Ibid., December 12, 1899.

67 Quoted from Dharmapāla's diary entry of April 16, 1907. It is interesting that there were five-hundred lay nuns in Burma in 1907.

68 "Miss C. Shearer," *The Mahā Bodhi and the United Buddhist World*, 15, nos. 1–3 (January-March 1907), 140.

69 She died in June, 1909. "The Late Miss Catherine Shearer," 131.

70 "A Buddhist Pilgrimage in Burma," *The Mahā Bodhi and the United Buddhist World*, 17, no. 3 (March 1909), 47–50.

71 See the letter from Shearer to Dharmapāla published posthumously in *The Mahā Bodhi and the United Buddhist World*, 17, no. 6 (June 1909), 132–133.

72 This passage from the "Mahāparinibbāna Suttanta" appeared, and continues to appear, on the covers of all MBS publications and thus identified the Saṅghamittā Upāsikārāmaya as one of its satellites.

73 Though the Countess gives Russell as *her* family name, in an interview with the *Ganartha Pradīpaya*, which appeared on 26 April 1900, she stated that her husband belonged to the Russell family.

74 This series of events corresponds to Dharmapāla's diary entries for the period in question.

75 *Pirit*, literally "protection," are auspicious Pāli verses.

76 According to the newspapers of the period, the campaigns for financial

support launched by the Upāsikārāmaya was well organized and very successful, as well. Requests for donations appeared in almost every issue of the Theosophical Society's newspaper, the *Sarasavisandaresa*, which often printed the names of those who contributed. The bi-weekly publication contained a plea for contributions for the Saṅghamittā Upāsikārāmaya and School in every issue in the months of January, February, and March of 1899. The editor also included a weekly list of contributions collected from different areas around the island (e.g., August 1, 1899, and August 15, 1899.) By September 19, 1899, 4,165.53 rupees had been collected – a considerable sum of money in 1899.

77 The *Tathāgata* is the "thus gone one" – the Buddha.

78 The Catholic terminology is striking.

79 "E. S. T." is unclear.

80 Not unlike Subhodānanda and the other itinerant lay preachers who had assumed the vocation of the ordained clergy in the 1890s, the Countess and her "nuns" also donned the ochre robe. This is substantiated by photographs of the Countess at the Upāsikārāmaya and, as we have seen, eye-witness accounts. According to a series of articles which was published in Sinhala newspapers, the Countess often appeared in the garb of a member of the monastic order. In articles that addressed the concerns of those who witnessed the emergence of laypeople appropriating the attire and vocation of the monk, mention is made of the Countess.

One writer, in a letter supporting the Countess's undertakings, cited historical precedence by mentioning Queen Anulā and King Milinda as fine examples of laypeople who wore the ochre robes. He then offers a contemporary example: "I have seen the woman from America, Canavarro *Upāsikā*, donning yellow robes over her clothing sometimes. I know that before doing this, she has talked about this to a *mahā nayaka sthavira* and he has told her that there is no harm in it. Whether this act leads to the decline of the Buddhism should be looked into by the learned great elder monks. My intention of writing was only to clarify matters in the eyes of those who will solve this problem" ("Donning of the Yellow Robe by Upāsikās," *Sarasavisandaresa*, 3 January 1899). A *mahā nayaka sthavira* is a monk who holds the preeminent position in any one of the three fraternities of Theravāda Buddhism in Sri Lanka.

81 The elder monk referred to above must have been Hikkaduwa Sumangala, who often advised the Countess concerning her role in Buddhist Ceylon. In his January 2, 1899 diary entry, six months prior to the appearance of the pamphlet, Dharmapāla wrote that the Countess had "gone to see the High Priest at Maligakanda ... where she had gone to get the consent to start the Sanghamitta order of *Upasikas*." In Dharmapāla's diary entries for October 29, 1897; November 16, 1897; January 2, 1899; and January 22, 1899, he established H. Sumangala as his advisor as well.

82 The rules required a quorum of monks to induct a novice into the sisterhood. Like the novice nun of ancient days, who was required to appear before nuns and monks as a necessary part of her ordination, the sisters of the Saṅghamittā Upāsikārāmaya, too, had to meet with the approval of the order of monks. This is one of the *garudhammas*, or eight weighty rules, which Mahāpajāpatī Gotamī accepted at the time of her initiation as the first *bhikkhunī*, a step in the development of insitutionalized androcentrism. For more on the *garudhammas*, see chapter 8. Moreover, as is the case with the lay nuns of present day Sri Lanka, a monk – a member of the *saṅgha* – rather than another lay nun was needed to "give" the ten precepts.

83 Not unlike the contemporary monks and lay nuns of Sri Lanka, the ordination ceremonies at the Saṅghamittā Upāsikārāmaya were conducted on days considered auspicious by Buddhists in Ceylon – Vesak and other full-moon periods (*pōya*), or important phases of the lunar cycle. I witnessed two separate ordinations of lay nuns, and a group ordination of 50 male novices, all of which were performed on *pōya* days.

84 Like the lace gown and expensive jewels the Countess wore at her induction into the Buddhist faith in 1897, the vestment the novitiate was required to wear at the Saṅghamittā symbolized lay life. In essence, the novitiate renounced all the finer things of life, symbolized by "silks and jewels" in favor of the life of the nun.

85 Oldenberg, ed., *Vinaya Piṭakam*, vol. 2, p. 266, states that it is an offense to wear a robe for the purpose of decorating the body; instead, it should be worn for modesty.

86 Chaplet is Catholic terminology for the rosary. Though beads are not traditionally used in Sri Lankan Buddhism, Dharmapāla encouraged the use of them as an aid in meditation, c.f., the *Sarasavisandaresa*, 3 January 1899; it is related here that he had sent beads (Sinhala: *nävagunavala*) to a Parisian Countess to aid her in her *bhāvanā* (meditation). Also, Dharmapāla had noticed the use of beads by Burmese nuns; see chapter 3. The kneeling cloth given as a requisite is called the *nisidānam* in the monastic code; see Oldenberg, ed., *Vinaya Piṭakam*, vol. 4, p. 123. It is used in Theravāda Buddhist meditation as the cloth upon which the meditator sits.

87 This meditation is an important feature in the *upasampadā* ceremony of monks today, though it is not chanted by the lay nuns at the time of their ordination. See chapter 8 for my descriptions of the two ordinations of lay nuns I witnessed.

88 It is possible that the "Lord" is the officiating monk (*upajjhāya*) of the texts. See, for instance, Oldenberg, ed., *Vinaya Piṭakam*, vol. 4, p. 86 (*pācittiya*, XXXVIII) for a reference to the *upajjhāya*.

89 The content of the five precepts is not clear, though the wording implies that the Countess referred to the traditional five precepts of the lay person. If this is the case, there is no apparent reason for requesting the

inductee to first chant the five precepts, and seconds later, the ten precepts. It may be that the Countess was aware of the tradition in the order of monks in which the novice monk, at the time of his higher ordination, symbolically becomes a layman by donning the white apparel of the householder. Having done this, he repeats the five precepts of the laity, which is an impressive and important part of the ceremony. He then chants the *pabbajjā dasasīla* (the ten precepts of the one who enters the *saṅgha*). In much the same way, the novices at the Saṅghamittā Upāsikārāmaya symbolically became laywomen again by richly dressing "in silks and jewels" and then chanting the five precepts. However, the chanting of the five precepts was to occur while the novice was dressed in the ochre robes, rather than when she was bejewelled. In other words, these events did not occur in a logical sequence.

90 This is the traditional Three Refuges of the laity and the *saṅgha* alike; it is chanted during every auspicious Buddhist event in contemporary Sri Lanka. However, the "dedication" is Christian.

91 We saw in chapter 3 that the Countess did not advocate celibacy.

92 It is not clear who the "Blessed Ones" were. The *Gāthās* are Pāli stanzas from the dialogues of the Buddha in verse form, traditionally sung at important events.

5 THE INSTITUTIONALIZATION OF TRADITION

1 Anyone reading the Sinhala or English newspapers of Ceylon in the 1890s would have been aware of the presence of Burmese monks and lay nuns in Kandy and Colombo. In a representative article from the period, we learn that Colombo was host to many Burmese world-renunciants: "Fifteen Burmese priests and laymen left this morning by the BL SS Stafordshire for Rangoon; the charitable lady P. P. Jayatilike Mahine and Sons Messrs. C. L. and C. H. de Silva, by whom large numbers of priests and priestesses [sic] were entertained on several occasions, and at whose residence several respectable Burmese parties stayed ... they gave valuable assistance ... The remaining three priests and eight priestesses [lay nuns], who are now staying at the Maligakanda Temple and the Pusparama Temple, Mount Lavinia, will not leave Ceylon for a year or two" ("Burmese Pilgrims in Ceylon Still," *Ceylon Examiner*, 13 March 1899). The pilgrims were guests of the Maligakanda Temple, the temple associated with the Saṅghamittā School.

2 It is not remarkable that Burma has played a role in the history of Buddhism in Ceylon. In fact, the two countries have a history of exchange – especially in regard to ordination – which dates back to 1070. According to the chronicles, when King Vijayabāhu brought stability after Cola invasions, he called upon the king of Burma to send monks to Sri Lanka to restore the monks' lineage. See Perera, *Buddhism in Sri Lanka: A Short History*, p. 46. Later, in 1476, when a revival of

Buddhism was well under way in Ceylon, the Burmese called upon Sri Lankan monks to ordain Burmese men in the tradition of the Mahāvihāra, so that they could return home and revive their own lineage (Ibid., p. 58). Still later in 1803, the Burmese established an ordination lineage in Ceylon after Buddhism had suffered under the colonial powers (Ibid., p. 70). Thus, the reciprocal relationship between Burma and Ceylon is an important chapter in the history of Buddhism in South Asia.

3 Like many Christian Ceylonese children of her period, de Alwis received an English-style education and upbringing. I have drawn much of what I know about de Alwis from Srī Sudharmā Samitiya, "Srī Sudharmācārī Upāsikā Mäniyan Vahansege Apadanaya" (Kandy: Srī Sudharmā Samitiya, 1939). I believe I consulted the only extant copy, which is in the possession of Kotmalee Sudharmā, the present incumbent of the lay nunnery de Alwis established. I also consulted a biography of de Alwis in V. S. Dharmabandhu, *Sinhala Virayo* (Colombo: S. B. Fernando Publisher, 1949), p. 315.

4 Srī Sudharmā Samitiya, "Mahānuwara Srī Sudharmā Upāsi-kārāmaya" (Kandy: Srī Sudharmā Society, n.d.), pp. 9–27. To my knowledge, I consulted the only extant copy. Like the pamphlet referred to above, it is in the possession of Kotmalee Sudharmā.

5 Ibid., p. 17.

6 Tissa Fernando, "The Western-Educated Elite and Buddhism in British Ceylon: A Neglected Aspect of the Nationalist Movement," in K. Ishwaran, ed., *Contributions to Asian Studies, Volume IV: Tradition and Change in Theravāda Buddhism* (Leiden: E. J. Brill, 1973), pp. 18–29.

7 Ibid., p. 22. Fernando quotes the *Ceylon Independent*, 19 April 1913.

8 Ibid., 23.

9 "Srī Sudharmācārī Upāsikā Mäniyan," written in 1939, states that "Catherine was born 90 years ago." Unfortunately, I have not been able to find sources which detail her life between the ages of twenty-five and fifty-six.

10 Ibid., p. 2.

11 "Burmese Upāsikā's Burial," *Sarasavisandarasa*. It is quite possible that de Alwis is the woman in Kandy about whom the Countess reminisces in her *Insight into the Far East*. According to the Countess, she met "an Upasika ... This lady was a very noble looking woman, and as I later had reason to know, was as noble as she looked. She was interested in the work I was doing. I wanted her for the head of the *Upasikarama* and finally she consented. This lady and myself opened the *Arama* (retreat) in the bungalow rented for the school ..." (p. 64).

12 "Srī Sudharmācārī Upāsikā Mäniyan," p. 4.

13 See below for more on the perception that cloisters for laywomen are part of traditional Buddhism in Ceylon.

14 That is, since the days recorded in the chronicles.

15 "Mahānuwara Srī Sudharmā Upāsikārāmaya," p. 1.

16 That is, the *upāsikā*.
17 *Vahansee* is a Sinhala title of respect.
18 "Srī Sudharmācārī Upāsikā Mäniyan," p. 1.
19 For instance, Kotmalee Sudharmā, the present incumbent of Lady Blake's, argued that Sudharmācārī did not wish to enter the *saṅgha*.
20 Hundreds and hundreds of years, of course, separate King Devānampi-tyatissa and King Dutugemanu from de Alwis.
21 "Srī Sudharmācārī Mäniyan," p. 1. The emphasis is mine.
22 *The Mahāvaṃsa*. ed. Geiger, p. 135.
23 That is, Catherine de Alwis.
24 "An Upāsikārāmaya in Kandy," *Diṇamina*, 20 June 1907.
25 Dharmapāla wrote in his diary entry for February 7, 1902, that he "addressed *Upasakas* and *Upasikas*, a decrepit, toothless, grey haired old lot they were. Idiotic and foolish are they ..."
26 See below.
27 "The Opening of a Buddhist *Upasika Aramaya* at Kandy by H. E. Lady Blake," *Weekly Times of Ceylon*, 4 July 1907. The parenthetical definition is in the original.
28 Dharmapāla's diary entry for December 14, 1897.
29 "Lady Havelock declined to visit the School lest her name should thereby be associated with Theosophy ... This is the kind of encouragement dealt out to Buddhists by their Christian rulers, but we take leave to doubt whether the Home Government would approve of the discourtesy on the part of its representatives" (The Sanghamitta School," *The Buddhist* (April 21, 1893), 127).
30 Quoted from Dharmapāla's diary entry of January 16, 1907. Dharma-pāla was in India during the years in which the Sudharmā Upāsi-kārāmaya project was inaugurated. However, he corresponded with Lady Blake from India.
31 Lady Blake's reference is to the *garudhammas* that Mahāpajāpatī Gotamī accepted from the Buddha as part of her ordination; they subordinated the order of nuns to the order of monks. For more, see chapter 8.
32 This gloss is Lady Blake's.
33 Edith Blake, "A Buddhist Nun," *The Buddhist Review: The Organ of the Buddhist Society of Great Britain and Ireland*, 7 (1915), 51. The parenthetical remarks are Lady Blake's.
34 Ibid., pp. 51–52.
35 Bella Sidney Woolf, *How to See Ceylon* (London: Blackfriars House, 1914), pp. 91–92. She also mentions Lady Blake's contribution to Sudharmācārī's project.
36 If Lady Blake had been a Theosophist, this would have been a major polemical issue for the Buddhists of Ceylon. No mention is made of her in regard to Theosophy in any of the sources.
37 Edith Blake, "The Sacred Bo Tree," *The Nineteenth Century and After*, 76 (July-December 1914), 660–673.

38 By *pansikas*, Lady Blake probably meant *pansilas*, that is, those who keep the precepts.

39 Blake, "The Sacred Bo Tree," 671.

40 Ibid.

41 They were also featured in "The Opening of a Buddhist *Upasika Aramaya* at Kandy," *Weekly Times of Ceylon.*

42 For elderly women, meditation and vows of renunciation constitute what Sherry Ortner has called a "ritual of postparenthood" (See Sherry P. Ortner, *Sherpas through Their Rituals* (New York: Cambridge University Press, 1978), pp. 35–60. An analogue of this practice can be found in the developed form of the Brahmanical *āśrāma* system in which the Hindu is to semi-retire from "the world" to practice yoga and to meditate; later, one is to renounce the world altogether, in order to pursue liberation from *saṃsāra*.

43 I would like to thank Kotmalee Sudharmā for giving me her only color photograph of Sister Sudharmācārī.

44 Bloss has discussed this point in his interesting article, "The Female Renunciants of Sri Lanka."

45 I was not able to refer to the letter as the issue of the *Ceylon Observer* in which it appeared is not part of the collection of the Ceylon Government Archives.

46 "The Education of Buddhist Girls," *The Buddhist* (March 11, 1916), 4.

47 *Mettā* is usually translated as loving-kindness.

48 "The Education of Buddhist Girls" (March 11, 1916), 4; the parenthetical remarks are in the original.

49 "Dear Sisters," *The Buddhist* (March 11, 1916), 5.

50 Personal communications from leading lay nuns in Sri Lanka.

51 "Residence for Buddhist Nuns at Anurādhapura," *The Buddhist* (March 24, 1917), 4.

52 Ibid., 4.

53 The Reverend Bhikkhu Silacara, "The Education of Buddhist Girls," *The Buddhist* (November 18, 1916), 1.

54 "The Dead Hand of Buddhism," *The Buddhist Chronicle* (December 12, 1923), 6.

55 For instance, "Upāsikārāmaya, Kandy," *The Buddhist Chronicle* (September 12, 1923), 6.

56 For example, "Katukele Buddhist Girls' School," *The Buddhist* (October 6, 1917), 2.

57 Here *Upāsaka* refers to Mr. Silva's piety.

58 For descriptions of the "ordination" of a lay nun, see chapter 8 of this work.

59 "The Only Daughter of Upāsaka Charles Silva Becomes an Upāsikāva," *Diṇamina*, 18 March 1907. According to "Charles Silva Upāsaka Becomes Ordained in Burma," *Diṇamina*, 25 June 1907, he became a *bhikkhu* having been inspired by his daughter's renunciant lifestyle.

60 She is not named in the articles.
61 The name was changed in 1961 from Sudharmācārī Upāsikārāmaya to Lady Blake's. Interestingly enough, the lay nuns of Sri Lanka refer to it as Lady Bloke's!
62 Sister Sudharmācārī, the founder, was followed by Sister Sumanā, who was followed by a Burmese lay nun, Māwicārī. I collected the data for this section during a series of interviews from October, 1988 to September, 1989. I gathered the bulk of Kotmalee Sudharmā's biography on May 8, and 9, 1989. Kotmalee Sudharmā and Kotmalee Dhīrā Sudharmā are not the same person. For more on Kotmalee Dhīrā Sudharmā, see chapter 7.
63 In the Sri Lankan system of education, it is possible for children to be educated until the tenth standard, at which time they sit for the Ordinary Levels and, if successful and willing, the Advanced Levels.
64 According to Kotmalee Sudharmā, Māwicārī came on a pilgrimge from Burma to Kandy in 1927 to visit the Temple of the Tooth. She returned to Ceylon in 1929; by the time of her death she had ordained seventy-two pupils.
   In the early 1930s, while Sudharmācārī was still living, Māwicārī ordained a young woman, Sīlavatī (formerly Miss Jayawardena), whose parents built them an *ārāmaya* in Moratunduwa. Sīlavatī eventually became the head lay nun and replaced Sudharmācārī's successor. Māwicārī became the *loku mäniyo,* or "chief mother," in the early 1940s.
65 Because the Upāsikārāmaya is built on a slope, the buildings are separated by an embankment. Approaching the Upāsikārāmaya from the Peradeniya road, the resident lay nuns make their way up an alley next to the school that used to be run by the Upāsikārāmaya, but was taken over by the state in the 1961. The alley passes by: the *pirivena* (where lay nuns come, from all over the county, to study a curriculum of Buddhism), the impressive Bō tree, the circular *ārāmaya* or the "down" section, and finally the two halls of rooms which are parallel to one another, or the "upper" section of the Upāsikārāmaya complex. The four lay nuns who do not associate with Kotmalee Sudharmā do their own cooking and lead a separate life.
66 Those who volunteered were of the *Goyigama,* or the highest, caste.
67 Mettā Mäniyo, who died in 1991, had a seventy year-old son and became a lay nun in her eighties upon the death of her husband. Her story is reminiscent of a few of the poems in the *Therīgāthā,* the poems attributed to the members of the *bhikkhunī sangha.* According to I. B. Horner, only three of the poems in the *Therīgāthā* can be attributed to widows. See *Women Under Primitive Buddhism,* p. 174.
68 In interviews with lay nuns islandwide, most of the *loku mātāvo* (head lay nuns) stressed the need to recruit younger women who are capable of leading a life of social service. They claim that in old age social work is impossible. We will see in chapter 6 that one objective of another

movement to re-establish the tradition of female renunciation, was to dispel the notion that the life of the lay nun was reserved for the elderly. I know of several cases of elderly "upset" female renunciants being sent away from the *upāsikārāmaya* in which they were ordained.

69 See chapter 7.

70 The term traditionally reserved for meals of the ordained clergy.

71 *Gilānpāsa* is a refreshment that is permitted to monks in the afternoon; as they are prohibited by *Vinaya* rules to eat in the afternoon, they are allowed a "medicine" (*gilāna*) to prevent them from becoming ill from not eating. As Charles Hallisey has pointed out to me, *gilānpāsa* is a legal fiction; that is, it has no basis in the *Vinaya* rules.

72 He wanted to build a hotel in the place of the nunnery.

73 According to Kotmalee Sudharmā, the present group of female renunciants suffer hardships unknown to Sudharmācārī.

74 See chapter 7 for more on the economic status of the lay nuns in contemporary Sri Lanka.

75 All the lay nuns I interviewed either volunteered this analysis or confirmed it.

76 For more on the social variables of women who entered the ancient order, see Horner, *Women Under Primitive Buddhism*, pp. 162–193.

77 They were part of the royal harem.

78 As Steven Collins has pointed out to me, most world-renouncers, in all religions, are drawn from the upper classes.

79 Sponberg, "Attitudes toward Women and the Feminine in Early Buddhism," p. 25.

80 Ibid., p. 11.

6 THE LAY NUN IN TRANSITIONAL CEYLON

1 Sponberg, "Attitudes toward Women and the Feminine in Early Buddhism," p. 17. Here Sponberg discusses the reasons why the ancient order of nuns was eventually brought under the control of the monks. His theory applies as well to the period under review in this chapter.

2 See chapter 5. It must be stressed here that many of those involved in politics, however, were Christians rather than Buddhists. According to Donald Smith, during the latter decades of the 1800s, "the Christians formed a minority of about 8%, but contributed a substantial number of its leading families to the elite." Though many Christian-educated, elite persons of Sinhala background remained nominaly Buddhist, "this was a vestige which bore little relationship to their highly Anglicized life." See Donald E. Smith, "Religion, Politics, and the Myth of Reconquest," in Tissa Fernando and Robert N. Kearney, eds., *Modern Sri Lanka: A Society in Transition* (New York: Syracuse University, 1979), p. 8. Yet, there were a few who remained loyal to Buddhism. See below.

3 Ibid.

4 See below for my discussion on the origin of societies of this type.
5 "Sanghamitta Day Celebrations," *The Buddhist Chronicle* (January 6, 1924), 1. *Bana* preaching refers to sermons by clergy.
6 "Sanghamitta," *The Buddhist* (June 1932), 1.
7 Ibid.
8 The origins of the Sinhala Buddhist conception of race were colonial. See Jonathan Spencer, "Introduction: The Power of the Past," in *Sri Lanka*, pp. 1–16.
9 "An Appeal to the Diyawadana Nilame and Other Members of the Buddhist Temporalities Committee, Kandy," *The Buddhist* (September 16, 1916), 3.
10 "Rules for the Vihāra Mahā Devī Samitiya," July 1938, cyclostyled.
11 J. R. Jayewardene was President of Sri Lanka from 1976–1988.
12 W. Harold Wriggins, *Ceylon: Dilemmas of a New Nation* (Princeton University Press, 1960), p. 83.
13 Also present at the inaugural meeting were Mrs C. Hewavitarane, Mrs. Raja Hewavitarane and Mrs. Neil Hewavitarane, Dharmapāla's sisters-in-law. They were elected as members of the Working Committee. "Minutes of the Vihāra Mahā Devī Upāsikārāmaya, 28.7.36," cyclostyled.
14 "Buddhist Nunnery Opened: Impressive Ceremony at Biyagama," *Ceylon Daily News*, 26 October 1936.
15 "Minutes of the Vihāra Mahā Devī Upāsikārāmaya, 1936–1945."
16 "Biyagama was selected owing to its proximity to Colombo and because it is within the precincts of Ceylon's erstwhile capital, Kalaniya, which tradition alleges was once the home of Ceylon's greatest queen, Vihara Maha Devi" ("A Nunnery for Ceylon," *The Buddhist* (September 1936), 347).
17 "Buddhist Nunnery Opened."
18 "Biyagama Upasika Aramaya," *The Buddhist* (September 1940), 74.
19 Ibid. According to nineteenth-century racial theories, the "*Ariyas*," or Ariyans, were the original Buddhists. These theories had permeated the ideology of most westernized Buddhists by this period. Sri Lankan Buddhists could thus boast that they, like their colonizers, were Aryan.
20 Biyagama Upasika Aramaya, *The Buddhist* (September 1940), 74. Note the usage of western words to describe the *dasa sil upāsikās* and their environs. Vidyalankara Pirivena continues to the present to attract highly cultivated *bhikkhus* for higher education. It, too, is located in Kalaniya.
21 "Rules for the Vihāra Mahā Devī Samitiya," 4.
22 I found the time table loose among the Vihāra Mahā Devī Upāsikārāmaya collection and cannot date it with much accuracy. However, Sister Visākhā, who was one of the two women ordained at the opening ceremonies and who served as the first chief lay nun, devised it.
23 This was a private worship; the nuns worshipped together at 6:00 a.m.
24 According to an undated newspaper clipping in the collection of the

Vihāra Mahā Devī Upāsikārāmaya, Sister Visākhā was originally a pupil of Sister Sudharmācārī of Lady Blake's Upāsikārāmaya in Kandy. I assume that like Sudharmācārī she was from a privileged Sinhalese family.

25 "Rules for the Vihāra Mahā Devī Samitiya," 1.

26 Ibid., 4.

27 "The Report of the Vihāra Mahā Devī Upāsikārāmaya Society, 1936–37," cyclostyled. Nissanka referred to the unordained female renunciants as "Nuns."

28 Ibid.

29 "The Report of the Vihāra Mahā Devī Upāsikārāmaya Society, 1936–1937." The parenthetical glosses are his.

30 Ibid., see rule 4 above which determines the age group of the *upāsikās*.

31 Personal communication from Sister Sudharmā, the present incumbent of Lady Blake's. The Vihāra Mahā Devī Samitiya seems to have been very familiar with the activities at Lady Blake's Upāsikārāmaya. According to one of their reports, it was held that "the immediate future calls for the training and education of the *Upasikas*. We have refused many applications because we are anxious to recieve only those who understand our ideals of renunciation and service. Too long have we thought that *Upasikas* should be the aged and the infirm, and *Upasikaramayas* fit homes for such." The "Report of the Vihāra Mahā Devī Samitiya, June 1936-June 1938," cyclostyled.

32 "Minutes of the Vihāra Mahā Devī Upāsikārāmaya, 29.9.40," cyclostyled. *Sāsana* here means "order."

33 "Buddhist Nunnery Opened."

34 "The Report of the Vihāra Mahā Devī Samitiya, June 1936–June 1938."

35 Ibid.

36 It can also be argued, however, based on Sri Nissanka's terminology such as "*ashram*," and the vocations that he considered admirable (spinning and weaving), that there was some Gandhian influence at this lay nunnery.

37 "The Report of the Vihāra Mahā Devī Upāsikārāmaya Society, 1936–37."

38 "Minutes of the Vihāra Mahā Devī Upāsikārāmaya," July 1, 1941, cylcostyled.

39 "All Ceylon Buddhist Congress: Diamond Jubilee Celebrations (1919–1979)," (Colombo: Metro Printers, 1980), 1, cyclostyled.

40 Ibid.

41 Ibid., 13.

42 "All Ceylon Buddhist Congress," 16.

43 "Minutes of the Vihāra Mahā Devī Upāsikārāmaya, 1.12.45," cyclostyled. According to the Minutes, four lay nuns were in residence in 1945: Visākhā, Sudharmā, Vimalā and Amarā.

44 Ibid.

45 They are both referred to as "Sister" in the literature of the period.

46 "Minutes of the Vihāra Mahā Devī Upāsikārāmaya, 12.9.38 and 25.10.38," cyclostyled. That the chief *upāsikā* had virtually no power in the decisions of the Upāsikārāmaya is further attested in these minutes.

47 "Minutes of the Vihāra Mahā Devī Upāsikārāmaya, 1.12.38," cylcostyled.

48 "Minutes from the Vihāra Mahā Devī Upāsikārāmaya, 20.12.38," cylostyled.

49 Upāsaka W. Persian, "Sister Uppalavanna," *The Buddhist* (July 1938), 46–47.

50 Ibid. The following biographical notes are taken from Persian's article.

51 For more on Gueth, see Michael Carrithers, "An Alternative Social History of the Self," in Michael Carrithers, Steven Collins, and Steven Lukes, eds., *The Category of the Person: Anthropology, Philosophy, and History* (Cambridge University Press, 1985), pp. 234–256; see also Carrithers, *The Forest Monks*, pp. 28–46.

52 Persian, "Sister Uppalavanna," 46.

53 "Sister Uppalavanna – Life of Renunciation," *Ceylon Daily News*, 15 July 1982. For more on Germans who were involved in Buddhism in the late nineteenth- and early twentieth-centuries, see *German Buddhist Writers* (Kandy: Buddhist Publication Society, 1964).

54 Persian, "Sister Uppalavanna," 46.

55 According to the *Daily News* article, her chief *dāyakas* were Mr. and Mrs. K. V. G. de Silva, prominent booksellers in Sri Lanka.

56 "Sister Uppalavanna – Life of Renunciation," *Ceylon Daily News*.

57 It is not clear who comprised the community of ascetics in which Uppalavaṇṇā seems to have been active.

58 Persian, "Sister Uppalavanna" 46.

59 Ibid., 47.

60 Francis Story, ed., *Early Western Buddhists* (Kandy: Buddhist Publication Society, 1962), p. 4. Story relates that the early European Buddhists did not "tamper with the Pāli texts and their meanings." Moreover, "their interpretation of Buddhism, leaned, if anything, rather too heavily on its purely rationalistic side" (p. 3). As we will see in chapter 8, this tendency continues among the western lay nuns.

61 Persian, "Sister Uppalavanna," 46. The present-day lay nuns I interviewed, save for those living at Uttama Sādhu's *vihāra* (See chapter 9), wear a robe, which they make by sewing various panels together rather than a patched robe.

62 This was related to me by former President J. R. Jayewardene, one of the few living members of the original Samitiya.

63 There are 100,000 *rupees* in a *läkh*.

64 This interview was conducted on May 3, 1989.

65 A female renunciant named Dhammawatī was very active at Lady Blake's in the years immediately after its establishment. She was an important liason between the Upāsikārāmaya and the laity. See chapter 5.

66 The Senanayake family was instrumental in establishing the Vihāra Mahā Devī Upāsikārāmaya. See above.

67 The interview was conducted on June 15, 1989, at the Vihāra Mahā Devī Upāsikārāmaya.

68 Sudharmā recalls that the nun whom she met on the road may have been a resident of Lady Blake's in Kandy.

69 "Minutes of the Vihāra Mahā Devī Upāsikārāmaya, 20.12.38," cyclostyled. Warakapola, Sudharmā's village, is located near Kegalle (between Kandy and Colombo).

70 "Minutes of the Vihāra Mahā Devī Upāsikārāmaya, 2.4.39," cyclostyled.

71 Self-ordination does not seem to have posed a problem for either the Vihāra Mahā Devī Samitiya or for Sudharmā. For the canonical view of self-ordination, see chapter 2 of this study.

72 "Report of the Vihāra Mahā Devī Upāsikārāmaya Committee, July 1938–July 1939," cyclostyled.

73 Ibid.

74 Ironically, the Countess, like contemporary Sinhala lay nuns, preferred the path of social service.

75 Wriggins, *Ceylon: Dilemmas*, p. 148.

76 A. Jayaratnam Wilson, *Politics in Sri Lanka*, 1947–1973 (London: The Macmillan Press, 1974), p. 16.

77 Ibid.

78 Here, "purification" means the support of Buddhism, with a strong spiritual and moral component also included.

79 "Biyagama Nunnery Second Anniversary Meeting," *The Buddhist* (August 1938), 74. It will be remembered that "purification" implies rejuvenation and purging.

80 K. M. De Silva, "Buddhism, Nationalism and Politics in Modern Sri Lanka," unpublished paper delivered at the South Asia Conference, Madison, Wisconsin, November 1984, p. 14, quoted in Bond, *The Buddhist Revival in Sri Lanka*, p. 64.

81 The 2,500 anniversary of the *parinibbāna* (final passing) of the Buddha.

82 Both Bandaranaike and his father studied at Oxford, while the elder Bandaranaike was knighted.

83 Michael Roberts, in "Elite Formation," *Collective Identities, Nationalisms and Protest in Modern Sri Lanka* (Colombo: Marga Institute, 1979), discusses the ways in which the gulf between the elite and the masses became more accentuated during the colonial domination of Ceylon.

84 Ibid., p. 32. That 1956 was the Buddhist Jayanti no doubt helped Bandaranaike in his campaign against the UNP.

85 See Obeyeskere, "Religious Symbolism," p. 62: See also Michael

Roberts, "Meanderings in the Pathways of Collective Identity and Nationalism," in *Collective Identities*, p. 60.

86 Sponberg, "Attitudes toward Women and the Feminine in Early Buddhism," p. 17.

87 Ibid.

7 THE DASA SIL MĀTĀ IN CONTEMPORARY SRI LANKA

1 After interviewing a hundred lay nuns, I was able to draw several general conclusions about them. The lay nuns we meet below voiced opinions that were generally accepted by many Sinhala women who have renounced lay life in Sri Lanka.

2 Here, *upāsikā* means "lay nun."

3 "Deaths," *Island*, 10 February 1989. Another example illustrates further: "The death occurred on Monday of Lucy Fernando Upāsikāwa [that is, lay nun] (88) of Charles Siriwardana Mawatha, Lunuwila Kirimetiyana West. She was the mother of Mr. A. S. Fernando, News Editor, Daily News" ("Death of Mrs. Lucy Fernando," *Daily News*, 30 June 1992).

4 "Deaths," *Island*, 22 August 1989.

5 I do not mean to imply that the laity compensated them with alms.

6 I do not suggest that there have not always been egalitarian tendencies in Sri Lanka. However, western liberal ideas can be said to have pervaded Sinhala society to a large degree during British colonization. Nor do I wish to imply that the status of women in the west is better than in the east.

7 For a similar appraisal of another traditional society see Ernestine Friedl, "The Portrait of Women: Appearance and Reality," *Anthropological Quarterly*, 40, no. 3 (July 1967), 97–108. In this work, Friedl argues that Greek peasant women have much more power than is usually ascribed to them: "If, as I hope to show, the women in a Greek village hold a position of real power in the life of the family, and, as I have shown earlier, the life of the family is the most significant structural and cultural element of the Greek village, then there is unmistakable need for a reassessment of the role of the Greek woman in village life" (97). A similar argument can be made of Sri Lankan rural society and culture, and probably most other rural areas of the world, as well.

8 This is probably also true of rural men.

9 However, she often feels pressured to marry and have a family. Personal observation and conversations with Buddhist friends and other informants during my period of field study in Sri Lanka led me to draw these conclusions.

10 This interview was conducted with Kotmalee Dhīrā Sudharmā on November 9, 1989, at the Madivala Upāsikārāmaya near Colombo.

11 *Ärräk* is coconut toddy, a very powerful intoxicant.

12 The interview was conducted on October 18, 1988, at the Madivala

Upāsikārāmaya. *Dukkha* is a Buddhist concept and is perhaps best left untranslated. However, Kotmalee Dhīrā Sudharmā was referring to the unsatisfactory situations that life can often offer us.

13 According to a recent study on the status of women in Sri Lankan Buddhist society, Kotmalee Dhīrā Sudharmā's vision of the life of the rural woman can be corroborated by empirical data. See Kumari Jayawardena and Swarna Jayaweera, *A Profile on Sri Lanka: The Integration of Women in Develoment Planning, Sri Lanka* (Colombo: Women's Educational Centre, 1986). In spite of the fact that Sri Lankan women have a "life expectancy of 67 years, a literacy rate of 82 per cent and a maternal mortality rate of 1.2 thousand births, ... these indications, however, reveal only the degree of physical well being; they do not reveal the real status of women ... which is one of general subordination." p. 1. The real status of the peasant woman, Jayawardena and Jayaweera argue, can be ascertained by looking at other statistics; according to them, the subordination of women in Sri Lankan society is a result of their own powerlessness over their procreative powers: "Age specific fertility rates show that the major contribution to total fertility rates had been by the 20 to 24, 25 to 29, and 30 to 34 age group females. Evidentally, the fertility of these females have not been exposed very much to effective use of contraceptives ... more than 50 per cent of the 25 to 29 age group do not want any more children. An important conclusion that could be drawn from this information may be that a large element of the married female population lack the capacity for decision making in married life, especially with regard to the size of their families" p. 25.

14 Carrithers, *The Forest Monks*, p. 9.

15 "Why We Became *Dasa Sil Mathas*," *Weekend* (Colombo), 29 April 1990.

16 This lay nun would prefer to remain anonymous. The interview was conducted in Kandy on May 15, 1989. While I was speaking to her, three other young lay nuns gathered around and agreed with her. Though this young lay nun does not cite disharmony as her reason for renouncing, but rather disinterest in shouldering family responsibility, she implied that such responsibility leads to misery for many women.

17 There is no difference in status between a formerly married and an unmarried lay nun; what is important, rather, is the purity of her practice. Just as in the early Encratite (celibate) Christian community in Syria, "It made little difference whether ... believers had remained virgins from birth, or whether they had decided to abstain from intercourse when already married." See Peter Brown, *The Body and Society: Men, Women, and Sexual Renunciation in Early Christianity* (New York: Columbia University Press, 1988), p. 93.

18 Kotagoda Dhammādinnā's life echoes that of women whose lives are immortalized in the *Therīgāthā*. Though in ancient India during the Buddha's career, most of the women "who went forth from home into homelessness" came from the royal or aristocratic families, there are records which indicate that a few were drawn from the rural classes.

These women, like Dhammādinnā, reflected upon their harsh lay lives. For instance, an anonymous poem in the *Therīgāthā* alleged to have been written by a *bhikkhunī*, highlights the difficult existence of a poor woman in ancient India before she renounced:
I have been well-released from the drudgery. My shameless husband, he disgusts me. My pots and pans stink.
I have meditated at the foot of a tree and have thus destroyed desire and hatred.
There, I meditate upon happiness, "Oh, the happiness."
See Hermann Oldenberg and Richard Pischel, eds., *The Thera-Therigāthā* (London: Luzac and Company, Ltd., 1966), p. 126.

19 The interviews with Kotagoda Dhammādinnā were conducted on August 3, and 7, 1989 at Dhammādinnārāmaya in Matiambalāma, Etulkotte, near Colombo.

20 "Why We Became *Dasa Sil Mathas*," *Weekend*.

21 Lawrence A. Babb, *Redemptive Encounters: Three Modern Styles in the Hindu Tradition* (Delhi: Oxford University Press, 1987), p. 95.

22 Ibid., p. 96.

23 Interview with Walpola Dhammāpālī at the Madivala Upāsikārāmaya on September 19, 1988. For more on Walpola Dhammāpālī, see below.

24 Careful observation of the ten precepts is Sumettā's "ideal expectation" of all female Buddhist renunciants. See Watson and Watson-Franke, *Life Histories*, p. 189.

25 For a translation of the Eight Rules, the *garudhamma*, see *Vinaya Texts*, I, pp. 323–324. Also, see below for more on the implication of the Rules.

26 The interview with Mahāgoda Sumettā was conducted at her Yaśodā-rādevī Upāsikārāmaya in Athidiya, Dehiwala, near Colombo, on May 16, 1989. For more on Mahāgoda Sumettā, see below.

27 For a translation of the story of the establishment of the order of nuns, see *Vinaya Texts*, I. Trans. Rhys Davids and Oldenberg, pp. 320–330.

28 Sponberg, "Attitudes toward Women and the Feminine in Early Buddhism," pp. 13–18. Other examples that further illustrate the institutional androcentrism of the early *saṅgha* are: the *Vinaya* injunction that the order of monks had to approve the ordination of a nun; and that the nuns had to spend the rainy season only at locations that were closely situated to a monastery. For futher examples, see Gunawardena, "Subtile Silks," 18–19.

29 The interview was conducted at the Madivala Upāsikārāmaya on October 24, 1988.

30 Jayawardena and Jayaweera, *A Profile on Sri Lanka*, p. 2.

31 This has not always been the case as our look at the late nineteenth century suggests.

32 The majority of lay nuns and monks in Sri Lanka do not "beg" for alms. By alms-rounds, I mean invitations to *dāyakas'* homes to chant *pirit*, and the *dānaya* given afterward.

33 This is Kotmalee Dhīrā Sudharmā's estimation.

34 However, Charles Hallisey has recently mentioned to me that monks seem to be part of wedding ceremonies in Cambodia, and I remember seeing monks participating in a December, 1987 wedding ceremony of a Theravādin Buddhist couple in Saranath, India.

35 See Gombrich and Obeyesekere, *Buddhism Transformed*, pp. 265–268.

36 Jäk fruit curry is the staple of most poor peoples in the rural areas.

37 In fact, following *Vinaya* instructions, they are supposed to take what they are given without regard for the content.

38 I insisted that I sit with the laity, but our hosts insisted that I sit with Kotmalee Dhīrā Sudharmā and the others.

39 I do not mean to imply that Sri Lankan Buddhists hold all monks in high regard. In short, they respect the institution of the *saṅgha*, rather than each and every monk. Neither I, nor any of my informants, have ever witnessed a lay person being served at the same time as a monk.

40 Just as not all monks are supported to the same degree, lay nuns too experience different levels of patronage. For instance, many consider it more advantageous to give to forest monks than village monks. As is the case with monks, the laity give to those lay nuns whom they consider to be most worthy; that is, to those who are the most observant of their precepts.

41 Carrithers, *The Forest Monks*, p. 111.

42 For more on the lay nuns' attitudes toward monks, see below.

43 Though the lay disciple observes the same ten precepts as the *sāmaṇerī*, the lay nuns are not novices because the ordination requires the presence of fully ordained nuns.

44 See the appendices for examples of the use of the term *upāsikā*.

45 Like the monks, they refer to their robes as *cīvara* (the accepted term for the robe of the *saṅgha*), their meals as *dānaya*, and their ordination as *pävidi kirīma*.

46 For an interesting discussion of the use of honorifics and the way in which they are useful indicators of status, see Hiroko Kawanami, "The Religious Standing of Burmese Buddhist Nuns (*thila shin*): The Ten Precepts and Religious Respect Words," in *The Journal of the International Association of Buddhist Studies*, 13, no. 1 (1990), 17–39. In Buddhist Sri Lanka, a special set of verbs is used when talking about, or addressing, monks and lay nuns to imbue their activities with a special religious significance. All the activities of monks and lay nuns – sitting, eating, sleeping – are considered to be religious activities. That the laity uses these verbs for both monks and lay nuns is significant; it suggests that the lay nuns are identified with the *saṅgha*, rather than with the laity. However, just as not all Buddhists use the religious respect words when addressing or refering to monks, not all conform to the convention when discussing or addressing lay nuns.

47 Bruce Matthews, "Sri Lanka in 1989: Peril and Good Luck," *Asian Survey*, 30, no. 2, (February 1990), 145

48 According to Indrāṇi Mäniyo, Hewavitarane Mäniyo is the first cousin of Anagārika Dharmapāla. I met Hewavitarane Mäniyo, who is very old and feeble. It seems impossible to me, however, that she could be Dharmapāla's cousin given the discrepency in their ages. I have included a translation of Hewavitarane Mäniyo's published biography in the appendices of this study.

49 The interview with Indrāṇi Mäniyo was conducted at Rahula Upāsi-kārāmaya, Grand Pass, Colombo 14, on July 6, 1989. While I chatted with her, Hewavitarane Mäniyo looked on.

50 An "*upāsikāva*," that is, a woman training to be a renunciant, prepared the meals at Lady Blake's.

51 In fact, the lay nuns who are mothers whom I interviewed all maintained a very motherly relationship with their sons and daughters; these children are very prevalent in the lay nunneries. The children continue to regard the renunciants as their mothers, but address them by their clerical name and grant them the traditional honor due to the clergy: upon greeting them and departing, the children, brothers, sisters, and parents of lay nuns fall to their knees and bow at the feet of the lay nuns.

52 However, in most cases, it takes a considerable time – sometimes decades and sometimes never – before a family is able to come to terms with their female loved one's decision to renounce the world.

53 Following the pattern of the monks, lay nuns usually take the name of their village as their first name.

54 An individual living quarter for a monk or nun.

55 This interview was conducted on May 16, 1990 at Yaśodārādevī Upāsikārāmaya. Other members of Sumettā's family have similarly been motivated to renounce; her mother decided recently to become a lay nun, and her brother is a monk.

56 See chapter 8 for a discussion of the lay nuns' ordination rite.

57 I take refuge in the Buddha, I take refuge in the *dhamma*, I take refuge in the *saṅgha*. Recitation of these "Three Refuges" defines a person as a Buddhist.

58 The end of each word is pronounced with an "ṅ" rather than an "ṃ." The latter has a much more dramatic effect. For more on the difference in pronunciation of the three refuges for the lay person and the novitiate, see Francois Bizot, *Les Traditions de la Pabbajja en Asie du Sud-Est* (Gottingen: Vandenhoeck and Ruprecht, 1988), pp. 22–23.

59 A *sāmaṇera* is a novice monk. That Kotmalee Dhīrā Sudharmā was invited to recite the Three Refuges as a *sāmaṇera* is of much significance to her; it is the standard by which she appraises her own life.

60 This extended interview was conducted on May 22, 1989 at Madivala. I would like to thank Ranmali Perera for helping with the translation of the interview.

61 Jayawardena and Jayaweera, *A Profile on Sri Lanka*, p. 6.

62 Moreover, there has been an increased participation of rural people in

the universities: "A little over 70 per cent of the university students have come from rural areas since the mid 1960s." Moreover, "... whereas 97 per cent of women students came from high and middle-income groups in 1950, only 36.1 per cent belonged to this group in 1977." See Jayaweera and Jayawardena, *A Profile on Sri Lanka*, p. 39.

63 The committee is no longer active in the affairs of the nunnery. Some of the members cite the present political troubles in Sri Lanka as the reason that they have not been able to meet and discuss the lay nunnery project; others related that Sudharmā would like to have more independence in matters relating to the lay nunnery. Interviews were conducted in November, 1988 and May, 1989. On November 22, 1988 the Vice-President of the committee discussed with me the goals of the members. In the beginning, the committee decided that the members would meet once each month and discuss the welfare of the lay nuns, *dānaya*, the buildings, and donations. They arranged that volunteer teachers would conduct classes in various subjects, including mathematics and English. A hundred lay nuns submitted applications and the committee accepted the most promising among them. The members hoped that the lay nuns would emerge educated enough to pass the GCE O level examinations – the minimum level of education in Sri Lanka. However, few people volunteered to teach and those who did were not able to make a lasting commitment. Today, six of the resident lay nuns attend the Maligakanda Pirivena in Maradana, Colombo (see chapter 4 for a discussion of this historic temple).

64 Ayyā Khemā became a *bhikṣuṇī* in a Mahāyāna ordination held in December, 1988 in Hacienda Heights, California. The ordination was sponsored by the Korean government. See chapter 9 for more on the ordination. I interviewed Ayyā Khemā on her Parappaduwa Nun's Island on April 20, 1989. Dhammāpālī Mäniyo of the Madivala Upāsikārāmaya accompanied me. Ayyā Khemā was flanked by westernnized, English-speaking laywomen seeking advice on meditation. For more on Ayyā Khemā, see Bloss, "Female Renunciants of Sri Lanka."

65 As we saw in chapter 6, the constitution of 1972 accorded Buddhism "the foremost place" and enjoined the state to "protect and foster" the religion. It is thus not coincidental that Kotmalee Dhīrā Sudharmā was allocated the land in 1972.

66 "Govt. Will Help to Revive *Bhikkhuni Sasana*," *Daily Mirror*, 16 January 1974.

67 May 22, 1989 interview at Madivala.

68 Kotmalee Sudharmā and Kotmalee Dhīrā Sudharmā are both from Kotmalee. The interviews with the two leaders were conducted independently of one another.

69 See the Epilogue to this study for more on the marked increase of similar women in the religious sites around the island.

70 Sinhala: *pissu*.

71 Many lay nuns in Sri Lanka have dedicated their activities to restoring pilgrimage sites. This is one of their maintenance and support roles.

72 For particular examples, see Gunawardena, "Subtile Silks," 21–22.

73 Interviews were conducted with Mr. Weerakoon on May 8, 1987 during a preliminary field trip to Sri Lanka, and on November 28, 1988, while conducting my field study.

74 A similar registration is incumbent upon the monks of Sri Lanka. Monks are entitled to free education, free travel, free medical advice, etc. The Ministry of Buddhist Affairs hopes that lay nuns who similarly carry identification cards will be granted the same privileges. Thus, it is considered necessary to find out who is a "real" renunciant. They also hope that registration of this sort will deter the insane from donning the robe.

75 I observed classes at two of these centers. Though the schools were closed during most of my stay in Sri Lanka due to civil strife, the lay nuns take their studies very seriously. During the few days of the year that their school was open, the Madivala group attended regularly, as did the renunciants at Lady Blake's (the school is on the premises). At both schools, the lay nuns are taught by monks on a voluntary basis. When the schools are closed, they continue with their studies in their respective lay nunneries.

76 By the term "order of nuns," *bhikkhunī* is not implied, but rather an order of lay nuns.

77 The sources do not indicate that purifications ever took place in the order of nuns. One reason for the silence could be that as the sources were written by men, we are perhaps given a biased view of history. Other reasons may be either that the *bhikkhunī saṅgha* was never considered absolutely vital for the welfare of Buddhism, or that nuns were never in need of reform.

78 Weerakoon, "Dasasil Mātā Vädapilivela" (1988, Ministry of Buddhist Affairs, Colombo, Sri Lanka), cyclostyled. I would like to thank Ranmali Perera and Abhaya Weerakoon for helping with the translation.

79 Ibid. Many of these rules, including 1, 2, 3, 5, 9, 10, and 11, are reminiscent of the *Vinaya* rules for *bhikkhunīs*.

80 Sister Sudharmā, the head lay nun of the Vihāra Mahā Devī Upāsikārāmaya, as did Kotmalee Sudharmā of Lady Blake's Upāsikā- rāmaya, gave similar explanations.

81 This interview was conducted on May 16, 1989 at Yaśodārādevī Upāsikārāmaya.

82 Mahāgoda Sumettā's work with orphans has attracted the attention of many; the former president of Sri Lanka, during his tenure as Prime Minister, was especially moved by her work. Sumettā was also lauded in the newspapers: "It was with a compassionate heart that she ventured

to give a helping hand to the destitute children who were rendered parentless due to the man-made calamity of terrorism at Kantale and the natural calamity of landslides of Maturata ... The Prime Minister released one *lakh* of *rupees* from the Terrorist Victims Fund launched in 1985 ... and offically handed over this amount to Rev. Sumeththa [sic] ... " ("'Yasorapura': a Village Born of a Nun's Compassion," *Island*, 1 February 1988; also "PM Sets Up "Yasorapura" in Response to *Dasasil Matha's* Plea," *Observer*, 17 January 1988; and "Nun's Compassion Brings New Life," *Daily News*, 23 January 1988).

83 The *dāyakas* of the Upāsikārāmaya grant the same amount of outward respect to the tiny lay nuns as they do to the older renunciants; even elder *dāyakas* bow at the feet of the child renunciants upon greeting and departing.

84 Weerakoon, "Dasasil Mātā Vädapilivela."

85 Service is Dhammādinnā's standard by which she measures the behavior of other lay nuns. This interview was conducted on August 3, 1989 at the Dhammādinnārāmaya.

86 Caroline Walker Bynum, *Holy Feast and Holy Fast* (Berkeley: University of California Press, 1987), p. 277.

87 For more on the rise of political monks, see Tambiah, *Buddhism Betrayed?*, pp. 122–123.

88 The newspapers covered the walk. It was reported in the *Island*, the *Daily News*, and all the Sinhala papers.

89 Gombrich, "From Monastery to Meditation Centre: Lay Meditation in Modern Sri Lanka," pp. 20–35.

90 See Bond, *The Buddhist Revival in Sri Lanka*, pp. 136–143.

91 However, though many argued that *nibbāna* is possible, they also argued that heaven is a more possible goal at this corrupt time.

92 Ibid., see especially chapter 7. The lay meditation movement in Sri Lanka can be traced to the Protestant Buddhism of the late nineteenth century.

93 For a discussion of religious women and symbolic maleness, see Bynum, *Holy Feast and Holy Fast*, p. 290.

8 NOVITIATES, WESTERN LAY NUNS, AND CAVE DWELLERS

1 That is, all the lay nuns with the exception of Ayyā Khemā. For more on Ayyā Khemā, see chapter 7.

2 We met Indrāṇi in chapter 7.

3 It is possible that the monk who administered the *dasa sil* was not aware of the distinction, or that he considered her an equal.

4 Sudharmā is the incumbent of the Vihāra Mahā Devī Upāsikārāmaya of Kalaniya (see chapter 6) and Anurādhapura. She spends most of her time these days in Anurādhapura.

5 Interviews with Sumanāsīlī were conducted on July 4, and July 6, 1989,

at the Dharmawatī Upāsikārāmaya in Maradana, Colombo, and on August 12, 1989, at the Vihāra Mahā Devī Upāsikārāmaya in Anurādhapura.

6 A Levels, or the Advanced Level examination, is taken after the O Level, or GCE Ordinary Level examination [now GCSE].

7 This is a fairly common practice among the lay nuns. Only three of the one-hundred Sinhala lay nuns I interviewed did not consult their horoscope before renouncing. Monks, too, follow this tradition.

8 In other words, meditation is the yardstick by which Sumanāsīlī assesses her own behavior, as well as the behavior of other lay nuns.

9 Though it looks as if the lay nuns drape their ochre robes in the same fashion as the monk (and ancient nun), they do not, see chapter 7. The only lay nuns I met who wear their robes like members of the monastic order were the western nuns, as well as Theranā, a disciple of Uttama Sādhu. For more on these renunciants, see below and chapter 9.

10 Sumanāsīlī is perhaps referring to one of the duties of the elder nuns in the *Vinaya*; at the time of the ordination of the novitiate, she is to be "duly provided with alms-bowl and robe" by her teacher. See Oldenberg, ed., *Vinaya Piṭakam*, vol. 2 (x, 17,7).

11 This interview was conducted on August 12, 1989.

12 The ceremony took place on May 20, 1989, on Vesak, at the Yaśodārādevī Upāsikārāmaya. The precepts were given by a monk at a nearby monastery.

13 The nine precepts exclude the regulation concerning the use of money.

14 I did not witness this event.

15 This is in keeping with the monastic code; see Oldenberg, ed., *Vinaya Piṭakam*, vol. 2, p. 271; for the translation, see Rhys Davids and Oldenberg, eds., *Vinaya Texts*, 3, p. 349.

16 This is standard practice in all the lay nunneries where I conducted research. The practice is based on canonical rules that declare that the novitiate must secure permission from her parents (or husband) to "go forth."

17 According to Līlāwatī's horoscope, 6:50 a.m. was considered to be the most auspicious time for the ordination.

18 The altar is outside and uncovered.

19 That Līlāwatī's eyes were covered until she was in Sumettā's sight is significant; it seems that she was not to look at lay people during her transition between lay, and monastic, life.

20 It will be remembered that the lay nuns all told me that the initiation of a novitiate is modelled upon the initiation of a *sāmaṇerī* into the monastic order. However, while the "going forth" ordination (*pabbajjā*) of a novitiate as a *sāmaṇerī* is not clear in the *Vinaya*, the process by which a candidate becomes a *sāmaṇera* is explictly stated. I assume that the process was the same for male and female candidates. In the *Vinaya*, the *pabbajjā* initiation is given as follows: "I prescribe, *bhikkhus*, the *pabbajjā*

ordination of novices by the threefold declaration of taking refuge. And you ought, *bhikkhus*, to confer the *pabbajjā* ordination in this way: Let him first have his hair and beard cut off; let him put on yellow robes, adjust his upper robe to cover one shoulder, pay respect to the *bhikkhus*, and sit down squatting; then let him raise his joined hands and tell him to say: 'I take refuge in the Buddha, I take refuge in the *dhamma*, I take refuge in the *sangha*.' 'And a second time, he is to do this, as well as a third. I prescribe, *bhikkhus*, the *pabbajjā* ordination of novices by this threefold declaration of taking refuge...' Then the novices thought: 'How many precepts are there for us, and how should we behave?' They told this to the Buddha. 'I prescribe, *bhikkhus*, ten precepts for the novice'." For a translation of these precepts, see the Introduction to this study. For the Pāli Text, see Oldenberg, ed., *Vinaya Piṭakam*, vol. I, p. 82. The lay nuns, too, take the Three Refuges as part of their initiation, in addition to asking for the ten precepts. The tradition of asking for the ten precepts thrice is not canonical, yet it is probably based on the Buddha's instruction to recite the Three Refuges "a second and a third time." In the ordination of several *sāmaṇeras* that I witnessed in Mahāragama on July 7, 1989, the same format was followed as in Līlāwatī's ordination, albeit with much more pomp.

21 "*Namo tassa bhagavato, arahato, sammāsambuddhassa*," that is, "Hail to him, the Blessed One, the perfected one, the fully enlightened Buddha."

22 I tape-recorded the monk's *bana* and later transcribed the contents. I would like to thank Ranmali Perera for helping with the translation.

23 Both the monk and Sumettā forgot to give Līlāwatī a new name. I reminded Sumettā as we were leaving the monastery that they had neglected to give the new lay nun a clerical name. It was a very awkward moment.

24 The ordination took place at the Susilārāmaya in Mahāragama on May 25, 1989. The Vesak holiday is the traditional season of ordinations for both the order of monks, and lay nuns.

25 According to Somā's preceptor, this was the proper training for a novice.

26 For more on Maitreya Buddha see the *Anāgatavaṃsa*, the "Chakkavati Sihānada Suttānta," and the *Buddhavaṃsa*.

27 Her father was worshipped first, and Sudāsī last. Whom she worshipped first and last did not seem to depend upon seniority, but rather upon the arrangement of the seating in the room.

28 "*Sādhu, sādhu, sādhu, sāāā*" is the response to the excitement caused by the moving words of a *bana*, or contact with a highly venerated religious person.

29 The Amarapura Nikāya is one of the three fraternities in contemporary Sri Lanka. The others are the Siyam Nikāya and the Rāmañña Nikāya.

30 D. Amarasiri Weeraratne, "*Bhikkhunī* Order: Case Goes By Default," *The Times*, 4 September 1988.

31 The implication is that the nuns' duty is to act as a role model for others

who are not yet strong enough to take all ten precepts on a permanent basis.

32 Sinhala, *ihala silayaka pihitiya.*

33 Sinhala, a *sāsanika* name, i.e., a religious name.

34 See chapter 5 for a discussion of the four "beams" of Buddhism.

35 That is, "You are a *bhikkhu* by this."

36 Pāli, "I will observe the 'going forth' precepts."

37 In other words, these precepts are not only easier to abide by, but are easier to remedy if broken.

38 The Venerable Paññāsīha ended the sermon with a warning about the direction in which Sri Lanka is headed as a result of people with selfish interests, and told the group how much merit had been made as a result of each person's participation in the Susilārāmaya event. His *bana* was not read from a text, but rather was given extemporaneously. Thus, there are gaps in its flow.

39 Tambiah, *Buddhism Betrayed?*, p. 103.

40 Ibid., p. 124.

41 The monks I interviewed were chosen randomly. I did, however, try to interview the most vocal and well-respected monks in Sri Lanka, most of whom are elderly, as well as the younger generation.

42 When I mentioned my interviews with junior monks to senior monks, the latter suggested that the newest generation among them does not understand the subtleties of the monastic code, which proscribes the resuscitation of the order of nuns without the necessary requisites.

43 The consecrated boundary is referred to as a *sīmā* (Pāli, Sinhala). For a discussion of the *sīmā* in the original Pāli, see Oldenberg, ed., *Vinaya Piṭakam*, vol. 1, p. 106 (ii.6–8). Madihee Paññāsīha's objections to the re-establishment of the nuns lineage are given in "*Bhikkhuni* Order: Case Goes By Default." Also, the Venerable Madihee Paññāsīha's "The *Bhikkhuni* Order: Can it be Reestablished," *Daily News*, 19 June 1986, contains more of his opinions about the contemporary tradition of female renunciation. The article continues in the June 20 issue of the *Daily News*, under the title "Virtues More Important than the Titles" [sic].

44 It is striking how similar Venerable Piyadassi's views about Maitreya and the order of nuns are to Sudāsī's, which are presented above. The Vajirārāmaya has been host to many European monks, and its members act as a "field of merit" for the most affluent Buddhist citizens of Colombo. In addition to hosting European monks, many western lay nuns have taken the ten precepts at the Vajirārāmaya (see below). The Venerable Piyadassi himself is a western-educated, English-speaking, Sinhala monk. The interview with the Venerable Piyadassi was conducted on June 30, 1989, at the Vajirārāmaya. I met with him informally on serveral other occasions, including the Convocation of Buddhist Nuns which was held in Beruwala in July, 1989 (see below).

45 The Venerable Piyadassi was referring to Ayyā Khemā, the lay nun who, it will be recalled, became a *bhikṣuṇī* in 1988.

46 For more on the Venerable Ānanda Maitreya, see Gombrich and Obeyesekere, *Buddhism Transformed*, pp. 299ff.

47 Venerable Ānanda Maitreya lives in the Cittavivekārāmaya, a heavily guarded *vihāra* about eight miles from Colombo in Battaramulla.

48 The Venerable Balangoda Ānanda Maitreya's views echo Sumanāsīlī's. See above.

49 The interview was conducted in English on January 8, 1989, at the Cittavivekārāmaya in Battaramulla.

50 Even Sinhala monks who do not live in Sri Lanka, are opposed to the re-establishment of the order of nuns. For instance, the Sinhala former incumbent of the London Buddhist Vihāra, the late Venerable Dr. Hammalawa Saddhatissa Nayaka Thera was opposed not only to the re-establishment of the order of nuns, but to most of the activities of the lay nuns, as well. In an interview, he argued that "These *Dasasil Mathas* wear robes cut and stitched like Buddhist priests and go chanting *pirith* [sic] and also attend almsgivings. They have no right to represent the *Maha Sangha* in any of those ritual ceremonies." See "*Dasasil Mathas* Doing Prohibited Duties," *The Daily Mirror*, 18 February 1982. There are a few Sinhala monks living abroad, however, who are in favor of re-establishing the Theravādin order of nuns. See chapter 9.

51 In addition to the Sinhala lay nuns at my primary research site who are in favor of the re-establishment of the order of nuns is Ambala Rohana Ñānasīlā Sil Mātā. A synopsis of her views is given in Rajitha Weerakoon, "Restore Bhikkhuni Order Plea," *The Observer*, 23 March, 1984. I interviewed her on several occasions.

52 One such foreign renunciant, Sister Uppalavaṇṇā, was discussed in chapter 7.

53 "First Englishwoman to Become Buddhist Nun: Kandy Home for Sister Vajira," *The Sunday Observer*, 17 January 1937.

54 Ibid.

55 Ayyā Khemā is a case in point. At her Nuns' Island, hundreds of Sinhala women (as well as foreigners) have studied and practised Buddhist meditation. It can be argued that while western lay nuns have helped to popularize lay meditation, the lay meditation movement in Sri Lanka has helped to legitimate the movement of lay nuns. In short, as the basic premise of the lay medition movement is that even laity can strive for *nibbāna*, it thus tacitly affirms the abilities of lay nuns.

56 Richard F. Gombrich, *Precept and Practice* (Oxford: Clarendon Press, 1971), p. 55.

57 Countless articles about the possibilities of re-establishing the *bhikkhunī sangha* appeared in both Sinhala and English newspapers while they resided in Sri Lanka.

58 Gombrich, *Precept and Practice*, p. 55.

59 The following synopsis of Jarcord and Heck's saga is taken from Rita

Sebastian, "They Want to Enter *Bhikkhunī* Order," *Observer*, 13 April 1986, and Rajika Wijenaike, "The Dilemma of the German Women Wanting to be Ordained," *Observer*, 20 April 1986.

60 "They Want to Enter *Bhikkhunī* Order," *Observer*.

61 Ibid. The two were eventually released from the institution, asked to sign a document promising that they would never step foot on the monk's premises again, and were encouraged to leave Sri Lanka. During my 1989 field study, it was rumored that one of the German women had returned to Sri Lanka, but was not permitted entry. I also learned that one of the women had later accepted the *bhikṣuṇī* (Mahāyāna) ordination at the Korean temple in Hacienda Heights, California, even though they are quoted as saying: "We know we can become Mahāyāna nuns. But we are not even considering it because we believe in Theravāda Buddhism."

62 Moreover, their story revived interest in the resuscitation of the Theravādin order of nuns. During the period in which they were in Sri Lanka, countless articles about its resuscitation appeared in both the Sinhala and English newpsapers.

63 This lay nun would prefer to remain anonymous.

64 That is, offering *gilānpāsa*, or refreshments, to the Buddha.

65 Ayyā Ñānasirī, formerly a professor of linguistics at a small college in New York, was first introduced to Buddhism in 1974, when she travelled to Malaysia in order to help the Malays revamp their education system. In 1978, she and her husband journeyed to Sri Lanka, where they meditated together for two years. Ayyā Ñānasirī's husband died in Sri Lanka in 1980, at which time she directed her attention more fully toward Buddhism. She renounced in 1987 after much contemplation and was ordained by the Venerable Ñānaponika and the American, Bhikkhu Bodhi. She has a grown son and daughter and is the grandmother of two. The interview with Ayyā Ñānasirī was conducted at her home in Aniwatta, Kandy, on May 9, 1989. She lives alone (but with many pets) in a very comfortable house and is supported by the neighboring *dāyakas*. She performs very few, if any, Buddhist rituals, rarely preaches *bana*, but spends hours alone meditating.

66 Ayyā Khemā and Ayyā Wimalā, an American, did not participate.

67 Bond, *The Buddhist Revival in Sri Lanka*, p. 192. Ironically, alienation from tradition connotes higher status.

68 Among these social problems, informants listed the political situation, rising divorce and alcoholism which the path of devotion and *pūjā* cannot address.

69 The canonical precedent for this term is found in Oldenberg, ed., *Vinaya Piṭakam*, vol. 4, pp. 320–323.

70 The western lay nuns, and Theranā, whom we meet in chapter 9, are the only female renunciants I witnessed using the begging bowl. See Sumanāsīlī's opinions about using the nuns' requisites above.

71 For more on the Venerable Khāntipālo and Wat Buddha Dhamma, see

Bronwyn Watson, "Actress, Became Candima, The Buddhist Nun" [sic], *The Sydney Morning Herald*, 5 August 1984.

72 That is, one object of meditation.

73 Located near Dodanduwa on the south-eastern coast of the island, Parappaduwa is an isolated island which can only be reached by boat. The island adjacent to Parappaduwa (but at some distance) is the abode of monks founded by the German monk, the Venerable Ñānaponika.

74 Piyaratna Mahāthera is the Chief Preceptor at Posgahauwala, the monks' island adjacent to Parappaduwa.

75 None of the women whom Ayyā Khemā ordained have remained at Parappaduwa, though none of them has disrobed.

76 Wimalā, a western, female renunciant from America who lives at Kanduboda Meditation Centre near Kalaniya, spends approximately six hours each day in meditation. Wimalā has a Masters Degree in Music from Missouri and was forty-six years old at the time of the interview on March 31, 1989. She has been married twice. Wimalā has been interested in meditation since 1980, when she was introduced to *vipassanā* meditation by a Burmese monk. She was ordained by Sister Sudharmā of the Biyagama Vihāra Mahā Devī Upāsikārāmaya in January, 1987, and is in charge of teaching meditation at the Kanduboda Centre, where foreigners study Buddhism.

77 Wikramasinghe's uncle, Sir John Kotalawala, was once prime minister of Ceylon.

78 See chapter 6.

79 My first interview with Wikramasinghe was conducted at the Hill Club, in Nuwara Eliya in April, 1989. The second interview was conducted on May 5, 1989.

80 I have located a newspaper clipping which recounts the adventures of a young woman from San Francisco, named Clariss van Strum. She became a Buddhist lay nun at the Sri Lankārāmaya Buddhist Temple in Singapore under the guidance of a Sinhala monk, the Venerable Chandrasiri Thero ("American Girl Becomes Buddhist Nun," *Ceylon Daily News*, 4 February 1944). As we have seen in previous chapters, other American women preceded Wikramasinghe's mentor to South and South-east Asia.

81 Brown, rather than ochre, is the color associated with meditative renunciants. A *sarong* is a floor length skirt, while a jacket is a tightly fitted upper garment which is commonly associated with the *sārī*.

82 See above for more on the Vajirārāmaya Temple.

83 This is Wikramasinghe's interpretation of the tenth precept which forbids the use of gold and silver.

84 That is, a primary level of meditative attainment.

85 Oldenberg, ed., *Vinaya Piṭakam*, vol. 2, p. 278 (x, 23).

86 Kataragama is the holy precinct of the eponymous god where hundreds of Hindus, Buddhists, and Muslims flock each July to perform painful

penance. It is located in the south-western most point of Sri Lanka, adjacent to the Ruhuṇu National Forest. For the phenomenon of renewed interest in the Kataragama deity among Sri Lankans, see Gananath Obeyesekere, "Fire Walkers of Kataragama: The Rise of Bhakti Religiosity in Buddhist Sri Lanka," *Journal of Asian Studies*, 37, no. 3 (1978), 457–476.

87 An anonymous informant told me that Uttarā Mäniyo won Premadasa's respect a few years ago when he ordered her off the property upon which she had simply squatted and set up residence. In an effort to refurbish the Kataragama area, the then Prime Minister Premadasa was apparently anxious to see her removed. She refused every effort he made to evict her and her students, and her tenacity finally won his respect.

88 Interviews were conducted with Uttarā Mäniyo from July 17, through to July 20, 1989.

89 Uttarā Mäniyo is one of the few lay nuns I interviewed who did not become part of a pre-existing lineage when she "went forth." However, she has established her own lineage, of which many lay nuns are proud to be a part.

90 Gananath Obeyesekere, *Medusa's Hair: An Essay on Personal Symbols and Religious Experience* (The University of Chicago Press, 1981), pp. 66–75.

91 For more on the evolution of Kataragama as the national god of Sri Lanka, see Obeyesekere, "Fire Walkers."

92 As we saw in chapter 7, most lay nuns do not actively engage themselves in politics. Uttarā Mäniyo is an exception. By associating her lay nunnery with Sri Lanka's legendary defender of Buddhism – especially in the context of the recent ethnic strife – Uttarā Mäniyo makes a racial and a political statement. For more on religion and politics in Sri Lanka, see Bruce Matthews, "The Janatha Vimukthi Peramuna and the Politics of the Underground in Sri Lanka", *The Round Table*, 312 (1989), 425–439; and Bruce Matthews, "Sinhala Cultural and Buddhist Patriotic Organizations in Contemporary Sri Lanka," *Pacific Affairs*, 61, no. 4 (Winter 88–89), 620–632.

93 Uttarā Mäniyo told me that the statue has been refurbished recently. The archaeologist, Arthur Jayawardena, visited the site and noted the statue in 1907. At that time, "almost all the caves were covered with jungle – thus rendering their enumeration difficult ... Down a ravine you come across, on your left, a large stone slab projecting like a roof. Under this stone canopy, there lies in recumbent posture, a colossal but mutilated figure of Buddha in dolamite." For more of this early description of Situlpavvihāra, see Arthur Jayawardena, "Some Ruins in the Ruhunu Rata," in Ananda Coomaraswamy, F. L. Woodward, W. A. de Silva, eds., *The Ceylon National Review*, no. 4, (July 1907), 23–24.

94 For more on Vihāra Mahā Devī, see chapter 6.

95 Ayyā Khemindā was born to Dutch parents in Indonesia in 1932. Her father, who was interested in Philosophy, converted from Protestantism

to Catholicism. At the age of forty-six Kheminda, like her father, changed her religion. However, she became a Buddhist.

Ayyā Kheminda attended the Dutch Academy of Fine Arts and was trained as an artist. By accident, she read a notice in her local newspaper advertising a series of talks by a Dutch Buddhist monk. She became involved in his Dutch Buddhist community and spent approximately ten years meditating under his guidance. In 1984, convinced that her only child was old enough to be on his own, she decided to divorce her husband, and accepted an invitation from a Sinhala monk to live at the Rockhill Meditation Centre, near Kandy.

Ayyā Kheminda returned to Holland after spending a few weeks meditating at Rockhill. While in Kandy, she decided that meditation is not something which can be done "half-way; it must be done properly," and she made the decision to "go forth." She returned to Sri Lanka, and was ordained in January, 1988. Since then, she has tried to keep each of the 311 *bhikkhunī* precepts. She recites the *Pātimokkha* (the core of the *Vinaya*) to herself every *pōya* (full-moon day). Like all of the western lay nuns, Kheminda told me that she feels "silly" doing Buddha *pūjā* and instead meditates the greater part of each day. She preaches *bana* and conducts a meditation once each week for an English-speaking audience in Kandy, where she has been offered a *kuṭī* by a *dāyaka*. For more on Rockhill, see Venerable P. Kassapa Nayaka Thera "The Story of Rockhill Hermitage," (Rockhill Hermitage Foundation), cyclostyled.

96 Gombrich and Obeyesekere, *Buddhism Transformed*, p. 216.
97 Ibid., p. 221.

9 THE SRI LANKAN BHIKKUNĪ SAṄGHA: TRENDS AND REFLECTIONS

1 This ascetic misogyny is full blow in the *Vinaya* story of the monks' rebuke of Ānanda, the monk who persuaded the Buddha to initiate Mahāpajāpatī Gotamī into the *saṅgha*. For the translation of the story, see *Vinaya Texts*, 3. Trans. Rhys Davids and Oldenberg, p. 380.

2 It will be recalled that *bhikkhunī* is Pāli, while *bhikṣuṇī* is Sinhala and Sanskrit.

3 At the time of the interview, which took place at the Sri Arunasīlārāmaya in Piliyandala on May 18, 1989, Dhammāsīlā had been a lay nun for eighteen years and was in her mid-thirties.

4 Visākhā Dhammāsīlā, who was thirty-five at the time of the interview, renounced aged fifteen.

5 Sanskrit, novice *bhikṣuṇī*.

6 For more on Uttama Sādhu, see Gombrich and Obeyesekere, *Buddhism Transformed*, see chapter 10.

7 This interview was conducted on November 30, 1989. Though Uttama Sādhu claims to know Sinhala, Sanskrit, Tamil, English, and Pāli (Magadha), he would agree only to speak in Sinhala. A few years earlier,

he told Gombrich and Obeyesekere that he knew neither Pāli nor Sanskrit (*Buddhism Transformed*, p. 323). He mentioned in the course of our first interview that he taught Richard Gombrich everything Gombrich knows about Buddhism!

8 Contrary to what he told me, he told Gombrich and Obeyesekere that he reads thrice a passage from the *Anguttara Nikāya* at the ordination of a *bhikkhunī* (*Buddhism Transformed*, p. 339).

9 In fact, he considers himself a Buddha. See Gombrich and Obeyesekere, *Buddhism Transformed*, p. 329. It will be recalled that both lay nuns and monks argue that only a Buddha can reinstitute the nuns' lineage. See chapter 8.

10 According to the traditional story, the Buddha was hesitant to admit women into his monastic community, as we saw in chapter 7. In addition, he made predictions about the ruin of his religion once women had entered his *saṅgha*.

11 According to a 1978 newspaper article, "Young Women Going the Buddha Way," *Weekend*, 15 January 1978, there were thirty-nine *bhikkhunīs* living at Sasuna Sänāsuma. In 1989, there were only two. In a subsequent interview with Theranā, she told me that it takes a strong personality to become a *bhikkhunī*, and that the others were just not suited to the activities of the hermitage. One by one, they returned to lay life. Theranā, by the way, is the daughter of the owners of the property.

12 In other words, she was dressed like an ascetic monk.

13 In an interview I conducted with Theranā on May 22, 1989 – seven months later – she told me that she only keeps the rules which apply to both the monk and the nun: most of the 227 rules of the monks' *Vinaya*.

14 "Young Women Going the Buddha Way."

15 Pāli, *iddhi*; Sanskrit, *siddhi*.

16 Dhammāpālī Mäniyo claimed this *en-route* to the interview with Uttama Sādhu.

17 Traditional Sinhala Buddhism, until very recently, did not accept "the doctrine of divine possession by women" (Gombrich and Obeyesekere, *Buddhism Transformed*, p. 184).

18 Nonetheless, Gombrich and Obeyesekere (*Buddhism Transformed*, p. 294) have documented cases of lay nuns who engage in practices normally associated with the priestess. My own research on Uttarā Mäniyo (see chapter 8 above) indicates that the two vocations are not always separate.

19 I asked other lay nuns around the island what they thought of Uttama Sādhu. Those who have heard of him do not condone his lifestyle or his teachings.

20 However, they do not feel the same way about forest monks, many of whom are self-ordained.

21 This invokes Sumanāsīlī's point of view. See chapter 7.

22 Theranā's "ideal-self" includes limited activity with the laity, and

extended periods of meditation. This is the opposite of the ideal-self of most of the Sinhala female renunciants I interviewed.

23 Many of the monks I interviewed in Sri Lanka are skeptical that the expatriate Sri Lankan monks really want to see the *saṅgha* opened to women.

24 "Buddhism Reaches Out in America," *Los Angeles Times*, May 30, 1988.

25 Quoted from a letter from Walpola Piyānanda, in Los Angeles, to Venerable Kurunegoda Piyatissa, President, Sri Lanka Saṅgha Council, April 10, 1988.

26 The Vesak Ordination, 1988. Produced by the Los Angeles Buddhist Vihāra. Videocasette.

27 Quoted from the letter from Walpola Piyānanda to Venerable Kurunegoda Piyatissa.

28 Interviews were conducted with the Venerable Gunaratana in September, 1989, and October, 1990.

29 "Four Ordained Monks in West Virginia," *Daily News* (Colombo), 24 August, 1989.

30 Ordination at the Bhāvanā Society, 1989. Produced by the West Virginia Bhāvanā Society. Videocasette.

31 Jane I. Smith, "Women, Religion and Social Change in Early Islam," in Yvonne Y. Haddad and Ellison Banks Findly, eds., *Women, Religion and Social Change* (Albany, New York: State University of New York Press, 1985), p. 19.

32 Ibid.

33 However, lay nuns would often write their names for me using male, rather than female, Pāli endings. This may have been due to sheer ignorance on their part.

34 I am indebted to Charles Hallisey for pointing this out to me. For more on instances of the Buddha as "mother," see *Butsarana* (Colombo: M. D. Gunasena Saha Samagamaya), p. 286; and Gombrich and Obeyesekere, *Buddhism Transformed*, pp. 162, 281.

35 Tambiah, *Buddhism Betrayed?*, p. 100.

EPILOGUE

1 Funding was provided by an Indiana University Faculty Development Grant.

2 I suspect lay nunneries appeal to many women who feel that they have few choices living in economically depressed and war-torn Sri Lanka. For more on nunneries as a safety-valve, see chapter 7.

3 See chapter 7.

4 The homeless lay nuns that I interviewed in Anurādhapura requested that I use fictitious names for them.

5 According to the *Mahāvagga*, living at the foot of a tree is one of the four requisites that the Buddha proclaimed for the "ideal" monk. The other

three include: using cow's urine as medicine, making one's robe from rags, and begging one's meals. Extra allowances were allowed for each of the four requisites. For more on the requisites, see Carrithers, *The Forest Monks*, p. 58.

6 It was founded by Sister Sudharmācārī of Lady Blake's in the 1920s.

7 In August, 1992, one United States dollar equaled forty-two Sri Lankan *rupees*. Not all lay nunneries require entrants to make a deposit. In fact, Kotmalee Sudharmā of Lady Blake's is opposed to the custom, as are many other leading lay nuns.

8 See chapter 7 for more on the Ministry of Buddhist Affairs.

THE LIFE OF DHAMMĀWATĪ HEWAVITARANE SIL MĀTĀ

1 "Hiththatiya Dhammāwatī Sil Mātā" (Colombo: Hevage Mudrana Kamitta, 1981), cylostyled. For more on Dhammāwatī Hewavitarane, see chapter 7.

2 That is, a place for distributing alms.

3 That is, robe distribution to monks.

4 See chapter 7 and chapter 8 for more on Ñānasīrī, known also as Indrāṇi.

5 It will be recalled that when Hewavitarane Mäniyo renounced (1916), women of her social status opted for the renunciant's life. It is striking that her biographers say that "though she was born in a respectable family..." suggesting that at present few women from the upper echelons renounce the world.

6 A list of lay nuns offering gratitude to Hewavitarane Mäniyo follows.

THE LIFE OF SIL MĀTĀ WADDUWA DHAMMĀCĀRĪ

1 I would like to thank Maureen Fernando for helping translate Dhammācārī Mäniyo's written biography.

2 In conversations with Dhammācārī Sil Mātā, I learned that "permission" meant her father's blessings to renounce the home life once proper training as a pious laywoman had been completed. In other words, her father wanted her to obtain an education first.

3 The Biyagama Children's Home has been a satellite of the Vihāra Mahā Devī Upāsikārāmaya. See chapter 6.

4 I would like to thank Dhammācārī Mäniyo for providing me with a copy of this unpublished, but printed, account of her life. Interviews with Dhammācārī Mäniyo were held at the Convocation of Buddhist Nuns in Beruwala, see chapter 8.

THE LIFE OF SĀRĀWATĪ SIL MĀTĀ

1 I would like to thank Maureen Fernando for helping me translate Sārāwatī Mäniyo's written biography.

2 Unlike the life stories of the two lay nuns I have offered in the previous appendices, Sārāwatī Sil Mātā's background is rural rather than urban.

3 See chapters 7 and 8, for more on the attitude of rural families toward the renunciation of the world by their daughters.

4 I learned in conversations with Sārāwatī Sil Mātā in Anurādhapura that she renounced when she was aged seventeen. Interviews were conducted with her in June, 1989. In one of our interviews, she related that she often has visions of Vihāra Mahā Devī, Dutugemenu's mother, who has been a constant source of support for her throughout her fifty years as a lay nun.

5 *Dānaya* legitimates her vocation to monks. Paragraphs about her students and their contribution to Buddhism follow.

6 Vajirā Sil Mātā, Pānaduree, "The Life of Sārāwatī Sil Mātā" (Anurādhapura: Gunasekera Saha Samāgama, 1989), cyclostyled.

Select bibliographies

SELECT BIBLIOGRAPHY OF SOURCES IN EUROPEAN LANGUAGES

All Ceylon Buddhist Congress: Diamond Jubilee Celebrations (1919–1979)," (Colombo: Metro Printers, 1980), cyclostyled.

Allen, W. Osborn, *A Parson's Holiday: Being an Account of a Tour in India, Burma and Ceylon in the Winter of 1882–83*, (Tenby, England: F. B. Mason, 1885).

Amarasingham, Lorna Rhodes, "The Misery of the Embodied: Representations of Women in Sinhalese Myth," in Judith Hock-Smith and Anita Spring, eds., *Women in Ritual and Symbolic Roles*, (New York: Plenum Press, 1978).

Aziz, Barbara Nimri, "Buddhist Nuns," *Natural History* 98 (March 1989), 41–48.

Babb, Lawrence A., *Redemptive Encounters: Three Modern Styles in the Hindu Tradition*, (Delhi: Oxford University Press, 1987).

Bartholomeusz, Tessa, "The Female Mendicant in Buddhist Sri Lanka," in Jose Ignacio Cabezon, ed., *Buddhism, Sexuality, and Gender*, (Albany, New York: State University of New York Press, 1992).

"Sri Lankan Women and the Buddhist Revival," *Iris: A Journal About Women*, 12, no. 1 (Fall/Winter 1991), 43–48.

Barua, Dipakkumar, *An Analytical Study of the Four Nikāyas*, (Calcutta: Rabindra Bharati University, 1971).

Bechert, Heinz, "Contradictions in Sinhalese Buddhism," in Bardwell Smith, ed., *The Religion and Legitimation of Power in Sri Lanka*, (Chambersburg, Pennsylvania: Anima Books, 1978).

Bhagavat, D. N., *Early Buddhist Jurisprudence*, (Poona: Oriental Book Agency, 1939).

Bizot, Francois, *Les Traditions de la Pabbajja en Asie du Sud-Est*, (Gottingen: Vandenhoeck and Ruprecht, 1988).

Blake, Edith, "The Sacred Bo Tree," *The Nineteenth Century and After* 76 (July–December 1914), 660–673.

"A Buddhist Nun," *The Buddhist Review: The Organ of the Buddhist Society of Great Britain and Ireland* 7 (1915), 47–58.

263

Bloss, Lowell, "The Female Renunciants of Sri Lanka: The *Dasasil mattawa*," *The Journal of the International Association of Buddhist Studies* 10, no. 1 (1987), 7–32.

Bode, Mabel, "The Women Leaders of the Buddhist Reformation," *Transactions of the 9th International Congress of Orientalists* (London: n. p., 1892), 341–343.

"The Women Leaders of the Buddhist Reformation," *Journal of the Royal Asiatic Society of Great Britain and Ireland* (1893), 517–566 and 763–798.

Bond, George, *The Buddhist Revival in Sri Lanka: Religious Tradition, Reinterpretation and Response*, (Columbia: University of South Carolina Press, 1988).

Bremer, M., *Ceylon Planter's Travels, 1851*, (London: Rivingtons, 1930).

Brown, Peter, *The Body and Society: Men, Women, and Sexual Renunciation in Early Christianity*, (New York: Columbia University Press, 1988).

Buddhist Publication Society, ed., *German Buddhist Writers*, (Kandy: Buddhist Publication Society, 1964).

Burghart, Richard, "Renunciation in the Religious Traditions of South Asia," *Man: The Journal of the Royal Anthropological Institute*, n.s. 18, no. 4. (December 1983), 635–653.

Bynum, Caroline Walker. *Holy Feast and Holy Fast*, (Berkeley: University of California Press, 1987).

Canavarro, M. de S., *Insight into the Far East*, (Hollywood, California: Strickland Publishing Company, 1925).

Order of the Sanghamitta Buddhist Sisterhood, (Colombo: Clifton Press, 1899, Colombo Museum Library, Colombo, Sri Lanka).

Canavarro, Countess Miranda de Souza (Sister Sanghamitta), to Paul Carus, "The Open Court Publishing Company Archives," (Special Collections/Morris Library, Southern Illinois University, Carbondale, Illinois).

Carrithers, Michael, *The Forest Monks of Sri Lanka: An Anthropological and Historical Study*, (Delhi: Oxford University Press, 1983).

Carrithers, Michael, and Steven Collins and Steven Lukes, eds., *The Category of the Person: Anthropology, Philosophy, and History*, (Cambridge University Press, 1985).

Carus, Paul, "A Modern Instance of World Renunciation," *The Open Court* 13, no. 2 (February 1899), 110–117.

"Sister Sanghamitta," *The Open Court* 15, no. 4, (April 1901), 251–252.

Che'en, Kenneth K. S., *Buddhism in China: An Historical Survey*, (Princeton University Press, 1964).

Cleary, Thomas, *Immortal Sisters: Secrets of Taoist Women*, (Boston: Shambala, 1989).

Copleston, Bishop Reginald Stephen, *Buddhism Primitive and Present in Magadha and Ceylon*, (London: Longmans, 1892).

Devendra, Kusuma, "The *Dasa Sil Matavo* of Sri Lanka," Unpublished M.A. thesis, Sri Jayewardene Pura University, Sri Lanka, 1986.

Dharmapāla, Anagārika, "The Diaries of the Anagārika Dharmapāla,"

Diaries in the Hands of the Directors of the Mahā Bodhi Society, Colombo, Sri Lanka.

"The Late Miss Catherine Shearer," *The Maha Bodhi and the United Buddhist World* 17, no. 4–5 (April–May 1909), 131.

"Miss C. Shearer," *The Maha Bodhi and the United Buddhist World* 15, no. 1–3 (January–March 1907), 140.

Dhirasekera, Jothiya, *Buddhist Monastic Discipline*, (Colombo: M. D. Gunasena, 1982).

"Women and the Religious Order of the Buddha," *Journal of the Mahabodhi Society* 75, nos. 5–6 (May–June 1967), 156–171.

Dumont, Louis, "World Renunciation in Indian Religions," *Contributions to Indian Sociology*, 4 (April 1960), 33–62.

"Education in Ceylon," *The Maha Bodhi and the United Buddhist World* 10, no. 3 (November 1898).

Elwood, Robert S., *Eastern Spirituality in America*, (New York: Paulist Press, 1987).

Endo, Toschiichi, *Dana: The Development of its Concept and Practice*, (Colombo: M. D. Gunasena, 1987).

Falk, Nancy Auer, "The Case of the Vanishing Nuns: The Fruits of Ambivalence in Ancient Buddhism," in Nancy Auer Falk and Rita Gross, eds., *Unspoken Worlds: Women's Religious Lives in Non-western Cultures*, (New York: Harper and Row, 1980).

Ferguson, John, *Ceylon in 1893*, (London: John Haddon and Company, 1893).

Fernando, Tissa, "The Western-Educated Elite and Buddhism in British Ceylon: A Neglected Aspect of the Nationalist Movement," in K. Ishwaran, ed., *Contributions to Asian Studies, IV, Tradition and Change in Theravada Buddhism*, (Leiden: E. J. Brill, 1973).

Fields, Rick, *How the Swans Came to the Lake: A Narrative History of Buddhism in America*, (Boulder, Colorado: Shambhalla, 1981).

Foley, Caroline A., "The Women Leaders of the Buddhist Reformation," *Transactions of the 9th International Congress of Orientalists* (London: n. p., 1892), 344–361.

Ford, Helen, *Notes of a Tour in India and Ceylon*, (London: Women's Printing Society, 1889).

Frank, Gelya, "Finding the Common Denominator: A Phenomenological Critique of Life History Method," *Ethos* 7, (1979), 68–94.

Friedl, Ernestine, "The Portrait of Women: Appearance and Reality," *Anthropological Quarterly* 40, no. 3 (July 1967), 97–108.

von Furer-Haimendorf, Christoph, "A Nunnery in Nepal," *Kailash: Journal of Himalayan Studies* 4, no. 2 (1976), 121–154.

Geertz, Clifford, *Works and Lives: The Anthropologist as Author*, (Stanford University Press, 1988).

"Genealogy of the Family of LaBrooy of Ceylon," *Journal of the Dutch Burgher Union* 24, no. 1 (July 1934), 69–81.

Godakumbura, C. E., "Sinhalese Festivals: Their Symbolism, Origins and Proceedings," *Journal of the Royal Asiatic Society* (Ceylon Branch) 14 n.s. (1970), 91–133.

Gokhale, B. G., "Anagārika Dharmapāla: Toward Modernity Through Tradition in Ceylon," in Bardwell L. Smith, ed., *Tradition in Theravada Buddhism*, (Leiden: E. J. Brill, 1973).

Gombrich, Richard, and Gananath Obeyesekere, *Buddhism Transformed: Religious Change in Sri Lanka*, (Princeton University Press, 1988).

Gombrich, Richard, "From Monastery to Meditation Centre: Lay Meditation in Modern Sri Lanka," in Philip Denwood and Alexander Piatigorsky, eds., *Buddhist Studies: Ancient and Modern*, (London: Curzon Press, 1983).

Precept and Practice, (Oxford: Clarendon Press, 1971).

Theravada Buddhism: A Social History from Ancient Benares to Modern, (Colombo, London: Routledge and Kegan Paul, 1988).

Gonzalez, Nancie L., "The Anthropologist as Female Head of Household," *Feminist Studies* 10, no. 4 (Spring 1984), 97–114.

Gross, Rita M., *Buddhism After Patriarchy: A Feminist History, Analysis, and Reconstruction of Buddhism*, (Albany: State University of New York Press, 1993).

Gunawardena, R. A. L. H., *Robe and Plough: Monasticism and Economic Interest in Early Medieval Sri Lanka*, (Tucson: University of Arizona Press, 1979).

"Subtile Silks of Ferreous Firmness: Buddhist Nuns in Ancient and Early Medieval Sri Lanka and Their Role in the Propagation of Buddhism," *The Sri Lankan Journal of the Humanities* 14, nos. 1 and 2 (1988), 1–59.

Guruge, Ananda, ed., *Anagarika Dharmapala: Return to Righteousness*, (Colombo: The Department of Cultural Affairs, 1967).

Haddad, Yvonne Y. and Ellison Banks Findly, eds., *Women, Religion and Social Change*, (Albany, New York: State University of New York Press, 1985).

Hall, Captain Basil, *Travels in India, Ceylon and Borneo*, (London: George Routledge and Sons, 1931).

Hare, E. M. trans., *The Book of the Gradual Sayings*, vol. 3, (London: Routledge and Kegan Paul Ltd., 1973).

The Book of the Gradual Sayings, vol. 4, (London: Luzac and Company, Ltd., 1965).

Havnevik, Hanna, *Tibetan Buddhist Nuns: History, Cultural Norms and Social Reality*, (London: Norwegian University Press, 1989).

Henry, Patrick G. and Donald K. Swearer, *For the Sake of the World: The Spirit of Buddhist and Christian Monasticism*, (Minneapolis: Fortress Press, 1989).

Hettiaratchi, S. B., *Social and Cultural History of Ancient Sri Lanka*, (Delhi: Sri Satguru Publications, 1988).

Holt, John Clifford, *Discipline: The Canonical Buddhism of the Vinayapitaka*, (Delhi: Motilal Banarsidass, 1981).

Horner, I. B., trans., *The Book of the Discipline*, parts 1–4, Sacred Books of the Buddhists, (London: Luzac and Company, Ltd., 1969–1971).

Milinda's Questions, vol. 2, (London: Luzac and Company, Ltd., 1969).

Horner, I. B., *Women Under Primitive Buddhism*, 2nd. edn., (Delhi: Motilal Banarsidass, 1975).

Jackson, Carl T., *The Oriental Religions and American Thought: Nineteenth Century Explorations*, (Westport, Connecticut: Greenwood Press, 1981).

Jayawardena, Arthur, "Some Ruins in the Ruhunu Rata," in Ananda Coomaraswamy, F. L. Woodward, and W. A. de Silva, eds., *The Ceylon National Review* 4, (July 1907), 23–31.

Jayawardena, Kumari, and Swarna Jayaweera, *A Profile on Sri Lanka: The Integration of Women in Development Planning, Sri Lanka*, (Colombo: Women's Educational Centre, 1986).

Kabilsingh, Chatsumarn, *Thai Women in Buddhism*, (Berkeley: Parallax Press, 1991).

Kassapa, Nayaka Thera, "The Story of Rockhill Hermitage," (Rockhill Hermitage Foundation, n.d.).

Kawanami, Hiroko, "The Religious Standing of Burmese Buddhist Nuns (*thila shin*): The Ten Precepts and Religious Respect Words," *The Journal of the International Association of Buddhist Studies* 13, no. 1 (1990), 17–39.

Kemper, Stephen, "Buddhism Without Bhikkhus: The Sri Lankan Vinaya Vardena Society," in Bardwell L. Smith, ed., *Religion and the Legitimation of Power in Sri Lanka*, (Chambersburg, Pennsylvania: Anima Books, 1978).

Keyes, Charles, "Mother or Mistress but Never a Monk: Buddhist Notions of Female Gender in Rural Thailand," *American Ethnologist* 11, no. 2 (May 1984), 223–241.

Khaing, Mi Mi, *The World of Burmese Women*, (London: Zed Books Limited, 1984).

Kirthisinghe, Buddhadasa, "Marie Musaeus Higgins: American Mother of Ceylon's Buddhist Womanhood," *The Mahā Bodhi Journal* 76, no. 11–12 (November–December 1968), 327–332.

Kirsch, A. Thomas, "Text and Context: Buddhist Sex Roles/Culture of Gender Revisited," *American Ethnologist* 12, no. 2 (May, 1985), 302–320.

Knighton, William, *History of Ceylon*, (London: Longman, Brown and Longmans, 1845).

Law, B. C., ed., *Buddhavamsa: the Lineage of the Buddhas and Cariyapitaka*, (London: H. Milford, 1938).

Law, Bimala Churn, "Lay Women in Early Buddhism," in G. C. Jhala and N. A. Gore, eds., *The Sardhaśatabdi Commemoration Volume*, (Bombay: The Asiatic Society of Bombay, 1959), 121–141.

Women in Buddhist Literature, (Varanasi: Indological Book House, 1927).

Layman, Emma McCloy, *Buddhism in America*, (Chicago: Nelson Hall, 1978).

List of Books Printed in Ceylon: 1899, (Colombo: 1899).

Malalasekera, G. P., ed., *The Dictionary of Pali Proper Names*, (London: Luzac and Company, Ltd., 1960).

Malalasekera, G. P., *The Pali Literature of Ceylon*, (Colombo: M. D. Gunasena, 1928).

Malalgoda, Kitsiri, *Buddhism in Sinhalese Society 1750–1900: A Study of Religious Revival and Change*, (Berkeley: University of California Press, 1976).

"Buddhism in Post-Independence Sri Lanka," in G. A. Oddie, ed., *Religion in South Asia*, (New Delhi: Manohar, 1977).

Marglin, Frederique Apffel, *Wives of the God-king: The Rituals of the Devadasis of Puri*, (Delhi: Oxford University Press, 1985).

Matthews, Bruce, "The Janatha Vimukthi Peramuna and the Politics of the Underground in Sri Lanka," *The Round Table* 312 (1989), 425–439.

"Sinhala Cultural and Buddhist Patriotic Organizations in Contemporary Sri Lanka," *Pacific Affairs* 61, no. 4 (Winter 1988–89), 620–632.

"Sri Lanka in 1989: Peril and Good Luck," *Asian Survey* 30, no. 2 (February 1989), 229–235.

Mernissi, Fatima, *Beyond the Veil: Male-Female Dynamics in Modern Muslim Society*, (Bloomington: Indiana University Press, 1987).

"Minutes of the Vihāra Mahā Devī Upāsikārāmaya 1936–1945," (Colombo, Sri Lanka: Ceylon National Archives).

Muller, Edward, *Ancient Inscriptions of Ceylon*, part 1, (London: Trubner and Company, Ludgate Hill, 1883).

Muller, Max, ed. *Vinaya Texts: Sacred Books of the East*, vol. 3, (Varanasi: Motilal Banarsidass, 1965).

Murcott, Susan, *The First Buddhist Women*, (Berkeley: Parallax Press, 1991).

Nichols, John and Lillian Shank, eds., *Distant Echoes: Medieval Religious Women, I*, (Kalamazoo, Michigan: Cistercian Publications, 1985).

Nissan, Elizabeth, "Recovering Practice: Buddhist Nuns in Sri Lanka," *South Asia Research* 4, no. 1 (May 1984), 32–49.

Norman, K. R., *Pali Literature*, (Leiden: E. J. Brill, 1972).

Obeyesekere, Gananath, "Fire Walkers of Kataragama: The Rise of Bhakti Religiosity in Buddhist Sri Lanka," *Journal of Asian Studies* 37, no. 3 (1978), 457–476.

Medusa's Hair: An Essay on Personal Symbols and Religious Experience, (University of Chicago Press, 1981).

"Religious Symbolism and Political Change in Ceylon," in Gananath Obeyesekere, Frank Reynolds, and Bardwell L. Smith, eds., *The Two Wheels of the Dhamma: Essays on the Theravada Tradition in India and Ceylon*, (Chambersburg, Pennsylvania: American Academy of Religion, 1972).

"Theodicy, Sin and Salvation," in E. R. Leach, ed., *Dialectic in Practical Religion*, (Cambridge University Press, 1968).

Olcott, Henry Steele, "The 'Wail' of Dharmapala," *Theosophist*, vol. 20 (1899), xxix–xxx.

Olivelle, Patrick, *The Origin and the Early Development of Buddhist Monachism*, (Colombo: M. D. Gunasena, 1977).

Vasudevasrama Yatidharmaprakasa: A Treatise on World Renunciation, (Vienna: E. J. Brill, 1977).

Ordination at the Bhāvana Society, 1989, Produced by the West Virginia Bhāvana Society, 1989, Videocassette.

Ortner, Sherry P., *Sherpas through Their Rituals*, (New York: Cambridge University Press, 1978).

Pachow, W., "Ancient Cultural Relations between Ceylon and China," *University of Ceylon Review* 7, no. 3 (July 1954), 182–191.

Paul, Diana, *The Buddhist Feminine Ideal*, (Missoula, Montana: Scholars Press, 1980).

Women in Buddhism, (Berkeley: University of California Press, 1979).

Perera, H. R., *Buddhism in Sri Lanka: A Short History*, (Kandy: Buddhist Publication Society, 1988).

Rahula, Walpola, *The History of Buddhism in Ceylon*, (Colombo: M. D. Gunasena, 1966).

"The Report of the Vihara Mahā Devī Upāsikārāmaya Society, 1936–37," (Colombo, Sri Lanka: Ceylon Government Archives).

"The Report of the Vihāra Mahā Devī Samitiya, June 1936–June 1938," (Colombo, Sri Lanka: Ceylon Government Archives).

"The Report of the Vihāra Mahā Devī Upāsikārāmaya Committee, July 1938–July 1939," (Colombo, Sri Lanka: Ceylon Government Archives).

Reynell, Josephine, "Women and the Reproduction of the Jain Community," in Michael Carrithers and Caroline Humphrey, eds., *The Assembly of Listeners: Jains in Society*, (Cambridge University Press, 1991).

Rhys Davids, T. W., and Hermann Oldenberg, trans., *Vinaya Texts: Sacred Books of the East*, part 3, (Delhi: Motilal Banarsidass, 1984).

Rhys Davids, T. W., and C. A. F. Rhys Davids, trans., "Introduction to the Sigalovada Suttanta," *Dialogues of the Buddha*, part 2, (London: Luzac and Company, Ltd., 1959).

Dialogues of the Buddha, part 3, (London: Luzac and Company, Ltd., 1957).

Rhys Davids, C. A. F., trans., *Psalms of the Early Buddhists*, vol. 1, (London: Luzac and Company, Ltd., 1964).

Richman, Paula, "The Portrayal of a Female Renouncer in a Tamil Buddhist Text," in Caroline Walker Bynum, Stevan Harrell, and Paula Richman, eds., *Gender and Religion: On the Complexity of Symbols*, (Boston: Beacon Press, 1986).

Women, Branch Stories, and Religious Rhetoric in a Tamil Buddhist Text, (Syracuse: Foreign and Comparative Studies Publications, 1988).

Roberts, Michael, ed., *Collective Identities, Nationalisms and Protest in Modern Sri Lanka*, (Colombo: Marga Institute, 1979).

Roe, Jill, *Beyond Belief: Theosophy in Australia, 1879–1930*, (Sydney: New South Wales University Press, 1986).

Rogers, Susan Carol, "Female Forms of Power and the Myth of Male

Dominance: A Model of Female/Male Interaction in Peasant Society," *American Ethnologist* 2, no. 4 (November 1975), 727–756.

Roth, Gustav, ed., *Bhiksuni Vinaya: Manual of Discipline for Buddhist Nuns*, (Patna: K. P. Jayaswal Research Institute, 1970).

"Rules for the Vihāra Mahā Devī Samitiya," (1938, Colombo, Sri Lanka: Colombo National Archives).

Saddhatissa, Bhikkhu H., trans., *Sutta Nipāta*, (London: Curzon Press, 1985).

Salgado, Nirmala S., "Custom and Tradition in Buddhist Society: A Look at Some *Dasa Sil Matas* from Sri Lanka in Relation to the Concept of Women in Buddhism," (Colombo: International Institute for Ethnic Studies, n.d. cyclostyled).

Sangharakhita, Bhikkhu, *A Survey of Buddhism*, (London: The Indian Institute of World Culture, 1957).

Sangharakshita, Bhikshu, *Anagārika Dharmapāla: A Biographical Sketch*, (Kandy: Buddhist Publication Society, 1983).

Senaveratne, John M., "Some Notes on the Chinese References," *The Journal of the Royal Asiatic Society* (Ceylon Branch) 24, no. 68 (1915–1916), 106–111.

Seneviratne, H. L., Review of *Buddhism Transformed*, *Journal of Ritual Studies* 4, no. 2 (Summer 1990), 398–402.

"Identity and the Conflation of Past and Present," in H. L. Seneviratne, ed., *Identity, Consciousness and the Past*, (The University of Adelaide Press, 1989).

Sharma, Arvind, "How and Why did the Women in Ancient India Become Buddhist Nuns?," *Sociological Analysis* 38–39 (Spring 1977–Winter 1978), 239–251.

Shearer, Catherine, "A Buddhist Pilgrimage in Burma," *The Mahā Bodhi and the United Buddhist World* 17, no. 3 (March 1909), 47–50.

"Letter to the Anagārika," *The Mahā Bodhi and the United Buddhist World* 17, no. 6 (June 1909), 132–133.

Sivaraksa, Sulak, "Buddhist Women: Past and Present," *Kahawai: Journal of Women and Zen* 1 no. 3 (Summer 1979), 3–11.

Smith, Donald E., "Religion, Politics, and the Myth of Reconquest," in Tissa Fernando and Robert N. Kearney, eds., *Modern Sri Lanka: A Society in Transition*, (New York: Syracuse University, 1979).

Spencer, Jonathan, ed., *Sri Lanka: History and the Roots of Conflict*, (London: Routledge and Kegan Paul, 1990).

Sponberg, Allan, "Attitudes toward Women and the Feminine in Early Buddhism," in Jose Ignacio Cabezon, ed., *Buddhism, Sexuality, and Gender*, (State University of New York Press, 1992).

Story, Francis, ed., *Early Western Buddhists*, (Kandy: The Buddhist Publication Society, 1962).

Swearer, Donald K., "Lay Buddhism and the Buddhist Revival in Ceylon," *Journal of the American Academy of Religion* 38, no. 3 (September 1970), 255–275.

Talim, Meena V., "Buddhist Nuns and Disciplinary Rules," *Journal of the University of Bombay* 34, no. 2 (September 1965), 98–137.

Tambiah, S. J., *Buddhism Betrayed?: Religion, Politics, and Violence in Sri Lanka* (University of Chicago Press, 1992).

The Buddhist Saints of the Forest and the Cult of the Amulets (Cambridge University Press, 1984).

World Conqueror, World Renouncer, (Cambridge University Press, 1976).

Thamel, K. M. Lilly, "A Study of the *Dasa Sil Mata* in the Buddhist Society of Sri Lanka," (Colombo: International Institute of Ethnic Studies, n.d., cyclostyled).

"The Religious Woman in A Buddhist Society: The Case of the Dasa- Sil Maniyo in Sri Lanka," *Dialogue* (Colombo), 11, nos. 1–3 (1984), 53–68.

Tillet, Gregory, *A Biography of Charles Webster Leadbeater*, (London: Routledge and Kegan Paul, 1982).

Tsomo, Karma Lekshe, "Tibetan Nuns and Nunneries," *The Tibet Journal* 12, no. 4 (Winter 1987), 1–14.

Turner, Victor, "The Center Out There: Pilgrim's Goal," *History of Religions* 12, no. 3 (February 1973), 191–230.

Tweed, Thomas, *The American Encounter with Buddhism*, (Bloomington: Indiana University Press, 1992).

The Vesak Ordination, 1988, Produced by the Los Angeles Buddhist Vihara, 1988, Videocassette.

Vimalananda, Tennakoon, *The State and Religion in Ceylon Since 1815*, (Colombo: M. D. Gunasena, 1970).

Walpola Piyananda Thera, Los Angeles, to Venerable Kurunegoda Piyatissa, April 10, 1988, Letter in the hand of Walpola Piyananda Thera, Los Angeles Buddhist Vihāra, Los Angeles, California.

Walshe, Manric, *Thus Have I Heard: The Long Discourses of the Buddha*, (London: Wisdom Publications, 1987).

Watson, Lawrence C. and Maria-Barbara Watson-Franke, eds., *Interpreting Life Histories: An Anthropological Inquiry*, (New Brunswick, New Jersey: Rutgers University Press, 1985).

Wax, Rosalie H., "Gender and Age in Fieldwork and Fieldwork Education: No Good Thing is Done by Any Man Alone," *Social Problems* 26, no. 5 (June 1979), 509–522.

Weeraratne, D. Amarasiri, "The *Bhikkhuni* Order in Ceylon," *Journal of the Mahābodhi Society* 78, no. 10–11 (October–November 1970), 333–337.

Welch, Holmes. *The Practice of Chinese Buddhism: 1900–1950*, (Harvard University Press, 1967).

Wickremasinghe, Don Martino de Zilva, trans. and ed., *Epigraphia Zeylanica*, 2, (London: Oxford University Press, 1928).

Wijayaratna, Mohan, *Buddhist Monastic Life*, Claude Grangier and Steven Collins, trans., (Cambridge University Press, 1990).

Les Moniales bouddhiste, naissance et developpement du monachisme feminin, (Paris: Editions du Cerf, 1991).

Wilson, A. Jayaratnam, *Politics in Sri Lanka, 1947–1973*, (London: The Macmillan Press, 1974).
Woodward, F. L., trans., *The Book of the Gradual Sayings*, vol. 2, (London: Luzac and Company, Ltd., 1973).
Woolf, Bella Sidney, *How to See Ceylon*, (London: Blackfriars House, 1914).
Wriggins, W. Harold, *Ceylon: Dilemmas of a New Nation*, (Princeton University Press, 1960).
Yalman, Nur, *Under the Bō Tree: Studies in Caste, Kinship, and Marriage in the Interior of Ceylon*, (Berkeley: University of California Press, 1967).

SELECT BIBLIOGRAPHY OF SOURCES IN INDIC LANGUAGES

Butsasarana, (Colombo: M. D. Gunasena Saha Samagamaya).
Carpenter, J. Estlin, ed., *Dīgha Nikāya*, vol. 3, (London: Luzac and Company, Ltd., 1960).
Chalmers, Lord, ed., *Majjhima Nikāya*, (London: Luzac and Company, Ltd., 1899).
"The Biography of the Venerable Sil Mātā Wadduwa Dhammācārī," Typed Biography in the Hand of Dhammācārī Silmātāva, n.d.
"Hiththatiya Dhammāwatī Sil Mātā," (Colombo: Hevage Mudrana Kamatta, 1981).
Dharmabandhu, V. S., *Sinhala Virayo*, (Colombo: S. B. Fernando Publisher, 1949).
Feer, M. Leon, ed., *Samyutta Nikāya*, vol. 1–4, (London: Routledge and Kegan Paul, Ltd., 1973).
Geiger, Wilhelm, ed., *The Cūlavamsa*, (London: Luzac and Company, Ltd., 1980).
Geiger, Wilhelm, ed., *The Mahāvaṃsa*, (Colombo: Government Press, 1986).
Hardy, E. ed., *Anguttara Nikāya*, vol. 3–5, (London: Luzac and Company, Ltd., 1958).
Jayawickrama, N. A., ed., *Vimāna Vatthu and Peta Vatthu* (London: Journal of the Pali Text Society, 1977).
Minayeff, J. ed., *Anāgatavaṃsa*, (London: Journal of the Pali Text Society, 1886), p. 33–53.
Morris, Richard, ed., *Anguttara Nikāya*, vol. 1–2, (London: Luzac and Company, Ltd., 1955, 1961).
Oldenberg, Hermann, ed., *The Dīpavaṃsa*, (New Delhi: Asian Educational Services, 1982).
Vinaya Piṭakam, vol. 1–4, (London: Luzac and Company, Ltd., 1964).
Oldenberg, Hermann, and Richard Pischel, ed., *Therā-Therīgāthā*, (London: Luzac and Company, Ltd., 1966).
Rhys Davids, T. W., and J. Estlin Carpenter, ed., *The Dīgha Nikāya*, vol. 2, (London: Luzac and Company, Ltd., 1966).
Saddhatissa, Bhikkhu H., ed., *Upāsakajanālankāra*, (London: Luzac and Company, Ltd., 1965).

Singh, Aruna Pratap, *Jain aur Bauddh Bhiksuni Saṅgha*, (Vāranasī: Parshva lath Vidhyāśram Shodh Sansthān, 1986).
Srī Sudharmā Samitiya, ed., "Mahānuwara Srī Sudharmā Upāsi-kāramaya," (Kandy: Srī Sudharmā Samitiya, n.d., Lady Blake's Upāsikāramaya, Kandy, Sri Lanka).
Srī Sudharmā Samitiya, ed., "Srī Sudharmācārī Upāsikā Mäniyan Vahansege Apadanaya," (Kandy: Srī Sudharmā Samitiya, 1939, Lady Blake's Upāsikārāmaya, Kandy, Srī Lanka).
Sugatadasa, K. B., *Anagārika Dharmapāla Apadanaya*, (Vallamapitiya, Srī Lanka: Somasiri Kasturi Aracci, 1986).
Taylor, Arnold C., ed., *The Kathāvatthu*, (London: Routledge and Kegan Paul Ltd., 1979).
Trenckner, V., ed., *The Milindapañho*, (London: Luzac and Company, Ltd., 1962).
Vajirā Sil Mātā, Panaduree, "The Life of Saravatī Sil Mātā," (Anurādh-apura: Gunasekera Saha Samāgama, 1989).
Weerakoon, Abhaya, "Dasasil Mātā Vādapilivela," (1988, Ministry of Buddhist Affairs, Colombo, Sri Lanka).
Woodward, F. L., *Paramattha Dipānī*, (London: Routledge and Kegan Paul, Ltd., 1977).

BUDDHIST NEWSPAPERS

THE BUDDHIST

(*1889–1940*)

1889, "A Retrospect and an Appeal," 246–247.
1889, "The Wesleyan Mission Report," 295.
1889, "The Work of Women," 295.
June 1889, "A Noble Project," 224.
22 July 1889, "The History of Princess Sanghamitta," 217–220.
16 January 1891, "The Work of Women," 32.
19 June 1891, "Reformation of the Priesthood," 206.
26 June 1891, "Burma and Buddhism," 210
3 July 1891, "Burma and Buddhism," 217.
3 July 1891, "The Cremation of Miss Pickett," 223.
10 July 1891, "Female Education," 229.
24 July 1891, "The Late Miss Picket," 246.
11 December 1891, "The Drowning of Miss Picket," 408.
10 June 1892, "The Maha Bodhi Society," 180.
9 December 1892, "Notes," 391.
21 April 1893, "The Sanghamitta School," 127.
22 December 1893, "The Women's Educational Society and the Sangha-mitta Girls' School," 388–390.
2 February 1894, "History of the Women's Educational Society," 25.
2 February 1894, "The Sanghamitta School," (February 2, 1894), 25.

2 February 1894, "Changes in Principals," 26.
22 June 1894, "The Sanghamitta Girls' School," 8.
13 July 1894, "Quarter Mile Clause," 207.
28 December 1894, "Pilgrims to Buddha Gaya," 400.
21 January 1898, "The Buddhist Countess and Her Work," 3–4.
11 March 1916, "Dear Sisters," 5.
11 March 1916, "The Education of Buddhist Girls," 4.
16 September 1916, "An Appeal to the Diyawadana Nilame and Other Members of the Buddhist Temporalities Committee, Kandy," 3.
18 November 1916, "The Education of Buddhist Girls," 1.
9 December 1916, "The Celebration of the Sanghamitta Festival," 4.
24 March 1917, "Residence for Buddhist Nuns at Anuradhapura," 4.
6 October 1917, "Katukele Buddhist Girls School," 2.
23 December 1923, "*Arahant* Sanghamitta and the Order of Nuns," 1.
June 1932, "Sanghamitta," 1.
September 1936, "A Nunnery for Ceylon," 347.
July 1938, "Sister Upalavanna," 446–447.
August 1938, "Biyagama Nunnery Second Anniversary Meeting," 74.
September 1940, "Biyagama *Upasika Aramaya*," 74.

THE BUDDHIST CHRONICLE

(1922–1938)

16 July 1922, "Is There a Buddhist Nunnery in Ceylon?" 9.
16 July 1922, "A Buddhist Nunnery," 9.
12 September 1923, "Upasikaramaya, Kandy," 6.
12 December 1923, "The Dead Hand of Buddhism," 6.
6 Januay 1924, "Sanghamitta Day Celebrations," 1.
August 1931, "A Women's Buddhist Association," 82.
August 1938, "Pilgrimage of Renunciation, Family in Yellow Robes," 73.

ENGLISH LANGUAGE NEWSPAPERS
(arranged by date)

7 August 1897, "Man of Asia Will Convert Us," *New York Journal*.
30 August 1897, "Buddha Gains a Convert," *New York Journal*.
31 August 1897, "Buddha's Fair Pale Convert," *New York Journal*.
31 August 1897, "She is Now a Buddhist: The Countess de Canavarro Received into the Faith with Impressive Ceremonies," *New York Tribune*.
31 August 1897, "Woman Vows to Follow Buddha," *New York Herald*.
12 October 1897, "A Countess Vows to Follow Buddha," *Ceylon Catholic Messenger*.
19 October 1897, "A Buddhist Countess in Ceylon," *Ceylon Catholic Messenger*.

30 October 1897, "Interesting to Buddhists," *Ceylon Examiner*.

21 January 1898, 3–4, "The Buddhist Countess and Her Work: Formation of a Sisterhood, Acquisition of a Convent, A Progressive Educational Scheme," *Ceylon Independent* (quoted in full in *The Buddhist*).

3 January 1899, "Burmese Pilgrims in Ceylon Still," *Ceylon Examiner*.

11 February 1899, "Countess Canavarro to Go to India," *Ceylon Examiner*.

13 March 1899, "Burmese Pilgrims in Ceylon Still," *Ceylon Examiner*.

19 October 1899, "Countess Canavarro and the Lanka Maha Bodhi Society: Why the Countess has left the Sanghamitta Upasikaramaya, Full Details," *Standard* (Colombo).

9 October 1900, "Madam Canavarro," *Ceylon Examiner*.

4 July 1907, "The Opening of a Buddhist *Upasika Aramaya* at Kandy by H. E. Lady Blake," *Weekly Times of Ceylon*.

26 October 1936, "Buddhist Nunnery Opened: Impressive Ceremony at Biyagama," *Ceylon Daily News*.

17 January 1937, "First Englishwoman to Become Buddhist Nun: Kandy Home for Sister Vajira," *Sunday Observer* (Colombo).

4 February 1944, "American Girl Becomes Buddhist Nun," *Ceylon Daily News*.

16 January 1974, "Govt. Will Help to Revive *Bhikkhuni Sasana*," *Daily Mirror* (Colombo).

15 January 1978, "Young Women Going the Buddha Way," *Weekend* (Colombo),

15 February 1981, "Buddhist Nuns in China Today," *Sunday Observer* (Colombo).

18 February 1982, "*Dasasil Mathas* Doing Prohibted Duties," *Daily Mirror* (Colombo).

15 July 1982, "Sister Upalavanna – Life of Renunciation," *Ceylon Daily News*.

23 March 1984, "Restore *Bhikkhuni* Order Plea," *Observer* (Colombo).

5 August 1984, "Actress, Became Candima, The Buddhist Nun," *Sydney Morning Herald* (Australia).

13 April 1986, "They Want to Enter *Bhikkhuni* Order," *Observer* (Colombo).

20 April 1986, "The Dilemma of the German Women Wanting to be Ordained," *Observer* (Colombo).

19 June 1986, "Bhikkhuni Order: Can it be Re-established?," *Daily News* (Colombo).

20 June 1986, "Virtues More Important than Titles," *Daily News* (Colombo).

14 July 1986, "Case for a Buddhist Order of Nuns," *Daily News* (Colombo).

7 June 1987, "Equal Rights for Buddhist Nuns," *Weekend* (Colombo).

7 June 1987, "A Welcome Move Towards Reviving Bhikkhuni Order," *Island* (Colombo).

17 January 1988, "PM Sets Up 'Yasorapura' in Response to a *Dasasil Matha's* Plea," *Observer* (Colombo).

23 January 1988, "Nun's Compassion Brings New Life," *Daily News* (Colombo).

1 February 1988, "'Yasorapura': A Village Born of a Nun's Compassion," *Island* (Colombo).

30 May 1988, "Buddhism Reaches Out in America," *Los Angeles Times*.

4 September 1988, *Bhikkhuni* Order: Case Goes by Default," *Times* (Colombo).

18 September 1988, Bhikkhuni Order-Questions Again," *Island* (Colombo).

10 February 1989, "Deaths," *Island* (Colombo).

11 June 1989, "Going Forth Into Homelessness," *Sunday Observer* (Colombo).

22 August 1989, "Deaths," *Island* (Colombo).

24 August 1989, "Four Ordained Monks in West Virginia," *Daily News* (Colombo).

17 September 1989, "125th Birth Anniversary of the Anagarika: Light of Lanka," *Sun* (Colombo).

29 April 1990, "Why We Became *Dasa Sil Mathas*," *Weekend* (Colombo).

11 August 1991, "Demoting Dasa Sil Matas," *Sunday Observer* (Colombo).

30 June 1992, "Death of Miss Lucy Fernando," *Daily News* (Colombo).

SINHALA NEWSPAPERS
(*arranged by paper and date*)
DINAKARA PRAKĀSAYA

17 November 1898, "Saṅghamittā Upāsikārāmaya."

13 October 1900, "Madam Canavarro."

DINAMINA

27 April 1898, "Saṅghamittā Shastra Shālawa."

19 November 1899, "Saṅghamittā Upāsikārāmaya."

25 November 1899, "Saṅghamittā Upāsikāva."

13 February 1900, "The Lady Canavarro Upāsikārāmaya."

22 February 1900, "Sil."

6 March 1900, "Anagārika Dharmapāla."

10 October 1900, "Canavarro Upāsikāva."

18 March 1907, "The Only Daughter of the Upāsaka Charles Silva Becomes an Upāsikāva."

20 June 1907, "An Upāsikārāmaya in Kandy."

25 June 1907, "Charles Silva Upāsaka Becomes Ordained in Burma."

GANARTHA PRADĪPAYA

27 September 1897, "Jokes."

11 October 1897, "Correspondences."

18 October 1897, "Saṅghamittā Upāsikārāmaya."
29 May 1899, "Countess Canavarro."
24 July 1899, "This and That."
23 October 1899, "Mahā Bodhi Sangamāya."
26 October 1899, "The Perishing of the Buddhist Camp."
27 November 1899, "Madam Canavarro and Buddhists in Ceylon: Reaching Great Poverty."
30 November 1899, "Letters to the Editor."
30 November 1899, "Madam Canavarro."
26 April 1900, "Miranda de Souza Canavarro."
15 October 1900, "Miranda de Souza Canavarro."

LAKMINIPĀHANA

19 June 1897, "Upāsakas."
8 January 1898, "Letter to the Editor."
19 February 1898, "Letter to the Editor."
6 August 1898, "Letter to the Editor."
13 August 1898, "Letter to the Editor."
10 September 1898, "Leaving the Robes of the Priesthood."

SARASAVISANDARESA

21 September 1897, "American Ladies Observing Ata Sil."
5 October 1897, "Madam Miranda Upāsikā."
8 October 1897, "Madam Miranda Upāsikā."
12 October 1897, "Lady Miranda Upāsikā."
29 April 1898, "Saṅghamittā Shastra Shālawa."
3 May 1898, "The Opening of the House of the Saṅghamittā."
5 July 1898, "Nuwara Upāsikārāmaya."
29 July 1898, "Saṅghamittā Shastra Shālawa."
9 August 1898, "Mr. Dharmapāla."
9 August 1898, "The Saṅghamittā Upāsikārāmaya of Colombo."
23 August 1898, "Mahā Bodhi Talks."
13 December 1898, "A Question to be Looked Into."
23 December 1898, "Questions Which Should be Addressed."
3 January 1899, "Donning of Yellow Robe by Upāsikās."
20 January 1899, "Burmese Upāsikās.
14 July 1899, "Dasasil Upāsikāvak."
18 July 1899, "Shearer Upāsikāva."
1 August 1899, "Saṅghamittā Upāsikārāmaya."
15 August 1899, "Saṅghamittā Upāsikārāmaya."
15 September 1899, "A Dasa Sil Upāsikāvak Who Dons Yellow Robes."
13 December 1899, "Upāsakas and Upāsikās Through Buddhist Schools."
12 October 1900, "Canavarro Upāsikāva."

Index and glossary